Paths to the Triune God

Paths to the Triune God

An Encounter between

Aquinas and

Recent

Theologies

Anselm K. Min

University of Notre Dame Press
Notre Dame, Indiana

Manufactured in the United States of America

Library of Congress Cataloging-in-Publication Data
Min, Anselm Kyongsuk, 1940–
Paths to the Triune God : an encounter between Aquinas and recent
theologies / Anselm K. Min.
p. cm.
Includes bibliographical references and indexes.
ISBN 0-268-03488-5 (cloth : alk. paper)
ISBN 0-268-03489-3 (pbk. : alk. paper)
1. Thomas, Aquinas, Saint, 1225?–1274. 2. Natural theology. I. Title.
B765.T54M49   2005
230'.2092—dc22

2005025279

∞ *This book is printed on acid-free paper.*

Societati Jesu

Grato Animo

Piaque Memoria

Contents

Acknowledgments

Part of chapter 1 was published as "Retrieving Aquinas's Natural Theology as a Trinitarian Theology of Creation" in *Issues in Medieval Philosophy: Essays in Honor of Richard C. Dales*, edited by Nancy Van Deusen (Ottawa, Canada: The Institute of Medieval Music, 2001), 153–176. Part of chapter 6 appeared as "The Dialectic of Divine Love: Pannenberg's Hegelian Trinitarianism" in *International Journal of Systematic Theology* 6, no. 3 (July 2004), 252–269. Both are included in this book with the permission of the publishers.

INTRODUCTION

Why Aquinas Today?

Gloria est finis operationis ipsius naturae per gratiam adjutae.
Glory is the end of the operation of nature itself assisted by grace.

ST, I, 62, 3, ad 3

This is a book I did not intend to write.

Having grown up on Aquinas's thought and his modern inter-preters as part of my philosophical training in the Society of Jesus in the first half of the 1960s, but like many, disenchanted with them in the critical ethos of postconciliar Catholicism in the second half, I decided to leave Aquinas and his school alone. I immersed myself in modernity, especially Hegel, Marx, existentialism, critical theory, deconstructionism, and contemporary theologies from Barth, Tillich, and Rahner through various political and liberation theologies. However, I have taught doctoral students in theology since 1992, and during this time it occurred to me that some of our students tended to be so preoccupied with things contemporary that they not only suffered a woeful ignorance of the classical tradition but also had a positive contempt for the theological past. Out of peda-gogical desperation, I thought I should offer a course in Aquinas so that at least some students might be able to remedy a critical deficiency in their theological training. I taught a course in his theology for the first time and was also invited to present a paper in a conference on medieval philosophy.[1] After some twenty-five years away from Aquinas in more than one sense, this gave me a chance to reread him and also to rediscover him, doing so with contemporary theological and philosophical sensi-bility and concern.

I do not mean to plead for a precritical return to the thirteenth century, which no person with a modern historical and critical consciousness could do, but to argue for a postcritical retrieval of certain insights a truly classi-cal thinker might still have for later generations increasingly tired with their own preoccupations and provincialisms. For all the simplicity, naivete, prejudices, and even plain errors and ideologies of his thought, which I cannot be accused of overlooking in this book, reading Aquinas was a broadening and liberating experience, broadening beyond our own contemporary preoccupations and liberating from our own contemporary prejudices. It was also refreshing to read a thinker who reflects and argues rather than shouts and claims, who withdraws himself so as to let the mat-ter speak for itself rather than intrude his own subjectivity at every avail-able turn, and who presents a balanced, comprehensive vision of the whole *sub ratione Dei*—or, in light of God's logic—without a selective, one-sided "concentration," whether christological, trinitarian, existentialist, or libera-tionist, making room for everything in its proper place in the divine scheme of things rather than reduce everything to its place in the human.

Aquinas is above all a preeminently human thinker. Aquinas does not claim to know more about God than can a finite spirit immersed in the *material* world; God's incomprehensibility remains the outer limit of all human knowledge, whose proper object is the essence of a material being. Nor does he claim to know less than can a finite *spirit* in the world of matter; a human being can know the existence and nature of God by way of analogy, and even provide extrinsic arguments for the plausibility or "fittingness" [convenientia] of revealed truths such as the trinity, incarnation, and salvation. Neither fideist nor rationalist, and self-conscious of both the limits and possibilities of human nature, Aquinas chooses to remain faithful to the human, without wallowing in its igno-rance but also without gloating in its pretensions. Neither modernist with triumphalist anthropocentric claims nor postmodernist with despairing negations of such claims, neither humanist nor anti-humanist, Aquinas is quite happy to be human, not unaware of human misery but without dwelling on it, nor ignorant of human grandeur but without being arrogant.

This is not to say that he has no eschatological hope. His trinitarian, incarnational vision allows him to see all created *nature* in the process of *graceful* self-transcendence toward *glory,* according to the divine exemplarity of the Word in the teleological power of the Holy Spirit leading all things to the glory of God. In a typical understatement, Aquinas says that "glory is the end of the operation of nature itself assisted by grace" [gloria est finis operationis ipsius naturae per gratiam adjutae].[2] Aquinas's is a profound theology of hope based on the trinitarian government of the world, but a government which deals with things according to the diversity of their natures. It is a theology of hope that is as profoundly realistic about human nature as it is profoundly optimistic about God's goodness and power gracious enough to assume human nature and give it a share in divine glory. It is not, however, a theology of hope that reduces all things to the horizon of hope, but rather a theology that welcomes the complements of faith and charity. It is a hope that quietly pervades all reality with proper respect for its diversity, not a hope that reduces all reality to itself in the name of historical relevance.

In short, what struck me most about Aquinas was his contrast with the ethos of contemporary theology. Contemporary theologies are activist in the sense of seeking to change reality through various political, liberating praxes. They are historicist in the sense of an all-determining consciousness of the historical conditioning, and thus ambiguity and relativity, of all human knowledge. They are deliberately one-sided in the sense of lifting up a particular theme or idea—such as obedience, transcendence, existence, hope, or liberation—as the ruling category of a whole theology and thus reducing everything else to that particular horizon. They are also increasingly fragmentary and heterocentric in the deconstructionist sense of giving up in the name of *differance* all attempts to grasp reality as totality.

In constrast, Aquinas's theology is a *theoria* or contemplation of God and all things *sub ratione Dei,* or, in light of God's logic. It is contemplative rather than activist in that it seeks to understand—rather than transform—reality precisely in its trinitarian movement from God and back to God through Christ in the power of the Holy Spirit. Without denying the need for active transformation, yet also without reducing the whole of theology to that need, it rather locates that need in the proper context of the divine totality. Aquinas's theology is historical but not historicist in that it is aware of change and diversity in human knowledge brought about by historical change but does not turn this into an absolute epistemological principle. It instead locates change in the context of a trinitarian history of salvation with hope in the enduring identity of the substance of inherited faith.

Aquinas's theology is also geared to the integrity of all things in their difference rather than a concentration of all reality on a particular theme or issue, no matter how central or compelling it may appear in the stress of a time; it does not reduce the whole of theology to a particular topic. Nor does it reduce the integrity of creation to God the creator as some theologies are tempted to do in the name of divine sovereignty or the triumph of divine grace. It tries to do justice to each thing according to the nature of each, to God as God, to humanity as humanity, to angels as angels, to creatures as creatures, in all the diversity of their being, according each its own "dignity of causality,"[3] with theological space for everything in its proper place. Aquinas's theology is above all a search for a comprehensive vision of God and all things in their reference and movement to God [ordo et motus ad Deum]. A quest for such a vision is rooted in the very nature of the human soul born with a "natural" desire for a "supernatural" vision of the divine essence. A quest for totality in God is connatural with our intellectual nature and a matter of our moral responsibility for our ultimate destiny. It should be pursued as far as it can. To stifle that quest in the name of *differance* would be to stifle our very nature as human beings. Aquinas's theological quest for a vision of the whole, however, is also only a human quest burdened with all the human limitations. His vision of the whole—embodied in the two *Summas*—is pervaded by the motif and acute sense of irreparable human ignorance and irrevocable divine incomprehensibility. Our knowledge "does not transcend the genus of the knowledge gathered from sensible things."[4]

It is this contemplative character of Aquinas's theology in its contrast with contemporary theology that struck me with a particular urgency and relevance. I am not naive enough to believe that we can simply abandon contemporary theology and return to Aquinas. The activist, historicist, unilateral, and fragmentary aspects of contemporary theology do have their own historical raisons d'etre that cannot be ignored. They are here to stay for the foreseeable future. What I am claiming is that

Aquinas's contemplative theology can provide a corrective counterbalance to contemporary theology with its fluctuations between activism and despair, its debilitating sense of sheer transience, its ultimately unsustainable and unhappy preoccupation with one thing considered necessary for the time, and its sense of sheer fragmentation and alienation. I am also claiming that theology after postmodernity is possible only in the constructive tension between theory and praxis, not as a theoretical theology alone, even if it is that of Aquinas, nor as a praxical theology alone, even if it is that of liberation theology, but only in the dialogical and dialectical tension between the two.

In addition to this contemplative, trinitarian dimension of theology in Aquinas, I also propose three particular aspects of his theology as especially relevant for today: his theology of reason and creation, the theological significance of the moral act, and his sacramental theology of religions. In fact, there is more than an accidental connection between his contemplative vision and his positive appreciation of the three universal dimensions of human existence, rationality, morality, and sacramentality. The contemplative vision of totality in God contains an inner dynamic to discern and appreciate God's salvific, theological presence as universally as possible, and certainly in such universal dimensions and functions as the teleological movement of creation as creation, the quest of the intellect for the ultimate intelligible object, the moral experience of the ultimate and unconditional, and the sacramental or liturgical embodiment of all religious quests for God.

In the contemporary pluralistic world with its overriding imperative for different peoples or others to live together in justice and peace, all sorts of fundamentalism stand in the way, especially and traditionally the denigration of reason in the name of a particularist revelation, the denigration of morality in the name of supernatural action directly related to God, and the denigration of other religions as means of salvation in the name of a uniquely valid line of salvation history. It is imperative, first of all, to recognize the value of a mode of public discourse—i.e., reason—that is not reducible to the language of a particular confession, and to appreciate the value of moral experience in the secular world in which we have to defend human dignity despite our religious differences. It is likewise imperative to respect the value of other religions because it is impossible to live together with others without respect, and there is no way of respecting others without also respecting the value of the religions from which they derive their ultimate, transcendent identity and dignity. It is equally imperative, however, secondly, to do all of these without denigrating one's own religious difference and particularity. As embodied beings we are, even in our deepest spirituality and religiosity, rooted in a particular tradition with its own different language, custom, institution, and horizon. Denying the value of particularity purely and simply and trying to level all differences in the name of an abstract universal are neither feasible nor desirable.

The third imperative is to bring the two imperatives, that of solidarity and that of otherness, together into a tensive synthesis or coordination in a "solidarity of Others." It involves, therefore, not so much a search for common denominators, which remain abstractions when separated from the contexts of their original traditions, as a search for the dynamism of self-transcendent solidarity internal to each tradition. The question is not primarily whether there are doctrines and rituals common to different religions but whether there is a dynamic in each religion which impels its own adherents from within and on its own particular theological ground to transcend their parochialism, purify themselves of any particularity that makes it impossible for them to live together with others with respect and justice, and welcome the other as creatures with a common destiny. This involves being able to distinguish between constructive particularity, the depth of one's own tradition in which our common humanity and creaturehood may be grounded, and destructive particularity that separates one group from another. This dynamic of self-transcending solidarity is particular insofar as it is rooted in what Aloysius Pieris calls "the soteriological depth"[5] of each religion, universal insofar as it impels each religion, without denying its own identity, to transcend itself in a solidarity of Others.[6]

The claim of this book is that Aquinas's theology does contain this dynamic of self-transcending solidarity with all humanity and creation, at least in three areas. First, Aquinas takes reason and creation, two areas of human life independent of a particular religious tradition, and liberates them from two traditional Christian attitudes that reinforce the separation of Christians from others—reason from fideistic denigration, and creation from the supernaturalistic *contemptus mundi* or contempt for the world. He frees reason and creation for human solidarity by legitimizing them precisely from the particular Christian standpoint as common spaces for discourse with others in a language other than the language of a particular faith and for living together with others under common historical and natural conditions. For

Aquinas, reason and creation are indeed "natural" as distinct from the "supernatural," but they are not only not opposed to the latter in an impossible dualism but positively "ordered" [ordinantur] to the latter as their own intrinsic dynamism. As mentioned earlier, in the trinitarian economy "glory is the end of the operation of nature itself assisted by grace" [gloria est finis operationis ipsius naturae per gratiam adjutae].[7] Christians are released by their own particularity to welcome and build reason and creation as bases of solidarity with others. This is the burden of chapter 1.

Second, nothing separates one group from another as much as the ultimate judgment that others as others cannot be "saved." For most of its history Christianity has been complacent about the impossibility of salvation in any name other than that of Jesus Christ or of "salvation outside the Church." The issue of salvation is the issue of our ultimate destinies, our ultimate success or failure as human beings, and involves our ultimate (self-)interests. The division between the saved and the damned is the ultimate in human separation because it deals with the absolutely final, definitive, and total disposition of our existence, compared with which divisions based on class, gender, race, origin, status, function, etc. are relative and provisional. To say that others as (religious) others are damned is to deliver the ultimate insult.

Still, religions do deal precisely with such ultimacies, and their particularity is often derived from the particularity with which such ultimacies are defined. Our contemporary (Christian) imperative, therefore, is to find out whether it is possible to allow for the possibility of salvation of the other without either denying the ultimacy of the ultimate in the Christian faith or weakening the "ultimate concern" with which the ultimate is taken; that is, by entering into the "depth" of Christian soteriology. This is precisely what Aquinas does. In anticipation of Karl Rahner he argues for the possibility and soteriological sufficiency of "implicit" faith for the non-Christian. Moreover, this implicit faith is present in the moral act. The moral act, therefore, precisely as a moral act common to all human beings in its form if not always in its content, is salvific. In allowing for the possibility of salvation in the non-Christian and removing one of the ancient walls of separation, Aquinas opens up another common space for human solidarity: the moral way to God empowered by the dynamic of universal grace, as distinct from the religious act in all its particularity and from which no human being is exempt. This is the burden of chapter 2.

Third, what about the respect for non-Christian religions precisely in their particularity? Certainly, the lack of this respect often expressed in the aggressive form of hatred has been a major divisive issue throughout human history. It is not enough to say that non-Christians as individuals can be saved by their "implicit" faith in Christ, nor is it enough to say that such religions as religions are authentic paths of "salvation." The first deals with non-Christians as isolated individuals, denies their basic sociality and historicity, and reduces them to asocial, ahistorical abstractions. The second recognizes the sociality and historicity of their existence as objectified in the particular religious traditions to which they belong, but it also subordinates their religions, reducing them to implicit, inferior variations on the Christian religion by measuring them by the Christian standard of "salvation." Such inclusivism in fact amounts to, in Hans Küng's phrase, "conquest by embrace, assimilation by exterior validation, integration by relativization and loss of identity."[8] Is it possible to find grounds within one's own faith for respecting the integrity of other religions precisely in their difference without attempting to reduce or subordinate them to one's own horizon? In other words, is it possible to be a genuine "pluralist" without ceasing to be a member of a particular religion, especially Christianity?

My claim in this book is that although Aquinas "explicitly" argues only for the possibility and sufficiency of "implicit" faith on the part of individuals, not for the pluralist position as such that recognizes the legitimacy of other religions as religions in their particularity, there are nevertheless certain principles and assumptions in his theology which can be retrieved and developed into a coherent pluralist position. These principles and assumptions include the epistemological function of "light," the sacramental necessity of the socio-historical embodiment of the spiritual, the ultimacy of the personal judgment of conscience, the providential principle of respect for difference, and the incomprehensibility of God who saves in ways of her own choosing. It is anachronistic to argue that Aquinas was *ex professo* a "pluralist" before his time, but it is not anachronistic to argue that there are resources in his thought that go beyond his intention, explicit and implicit, that can be developed into a kind of contemporary pluralism. This is the burden of chapter 3.

What makes Aquinas's universalist vision of salvific significance possible is his conception of theology as contemplative wisdom. As wisdom theology seeks a vision of the whole in its ultimacy and universality, of God, therefore, as the ultimate origin and end of all things and of all things precisely in their teleological, theological movement to God. It is a theology of creation, of all creation in its movement of assimilation and participation in God as her image, and in the theological, salvific significance of its ontological dynamics. It includes a theology of redemption, but as a subordinate moment of a theology of creation. This universalist vision is possible only to contemplation or the speculative intellect, whose nature is to know reality as given in its ultimacy, breadth, and depth, for the sake of truth as such, not to transform reality in the contingencies and particularities of history, which is the function of the practical intellect. To discuss Aquinas's vision of theology as contemplative wisdom, against the background of the contemporary debate on the nature of theology as theory, praxis, aesthetics, and doxology is the burden of chapter 4.

Behind the rational way to God with its trinitarian theology of the goodness of all creation, the moral way to God with its theology of implicit faith and grace in the non-Christian, and the religious way to God with its trinitarian theology of salvation and its sacramental theology of religions, is the God who empowers all things in their *nature* to share in her *glory* through her *grace* meted out to each according to its measure, the God whom theological wisdom contemplates as the origin and end of all things. This God, whose "economy" or saving activity in creation we will have studied in the preceding chapters, is not only a "God for us" but also a "God in herself" with a life of her own independent of and "infinitely" transcending her economic life. This is the life of the "immanent trinity" whom Christians worship.

What is the intrinsic nature of God such that he can manifest himself as creator in things other than himself and reveal himself as Father, Son, and Holy Spirit in his redeeming activity in the world? Already two generations of theologians have been brought up completely alienated from the classical doctrine of the immanent Trinity from Athanasius to Aquinas and incapable of appreciating its depth, richness, and nuances, in part because they can no longer understand the technicalities of the metaphysics underlying that tradition. How many students today come to theology equipped with the knowledge of the classical concepts of "being itself" [ipsum esse], "substance," "accidents," "relation," "person," "supposit," "essence," "nature," "procession," "notion," "appropriation," "substantive predication," "relative predication," etc., that make up the vocabulary of classical trinitarianism? It is the burden of chapter 5 to present the classical doctrine of the immanent Trinity, whose synthesis Aquinas provides, with as much elaboration and detail as possible.

The classical doctrine of the Trinity has recently come under many different kinds of criticism. Some object that it is too abstract and abstruse, that it is too metaphysical and not practical enough. Others object that it contains sexist language. "Social" trinitarians object that once we begin, as does classical trinitarianism, with the *one* divine nature or the *one* divine subject, i.e., the Father, we necessarily fall into either modalism or subordinationism; we must begin with the *three* persons in their distinctness and look for a unity appropriate to the three. The burden of chapter 6 is to engage these issues with some thoroughness. I present the criticisms of the classical position, especially by the social trinitarianism of Jürgen Moltmann, Wolfhart Pannenberg, and Cornelius Plantinga, Jr., at some length, while also confronting them with counter-criticisms from the classical position. This chapter analyzes contemporary trinitarian discussions and exposes their inadequacies and incoherences in light of Aquinas.

The burden of chapter 7, the last chapter, is to plead for a new theological approach today, a methodological tension between sapiential and prophetic theology. Contemporary theologies are largely theologies of prophetic action oriented towards a particular historical issue (e.g., liberation), one-sided in its attention (e.g., liberation as central), based in a particular group (e.g., white women, African Americans), activist (e.g., removal of oppressive conditions), suspicious of tradition (e.g., the past as patriarchal), and anthropocentric. Classical theologies are largely theologies of sapiential contemplation oriented towards a vision of the whole in God, comprehensive in its attention, universal in its addressee, contemplative of reality, affirmative towards the past, and theocentric. Each type has its own merit and its own pitfall. The merit of sapiential theology is its vision of totality and universality, its pitfall the ideological justification of human oppression. The merit of prophetic theology is its overriding concern for human liberation, its pitfall the absolutization of particularity and the fragmentation of human unity. The strength of one is the pitfall of the other.

What we need today, I propose, is a creative tension between the two where each is prevented by the challenge of the other from being complacent in its identity. Without the theocentric, universal vision of sapiential theology, prophetic theology ceases to be *theology* and becomes humanitarian sociology. Without the burning concern for the liberation of the oppressed and suffering of prophetic theology, sapiential theology ceases to be *Christian* and becomes aesthetic contemplation. Only in this creative tension can each remain both theology and Christian. This creative tension is all the more compelling as the *kairos* of the twenty-first century demands a greater sense of the solidarity of human beings both among themselves and with all creation in a theocentric vision of the whole. Prophetic theology needs the challenge of sapiential theology to broaden and universalize its sympathies and concerns, as sapiential theology needs the shock of prophetic theology to remain attentive to the cry of the poor, oppressed, and persecuted. It is in this creative tension with contemporary prophetic theologies and as their corrective that I also propose to retrieve the classical vision of St. Thomas Aquinas.

This book does not claim, as is rather obvious, to be a comprehensive presentation of Aquinas in the fashion of Garrigou LaGrange, although I do see an urgent need for an updated, comprehensive commentary on his thought.[9] Nor is it an exegesis of Aquinas on a special topic, although I do see an equally urgent need for insightful and historically sensitive exegesis of Aquinas on many topics. Instead, it is an attempt at a hermeneutic retrieval of Aquinas on some compelling contemporary issues in the context of his overall trinitarian vision, taking his thought and developing it beyond his intention but, hopefully, without betraying it. It is a study of the four ways or paths to God, the rational, the moral, the religious, and the contemplative, and of the triune God to which they lead, in the theology of Aquinas. Hence the title, "Paths to the Triune God." It is also a study of Aquinas in the context of and in dialogue with certain contemporary concerns and perspectives on all the major topics covered. Hence the subtitle, "An Encounter between Aquinas and Recent Theologies." In short, the book is half exegesis of Aquinas and half contemporary theology.

A word on the use of gender in referring to God and human beings in this book. I refer to the first and second persons of the Trinity as Father and Son, in the masculine, while using the feminine to refer to the Holy Spirit and to God taken simply as God, except where the context dictates otherwise. This has the virtue of preserving the traditional way of referring to the triune God, balancing the distribution of masculine and feminine pronouns, and avoiding awkward neologisms such as "Godself" and stylistic infelicities such as "he/she." I also simply vary between feminine and masculine pronouns in referring to the human being. For a theological justification of this approach, please consult "The Problem of Sexist Language" in chapter 6.

Chapter One

REASON AND CREATION
IN THEOLOGY AND FAITH

The Rational Way to God

The Contemporary Relevance of Natural Theology

More than fifty years ago, insisting on the essential importance of
natural theology for ethics, dogmatics, proclamation of the word,
and dialogue with unbelievers, Emil Brunner argued that the recovery of "true" natural theology was the task of his theological generation.[1] To which, as we know, Karl Barth responded with his
thunderous No! For Barth, natural theology was an attempt to know
God solely on the resources of human reason by analogy with creation, independent of yet claiming equality with divine revelation.
Natural theology ignores the infinite qualitative difference between
God and human beings by falsely positing analogy between them, and
reduces God to a human projection, an idol which we can manipulate.
For Barth, natural theology has in principle been annulled since the
revelation of God in Christ, and its only theological destiny is to

"disappear." We should learn not to argue with or even to reject but simply to ignore it. Theology is in no way mediated by natural theology, not even by its negation.[2]

Almost forty years ago, John Cobb, Jr., called attention to the challenge of religious diversity and interreligious dialogue and argued for the necessity of a "Christian natural theology." By this he meant any responsible philosophical reflection on matters of ultimate concern that is based on general human experience and employs criteria of judgment that are independent of any particular community of faith (including the Christian community) and yet are also expressive of the Christian vision of reality. Such a theology fully recognizes that its reflection will be historically conditioned, not ahistorical and purely universal.[3]

Most recently, James Barr has revived the question of natural theology with a sustained critique of Barth and biblical theology from the biblical perspective itself. Barr takes natural theology broadly as any reflective knowledge of God derived from sources other than the biblical revelation, including non-Christian religions and philosophies. Such knowledge is not a product of "pure" reason but is necessarily culturally mediated, with a much broader function than that of providing the proofs of God's existence. Such a natural theology is not only a condition for the possibility of special revelation but is also valid in its own right. For Barr, the Bible already contains plenty of natural theology, often as its structuring principle, in such places as Acts 17, Romans 1, the Wisdom of Solomon, and many of the Psalms and the laws. It is not valid to sharply separate biblical theology and natural theology or to associate Hebrew thought with revelation and Greek thought with natural theology. Natural theology is also a valid kind of revelation of God for those outside the Judeo-Christian tradition and often serves as a principle of criticism for the biblical revelation itself, raising questions, for example, about the morality of genocide by divine command. The Bible cannot be the only horizon or criterion for theology, just as many important theological questions lie beyond the purview of biblical theology.[4]

There are many pressures today for a revival of natural theology of some sort. The Scripture principle and the paradigm of salvation history, which limit the possibility of revelation and salvation to the narrow stream of the Western Christian tradition, have lost their intellectual credibility.[5] The need for dialogue with other religions and cultures and the increasing concern for the ecological integrity of nature have led to the search for a possible common ground within the limits of cultural differences and to the revival of a theology of creation as distinct from a theology of revelation. Many Asian theologians and Jürgen Moltmann have pointed out that the traditional emphasis on revelation and redemption in Christ has led both to exclusivism in relation to other religions and to anthropocentrism in relation to the rest of creation.[6] Biblical studies have also exposed the many forms of cultural mediation of Christian revelation itself. Another source of urgency is the renewed quest for a metascientific understanding of nature based on a theological interpretation of contemporary cosmology.[7] Finally, the need of human liberation from all forms of oppression—racism, classism, sexism, and others—demands dialogue with secular sciences such as economics, psychology, sociology, anthropology, and politics, beyond the word of Scripture.

The recovery of some sort of natural theology, then, has now become a question of how far Christian theology is willing to go in engaging the many Others of the contemporary world and searching for grounds of solidarity with them without losing its Christian identity. What is required for dialogue and solidarity among people with different ultimate commitments, concerns, and methods of inquiry is the recognition of a mode of knowing God that is not so tied to a particular religious tradition as to exclude all common ground, yet that is also capable of justification from within the perspective of the particular tradition itself in such a way that the tradition can accept it for its own reasons and therefore without losing the integrity of its specific religious identity. Both conditions are necessary: It must be a mode of knowing that transcends religious particularity and is accessible to others in principle, at least in some significant ways; otherwise, it cannot provide a ground of solidarity. It must also be rooted in and justifiable on the ground of particular religious traditions; otherwise, it will be resisted as an alien imposition by the traditions themselves. What is required, then, at least from the Christian perspective, is something like natural theology in the traditional Thomistic sense: any knowledge of God which reason can acquire on the basis of its reflection on the created world, both nature and history, whose validity is (relatively) independent of the Christian (or any other) divine revelation, yet whose role is also justified and given theological significance on the specific ground of Christian theology itself.

In this chapter I focus on Aquinas's conception of natural theology, and try to retrieve its systematic possibilities for the needs of contemporary theology. I am not going to repeat the old controversies with all their pros and cons; many of them, I am afraid, have been rendered obsolete by the changing times.[8] Rather, I concentrate on drawing out the relevant possibilities of Aquinas's conception for today. As reason reflecting on creation for traces and images of God, natural theology contains two essential components, namely, reason as subject of theology and creation as object of theology. The peculiarity of Aquinas's theology is the claim that this natural theology is not just natural but is an integral part of revealed theology or *sacra doctrina*. It is precisely this claim, the discovery of reason and creation in and for theology along with their trinitarian justification, that I find especially relevant today.

This also means that I am using "natural theology" in a much broader sense than has been customary among philosophers and theologians. Natural theology in the conventional sense refers to a specific content of conclusions that reason can draw about God from its reflections on human experience in general. It is traditionally limited to the proofs of God's existence and the demonstrations of various attributes of God, which today may be extended to include any religious reflection not limited to a particular religion. In this conventional sense natural theology is limited to the prerequisites for faith [praeambula fidei], the content of the preparatory or preliminary function reason performs for theology proper. As will be discussed, however, reason also performs many other functions for theology. Reason, although informed by faith, remains the subject of theology, finding itself, therefore, wherever theology is at work. Reason is operative in the apologetic functions of theology, where it seeks to defend the content of faith against criticisms of unbelievers and heretics; in the deductive functions, where it draws inferences from the articles of faith; and in the clarifying or elucidating functions, where it seeks to make the content of faith humanly plausible by means of analogies and congruent reasons.

There is some difference, of course, between the preliminary function of reason on the one hand and all its other functions: in the former function reason, although subject to theological intentionality, preserves its autonomy by relying only on philosophical criteria and resources of human experience in the created world of nature and history; in the latter functions reason directly serves theological purposes by taking the articles of faith as both criteria and sources and seeking only to defend, infer from, or clarify them. These differences are important but not absolute differences. As we know very well today, and as will be pointed out later, reason does not leave its habits, presuppositions, and interests at the door when it enters its non-preliminary functions. Reason does not cease to be reason in every exercise of apologetic, deductive, and clarifying function, but operates, perhaps unconsciously, with its full set of habits, presuppositions, and interests, which enter into the very determination of the content. The question, therefore, is not only whether there is a theological justification for natural theology in its narrow, preliminary function but whether there is a theological justification for reason—and created experience—as such in all its functions in elaborating the very *content* of faith itself. The issue is the broader one of the significance of reason and creation for theology, the reflection on God, and thus of the very justification of the theological significance of reason and creation or the significance of reason and creation for God. The question of natural theology is also a question of the theology of reason and creation. In this chapter I take natural theology in this broad sense of the theology of reason and creation as such.

I proceed in three steps. First, I summarize the high points of Aquinas's conception of theology and of the role of reason and creation in that theology. Second, I go on to discuss the ontological-christological-trinitarian foundation of his confident theological embrace of reason and creation. Third, I reflect on the relevance of his trinitarian theology of reason and creation for a broad conception of theology as it is appropriate in today's world beset with global issues such as justice, ecology, and pluralism, issues on which biblical revelation alone does not provide adequate guidance and which demand all the resources of reason that we can muster in its social-scientific, cosmological, and comparative-religious potentialities. Contemporary theology can incorporate these resources of reason and consider them *sub ratione Dei,* confident in the trinitarian identity of the human and the divine *ratio.*

The Role of Reason and Creation in Theology and Faith

For Aquinas, theology as *sacra doctrina* is principally the science, knowledge, or doctrine of God as our ultimate end, the source of our eternal happiness or salvation.[9] In order to be able to direct our thoughts and actions to that end, we must have access to the salvific truths about God, her essence, her trinitarian life, her salvific will, the Incarnation. Insofar as these truths are intrinsically beyond the grasp of human reason, they can be known only through revelation and our acceptance of it in faith. Salvation requires God's twofold initiative. God must, first, reveal herself and propose what is to be believed, and, second, internally move the will of the believer to assent to what she proposes. We depend on God's grace both for the content proposed to faith—revelation—and for the motive for its acceptance—faith.[10]

It is God who infuses us with the virtue and "light" of faith, elevating us above our natural powers and inclining us to believe. Of the content of belief we have only acquaintance or awareness [notitia], not demonstrative knowledge, which would make the assent of the intellect necessary, not voluntary, and deprive faith of its merit. It remains an object of belief [creditum], not an object of vision [visum]. As an activity of human reason intrinsically conditioned by materiality, theology enjoys neither the intellectual intuition of God's essence nor the capacity to demonstrate the intrinsic intelligibility of the articles of faith. Our faith proceeds "not from the vision of the believer but from the vision of the one believed [non ex visione credentis sed a visione ejus cui creditur]."[11] Just as the "light" of natural reason enables us to assent to self-evident first principles, only the grace of the "light" of faith, "a faint stamp of the First Truth in our mind"—not our own capacity or any external cause such as miracles, preaching, or examples of holy life—enables us to see the *credibility* of the revealed content and assent to it whose *intelligibility* remains beyond human reason. Aquinas notes that this "light" or "habit" of faith does not move us by way of the intellect but by way of the will, which means that such a light does not make us "see" what we believe, which would force our assent, but only makes us assent to it voluntarily by promoting the will to believe.[12]

In this sense, the first principles of theology are neither self-evident nor rationally demonstrable in the way of other sciences but are derived from a higher science, the *scientia Dei et beatorum* or knowledge possessed by God and the blessed in heaven, and contained in the biblical testimonies and articles of faith. Theology is possible only as participation through faith in this revealed knowledge of God. Any attempt to "demonstrate" the truths of faith such as the Trinity by natural reason only exposes the theologian to the ridicule of unbelievers and does a disservice to the cause of faith. Aquinas's theology is totally opposed to a rationalism that seeks to reduce the content of faith to what is humanly intelligible.[13]

In short, for Aquinas, the principal object of theology is the God of glory whose vision constitutes our beatitude and salvation. Its basis lies in revelation, and its horizon, perspective, or "light" is that of faith and salvation. What, then, is the theological relevance of creatures and creaturely experience? Can these also become objects of theology proper? Likewise, what is the theological relevance of reason itself, its various activities and the fund of knowledge about God and creatures that it can acquire on its own resources, apart from divine revelation although never apart from the grace of divine motion? Furthermore, can creation and reason become part of theology proper without impairing its unity as a science?

The proper object of theology is indeed God as the ultimate end of all things and the source of our salvation, which constitutes theology as wisdom, indeed the highest and most comprehensive wisdom. Theology deals with God as the highest cause not only as knowable through creatures but also as "known to himself alone and revealed to others,"[14] and is, in this sense, participation in God's self-knowledge. For Aquinas, however, all things or the whole of creation can themselves become the proper object of theology. What distinguishes theology from philosophy and other sciences is not so much its material object—or *what* it deals with, which can be common to several different disciplines—as its formal object, its *formalis ratio objecti*—or *how* it deals with its material object, the perspective or horizon from which it treats its material. The defining horizon of theology is that of God as the ultimate end of all things and the source of salvation knowable only through faith in revelation. The same thing can be studied in itself, in its immanent nature and properties, in light of natural reason [lumine naturalis rationis] as philosophy does, or in its reference to God [ordo ad Deum] as its origin and end, in light of divine revelation [lumine divinae revelationis][15] as theology does. While philosophy considers creatures in themselves, their various *genera,* proper causes, and what belongs to them by nature, and terminates in God as the first cause, theology begins with God as the first cause and moves to creatures in light of their relation to God.[16] In this regard, theology is similar to God's own knowledge, for God, in knowing herself, knows all other things as well.[17]

In this sense, then, although theology indeed deals with God "principally," it can deal with the whole of creation as its proper object as long as it does so from its own distinctive horizon or "light" of salvific finality, revelation, and faith, or, in Aquinas's typical, pregnant phrase, "under the intelligibility or logic of God [sub ratione Dei]." It is because of this properly theological horizon that "theology included in sacred doctrine differs in kind [secundum genus] from that theology which is part of philosophy."[18]

This identity of its formal object or horizon provides unity to theology as a science despite the diversity of its material objects. Theology deals with the creator and creatures, angels, corporeal creatures, human morality, speculative and practical sciences, which, not belonging to the same class of objects, are handled by different philosophical sciences. Theology, on the other hand, deals with them according as they are divinely revealed [divinitus revelata] and thus with all things insofar as they are divinely revealable [divinitus revelabilia] or knowable by divine light [divino lumine cognoscibilia].[19] Likewise, although theology deals more with divine things than with human acts and is thus more speculative than practical, it also deals with human acts and practical sciences "according as a human person is ordained through such acts to the perfect knowledge of God, in which consists eternal beatitude,"[20] the ultimate end to which all the ends of the practical sciences are themselves ordained.[21]

God is truly *the* object of theology, then, not because God is the only object exclusive of all creatures but because God provides the one *ratio*— the *ratio Dei* or *ordo ad Deum*—for the inclusion of all things in theology, which treats all things *sub ratione Dei* "either because they are God herself or because they refer to God [habent ordinem ad Deum] as their beginning and end."[22] Anything can become a proper object of theology as long as it shares in the *ratio* of the formal object, i.e., as long as it is ordained to God "in some way," and "any creatures whatever come under faith, insofar as by them we are directed [ordinamur] to God, and in as much as we assent to them on account of the divine truth."[23] By virtue of this *ratio* of God and faith, all theological relations to creation, for Aquinas, are not just "natural" relations but relations based on what Barth would call the "analogy of faith." By the same token, all creatures can become *revelabilia*, or objects of theology, not only *intelligibilia*, or objects of metaphysics.[24]

In light of this comprehensiveness of the theological horizon and the universality of its subject matter, it is important to note that the distinction between philosophy and theology is not identical with the distinction between reason and faith. Theology, of course, includes the content of revelation [revelata] accepted by faith, which constitutes the principles [principia] of theology, but it also includes rational or philosophical knowledge of all things *sub ratione Dei,* in relation to their ultimate end in light of divine revelation.[25] In this sense, even "things which can be proved by demonstration are reckoned among the objects of faith [credenda], not because they are believed simply by all, but because they are a necessary presupposition to matters of faith [praeexiguntur ad ea quae sunt fidei]."[26]

Thus, theology deals with both the Trinity and sacramental symbols, both the works of redemption and the mystical body of Christ in its head and members, precisely according to their ordination to God [secundum ordinem ad Deum].[27] It is this same formal horizon which makes it possible for theology, without prejudice to its unity, to include in its *Summa* both the revealed knowledge of the triune God and the rational, philosophical knowledge of the one God, her existence and nature, both theological and philosophical anthropology and epistemology (Part One); both Christology and sacramental theology (Part Three); and also both philosophical and theological ethics, doctrines of virtue, law, sin, and grace, and theological and natural virtues, which describe the dynamics of human praxis interpreted as a movement to God [motus ad Deum] (Part Two), without sharply separating what is revealed and what is rational. The perspective of theology is *ratio Dei*, and there is nothing in the universe which does not fall under this *ratio*: all things other than God are at least related to God as their origin and end and can, therefore, be included in theology.[28]

It is useful to remind ourselves here of the important distinction Etienne Gilson makes between the "revealed" [revelata] and the "revealable" [revelabilia]. The essence of the "revealed" does not lie in the mere fact that they have been revealed but in the fact that they are accessible through revelation alone. All knowledge about God beyond the grasp of human reason, such as the Trinity, the Incarnation, the content of faith, hope, and charity, of sin and grace, belongs to the revealed. The "revealable" refer to the totality of knowledge of God and creatures accessible to reason, interpreted in light of the theological horizon of faith or *sub ratione Dei*, and integrated into theology, which Gilson also calls "Christian philosophy." They include philosophical knowledge of the existence and attributes of God, the identity of existence and essence in God, the immortality of the soul, the nature of the human soul as the form of the body, the ways and limits of human knowledge, the nature of moral virtues and vices, and in fact the totality of purely rational knowledge included in the *Summa*. These are in principle capable of being known by natural reason, yet some of them have also actually been revealed for the sake of the salvation of those who otherwise cannot attain certain knowledge of such things because of various intellectual defects.[29] These elements of purely philosophical theology, anthropology, epistemology, and ethics can be integrated into and become an authentic part of theology without losing their purely philosophical nature when they are directed and subordinated to the theological horizon of revelation, when they are clarified in light of the revealed. The revealable in this sense belong to theology no less than do the revealed.[30]

The whole of creation, then, is theologically relevant, and so is the activity of reason in interpreting and integrating it as a proper object of theology in the light or horizon of faith in the revealed. We may now ask how reason goes about performing these functions as the human subject of theology.

For Aquinas, theology is not only wisdom that studies God as the ultimate end of all things and all things in their ordering to that end, but is also a science.[31] It is not, of course, a science like arithmetic, which proceeds from principles known by the light of natural reason, but a science more like music, which accepts on authority principles taught by a higher science, arithmetic. The first principles of theology are neither self-evident nor rationally demonstrable, as are those of other sciences; they derive from a higher science, the knowledge of God and the blessed [scientia Dei et beatorum] revealed in Scripture and contained in the "articles of faith," a term which became prevalent only in the twelfth and thirteenth centuries as a reference to the irreducible elements of faith.[32] In this sense, divine revelation remains the principal source and the controlling norm and horizon of all theology. Only the arguments from the authority of Scripture and the articles of faith are strictly "proper" [proprie] and lead to "necessary" conclusions and proofs. Subject to this norm and source, however, theology can also use other resources such as the teachings of the doctors of the church and the insights and truths of natural reason and philosophies. Arguments from the authority of the doctors of the church are "somewhat proper" [quasi ex propriis] but lead only to "probable" conclusions; our faith rests on the revelation made to the apostles and prophets, who wrote the canonical books, not on any revelation made to the doctors. Arguments from resources of natural reason are "extrinsic" and "probable"; they cannot "prove" what is of faith to those without faith, although they can perform other functions in the service of theology.[33]

What, then, does theological reason do on the basis of these principles and resources? What are its functions, and how does it fulfill these functions? Following Yves Congar, we can classify the functions of theology as preliminary, defensive or apologetic, deductive, and explicative.[34]

The preliminary function of theology consists in demonstrating the truths which, though not part of the articles of faith, are nevertheless presupposed by them, the *praeambula fidei*, such as the existence and attributes of God, the immortality of the soul, and the impossibility of finding ultimate happiness in a created good. These necessary presuppositions of faith may also be believed by those who do not know them by demonstration. This preliminary function proceeds from the principles and resources accessible to human reason as such. This, as noted earlier, is "natural theology" in its conventional sense.[35]

The defensive or apologetic function may be of two sorts. It may be directed against unbelievers, in which case theology tries to show why the content of faith is not impossible and to refute whatever arguments they bring against the credibility of faith. The basis of both defense and refutation is that of rational knowledge itself, the only ground common to believers and unbelievers. It is important to note here that strictly speaking, it is not possible to demonstrate that the content of faith is not impossible, for such a demonstration presupposes knowledge of the intrinsic intelligibility—the possibility and necessity—of the content of faith, a knowledge not available here below. Such defenses of faith are rather persuasive [persuasiones], not demonstrative, and the purpose of such defense is only negative, that is, to remove the obstacles or impediments of faith.[36]

The refutation of arguments against faith, on the other hand, has the force of a demonstrative argument. For Aquinas, there cannot be any contradiction between the truths of faith and the truths of reason. Likewise, there can be no demonstration of the contrary of the truth of faith any more than there can be a demonstration of the truth of faith by reason alone. Any argument against the truths of faith, therefore, must be an incorrect argument from the first principles of rational knowledge. Its conclusions are either sophistical or at best probable. It is possible, therefore, to refute such an argument by demonstrating it to be either impossible (e.g., atheism) or unnecessary (e.g., eternity of the world).[37]

The apologetic function may also be directed against heretics who, unlike the unbelievers, accept at least some articles of faith, in which case the theologian can show how the articles of faith they reject necessarily follow from the articles which they do accept.[38]

The deductive function of theology, which is its main function for Aquinas, consists in inferring further truths from the articles of faith, thus making explicit what is implicitly contained in the formal facts of revelation. Examples of this function are the proofs of our resurrection from the resurrection of Christ, the distinction of the virtues and gifts, and the unity of being in Christ. This process of inference from the well known articles of faith to the less known or unknown, from the explicit to the implicit, is mediated by the use of rational principles and philosophical (metaphysical, ethical, anthropological) premises. Such inferences, for Aquinas, derive their cogency from the principles of faith and are as demonstrative for those who believe as conclusions drawn from self-evident principles are for all. This sort of demonstration constitutes the proper scientific character of theology, i.e., theology as a science or knowledge of necessity. It is not possible to demonstrate the articles of faith themselves, but it is possible to demonstrate other truths on the basis of such indemonstrable principles. What is demonstrated here is not the intrinsic necessity of the articles of faith from which the argument proceeds but the logical necessity, once the principles are granted, of the conclusions so reached. Theology as a science in this sense is compatible with faith: what it makes evident is not its principles, the articles of faith, but only its conclusions about other related matters.[39]

The explicative or clarifying [manifestare] function of theology consists in trying to comprehend, clarify, and penetrate the meaning of the articles of faith themselves by means of the resources of human reason, especially through analogies and congruent reasons based on human experience. This explicative function, of course, does not provide demonstrative but only "extrinsic" and "probable" arguments, which nevertheless have real apologetic value and nourish the faith. The data of revelation, found loose and unsystematized in Scripture, are interpreted, correlated, and systematized by means of philosophical categories: metaphysical categories in trinitarian theology, anthropological categories in Christology, the categories of cause and sign in the theology of sacraments, and so on. In this way, without pretending to comprehend the intrinsic intelligibility of the content of revelation, theology nevertheless seeks to provide the motives of credibility by making it humanly intelligible, plausible, and persuasive. This sort of "persuasive," not "demonstrative," reasoning "does not take away the nature of faith because it does not render them [the truths of faith] evident, for there is no reduction to first principles intuited by the mind. Neither does it deprive faith of its merit, because it does not compel the mind's assent but leaves the assent voluntary."[40]

If Aquinas is not a rationalist who reduces the revealed content of faith to the principles and criteria of human reason, it is equally clear that he is not a fideist who leaves the activity of human reason no scope in the process of appropriating the content of faith beyond that of self-negation for the sake of a leap of faith. There is plenty that human reason can and should do in the service of theology as "faith seeking understanding [fides quaerens intellectum]." The content of faith is indeed "above" reason, but it need not be "against" reason, which is precisely what theology seeks to show in its many diverse functions.

In postulating these functions of theology, Aquinas is convinced that there is an inner harmony between reason and faith, between the truths and functions of reason which enter into theological reflection and the truths of faith which theology accepts while also seeking to understand them according to its own human mode of knowing. According to a statement of Aquinas that has become so familiar through constant quotation yet also penetrates to the heart of his theology, "grace does not destroy but perfects nature [gratia non tollit sed perficit naturam]," which therefore preserves its proper function even while being perfected by grace and is perfected by grace precisely in its proper function. The light of faith does not do away with the light of natural reason, both coming to us as gifts from God. Furthermore, as the natural inclination of the will serves charity, so natural reason serves faith.[41] "Just as nature itself is a preamble to grace," so the truths of reason bear certain "likenesses" to the truths of faith and also contain certain "preambles" to them.[42]

This means, for Aquinas, that should there be a conflict between reason and faith, such a conflict could only be apparent, not real. The truths of reason cannot be opposed to the truths of faith; if they are, they are corruptions and abuses of reason arising from faulty reasoning. Even "secular" wisdom is "opposed to God in regard to its abuse, as when heretics misuse it, but not in regard to its truth."[43] Only the false is opposed to the true. After all, God is the author of both nature and grace, both reason and revelation, and God cannot contradict herself. For Aquinas, "all truths, no matter by whom they are spoken, are from the Holy Spirit," who enables us either to understand them by bestowing natural light [lumen naturale] as in the case of natural truths or to appreciate them by sanctifying grace or special gifts as in the case of supernatural truths.[44] The knowledge of the principles known to us naturally has been implanted in us by God as author of our nature, in whose divine wisdom such principles preexist. Whatever is opposed to such principles, therefore, is opposed to divine wisdom. Likewise, the human subject of both faith and reason is one; it is impossible that contrary opinions exist in the same subject at the same time. In case of seeming conflicts, however, Aquinas states that we have to examine the truths of reason, not the truths of faith, to determine whether they are really true. Whatever is opposed to revealed truths cannot be true and must be condemned as false. For theology receives its principles from divine knowledge through revelation and is superior to all other human sciences—inferior only to the *scientia Dei et beatorum*—and performs the task of judging them and condemning as false whatever in them is opposed to the truths of sacred doctrine. This is precisely the function of theology as the highest wisdom.[45]

For Aquinas, there are three ways in which the use of reason or philosophy in sacred doctrine can go wrong. The first way is to make use of philosophical doctrine that is contrary to faith, as in the case of Origen, who, according to Aquinas, applied the Neoplatonist doctrine of three substances, God, the divine mind, and the world soul, to the Trinity and fell into subordinationism. The second way is to include the contents of faith within the limits of reason, willing to believe only what can be established by reason. This rationalism makes reason precede and determine faith, not the other way around. The third way is that of presumption, the arrogance to overstep the limits of finite knowledge and to try to grasp the divine realities fully rather than understand that they are incomprehensible. It is the function of theology as science to refute philosophical errors, the function of theology as the highest wisdom to judge and subordinate philosophy to itself, and the function of theology as human knowledge to seek to "know more and more about God in the manner proper to the human mind."[46]

The basic harmony between reason and faith makes it possible for theology to borrow philosophical arguments and principles for its own theological purpose of more clearly explicating the things of faith, provided, of course, that philosophy remains subject and secondary to the principles and light of faith, which should remain the ultimate controlling principle of theological reflection. In thus being used for theological ends and integrated into the theological context, philosophy undergoes a substantial transformation, a redirection in its motivation and a strengthening in its insights.[47] Those who use philosophy for theological ends "do not mix water with wine, but turn water into wine."[48] Theology borrows from philosophy and other human sciences, not as from superiors but as from inferiors and servants, in the same way as architects use tradesmen, or as statesmen use soldiers. Theology uses philosophy as philosophy itself often uses other sciences for its own superior purpose, and if it does so, it is not because of the intrinsic defect of theology but because of the defect of our own intellect, which is more easily introduced to suprarational truths through what is knowable through natural reason.[49]

Whether Aquinas was a theologian or a philosopher has been a longstanding controversy. The preceding discussion should make it clear that at least in the two *Summas* he was primarily a theologian, using philosophy as an instrument of theology and subjecting it to the light and criteria of theology. Operative *sub ratione Dei,* all the philosophy in the *Summas* is, in Anton C. Pegis's phrase, "*formally* theology and *only materially* philosophy." It may be going a little too far to deny, with Jacques Maritain, the authenticity of "Thomistic philosophy" because it exists in Aquinas only as matter formed by theology, and to call such philosophy, withdrawn from the light and context of theology, "a lifeless theology passing as a philosophy." Such a philosophy, I think, is still profoundly meaningful in itself. It is also clear, however, that both the overriding purpose and form of Aquinas's reflections were theological.[50] Missing this theological *form* and intentionality has generated countless misinterpretations of the philosophical content (such as the "proofs of God's existence") in the *Summa,* to the point of regarding such proofs as a claim to a self-sufficient foundation of an autonomous "natural" theology divorced from faith and revelation. Aquinas indeed respects the autonomy of human reason—it cannot simply be "beaten" into the service of theology—but he always places it *sub ratione Dei,* into the theological context, giving it theological form and thereby transforming it.[51] Whether this theological function and limitation of whatever natural theology there is in Aquinas will allay the fears of a Barth is a question too complicated to get into here.[52] What is clear is that he was primarily a theologian.

A Trinitarian Theology of Creation

For Aquinas, then, all creation can become the proper object of theology *sub ratione Dei.* Reason, too, can fulfill its properly theological role as reason as long as it remains faithful to the "light" of revelation and faith. Theology deals with God and creatures, contains divine revelation and rational reflection, and requires faith and rationality; these pairs remain part of one and the same science and wisdom within the unity guaranteed by the formal object of theology. Aquinas's profound conviction about the ultimate harmony of reason and revelation has long been noted as a distinctive mark of his theology. The basis of his conviction, however, has generally been traced only as far as his faith in the identity of the God of reason and the God of revelation and the principle of the impossibility of God's self-contradiction, which is a rather formal and abstract justification of his confidence.[53]

I think we can and must go much further. Aquinas's confidence in reason and creation as sources of theology is derived not only from the formal identity of the God of revelation and the God of reason but also from the concrete ontological orientation of all creation to God and of the rational creature in particular to the beatific vision of God. Even in their very naturality all creatures including reason are ordered to God as to their origin and end. It is this *ordo ad Deum* established by the triune God in Christ which constitutes their very being and which makes it possible for theology to consider them in their reference to God. Reflection on creation *sub ratione Dei,* then, is not something extrinsic to creation, any more than divine revelation is foreign to reason. Inclusion of all creation in theology only fulfills its teleological intelligibility, just as the "light" of revelation only "perfects" the dynamism of reason, whose "light" is nothing other than "the imprint of the divine light in us" [impressio divini luminis in nobis].[54] Aquinas works out this theological-ontological ordination of all things to God in terms of a christological, trinitarian, iconic theology of creation and reason, or a theology of all things created to "image" God through the Son in the power of the Holy Spirit.

In this iconic theology, all things are created by God as the first agent to tend to God as their ultimate end. As the effect of an agent is similar to the agent [omne agens agit simile sibi], creatures bear a certain similarity to the creator and are in a sense "images" of God the creator. The function of a perfect image is to represent its exemplar through similitude. God is not only the exemplar of creatures but also their end, for the agent is the end of the effect insofar as the effect tends to become like the agent [tendit in similitudinem agentis]. The form of the one generating is the end of generation [forma generantis est finis generationis]. As the most liberal giver [maxime liberalis], God creates all things "solely to communicate his perfection, which is his goodness."[55] The ultimate end of all creatures is to fulfill themselves by participating in God's own being and goodness and becoming like God [Deo assimilari]. God not only creates beings to share his goodness with them but also leads them through providence and government to their ultimate end. Thus, "all things tend through their movements and actions toward the divine likeness as toward their ultimate end."[56] When they desire their own perfection and precisely by doing so, they "desire God himself, inasmuch as the perfections of all things are so many similitudes of the divine being [similitudines divini esse]."[57] "From the first being that is a being and good through its own essence, everything can be said to be good and a being, inasmuch as it participates in that being by way of a certain likeness [assimilatio]."[58]

In seeking the divine likeness as the most fundamental tendency of their being, not all creatures do so in the same way or to the same degree. As Aquinas speaks of the analogy of "being," we may also speak of an analogy of "imaging" in him. In fact, we can say that the analogy of being is founded on the analogy of imaging; it is the degree of "likeness" to

God constitutive of the image that makes the analogy of being possible.[59] At the same time, we can similarly speak of an "analogy" of imaging, since creatures are images of God seeking to represent and participate in the divine exemplar and become like God in varying ways and degrees. The diversity of imaging God depends on the diversity of ways in which creatures participate in God's own being and goodness, for "each thing imitates divine goodness according to its own mode" [secundum suum modum].[60]

For Aquinas, there are basically four different degrees or ways of representing and imaging God. The lowest is the way non-intellectual creatures imitate God. Theirs is likeness to God by way of "vestige" or "trace" [per modum vestigii]. As God's effects, they represent God's causality, not God's specific form or nature, and bear divine likeness in a generic way as existing and living beings. Higher than the mode of vestige is the mode of "image" in the strict sense, representing something not only in its causal activity but in its own specific form or nature. Imaging God precisely in her own intellectual nature, in her activities of understanding and loving herself, is the very nature and privilege of intellectual creatures. The mind represents and images the Trinity primarily— "according to conformity"—when it knows God and assimilates itself to the form of God, and secondarily—"according to analogy"—when it knows itself and, in begetting and loving a self-expressive word, represents the immanent processions of the Trinity. (The mind only represents God as "vestige" when it is concerned with temporal things.)[61] Higher than the mode of image, however, is the mode of adoptive filiation through grace, through charity and faith. The highest mode of assimilation and participation in God is the mode of eternal life or the beatific vision of God's own essence through glory.[62]

Creatures are not images of God as accomplished facts but as teleological "tendencies" or "movements" seeking to participate in God ever more closely, become ever more like God, and thus image God ever more deeply. They are not images of God in the perfect tense of having already become such but in the imperfect tense of being in the process or movement of becoming such. It is precisely "through their own movements and actions" that "all things *tend* to divine likeness as to their ultimate end."[63] Creaturely imaging of God always remains imperfect—only the Son is the perfect Image of God—and creatures are in perennial need and process of becoming more perfect. This is why, for Aquinas, Scripture says that humans are made "to" [ad] the image of

God[64] in the sense of "a certain *movement* of a thing tending to perfection" [motus quidam tendentis in perfectionem][65] *so that* [ut] God's image may be in us.[66]

It is important, then, to take care neither to sharply separate the four levels of imaging as though they had nothing to do with one another nor to see them as sharing a common characteristic, the power to image God, in a static way. It is essential to see the different levels as progressive stages in the single cosmic movement of returning to God according to God's own teleological providence and government, and to see each of them as ordained to the next stage.

Thus, in discussing the human being as imaging God by imitating God's understanding and loving herself, Aquinas refers to the first stage of intellectual existence as "the natural aptitude for understanding and loving God," which is founded on the very nature of the mind [ipsa natura mentis]. He refers to the second stage of grace as "knowing and loving God actually or habitually [actu vel habitu], although imperfectly," and to the third stage of glory as "actually [actu] knowing and loving God perfectly." The first type of imaging is found in all human beings, the second in the just, the third in the blessed.[67]

We should note here not only that the first stage of intellectual existence as such—even prior to grace—is already described as containing the tendency to understand and love God, but also that this tendency is called "aptitude," a sort of potentiality, which then is fulfilled by the next stage of grace that "actually" realizes the aptitude of knowing and loving God, whose "imperfect" mode is in turn finally perfected in the glory of loving God "actually" and "perfectly."[68] Glory is the perfection of grace, as grace is the perfection of nature.[69] The adoptive children of God according to the likeness of grace are "ordered [ordinantur]" to the inheritance of the likeness of glory,[70] as "grace is a disposition for glory."[71] As grace perfects nature by healing the wounds of original sin, restoring its natural integrity and raising it beyond itself to a union with God as the object of beatitude, so glory perfects grace by leading it to eternal life. One might note here the mediating role of grace: precisely by perfecting nature, grace prepares nature for glory, for "glory is the end of the operation of nature itself assisted by grace [gloria est finis operationis ipsius naturae per gratiam adjutae]."[72]

Each stage is thus ordered to the next as potentiality to actuality, imperfection to perfection, in a single cosmological movement empowered by God's saving providence to share in the predestination of the Son and God's own life in the glory of God's children. The three stages are stages, in Yves Congar's words, "within the process of realization of the image of God, and of the growth in likeness to God."[73] Human life, then, is a *process* in which our "natural aptitude" is being actualized and perfected by grace for the end of glory. Just as there is no pure potentiality in nature but only potentiality in the process of actualization, so there is no purely natural aptitude that is not already in the process of being actualized and perfected by grace.[74]

In this sense we can easily understand how Aquinas could say that "the soul is naturally capable of grace [naturaliter gratiae capax]; since from its having been made to the image of God [ad imaginem Dei], it is fit to receive God by grace [capax est Dei per gratiam]."[75] For him, the justification of the sinner is *not* miraculous in the way that the resurrection of the dead is miraculous: life is beyond the natural power of a dead body, but the "capacity for grace"—note, not grace itself—is not beyond the natural power of the soul. In fact, "a certain suitability for the reception of grace" constitutes the nature of the soul and all rational beings, which can be "diminished" but "not totally destroyed" by sin.[76] As an intellectual creature with the capacity for transcendence, which material creatures lack,[77] the human soul possesses "the natural aptitude for understanding and loving God" and thus "imaging" God. This "natural" aptitude or capacity for God, however, can be actualized only "by grace." In other words, human beings are by nature destined for a supernatural destiny: human nature is from the beginning a nature oriented or ordered toward grace or "graced" nature.[78] Cornelius Ernst's comment is apt: "The human 'nature' about which St. Thomas is speaking here is not a pure Aristotelian nature, but a 'nature' created by God as part of a total divine plan for its final transfiguration into glory."[79] The distinction between "nature" and "grace" is itself a distinction posited by the grace of the triune God who seeks the participation of the human creature in her own life in glory.

It is important now to locate and understand this universal teleological movement of being as imaging God through assimilation and participation in the christological context of the creation of all things after the divine exemplar of the Word and the involvement of all humanity in the predestination of the Son as head of recreated humanity. Aquinas's discussion of the christological mediation of the movement of all creation from and to God can be reviewed under three headings: the special affinity of Christ with all creation as exemplar and mediator of both creation and redemption; Christ as head of the Church and all humanity; and the participation of all creation in the predestination of Christ.

Most fundamental to the christological mediation of all creation is the role and status of Christ in the Trinity. As the Word of the Father in which the Father knows himself, the Son, the Holy Spirit, and all creatures, Christ is the "connatural," "altogether similar," and "perfect" Image of the Father and the primordial model or prototype of all creation, God's own eternal concept of all things to be made.[80] As such, the Word is "expressive not only of the Father but also of creatures," "indeed only cognitive of God but cognitive and productive [factiva] of creatures."[81] He is the "exemplar likeness of all creatures," and "creatures are established in their proper species, though movably, by the participation of this likeness."[82] "The Word contains the essences [rationes] of all things created by God, just as artists in the conception of their intellects comprehend the essences of all the products of art."[83] Thus, all creatures are "nothing but a kind of real expression and representation of those things which are comprehended in the conception of the divine Word."[84] Christ is "the primordial exemplar [primordiale exemplar] that all creatures imitate as the true and perfect image of the Father."[85]

In this sense, the Word is "the principle of the production of creatures" and "the productive reason [ratio factiva] of those things that God makes," and enjoys "a certain common agreement with all creatures" [communis convenientia ad totam creaturam].[86] As such, the Word also contains and "is himself the eternal law by a kind of appropriation,"[87] i.e., the *ratio* or plan of the divine government of the universe, of the divine wisdom creating and directing all things to their proper acts and ends.[88] All things are ruled and measured by the eternal law imprinted in their "nature," the intrinsic principles of their action. Things have their truth only insofar as they imitate the eternal law.[89] All just laws are derived from the eternal law insofar as they partake of right reason. All laws that deviate from the eternal law are unjust.[90] It was only fitting that creatures should be restored to their original perfection precisely through the incarnation of the divine exemplar in whose likeness they have been made. "The first creation of things was made by the power of God the Father through the Word; hence the second creation ought to have been brought about through the Word, by the power of God the Father, in order that restoration should correspond to creation" [ut recreatio creationi responderet].[91]

The divine Word has not only a universal agreement with all creatures but also "a particular agreement with human nature."[92] This special affinity derives from the fact that "human beings get their proper species from being rational," while "the Word is akin to reason" in the sense that both "word" and "reason" are related to *logos* in Greek. Because of this common rationality, "image" can be predicated of both, of the Son as "the image of the invisible God" and of humanity as "the image of God."[93] Furthermore, the Word is the eternal Wisdom from whom all human wisdom is derived. As the proper perfection of human rationality, wisdom is fulfilled only by participating in the eternal Wisdom of the Word. For the perfection of human reason and human nature, therefore, it is fitting that the Word of God be personally united to human nature.[94] The ultimate salvation of a human being as an intellectual being lies in the contemplation of the First Truth, and it was only proper that "it should have been by the Word who proceeds from the Father by an intellectual emanation that human nature was assumed."[95]

Christ, then, is united with all creatures, especially humanity, as the primordial exemplar of both creation and redemption. Redemption does not lie in the destruction of the old creation and the construction of a wholly new creation but in the restoration and perfection of creation, and the model of both creation and redemption is the same Christ, in whom creation and redemption constitute a single teleological movement or *motus ad Deum.* Christ redeems the world as head [caput] of the church which, for Aquinas, is made up potentially of *all* humanity—and angels—from the beginning of the world to its end. As a human being personally united to the Son and thus enjoying the highest possible union with God, Christ in his humanity models the perfection of redeemed humanity and constitutes the exemplary source or *principium* of all grace. He enjoys the fulness of all grace and has the power to bestow grace on all his members.[96] "Grace was bestowed upon Christ, not only as an individual, but inasmuch as he is the head of the church, so that it might overflow into his members," for by his passion he "merited salvation, not only for himself, but likewise for all his members."[97] Christ leads others to the glory of eternal life "insofar as he is the head of the church and author of human salvation."[98]

Christ is not only the primordial exemplar of creation and redemption or the source of salvific grace offered to all as members of his body. For Aquinas, as for Paul, Christ also involves us in the solidarity of his own predestination and constitutes the very goal of our destiny. Our destiny is to be assimilated [assimilari] to the Word not only in form, as are all creatures, or in intellectuality, as are all rational creatures, but precisely according to the unity of the Word with the Father. We are preordained from all eternity to be conformed to the image of the Son by sharing as adoptive children in the likeness [similitudo] of the Son and thus in his own inheritance.[99] In this sense, too, "it was fitting that by him who is the natural Son, human beings should share this likeness of sonship by adoption."[100]

The exemplar of our destiny to adoptive divine filiation is Christ in his human nature, who was preordained from all eternity to be the natural Son of God by being united to the divine Son. It is in "one and the same act" [uno modo et eodem actu] that God predestined both Christ and us, Christ to be the natural Son of God and us to be children *in* the Son [filii et filiae in Filio] or adoptive children of God by participating in the likeness of Christ's natural filiation. Christ's predestination is the cause of our own predestination because his own eternal destiny as Son is the exemplar of our own and because his own death on the cross was preordained from all eternity to be the cause of our salvation. Our human destiny is not to a purely natural fulfillment but to participation in the likeness of the Son through the Spirit and thus in the inner life of the Trinity.[101]

It is no wonder, therefore, that Christ in his humanity is "our way of moving into God [via nobis tendendi in Deum]" and the "personal demonstration of the way of truth [viam veritatis nobis in seipso demonstravit]" leading to the beatitude of immortal life, just as for John he is "the way, the truth, and the life" (John 14:6).[102] His humanity actualizes our potentiality in relation to the beatific vision of God, the *scientia beatorum*, which is our ultimate end as creatures made to the image of God.[103] The union of the divine and the human in the incarnation is a concrete demonstration—"an example and testimony of a sort"—of the possibility of fulfilling the ultimate human vocation, union with God in the beatific vision.[104] As Christ is the mediator of creation, redemption, and glorification, of nature, grace, and glory, all theology for Aquinas must be "christomorphic" or "christoform."[105] As the revelation of both divinity and humanity, Christ effects the unique mediation of God the exemplar—of which the First Part of the *Summa Theologiae* treats—and humanity the image—the subject of the Second Part—and thus the crowning consummation of all theology—the content of Part Three.[106]

Aquinas's christological iconic theology of participation is thoroughly rooted in his theology of the Trinity. From all eternity, creation was oriented toward redemption and glorification in a single teleological movement, and the author, exemplar, and end of this movement is the triune God. The destiny of the creature is already implicated in the eternal life of the immanent Trinity: "As the Father speaks himself and every creature by his begotten Word, inasmuch as the Word begotten adequately represents the Father and every creature; so he loves himself and every creature by the Holy Spirit, inasmuch as the Holy Spirit proceeds as the love of the primal goodness [amor bonitatis primae] whereby the Father loves himself and every creature."[107]

God is the cause of things by his intellect and will, making creatures through his Word, which is his Son, and through his Love, which is the Holy Spirit. The eternal, immanent processions of the divine persons are the *rationes* of the production of creatures. Creation is appropriated to the Father as power, to the Son as wisdom, and to the Holy Spirit as goodness that gives life to things and governs them by bringing them to their proper ends.[108] Creation is not a necessary emanation from God's own essence; it is a product of God's self-knowledge in the Word and self-love in the Spirit, freely created to share in God's own goodness by participating in the exemplarity of the Son.[109]

As God's own will and love, "a kind of driving and moving force" [vis impulsiva et motiva], the Holy Spirit is not only the principle of movement and finality in God but also the principle of creation and the teleological government of the world whereby all things are directed to God as to their proper end. She enables us to love and be like God, "disposing all the powers of the soul to be amenable to the divine motion" through the seven gifts,[110] "configuring" [configurare] us to God, leading us to adoption as children of God, remitting our sins, renewing and cleansing us, giving us joy and security in God, driving us to fulfill God's commandments, and liberating us from both the slavery of passion and that of the law.[111] By the same Holy Spirit the Father loves himself, the Son, and all creatures. As love, the Spirit is the Father's primordial gift, the eternal "aptitude to be given" [aptitudo ut possit dari].[112] The Spirit manifests the Son as the Son manifests the Father.[113] Life according to the new law is based on the grace of the Holy Spirit given through faith in Christ.[114]

As created by God, non-intellectual creatures contain the "vestiges" of the "causality" of God, but not of God's "form," as do intellectual creatures, who alone are "images" of God in the strict sense. Non-rational creatures represent the Father, "the principle from no principle" [principium non de principio] insofar as they are themselves substances capable of exercising causality. They represent the Word, the primordial exemplar of all creation, insofar as they have their own specific forms.

They represent the Holy Spirit, the primordial (self-)love of God, inso-far as they enter with other creatures into mutual relations of a teleo-logical "order," which is ultimately derived from the will of the creator.[115]

The teleological destiny of intellectual creatures and especially human beings—to share in the predestination of the Son as head of the human race—is the work of the whole Trinity. The call to adoptive fili-ation, however, can be appropriated to each of the divine persons differ-ently. Aquinas attributes it to the Father as author [auctor], to the Son as exemplar, and to the Spirit as "imprinting on us the likeness of this exem-plar."[116] Human beings have been predestined to become the adoptive children of the Father by sharing in the likeness of the Son or "being assimilated [assimilari] to the splendor of the eternal Son through the brightness of grace attributed to the Holy Spirit."[117] As Christ is the hier-archical "head" of the church and the human race, the Holy Spirit is the "soul" and "heart" that invisibly vivifies and unifies the church.[118]

In Aquinas's christological, trinitarian, iconic theology of participa-tion, then, human beings are not created for purely natural ends; they are created for the supernatural end of glory and empowered to seek that end by the Holy Spirit who incorporates humanity into the Body of Christ who is the exemplar and cause of both creation and salvation and who guarantees the unity of the two. It is the triune God who has predestined and empowered all reality, especially human reality, in a sovereign econ-omy of grace, to transcend itself towards sharing in God's own life through the Son in the Holy Spirit. Whether we are conscious of it or not, our life is already immersed in the economic movement of the Trinity motivating, directing, empowering, and otherwise embracing us in the élan of divine grace, in "the very mission [ipsa missio] of the divine persons" that "leads us to beatitude."[119] In this sense, "creation is not meant as the basis of a natural theology, much less of a natural religion. Creation is not one sepa-rate form of revelation, a natural revelation. Creation is part of God's *one* revelation, consummated in Jesus Christ."[120] Precisely because we are cre-ated "to" the image of God, our *entire* life including both the "natural" life of decisions, passions, habits, laws, and the cardinal virtues, as well as the "supernatural" life of sin and grace, practice of the Gospel, and the theo-logical virtues—the entire Second Part of the *Summa*—constitutes "the movement" [motus] of the rational creature to God.[121]

One of the burdens of pre–Vatican II Catholicism was the purely extrinsic, dualistic relation between nature and grace, creation and re-demption. In light of the preceding discussion of the profound ordination of all nature to glory through grace, it should be clear how foreign such dualism would be to Aquinas's position.

In an approach that is unconventionally Thomistic yet deeply insightful and faithful to Aquinas, Joyce Little retrieves his position on the subject in the most succinct but also revolutionary way. For Aquinas, creation means the production of the act of existing itself, the most intimate and foundational reality of all created things. This act of existing is produced by the Father in the teleological power of the Holy Spirit to participate in the Word. Our very existing is thoroughly "relational" to the creator, to the primordial power of the Father, the cosmic wisdom of the Word, and the teleological goodness of the Holy Spirit.[122] At the same time, as the foundational reality of all created things that provides actuality to created essences and without which nothing is real, this graced act of existing is most internal or intrinsic to an entity, thus overcoming dualism and extrinsecism. As there is a real distinction between the act of existing and essence in all finite beings, the gracing of the act of existing also preserves the gratuity of divine grace; it is not owed to a finite essence as finite. As Aquinas put it, beatitude "is not of the nature of the creature, but is its ultimate end."[123] This view also overcomes the profoundly unsatisfactory traditional notion that grace is an accident. As embodied in the act of existing itself, grace is substantial, not accidental, as it is the whole existence that is graced by the gratuitous act of existing that actuates and finalizes the whole being, substance and accidents, essence and existence, toward the triune God. In Karl Rahner's language, grace is *intrinsic* to the existence of finite beings but not *constitutive* of their essence.[124]

An enduring issue of debate among Thomists has to do with the center and structure of Aquinas's theology in *Summa Theologiae*, in particular the place of Christ in that structure. Most scholars seem to agree on the—trinitarian—theocentrism of his theology which deals with God as the ultimate origin from which all things emerge and as the ultimate end to which all things return, and to concur that the *exitus* and *reditus* scheme originally expounded by M.-D. Chenu some five decades ago accurately explains the nature of Part One and Part Two.[125] The issue has to do rather with how Christ fits into that scheme, and especially with why Christ has been assigned to a separate Part Three rather than to a central place in Part Two dealing with the return of all things to God. Both Chenu and Otto Pesch argue for the appropriateness of such an arrangement on the ground that the incarnation was a free, contingent act of God that could not be integrated into the necessary, ontological, scientific structure of the first two Parts. As Chenu put it, the transition from Part Two to Part Three is "a passage from the order of the necessary to the order of the historical, from an account of structures to the actual story of God's gifts."[126] In contrast, Michel Corbin argues for a different interpretive scheme, that of divine exemplar and human image dealt with in Part One and Part Two, respectively, and thus for the appropriateness of discussing Christ, the revealing unity of God and humanity, exemplar and image, in Part Three, the last, crowning part of theology.[127]

On the other hand, in the view of Jean-Pierre Torrell, Aquinas did not precede his moral theology of Part Two with a Christology and try to organize it as a function of Christ, the Son of God and absolute model for all creatures, because this would give the center to Christ and contradict Aquinas's absolutely theocentric vision of *sacra doctrina*. Instead, Aquinas took the scheme of the human image and the divine exemplar and interpreted Christ as the unique mediator of grace who makes possible the resemblance of the divine exemplar and the return of the image to God. Christ is present, as is the Holy Spirit, even if his name is not mentioned, wherever that grace is present. Furthermore, instead of seeing satisfaction and reparation for sin and the establishment of strict justice as the overriding motif for the incarnation, a view that tends toward the anthropocentric, Torrell sees the Incarnation as necessary for the fulfillment of our ultimate end, the union with God in the vision of the divine essence. As the practical demonstration of the possibility of union of the human and the divine, the Incarnation was necessary for our attainment of the beatific vision. The Word incarnate is indeed our way to God. Aquinas's theocentrism, then, does not relegate Christ to the periphery. "Christ is exactly at the place where he ought to be: at the perfect center of our history, at the junction between God and human beings."[128]

In light of our whole preceding discussion of Aquinas's trinitarian, christological, iconic theology of participation, I think it is quite possible to produce a reasonable solution to the two issues at stake: that of the opposition between the exitus/reditus scheme and the image/exemplar scheme, and that between theocentrism and christocentrism. First, the two schemes are not mutually exclusive or contradictory but presuppose each other. Under the theocentric perspective, creatures come from God as their origin and return to God as their ultimate end. This, however, is to regard the relation purely formally. If we ask about the content of the relation, creatures come from God precisely as images of God and return to God precisely as their exemplar. Being created means bearing a certain image or likeness to God, while returning to the creator means participating in the divine exemplar. The form of the one generating is the end of generation [forma generantis est finis generationis]. The form of the one generating, i.e., his exemplarity, is also the end of generation, i.e., the end to be achieved by the generated, the images. The end of the generated is precisely to image and participate in the exemplar. To return to one's end is to participate in the likeness of the exemplar, just as to be generated is to be generated as the image of the exemplar. To speak of emergence and return is to speak formally about what the talk of image and exemplar tries to convey materially. Both are speaking about the one and the same reality. As Aquinas put it, "all things tend through their movements and actions toward the divine likeness as toward their ultimate end."[129]

Likewise, theocentrism and christocentrism need not be mutually exclusive. The triune God is at the center because God is the origin and end of all things, governing and providing for all things. The Father represents the primordial power of creation, the Word represents the divine reason or wisdom of creation, and the Holy Spirit represents the divine love that brings all created things back to their ultimate end. Theology, therefore, regards all things from the perspective of this trinitarian God. Christ, the Word incarnate, is likewise at the center because the humanity of the Word, the perfect image of the Father and exemplar of all created things, is the perfect incarnation or concretization of the union of the divine and the human, of the perfect divine image and the perfect human exemplar, of the perfect image of God the Father for us human beings and the perfect exemplar of humanity for God, and of the divine ideal for created humanity and the concrete example of recreated, redeemed humanity. As such, he is the sole mediator of grace that brings creatures back to their origin and end, the triune God. He is indeed "the way, the truth, and the life." It makes perfect sense, therefore, as Corbin argues, that Aquinas assigns Part Three to Christ: as Christ is the concrete unity of the divine exemplar and the human image, an exemplary, divinely inspired unity to empower and guide all human attempts to achieve union with the Father, so Part Three is the concrete unity of Part One and Part Two. It is clear, however, that theocentrism and christocentrism in this sense are not mutually competitive. Christ is at the center precisely as the way back to the divine origin and end of all things, while the triune God is at the center precisely as that origin and end.

The relation between theocentrism and christocentrism in this sense also manifests the centrality of the perspective of creation as the ruling theological *Denkform* of Aquinas, earning for him the theological name of "Thomas of God the Creator" from Otto Pesch.[130] The christocentrism of saving history is itself derivative from the triune God as creator of the world. The Word incarnate is precisely the eternal Word that contains the *rationes* of all things to be created. Salvation or redemption does not have its own end different from the original end of creation but has exactly the same end: the dualism of creation and redemption is foreign to Aquinas. Human beings were not first created for a purely natural end and then somehow given an additional, supernatural end through redemption. This is why redemption is referred to as "reparation" [reparatio]" and fulfillment of the original integrity of nature with its supernatural destiny. This is also why it was fitting and necessary for the original creative Word to become incarnate and redeem humanity, that is, "in order that restoration should correspond to creation" [ut recreatio creationi responderet]."[131]

It is remarkable that out of the twelve reasons for the necessity of the incarnation mentioned in the two *Summas,* only two are related to the remission of sins and certainty about that remission, while all the others have to do with the fulfillment of the ultimate end for which human beings have been created, the attainment of union with God in the beatific vision of the divine essence. Even the remission of sins and certainty about that remission are regarded as necessary only as a means to that ultimate end, sin being the greatest obstacle to that end.[132] Redemption itself is significant as an internal moment of the fulfillment of the original end of creation. Aquinas's theocentrism is precisely the theocentrism of the triune God as creator. His christocentrism too is significant as an internal moment of that theocentrism. The God to whom Christ is the way is precisely the triune God as the origin and end of all created things.[133]

Aquinas's Theology of Reason and Creation for Today

For Aquinas, theology considers not only God but also all of creation in their *ordo* and *motus* to the triune God. "Glory is the end of the operation of nature itself assisted by grace."[134] The locus or source of theology, then, is not limited to biblical revelation but is also extended in principle to revelation in all of creation, including both contemplation of physical nature and reflection on the histories and cultures of different peoples, their experiences of oppression, philosophies, sciences, and religious experiences. It is legitimate to look for the traces, images, and graces of the triune God in all of these because they belong to God's graced creation. The pneumatically motivated teleological ordination of reason to the beatific vision is as operative in non-Christian religions as in the Christian. The Holy Spirit is operative everywhere in both nature and history to bring about the "assimilation" of all things to the divine Exemplar to the glory of the Father. Aquinas's discovery of reason and creation as theological categories means the explicit universalization of the theological loci, the opening of theology to the whole of creation, and the placing of a significant portion of theology on the common ground with other experiences and religions. The task of theology need not be limited to an extended commentary on Scripture, as Aquinas's two *Summas* superbly illustrate.

In this regard it is worth noting what Wolfhart Pannenberg has to say about natural theology in the context of its history and his critique of Karl Barth. According to Pannenberg, the appropriation of the natural theology of the Greek philosophers by the Fathers of the church was not just a matter of a pedagogic adjustment to the intellectual climate of the culture in which the Christian message had to be proclaimed, but was much more importantly a matter of the very truth of the Christian God as the universal God of all nations, not just of the Jews, in a religiously plural world. Natural theology provided a criterion for judging whether any God could be seriously considered the author of the cosmos in its unity and totality, and Christian theology had to meet this criterion if it could really claim that the God who redeems us in Christ is the creator of heaven and earth and thus the one true God of all nations. A "pre-Christian" and "extra-Christian," that is, philosophical, understanding of God, no matter how much this must be subjected to later theological correction, is the very condition for making sense of the divinity of Yahweh and the triune God of Christian faith. Contrary to Barth, divine revelation is not only compatible with but presupposes a preceding knowledge of the same God without which the self-revealing God cannot be recognized or encountered precisely as God.[135]

Furthermore, according to John's prologue, the Word came to his own possession, not to a foreign territory. Of course, "his own" did not receive him, but the real pathos here is not simply that they rejected him but that those who rejected him were nonetheless his own, not strangers. His coming, therefore, could not have been completely alien to their being or knowledge, for "the being of creatures, even of sinners, is constituted by the creative presence of God, his Logos, and his Spirit among them."[136] In Romans 1:20 Paul refers to the knowledge of the power and deity of God gleaned from creation as itself a "divinely disclosed knowledge," not something we can acquire through "pure" reason; this knowledge makes possible the guilt we feel when we turn to idolatry. A Barthian dichotomy of natural and revealed knowledge of God is not quite Christian.[137]

One of the theological breakthroughs in recent decades has been the overcoming of the dualism of sacred and profane. Theologies of the "secular city," "the world," "history," and the "divine milieu" have been attempts in this direction. On the Roman Catholic side it culminated in the declaration on *The Pastoral Constitution on the Church in the Modern World* of the Second Vatican Council, which announced that the grace of the Holy Spirit is operative in all of humanity and creation albeit "in a manner known only to God" and that we should try to "decipher authentic signs of God's presence and purpose in the events, needs, and desires" of our times.[138] In this regard, it seems safe to say that the real breakthrough had already occurred with Aquinas when his trinitarian, christological theology of creation saw all nature graced for the sake of glory and made it possible to include *all* things *sub ratione Dei* in theology.

Historians point out that by discovering reason and providing a rational basis for theology, Aquinas overcame the crisis of Augustinian theology, which was being increasingly challenged by the discovery of Aristotle and Muslim culture. The challenge could not be met by simple appeal to previous authorities such as the Bible, church Fathers, councils, and popes.[139] Aquinas did not consider Aristotle's "ambitious and confident rationalism" a threat from which to retreat but a promise to explore. For Aquinas, as for Hegel, theology was not meant to withdraw into a special area of religious conviction and feeling but rather, as Thomas Gilby put it, "to advance into the whole world of human experience, and in particular of reasoned experience," based on the recognition of the unity in difference of nature and grace, which are "two in one flesh, real only in a single substance, married by the Word made flesh, the Son of God and the son of man."[140] It is clear that theology today is faced with far greater challenges and that its need for the resources of reason in all its competencies and resourcefulness is likewise far greater, especially in the areas of basic theological method, social-scientific analysis of scandalous suffering, natural-scientific exploration of physical nature, and comparative and dialogical analysis of the human movement to God in Christian and other religions.

Aquinas's profound confidence in the presence of grace in nature also enables him to accept, in a serene yet joyful way, the fundamental goodness of all creatures, each according to its own nature and particular role in an ordered cosmos. Yes, human nature has been wounded by original sin, but it has not been destroyed. Yes, grace does transcend nature, but it does so by perfecting nature through healing its wounds and preparing it for glory. Totally absent in the thought of Aquinas is the Kierkegaardian fear of aesthetic immediacy, the Barthian anxiety about idolatry of the finite, or Tillich's Protestant Principle. "God provides for everything according to the capacity of its nature" and "according to the nature of each thing."[141] God does not devour her creatures; her primary causality respects the secondary causality of creatures, allowing each to enjoy its own "dignity of causality."[142] Aquinas exaggerates neither the temptations nor the merits of creatures. He does not smother them with the sovereign majesty of the Barthian God, nor reduce their integrity by seeking to bring all under one organizing principle, such as grace, hope, existence, or liberation.

As Cornelius Ernst pointed out, the unity of the *Summa* is not "systematic" in the sense of subordinating all things to a single principle but "thematic" in the sense that the theme of *esse* in all its intrinsic variability provides the unifying topic of the whole.[143] There are sections in the *Summa* on the triune God, sin and grace, and the Incarnation, but we are not reminded of them in every section in the name of either the trinitarian or the christological "concentration" in Barthian fashion. The "light" of grace is indeed there, but it is there more like the light of the sun—a metaphor Aquinas loves—which illumines everything without always intruding itself, without always calling attention to itself or competing with other lights.

Aquinas's respect for nature and reason goes so far as to hold them up as standards of theological judgment. If nature is indeed oriented to glory through the aid of grace, "to sin is nothing else than to fail in the good which belongs to any being according to its nature," or "nothing else than to stray from what is according to our nature."[144] "Nature" is not just a "natural" but also a "supernatural" category. In the same vein, just as violation of nature is a sin, "those things that are opposed to reason are prohibited by divine law."[145] Not only does whatever contradicts divine revelation also contradict reason, but in addition whatever contradicts reason also violates divine law. Divine revelation and divine law provide norms from above; reason and nature provide them from below.

Aquinas's balanced appreciation of the respective roles of reason and faith within the unity of the theological horizon also makes it possible to avoid the dichotomy of rationalism and fideism. He rejects arrogant rationalism by insisting on the subordination of reason to the principles of faith as a servant to a master. He rejects fideism by insisting on the essential role of reason in supplying the philosophical presuppositions of faith, defending faith against its opponents, deducing other truths from the *revelata*, and in general rendering the content of faith humanly intelligible and plausible. Nor does Aquinas overcome the dichotomy simply by keeping nature and grace, reason and revelation, creation and redemption, as Brunner wrongly put it, "neatly divided by a horizontal line, distinguished from one another like the first and second storeys of a building."[146] It is a matter of mediation and interaction, not of division and juxtaposition. All things can be interpreted in light of faith, faith can be made humanly plausible in light of reason, and the role of reason in mediating faith is indispensable. Fully aware of the rationalist excesses of his day, Aquinas was convinced, nevertheless, of the ultimate harmony of God and creatures, revelation and reason, because the economic Trinity and the christological solidarity of all creation guarantee that harmony.

It is important to remember, however, that the actual overcoming of the dualism of reason and faith is not always easy to accomplish. In all its functions in and for theology, especially in its preliminary, deductive, and explicative functions that use analogies and congruent reasons, the "light" or horizon of reason is not merely external or instrumental to the articles of faith. As we are keenly aware in our hermeneutical age, concepts, metaphors, and paradigms do not merely explicate the content from outside; they also constitute and determine the content from within. It is one thing to recite the Apostles' Creed and another to explain the Trinity in terms of such metaphysical categories as being, essence, procession, person, relation, notion, mission, intellect, and will. When root metaphors and models change, the whole theology also changes. I am not sure whether Aquinas was aware of this deeper constitutive implication of the use of reason in theology.

Furthermore, Aquinas did not have our contemporary sense of the historicity of both reason and faith and tended, as a result, to reify both as *given* in isolation from the concrete historical conditions that constitute them. The articles of faith are taken in their purely intellectual content abstracted from the concrete historicity of faith and revelation. When such articles contradict reason, it is reason, for Aquinas, not the articles, which must be looked into. It does not occur to Aquinas to ask how historical assumptions and values might have entered into the very formulation and content of such articles themselves. The only historicity he admits is the possibility of progress from the implicit to the explicit, from the partial to the complete, and this on the occasion of either the perception of the inherent *intellectual* obscurity of the articles or the *intellectual* challenge posed by heretics. Such a development of dogma, however, is no more than the same faith simply more elaborated [magis exposita].[147] As far as the historical content of revelation is concerned, such content does not belong to faith intrinsically but only accidentally [per accidens] or secondarily [secundario]. It only provides examples of holy life and proclaims the authority of those who mediate revelation but does not constitute the essential content of faith as such. Revelation does not come *as* history (Pannenberg), which remains the realm of contingent singular events and thus incidental to the beatifying content of faith.[148]

Aquinas also fails to take reason historically enough. He is fully cognizant, of course, of the fact that human reason operates only within the limits of human nature. Things known are in the knower according to the mode of the knower [cognita sunt in cognoscente secundum modum cognoscentis].[149] Reason has no intellectual intuition of pure intelligibles; any knowledge of separated substances and a fortiori God is based on analogy with our knowledge of sensible things [sensibilia]. It is also limited by the subjective conditions of passion and ignorance. He is not however, also aware of the socio-historical limits of human reason; he does not take the senses and sensible things which limit human reason in their fully human, that is, historical and social, significance, *as* socialized and historicized sensibility. The social location of the theologian, the ideologies of the established order, the conflicts in the sphere of our social praxis: none of these is taken into account as the *intrinsic* condition of both the activity and content of theological reason as *human* reason. In itself "above time," it is only "accidentally" [per accidens] that human reason is subjected to time.[150]

Today, we are not so sanguine about the unity of reason and faith as Aquinas was. The history of modernity has been one of the progressive divergence and conflict of reason and faith, often verging on a life-and-death struggle between master and slave on issues ranging from evolution to atheism, historical criticism, political praxis, and the archaeology of knowledge. We are also increasingly confronted with the unsublated pluralism of reasons and religions in the world. The "light" of Christian faith and the "light" of reason in its historically conditioned diversity, the *ratio Dei* as interpreted in faith and the *ratio Dei* disclosed by reason in creation and history, do not always seem to coincide. Natural theology as reflection on all creation in its *ordo ad Deum* by a reason destined to the beatific vision but also culturally shaped and often ideologically tainted is not always agreeable to the "light" of revelation. All the more so because the integration proposed is not between unmediated, pure, universal revelation and historically conditioned reason but between revelation whose very content and light are interpreted precisely by historically ambiguous reason and that reason in all its diversity reflecting on God's creation. There is no way of returning to the Scripture principle in our "critical" age.

It is rather nostalgic of many contemporary trinitarian theologians, such as Karl Barth, Karl Rahner, Jürgen Moltmann, Wolfhart Pannenberg, Vladimir Lossky, Thomas F. Torrance, and Catherine Mowry LaCugna, among others, to lament the traditional separation of *de Deo uno* and *de Deo trino* given its classical form by Aquinas, arguing that such a separation reduces revelation to reason, denies the specificity of the Christian concept of God, and renders the economic importance of the Trinity otiose.[151] In Barth's language, the content of the trinitarian doctrine must remain "decisive and controlling for the whole of dogmatics."[152] It is questionable, however, whether the kind of total subordination of reason to revelation or the totalizing unification of reason and revelation they desire is possible today. Our intellectual situation is such that we may have to frankly recognize two kinds of revelation, "general" revelation of God in nature, conscience, history, and other religions independent of biblical revelation, and "special" revelation in Jesus Christ, without necessarily being able to settle the further question of whether general revelation is "salvific" enough.[153] At the present time we simply do not know how to relate one to the other, still less how to reduce one to the other. The only choice, it seems, is to pursue both reason and revelation, natural theology and revealed theology, and learn to live with a certain amount of tension, even conflict, between the two, for the foreseeable future.

It is precisely the contribution of Aquinas's trinitarian theology of reason and creation that it can enable us precisely *as* Christians to accept both reason and revelation along with their tensions and even learn from "other" reasons and revelations, without a debilitating Barthian anxiety and with the eschatological hope in their ultimate harmony. For the foreseeable future, the difference of reason and faith seems irreducible, and the ultimate harmony of the two may indeed have to remain an eschatological hope. This does not mean that natural theology becomes, as Brunner says about the Catholic conception, "a self-sufficient rational system of natural knowledge of God."[154] Reason as knowledge is indeed independent of divine revelation, but as theological reason, it is in constant dialogue, even if tensive at times, with the "light" of revelation, under the divine grace already operative in the theological depth of reason and creation, and the ground for the ultimate harmony of reason and revelation is the triune God operative in all creation.

It is also remarkable that in appreciating the role of reason, Aquinas does not turn reason into the constitutive principle of all knowledge and all being in the manner of modern European philosophy since Descartes. He was aware of the essential role of reason but never thought of erecting the *Cogito* of the isolated individual into a "first principle of philosophy" as did Descartes. He was certainly aware of the limits of human reason. Whatever is known is known according to the mode of the knower, and the human knower as a composite of matter and form can only know on the basis of material things. As sinful reason, it is also wounded by original sin and vices. Yet, he did not humiliate reason by writing *An Inquiry Concerning Human Understanding* like Hume or *Critique of Pure Reason* like Kant or *Concluding Unscientific Postscript* like Kierkegaard. He simply was not obsessed with either the glories or limitations of human reason. He took reason seriously, but not too seriously, and certainly not in any self-conscious way. Human reason is neither the constitutive source of all things in the manner of idealism, nor the absolute moral norm before whose bar everything must justify its existence in the manner of Kantian rationalism, nor yet the "whore" that Luther declared it was.

Aquinas, then, was precritical in the sense of not instituting a self-conscious critique of reason. He was also precritical in the sense that he was not systematically aware of the socio-historical, ideological conditioning of human knowledge. In an important sense, however, he was also post-modern and postcritical, insofar as he does not absolutize human reason and human existence in the homocentric fashion of Western philosophical modernity. Human beings are indeed rational creatures, but they are not thereby so privileged as to be the center of the world. Aquinas would not accept the Kierkegaardian and existentialist notion that God and things "are" but that human beings "exist." He does not apply special anthropological categories to the analysis of human nature, as Heidegger, for example, insisted on applying "existentials" to human existence and "categories" to things.[155] Important as a human being is in the hierarchy of beings, a human being is still fundamentally one being among others, to whom Aquinas applies exactly the same ontological categories—act and potency, existence and essence, matter and form—that he does to everything else.

Of course, Aquinas did claim that as rational creatures made in the image of God, human beings possess natural dominion over the non-human creatures, but this claim was simply an extension of the natural subjection of the non-rational (e.g., passions, appetites) to the rule of reason in a human being.[156] Only a rational being can exercise power with knowledge, freedom, and responsibility. The injunction to rule over the earth was hardly an authorization to plunder it with rapacious greed and technological violence as we moderns have been doing for centuries, but a responsibility to govern it with due respect for nature, order, and the common good. Human reason, the rule and measure of human action, is not the rule and measure of things; it is itself measured by things and subject to the law of nature, "the first rule of reason," which is a participation of the rational creature in the eternal law of God, whose intellect, as truth itself, is the measure of all things.[157] Furthermore, human beings are the "lowest" among intellectual creatures, who are themselves part of the universe and subordinate to the divine government to which all things are subject. Human beings are hardly the center of the universe; God alone is.[158]

In the most fundamental sense, all finite beings are equal; they are beings by participation, not by essence, beings by grace, not by merit. "Being is found to be common to all things, however otherwise different. There must, therefore, be one principle of being from which all things in whatever way existing have their being, whether they are invisible and spiritual, or visible and corporeal."[159] This ontological equality of all creatures, spiritual and corporeal, the equal contingency of their existence, excludes all possibility of arrogant homocentrism. The incarnation shows something special about humanity, but what it does show is not the greatness of humanity but the greatness of God's love. Aquinas certainly does not use the incarnation as an excuse for turning humanity into the center of the universe. "As to the condition of nature, an angel is better than a human being. God therefore did not assume human nature because he loved human beings, absolutely speaking, more; but because the needs of human beings were greater; just as the master of a house may give some costly delicacy to a sick servant that he does not give to his own son in sound health."[160] Furthermore, even an angel is better than a human being as to its "natural" condition only because of God's love: "Since God's love is the cause of the goodness in things, . . . no one thing would be better than another, if God did not will greater good for one than for another."[161] In their *ordo* to grace and glory, angels are only "equal" to human beings.[162] What is primary is being [esse] common to all things that are; what is ultimate is God alone as the existence itself subsisting through itself [ipsum esse per se subsistens].

It is as nonsensical and anachronistic to blame Aquinas for theologically justifying domination of nature by granting human beings dominion over other creatures, as it is to make him an ecological theologian before his time for insisting on the ontological equality of all creation before God. In his day the technological power of human beings to dominate nature was so meager that human dominion was limited to farming, cattle raising, road building, and some elementary modifications of nature absolutely essential for survival. In fact, human beings throughout history were victims of the violence of nature through earthquakes, floods, drought, hurricanes, snowstorms, and plagues, more than the tyrants over nature that we have lately become. The idea of ever "dominating" nature would have been simply unthinkable for people who would have counted themselves lucky if they "survived" the ravages of nature to the age of forty. Aquinas could not have had the kind of ecological consciousness that we today find so compelling, given our demonic capacity to pollute and destroy.

Still, Aquinas's theology does present a sacramental vision of the universe quite relevant to contemporary ecological concerns. All things possess existence and goodness only in proportion as they participate in God, in her being and her goodness, by way of a certain likeness. They do so as movements: "all things tend through their movements and actions towards the divine likeness as toward their ultimate end."[163] Creatures are, each in their own way, "so many similitudes of the divine being" [similitudines divini esse].[164] The whole universe expresses the power of the Father, the wisdom of the Son, and the goodness of the Holy Spirit, and consists of the dynamic movement of all creatures tending to their ultimate divine end through assimilation and participation under the direction of the Holy Spirit. Creatures are not just themselves but images, similitudes, or signs of the triune God preparing nature for glory through grace. "Glory is the end of the operation of nature itself assisted by grace."[165] The universe is a sacrament of God's grace moving all things to their divine end. To violate the "nature" of this graced nature is the very definition of sin, to sin against the creator whose sacrament it is. A sacramental universe demands awe and respect, not degradation and exploitation.

There is a discernible shift today, under the impact of the ecological movement, away from the historical, humanistic, and existentialist categories of modern theology to more inclusive, cosmological categories such as "life," "body," and "nature." It is problematic, however, whether each of these can really fulfill the comprehensive function assigned to it. "Life" is either a biological category when used in a narrow sense or a more inclusive category when used broadly enough to comprehend human and divine life, but in either case it also excludes non-organic, material realities. Both "body" and "nature" may be conceived broadly enough to include all creation, but they are not really applicable to God.

"Being," on the other hand, is simply all-inclusive, since it comprehends all things that "are," from God to angels, human beings, and the smallest particle of matter in the vast universe. Actual and potential, real and ideal, beings are all included. Furthermore, "being" comprehends all things that "are" with all their intrinsic differences: each being "exists" differentiated according to its own "essence." The category of being is comprehensive without denying the essential differences that do exist among different kinds of beings and therefore without being reductionist, as the categories of "life," "body," and "nature" tend to be when applied to all reality. "Being" is not only the most comprehensive and intrinsically differentiated but also the deepest category of all: all the perfections and qualities of beings presuppose and express the most fundamental act of beings, their "act of existing" that actualizes the totality of their reality from the depth of their being. To an activist, pragmatic mind "being" does appear abstract, as it does to much modern consciousness, but such "abstraction" may be precisely what the overcoming of homocentrism requires. It does take a contemplative mind to appreciate the existential concreteness of what it means to "be."[166]

Aquinas was able to appreciate reason without turning it into a homocentric transcendental principle of all reality because he never forgot the ultimate finality of all things, the *ratio Dei* to which all theological reflections must be brought back. Before the *ratio Dei,* Aquinas also had an incomparable sense of the sheer finitude of human reason in its irrevocable limitation to the sensible, as well as of the infinity and incomprehensibility of God. Our knowledge of God "does not transcend the genus of the knowledge gathered from sensible things."[167] At best, we know God as we know the cause from its effects, from God's effects in nature as in philosophical knowledge, or from God's effects in grace as in faith.[168] These effects indeed bear traces of likenesses to God, but such likeness is so imperfect as to be "absolutely inadequate [omnino insufficiens] to manifest God's substance."[169] In this life, "what God is not [quid non est] is clearer to us than what God is [quid est]," for God is above what we may say or think of him [quod sit supra illud quod de Deo dicimus vel cogitamus]."[170] God surpasses all things "infinitely according to every mode of transcendence [in infinitum secundum omnimodum excessum]."[171] In fact, "what is ultimate in human knowledge of God" is the Socratic confession that "one knows that he does not know God, because he knows that what God is exceeds everything that we can understand of him."[172] As long as we live in this world, even with the revelation of grace we cannot know what God is, and we are only "united to him as to one unknown [quasi ignoto]."[173]

It is to the vision of the essence of this God that all intellectual creatures including human beings are called. What no creature can "see" in this world will indeed be "seen" by the blessed in heaven by virtue of the "light of glory," but what they see is not the comprehensibility but precisely the incomprehensibility of God in her infinity. The *lumen gloriae* does not render God comprehensible to finite intellects; in the beatific vision God does not cease to be infinite any more than finite intellects cease to be finite. As Karl Rahner used to argue, divine incomprehensibility "does not really decrease, but increases, in the vision of God."[174] We are compelled to recognize that the God whose *ratio* constitutes theology is not only a God who creates, redeems, and glorifies us but also an incomprehensible God who cannot be reduced even to her love of us or our need of her in creation and salvation. God is "always more" than what she is *for us. Deus semper major.* God deserves praise and glory for her own sake in her own incomprehensible infinity. To consider all things *sub ratione Dei*, then, is not only not to forget God as their ultimate origin and end but also to pass into the doxology of a God whose very incomprehensibilty constitutes the inexhaustible source of our eternal beatitude.[175]

Chapter Two

THE IMPLICIT SALVATION
OF NON-CHRISTIANS

The Moral Way to God

The Debate on the Salvation of Non-Christians

Aquinas has made it possible, in terms of a trinitarian theology, for Christians to accept reason and creation without guilt or apology by providing both with a teleological theological significance in the cosmic scheme of creation and redemption. In doing so, he has also provided theological justification for universal human solidarity in two of the theologically most contested areas of human experience. Reason has always been suspected of complicity with paganism, and creation of complicity with "the world, the flesh, and the devil." These polemical views, always there in Christian attitudes with varying degrees of explicitness, have perhaps been the most potent factors in isolating Christianity from the rest of the world, condemning reason in the name of a unique revelation and the world in the name of a divine judgment, and adding to the division and fragmentation of the world in the process. By locating both within the trinitarian dynamic of grace Aquinas has made it possible for Christians to meet with others on the non-sectarian grounds of reason and creation. However conditioned historically, ideologically, and otherwise, reason still provides the only capacity and ideal of a way of knowing that is independent of and less particular than a particular religion. Creation in the sense of the totality of history and nature simply provides the common space in which different groups have to live together for all their differences. Christians, precisely as Christians and without negating any of their beliefs but precisely because of them, can now relate with others, without apology and reservation, in the public discourse of reason in the common space of creation.

Another factor in the relation among different human groups has been the regard in which one religion is held by another, particularly concerning the capacity of other religions for fulfilling the ultimate end of human existence as defined by one religion. From the standpoint of Christianity the issue has always been the possibility of "salvation" in and through another religion. The issue involves ultimate human destinies, the fulfillment or frustration of our ultimate ends, and thus the ultimate meaning of our identities. To say that there is no salvation in and/or through other religions could mean the ultimate in both loyalty to one's own religion and insult to another. It involves accepting one's own religion with an ultimate concern. It also involves making a final judgment of the ultimate worthlessness and transcendent futility of the other. No wonder that the issue has historically been most divisive.

From the Christian standpoint the prevailing alternatives in interreligious relations have been exclusivism, inclusivism, and pluralism. Exclusivism and inclusivism agree that there is one common, ultimate end to all humanity—salvation—and that salvation is ontologically derived from the atoning death of Jesus Christ on the cross. As Peter says, there is "no other name" than that of Jesus in which we can be saved (Acts 4:12), and Jesus remains the unique, universal, and definitive savior of all humanity. The difference between the two is that exclusivism insists on an additional, epistemological condition for salvation, explicit acceptance of Jesus in faith and conversion, while inclusivism does not, content as it is with "implicit" faith. Exclusivism thus "excludes" from the possibility of salvation all who do not profess their faith in Christ through conversion and baptism. Theologically, exclusivism is Christocentric or even Christomonistic. Aware of the fact that it is simply impossible for many to have an historical access to the Christ event existentially con-

crete enough to compel a decision of faith, and insisting on the universality of God's love, inclusivism looks for implicit moral equivalents of
Christian faith in other religions, interpreting them from the trinitarian
perspective as seeds of the Word sown by the Holy Spirit in the economy
of salvation. Inclusivism "includes" non-Christians and non-Christian
religions within the possibility of salvation, even regarding the religions
themselves as paths of salvation whose validity is ultimately derived from
the hidden presence of the Word through the Holy Spirit.[1]

Pluralism is itself pluralistic and admits of no easy definition. The only
common factor among its varieties is the insistence on respect for the self-
understanding of each religion in its difference and autonomy and the need
for interreligious dialogue and cooperation. Depending on the reasons given
for that respect, I discern five types of pluralism. First, there is the "phenomenalist" pluralism of John Hick and Paul Knitter, who regard different
religions as different phenomenal responses to the same ultimate noumenal
reality. Second, there is the "universalist" pluralism of Leonard Swidler,
Wilfred Cantwell Smith, Ninian Smart, Keith Ward, and David Krieger,
who stress the insufficiency of each religion taken in isolation and the necessity and possibility of a universal theology based on the mutually complementary insights of the different faiths. Third, there is the "ethical" or
"soteriological" pluralism of Rosemary Ruether, Tom Driver, and Paul
Knitter, who deny the ethical superiority of any one religion and accept
more or less the equality of all religions in the matter of moral achievements.
Fourth, there is the radical, "ontological" pluralism of Raimon Panikkar, for
whom being is pluralistic in itself, not only in relation to our perspectives
and horizons. Fifth, there is the "confessionalist" pluralism of Hans Küng,
John Cobb, Jürgen Moltmann, John Milbank, Mark Heim, and Kenneth
Surin, who consider each religion as an irreducibly particular confessional
totality and regard themselves as true pluralists because they refuse to reduce or subordinate religious differences to the same ultimate reality, the
ideal of a universal theology, or the single moral criterion of justice.[2]

Where does Aquinas fit in this spectrum? Did he believe in the necessity of explicit faith in Christ for all as a condition of salvation? Or, did
he consider implicit faith sufficient? Was he an Augustinian pessimist or
a modern-day optimist regarding the salvation of humanity? Why did he
not devote a single *questio* out of some 611 in the *Summa Theologiae* or
a single chapter out of some 463 in the *Summa contra Gentiles,* which
indeed would have been a most appropriate place, to a formal, systematic
treatment of the salvation of non-Christians? After all, with the increasing

cultural contact with Muslims across the Mediterranean, crusaders returning from the Middle East, incipient missionary journeys to Asia, and the Mongolian armies in Poland and Hungary, horizons were expanding and new frontiers opening up in the consciousness of non-Christian cultures, religions, and peoples.[3]

If Aquinas did not devote a question or a chapter to the issue of the salvation of non-Christians as such, he did write many articles and make a number of remarks with direct, explicit bearing on the subject. There are also certain general orientations and trajectories in his trinitarian theology, Christology, and theology of saving providence as well as in his near-Augustinian doctrine of reprobation that make his position on the subject reasonably clear even if it is burdened at times with tension and ambiguity.

In this chapter I will discuss Aquinas's approach to the salvation of the non-Christian in three stages. First, I present Aquinas's argument that salvation does normally require explicit faith in Christ as our mediator and way to God, but that for the non-Christian who has never had a real encounter with Christ, implicit faith in God's saving providence—the primordial hope that God will liberate us in her own mysterious ways—can substitute for the explicit faith in Christ.

Second, I discuss what I would call "the principle of nature" in Aquinas as basis for God's saving providence. Aquinas's God is a supremely "reasonable" God, who provides the means of salvation for everyone according to the nature of each, with full respect for the differences of times, persons, and conditions, never requiring the unnatural or the impossible of anyone. As discussed in the preceding chapter, Aquinas's "iconic" theology of participation looks upon the entire creation as a dynamic movement of "images" returning to their trinitarian source, exemplar, and end. From the very beginning, creation was never meant to be purely "natural"; it has always been "graced" nature, part of a larger trinitarian movement internally sustaining and orienting it to glory through grace. Human beings have always been called to share in the predestination of Christ by being incorporated into his body and conforming to him in his life, passion, resurrection, and glory. At the same time, this universal trinitarian call to grace and glory only occurs with full respect for the *differences* of historical circumstances. The grace of salvation is indeed offered to all, but to each in a different way.

Third, I discuss how, for Aquinas, this implicit faith becomes concrete in the moral act, which already embodies the dialectic of sin and grace in the trinitarian economy of universal grace. The good moral act—

doing what lies in us—is already salvific, and for the non-Christian this moral way to God is available. This chapter shows Aquinas to be at least an inclusivist, even a pluralist inclusivist, given his unfailing theological respect for diversity of situations. Whether he could also be regarded as a pluralist (of the confessionalist sort mentioned above) will be discussed in the next chapter, where I develop a sacramental theology of religions out of Aquinas's own principles and assumptions.

Dialectic of Implicit and Explicit Faith

For Aquinas, salvation means the attainment of one's ultimate end, the enjoyment of the vision of God in her own essence, and requires knowledge of the mystery of God and the way to the beatific vision. Such knowledge exceeds the capacity of natural reason and requires divine revelation and faith in that revelation.[4] Holding the right faith about God is necessary because loving God as one's ultimate end is not possible without the true knowledge of God. Aquinas opposes "the error of those who say that it makes no difference to the salvation of human beings whatever be the faith with which they serve God."[5] Aquinas is not an indifferentist.

Aquinas distinguishes between the essential object of faith, that which belongs to faith properly [proprie] and per se, and the secondary object of faith, that which belongs to faith accidentally [per accidens] or secondarily [secundario]. The essential object of faith consists of those mysteries of God which have directly to do with our eternal salvation: first, the mysteries of God the sight of whom constitutes our eternal happiness, such as the existence and unity of God, the trinity of persons, and the divine works such as creation, sanctification, and glorification; and second, the mysteries of Christ as the way to eternal life, which comprise all the events of his incarnation—his conception, birth, passion, death, burial, descent into hell, resurrection, and ascension, and extending to his second coming for the last judgment.[6]

The secondary objects of faith are those historical events recorded in Scripture which, however, have only an accidental relationship to eternal life, such as Abraham having two sons or David being the son of Jesse. With regard to these secondary objects of faith, Aquinas says that it is sufficient to believe them implicitly or "to be ready to believe them," insofar as we are prepared to believe "whatever is contained in the divine

Scriptures." We are bound to believe such things explicitly "only" when it is clear to us that "they are contained in the doctrine of faith."[7]

What about the essential objects of faith? Are we bound to believe in them explicitly? Here Aquinas's answer is thoroughly nuanced and intrinsically differentiated. So much here depends on whether we grasp all the nuances and distinctions he introduces into his answer.

First of all, within the group of essential objects of faith Aquinas further distinguishes between what he calls "primary objects of faith" (*prima credibilia*) and the articles of faith. The articles of faith are to theology, the doctrine of faith, what self-evident principles are to the sciences of natural reason. Now, there is a certain order among such self-evident principles according to which some are implicitly contained in others. All such principles are, in fact, contained in and reducible to the principle of non-contradiction (the logical impossibility of affirming and negating the same thing at the same time) as to a first principle.

Similarly, for Aquinas, all the articles of faith that constitute the essential objects of faith are implicitly contained in the two objects of belief according to Hebrews 11:6: "Without faith it is impossible to please God. For whoever would draw near to God must believe that he exists and that he rewards those who seek him." All the articles of faith are reducible to this faith in God's existence and God's saving providence. In a masterstroke of simplification, Aquinas calls these two the primary objects of faith (*prima credibilia*) and the *substantia* of faith. "For the existence of God includes all that we believe to exist in God eternally, and in these our happiness consists, while belief in His providence includes all those things which God dispenses in time, for man's salvation, which are the way to that happiness; and in this way, again, some of those articles which follow from these are contained in others: thus faith in the redemption of humanity includes belief in the incarnation of Christ, his passion and so forth."[8] The articles of faith only explicate these primary objects.

Is it, then, sufficient to believe explicitly in the primary objects of faith, or is it also necessary to believe explicitly in those articles that define and explicate the primary objects of faith? Aquinas's answer seems rather ambiguous at first. In response to the question of "whether we are bound to believe in anything explicitly,"[9] he makes a distinction—noted above—between the essential and the accidental objects of virtue and argues that the essential object of the virtue of faith comprises that by which humans are rendered blessed. As we are bound to have faith, so we are bound to believe explicitly in the *essential* object of faith, because there can be no faith without it. What, then, is the essential object of faith which must be believed explicitly?

As we have just seen in II-II, 1, 7, Aquinas makes a clear distinction between the primary objects of faith, the two things mentioned in Hebrews 11:6, and the articles of faith defined in the Apostles' Creed, yet also insists that "all the articles of faith are implicitly *contained* [continentur] in certain primary objects of faith [primis credibilibus]." In II-II, 2, 5, however, he simply equates the two and says that "regarding the primary objects of faith, which *are* [sunt] articles of faith, we are bound to believe explicitly." Insofar as he assumes an implicit identity of content or substance between the two, it can be said that there is nothing improper with such an identification. But to the reader of II-II, 1, 7, it remains unclear whether the obligation of explicit faith extends only to the primary objects of faith or also includes the articles of faith.

Aquinas removes all ambiguity regarding the object of explicit faith in the immediately subsequent articles. In II-II, 2, 6, dealing with the question, "whether all are equally bound to have explicit faith," he responds by saying that not all are so bound. Those who have the task of instructing others are obligated to "have a fuller acquaintance [pleniorem notitiam] with the objects of belief and to believe more explicitly." "The explication of the objects of belief [explicatio credendorum] is not equally necessary for salvation with regard to all, for the *majores* [the educated ones] entrusted with the task of teaching others are bound to believe in more things explicitly than do others," that is, the *minores* [the uneducated] and simple folks [simplices]. If this article introduces degrees of explicitness according to one's intellectual attainment, the following article introduces further gradations of explicit faith—and of the content of such faith— according to one's proximity to Christ in the history of salvation.

In responding to the question, in II-II, 2, 7, of "whether it is necessary for salvation for all people to believe explicitly in the mystery of Christ," Aquinas begins by stating the formal norm that the essential object of faith consists of "that through which we attain beatitude" and that the incarnation and passion of Christ is precisely the way to that beatitude. As according to Acts 4:12, there is "no other name" for human salvation. His conclusion is that the mystery of the incarnation must be believed "at all times" "among all." It is crucial, however, to note his sensitivity to difference and the decisive qualifiers he introduces. It is necessary for all at all times to believe in the mystery of the incarnation, but note, not "explicitly" but only "in some way" [aliqualiter], meaning "in different ways according to the difference of times and persons" [diversi-mode tamen secundum diversitatem temporum et personarum].

Aquinas showed the same sensitivity to difference as early as *De veritate*, 14, 11. While insisting that there are some things that *all* have to believe *explicitly* at *all times,* namely, the content of Hebrews 11:6, God's existence and God's saving providence, which he would later call *prima credibilia* in the *Summa Theologiae,* he also introduced gradations of explicitness according to the "diversity of times and persons." There are some things that have to be explicitly believed at all times but not by all, some things to be believed by all but not at all times, and some things that need to be explicitly believed neither at all times nor by all. The perfection of faith that consists in the full explication of faith does not belong to all. Not all are bound to believe explicitly in all things that are of faith; only the teachers of faith are so bound. Even these teachers, however, are not bound to believe in all things explicitly at all times.

For Aquinas, our faith or knowledge of divine things does grow through the passage of time [per successiones temporum]. Such growth reaches fullness and perfection at the time of grace, i.e., the time of God's revelation in Christ. At this time, then, the educated ones are bound to believe explicitly in all things that are of faith. *Before* this time of grace, however, even the educated are not bound to believe in all things explicitly. Still, more things were believed explicitly *after* the time of the law and the prophets than *before. Before* the fall, there was no obligation to believe explicitly in those things concerning the redeemer because there was as yet no need of redemption. Nonetheless, there was an implicit faith in divine providence insofar as Adam and Eve believed that God would provide all things necessary for salvation to those who love God.

Both before and after the fall, however, and at all times, the educated had the obligation to hold an explicit faith in the Trinity. The uneducated did not have this obligation between the fall and the time of grace. (Before the fall, there was no distinction between educated and uneducated.) Likewise, between the fall and the time of grace, the educated were bound to hold an explicit faith in the redeemer, while the uneducated were bound only to an implicit faith, such as faith in the patriarchs and prophets or in divine providence.

At the time of grace, however, *all* are bound to have an explicit faith in the Trinity and the redeemer. The uneducated, however, are not bound to believe explicitly in all things that can be believed [credibilia] regarding the Trinity and the redeemer; only the educated are so bound. The uneducated are to believe explicitly in general articles such as the unity and trinity of God, the incarnation, death, and resurrection of the Son, and other things of this kind that the church has established.

Aquinas's discussion of the "diversity of times and persons" in the *Summa Theologiae* follows lines similar to those in *De veritate*, but with subtle differences. Aquinas said in the earlier work that before the fall there was no obligation to hold an explicit faith in the redeemer but that there must be at least an implicit faith in God's saving providence. In the later work, however, Aquinas says that it appears (*videtur*) that the man had an explicit belief in Christ's incarnation as part of the consummation of glory, although not as a means of redemption from sin. How did Adam know this when he did not have a foreknowledge of his own sin? Aquinas holds that he could not have known about a man leaving father and mother and cleaving to his wife without also knowing about Paul's interpretation of marriage, in the Ephesians, as bearing on the mystery of Christ and his church.[10]

After the fall, the mystery of Christ was explicitly believed not only regarding the incarnation but also the passion and resurrection as means of human redemption from sin and death. How does Aquinas know this? From the fact that the various sacrifices both before and under the law "prefigured" Christ's passion. The educated had an explicit knowledge of the christological significance of the sacrifices both before and under the law, the uneducated a veiled (*velata*) knowledge. The ease of knowledge of the mystery of Christ was directly proportionate to the nearness of Christ.[11]

After the revelation of grace, both the learned and the uneducated are bound to have an explicit faith in the mysteries of Christ, especially those celebrated throughout the church and proclaimed publicly. Central here are the articles mentioned in II-II, 1, 8, that refer to the incarnation, i.e., Christ's conception, birth, passion, death, burial, descent into hell, resurrection, ascension, and coming for the last judgment. The degree of explicitness with which any given person must accept the more subtle points of the articles of the Creed "depends on what is appropriate to the status and office of each [secundum quod convenit statui et officio uniuscujusque]."[12]

What is most relevant here is Aquinas's response to the objection that explicit faith in Christ's incarnation was not necessary for everyone for salvation because many pagans received salvation through the ministry of angels. Having received no revelation, they had neither implicit nor explicit faith in Christ. His response is twofold. First, he believes that many pagans did receive revelation about Christ. Second, however, if some had been saved to whom no revelation had been made, "they had not been saved apart from the faith in the mediator" [non fuerunt salvati absque fide mediatoris]. If they had no explicit faith, "they had at least implicit faith in divine providence, believing that God was the liberator of humanity in ways of his own choosing and according as the Spirit would reveal to those who know the truth" [secundum modos sibi placitos et secundum quod aliquibus veritatem cognoscentibus Spiritus revelasset].[13]

It is crucial to note three things here. First, Aquinas allows that for those pagans who have received no revelation about Christ, faith in God's saving providence, i.e., the "primary objects of faith," can substitute for explicit faith in Christ as a condition of salvation, and that this faith in God's providence may only be implicit. Second, here in the *Summa Theologiae,* his most mature work, Aquinas no longer mentions, as he did in his previous works, the possibility of private revelation or the miraculous sending of a preacher in the case of those sincerely seeking salvation without ever hearing about Christ.[14] Third, the criterion of implicit faith in saving providence as a condition of salvation would apply to anyone who has had no effective access to the revelation about Christ, regardless of when the person lived. The decisive issue is not whether a person lived before or after Christ but whether the person has had effective access to that revelation. Aquinas considers Cornelius a "believer" by virtue of implicit faith even though he lived after Christ but without hearing his Gospel.[15] Even after the Christian revelation, not all are bound to have an explicit faith in Christ.[16]

In his commentary on Hebrews 11:2 Aquinas repeats much the same idea. After the fall of Adam salvation is not possible without faith in the mediator, but the mode of believing in the mediator is made diverse "according to the diversity of times and conditions [secundum diversitatem temporum et statuum]." Those who have seen the benefits of Christ are obligated to believe more than those who lived before Christ, just as educated ones and those under the law are respectively obligated to believe more explicitly than uneducated ones and those before the law. "With regard to the pagans who were saved, it was sufficient for them to believe that God was a rewarder, which is not possible except through Christ. Thus, they implicitly believed in the mediator."[17]

It is important here to call special attention to a passage of *Summa Theologiae* that has been scarcely noted in the debate. In I-II, 113, 4, written shortly prior to the above passage (II-II, 2, 7) about implicit faith in saving providence as a sufficient condition for the salvation of the pagan,

Aquinas does require the movement of faith as an act of turning to God for the justification of the ungodly [impii]. The content of this faith, however, is indicated by a simple reference to Hebrews 11:6, the faith in saving providence. Even in response to the question of whether one ought to think about [cogitare] *all* articles of faith in the required act of faith, Aquinas does not say that one ought to but that we must believe that God justifies human beings "through the mystery of Christ." The *prima credibilia* and substance of faith do remain faith in God's saving providence.

This also demands a more nuanced understanding of Aquinas's doctrine concerning unbelief. In II-II, 10, dealing with unbelief, he begins by noting two kinds of unbelief: unbelief as *ignorance* of divine things [ignorantia divinorum] in the sense of the simple absence of faith arising from the fact that there has been no opportunity to hear about them, and unbelief as *resistance* to faith [contrarietas ad fidem] arising from the pride unwilling to subject one's intellect to the rules of faith. For Aquinas, resistance to faith is a sin, but ignorance of faith is not so much a sin as a punishment for original sin. Unbelief in this latter sense is not of itself damning. "If such like unbelievers are damned, it is on account of other sins, which cannot be taken away without faith, but not on account of their sin of unbelief."[18] Unbelievers may be damned not for their unbelief due to their original sin but only for their personal sins, which, however, "cannot be taken away without faith." Unbelief as invincible ignorance is not unbelief in the proper sense; only unbelief as resistance to faith "fulfills the notion of unbelief [perficitur ratio infidelitatis]."[19]

Regarding the ambiguous status of those who do not believe because of ignorance, yet who may be damned for personal sins unless they have faith, Francis Sullivan asks: "Does this mean that everyone lacking faith would inevitably be damned for personal sins? Or would St. Thomas still admit that an individual whose lack of faith was inculpable might 'do what lay in his power,' and that to such an individual God would provide the means by which he could arrive at an act of saving faith?"[20] In light of the preceding discussion about the salvation of non-Christians in terms of implicit faith in God's saving providence—the *prima credibilia*—the answer has to be the second alternative, and the "means" provided would be implicit faith. This, I think, is confirmed by Aquinas's denial that Cornelius was an unbeliever, even though he had not yet heard the truth of the Gospel. Cornelius was ignorant of the content of faith, yet "he was not an unbeliever, else his works would not have been acceptable to God, whom none can please without faith. Now he had implicit faith, as the truth of the Gospel was not yet made manifest."[21]

This also means that Aquinas is postulating an intermediate state between the unbelief of invincible ignorance as a state of original sin but without further personal sins and the unbelief of resistance to faith as a state of culpable personal sins. Cornelius provides the model of a pagan who is indeed invincibly ignorant yet acquires at least implicit faith due to his trust in God's saving providence and openness to divine grace. Between ignorance of the content of faith and resistance to it, there is also resistance to—or acceptance of—*implicit* faith. The situation of the pagan unbeliever who has never heard of the Gospel is neither that of pure nature nor that of original sin alone; it is a situation marked by the dialectic of personal sin and divine grace with at least an offer of implicit faith.

I think it is this third possibility that Aquinas is referring to in his otherwise rather puzzling threefold typology of unbelief as resistance to faith. For him, faith can be resisted *before* it has been accepted, which is the unbelief of pagans, or *after* it has been accepted, either "in the figure," which is the unbelief of the Jews, or "in the very manifestation of truth," which is the unbelief of heretics.[22] The unbelief of heretics is the most grievous, that of pagans the least.[23] I wonder what sense it makes to speak of resisting something even *before* one accepts it, unless one is speaking of resistance to *implicit* faith—that is, of implicit unbelief—blocking explicit acceptance or explicit faith, which also allows the possibility of implicit acceptance of faith or implicit belief.

We cannot obviously share the assumption that Aquinas makes in this discussion about the extent to which the knowledge of the Christian revelation had spread in both time and space. As we have seen, Aquinas assumed that the educated had known about the Trinity before and after the fall and indeed at all times, and had known about the redeemer before the incarnation.[24] Even Adam had known about the incarnation, before his fall as part of the consummation of glory, and after his fall as the means of human redemption. Aquinas also assumed that many pagans received the revelation about Christ.[25] Some of the inferences underlying these assumptions—e.g., that Adam knew about Christ because his marriage "prefigured" the union of Christ and the church according to Ephesians, or that pagans and Jews knew about Christ's passion because the various sacrifices before and under the law "prefigured" it—certainly appear fantastic to us brought up on historical criticism.

In this regard I do not share Max Seckler's view that Aquinas does not base his discussion of the need for explicit faith on "intrinsic fittingness or the consequence of a once established salvific order." Our discussion of his distinction between essential and secondary objects of faith, between *prima credibilia* and articles of faith, between implicit and explicit faith, together with the principle of nature and difference, should clearly show that Aquinas did base his discussion on considerations of intrinsic fittingness and not solely on the assumption about the extent of the spread of the knowledge of the Christian revelation, as Seckler seems to argue. But Seckler is quite right in saying that the assumption did contribute to the discussion and that it is false. He is also right that Aquinas does provide a more organic, less miraculous, and more thoughtful solution than that of the emergency preacher and a private revelation, although this position is not yet fully formulated conceptually.[26]

The Principle of Difference in Saving Providence

Turning now to the nature of this implicit belief and unbelief in the case of the pagan, we recall that for Aquinas, explicit faith in the revealed mysteries of God and Christ as set down in the articles of the Creed is the normal requirement for salvation, that is, for those who have heard the Gospel. For those who have not, implicit faith in God's saving providence is sufficient. This *differentiation* of requirement is itself derived from a more fundamental principle which Aquinas attributes to divine providence, which I call the "principle of nature." This principle states that "God provides for all things according to the nature of each thing [Deus providet omnibus secundum uniuscujusque modeum]"[27] and that "God provides for each nature according to its capacity."[28] "God moves all things according to the nature of each [secundum modum uniuscuiusque]," which means that in matters of saving justification, God "moves human beings to justice according to the condition of human nature [secundum conditionem naturae humanae]." If it is the proper nature of a human being to have free will, then, "in someone who has the use of free will, the motion from God to justice does not occur apart from the movement of free will."[29] "It belongs to divine providence to provide for each one according to the mode of its condition [secundum modum suae conditionis]," and "God's grace is a sufficient cause of human salvation. But God gives grace to human beings

in a way which is suitable to them [secundum modum eis convenien-
tem]."[30] "Grace perfects nature according to the mode of the nature
[secundum modum naturae][e.g., human, angelic], just as every perfection is received in the perfectible according to its mode."[31] Likewise, "it
is a law of divine providence that nothing shall act beyond its powers."[32] For Aquinas, "divine wisdom requires that provision be made
for the various classes of things in harmony with themselves [secundum
earum congruentiam]."[33]

In other words, God deals with things according to their distinctive
nature and capacity, requiring different things of different people in their
different circumstances. With unfailing respect for difference in nature,
capacity, and situation, God refrains from demanding the unnatural or
the impossible by demanding the same of all peoples. God's saving grace
is offered to all human beings precisely as they concretely exist in all the
differences of their history, culture, and religion. God is not a totalitarian
despot demanding uniformity at all times and places.

We have already seen Aquinas's sensitivity to difference in arguing
for differential requirements in the matter of faith as a condition of salvation. He made a distinction not only between educated and uneducated, those with teaching responsibilities and those without, but also
among different periods in the history of salvation such as the fall, the
giving of the law, and the time of revelation in Christ, and between Christians who have heard the revelation and pagans who have not. Aquinas
assigns differential requirements for salvation "according to the diversity
of times and persons" or "according to what is appropriate to the status
and office of each [secundum quod convenit statui et officio unius-
cuiusque]."[34]

It is in terms of this principle of nature—and difference—that
Aquinas argues for a gradualist, evolutionary understanding of revelation. Before the law, only some families such as the patriarchs were
taught to believe in God in a general way, as one and almighty. Under the
law, a whole people were taught about God in a more excellent way, with
Moses receiving even a fuller instruction about the simplicity of the
divine essence. Under grace, the mystery of the Trinity was revealed by
the Son of God himself.[35] Like a good teacher, the divine pedagogue
"condescends to the disciple's capacity and instructs him little by little. It
is in this way that human beings made progress in the knowledge of faith
as time went on." The knowledge of faith necessarily proceeds from
imperfect to perfect, because in regard to divine knowledge, human

beings are like matter, a potential principle, receiving the influx of divine action.[36] Human beings learn "not indeed all at once, but little by little, according to the mode of their nature."[37]

Aquinas's sensitivity to difference is radically consistent to the point of defending the right of erroneous conscience to reject the belief in Christ when reason judges it to be evil. Human will can only act according to the object as proposed by reason. Now, erring reason can accidentally find what is evil in itself to be good, as it can also accidentally find what is good in itself to be evil. Since the will according to its own nature tends to its object only as proposed by reason, there is no alternative but for the will to follow reason, even erring reason. Thus, "to believe in Christ is good in itself, and necessary for salvation: but the will does not tend thereto, except inasmuch as it is proposed by reason. Consequently, if it be proposed by reason as something evil, the will tends to it as to something evil: not as if it were evil in itself, but because it is evil accidentally, through the apprehension of reason. . . . We must therefore conclude that, absolutely speaking, every will at variance with reason, whether right or erring, is always evil. . . . When erring reason proposes something as being commanded by God, then to scorn the dictate of reason is to scorn the commandment of God."[38] In other words, those who feel bound by their conscience to reject Christian faith as evil—such as twentieth-century protest atheists—are morally bound to follow that conscience.

It is significant to note that Aquinas uses the principle of nature in arguing for the appropriateness of incarnate and material manifestations of the divine and the necessity of sacraments. Regarding the fittingness of visible signs of the trinitarian missions and the incarnation, he states: "God provides for all things according to the nature of each thing. Now the nature of human beings requires that they be led to the invisible by visible things, as explained above [I, 12, 12]. Wherefore the invisible things of God must be made manifest to human beings by the things that are visible."[39] As will be discussed in the next chapter, most of his arguments for the necessity or fittingness of the incarnation are arguments based on "harmony with human nature [congruebat humanae naturae]."[40] One of his arguments for the necessity of the sacraments is "from the condition of human nature which is such that it has to be led by things corporeal and sensible to things spiritual and intelligible. Now it belongs to divine providence to provide for each one according as its condition requires. Divine wisdom, therefore, fittingly provides humanity with means of salvation, in the shape of corporeal and sensible signs that are called sacraments. . . .

God gives grace to human beings in a way which is suitable to them [Deus dat hominibus gratiam secundum modum eis convenientem]. Hence it is that human beings need the sacraments that they may obtain grace."[41]

Likewise, regarding the availability of baptism: "It is due to the mercy of him who will have all human beings to be saved (1 Timothy 2:4) that in those things which are necessary for salvation, they can easily find the remedy. Now the most necessary among all the sacraments is baptism, which is man's regeneration unto spiritual life. . . . Consequently, lest human beings should have to go without so necessary a remedy, it was ordained, both that the matter of baptism should be something common that is easily obtainable by all, i.e., water; and that the minister of baptism should be anyone, even not in orders, lest from lack of being baptized, human beings should suffer loss of their salvation."[42]

The principle of difference also means that "diverse sacraments suit different times [diversa sacramenta diversis temporibus congruunt]. . . . Just as under the state of the law of nature man was moved by inward instinct and without any outward law, to worship God, so also the sensible things to be employed in the worship of God were determined by inward instinct. But later on it became necessary for a law to be given from without: both because the law of nature had become obscured by human sins; and in order to signify more expressly the grace of Christ, by which the human race is sanctified. And hence the need for those things to be determinate, of which men have to make use in the sacraments. Nor is the way of salvation narrowed thereby: because the things which need to be used in the sacraments, are either in everyone's possession or can be had with little trouble."[43]

Now, if God wishes human beings to be saved, and yet there are human beings who cannot reasonably be expected to know anything of the Christian revelation because of their "diversity of times and persons," how would the eminently reasonable God of Aquinas provide for their salvation? What do "nature" and "difference" require with regard to this theologically most important difference, that between Christians and non-Christians? To ask with Seckler, how is the implicit faith of good pagans such as Cornelius concretely mediated?[44]

Dialectic of Nature and Grace in the Moral Act

As early as his commentary on the *Sentences,* Aquinas operates with the assumption that God wishes all human beings to be saved and that God is reasonable enough to provide whatever in the conditions of salvation does not depend on the free will of an individual; in any event, God does not demand more than what lies within the power of one's free will. Thus: "In those things which are necessary for salvation God is or never was absent to the human being seeking salvation, unless something might remain from that person's own fault. So the presentation of those things which are necessary for salvation either would be provided for a person by God through a preacher of faith (as with Cornelius) or by revelation. Having presupposed this, it then lies in the power of free will for one to enter into an act of faith."[45] That is, salvation requires an act of faith, which in turn requires contact with revelation. For those who do "what lies in them [quod in se est],"[46] God will fulfill this condition by sending a preacher or granting a revelation, which, as we saw, was replaced by implicit faith in the *Summa Theologiae.* Thus, an act of faith remains in the power of free will. If we do not make an act of faith, it is our own fault.

Some years later in *De veritate,* posing the objection that it is unreasonable [inconveniens] to require an explicit faith of someone who has grown up in isolation in the woods or among animals, Aquinas provides fundamentally the same answer: "Granted that everyone is bound to believe something explicitly, no unsuitability follows [non sequitur inconveniens] even if someone ended up growing up among animals or alone in the woods. For it pertains to divine providence to furnish everyone with what is necessary for salvation, provided on his part there is no hindrance. Thus if someone so brought up followed the direction of natural reason desiring good and fleeing evil, it is most certain that God either would reveal through internal inspiration those things necessarily to be believed or would direct a preacher there (as Peter is sent to Cornelius)."[47] Again, our responsibility is to do what lies in our own free will, i.e., not to place any impediment in the way of divine grace, to follow the guidance of natural reason [ductum rationis naturalis], and to do good and avoid evil. God will provide the rest. "Although it is not in our power to know by our own effort those things that are of faith, still, if we did what lies in us [quod in nobis est], that is, follow the lead of natural reason, God would not abandon us in what is necessary for us."[48]

The reason for Aquinas's confidence is that saving grace is already operative in every genuine moral act through which we do "what lies in us." We "cannot perform any good work without God's grace,"[49] and by the same token, wherever there is good work, there is God's grace. Once we reach the use of free will, it is not possible, without grace, to remain solely in the state of original sin alone (i.e., not committing personal sins). Either we prepare ourselves for the reception of sanctifying grace through good moral acts (which itself requires the grace of divine providence mercifully converting and directing us to the good), in which case we will receive sanctifying grace; or we neglect to do so, in which case we will be guilty of mortal sin.[50]

Again, in his commentary on the Romans, Aquinas argues that those who have never heard about Christ are excused from the sin of unbelief but that by the same token, they cannot attain the forgiveness of their original and personal sins. "If, however, any of them do what lies within them, the Lord would provide from his mercy by sending them a preacher," while their doing what lies within them in order to turn to God "is itself from God moving their hearts to good."[51] Later, commenting on the tenth chapter of Romans, Aquinas claimed that pagans were saved *naturaliter,* that is, "through nature reformed by grace [per naturam gratia reformatam]" or acting according to the light of natural reason under the prevenient impact of divine grace.[52]

It was noted earlier that in *Summa Theologiae* Aquinas never mentions the possibilities of private revelation or a special preacher that he consistently mentioned in his previous works. I do not know how to explain this, but it seems a reasonable conjecture to suppose that in his final maturity, he no longer felt the need for extra-natural hypotheses, what Seckler calls "illuminism of faith."[53] He was so convinced of the presence of grace *in* nature that he now considered it sufficient within the overall economy of grace for both Christians and non-Christians to live according to "nature" by following the lead of "natural" reason. This is not to deny the necessity of explicit faith for the former and implicit faith for the latter.

Central to Aquinas's teaching here is the salvific significance of the first moral act. In dealing with the case of the unbaptized, the case most relevant to the non-Christian, Aquinas argues that once a person reaches the age of reason, the person cannot remain in the pure state of original sin alone or in the state of original sin with only venial sins. The person necessarily faces a choice between mortal sin and forgiving grace. The reason: "The first thing that occurs to a person to think about then is to deliberate about oneself. And if one then directs oneself to the due end [ad debitum finem], one will, by means of grace, receive the remission of original sin: whereas if one does not then direct oneself to the due end, as far as one is capable of discretion at that particular age, one will sin mortally, through not doing that which is in one's power to do [non faciens quod in se est]."[54]

To deliberate about oneself is to decide between ordering one's life to one's ultimate end and deviating from that end, and thus between accepting one's ordination to God and rejecting that ordination. To do the first, for Aquinas, results in the remission of original sin by means of grace; to do the second and incur "the loss of the ordination to the ultimate end" [defectus ordinis ultimi finis] is "to sin mortally, through not doing that which is in his power to do."[55] Either case involves what Sartre and Rahner would call the "fundamental option" whereby one disposes of one's total existence in a definitive choice. The first moral act of "doing what is in our power" regarding our ultimate end is already a graced act, not a purely natural act. Within the single economy of grace, we prepare ourselves for the reception of justifying grace precisely by doing what we can for the right ordering of our moral priorities. Ordering our lives to God as the ultimate origin and end of all things is already, under grace, ordering ourselves to God as the object of beatitude and cause of justification, just as the failure to do what lies in our power in order to live in accord with our natural orientation to the good is already a mortal sin even without the explicit rejection of God or the Gospel.[56]

For Aquinas, the preparation for grace by the moral exercise of free will is itself always the work of (prevenient) grace. "The human being, by his will, does works meritorious of everlasting life; but . . . for this it is necessary that his will should be prepared with grace by God."[57] Again, "a human being's turning to God is by free will; and thus he is bidden to turn himself to God. But free will can only be turned to God, when God turns it. . . . It is the part of the human being to prepare his soul, since he does this by his free will. And yet he does not do this without the help of God moving him, and drawing him to Himself."[58]

In addition to the sanctifying grace that heals and elevates human nature, we depend on the prevenient, operative grace of divine motion, the motion of God as the first mover and the first act, the precondition of *all* movements and actions, corporeal and spiritual, natural *and* supernatural. We need divine motion to move us from potency to act and to act according to our form or nature;[59] to "do or wish any good whatsoever" and to "act well"; "to be preserved [conservari] in the good which pertains to our nature" as well as in being; [60] and to maintain our order to the ultimate end and "love God above all things naturally."[61] Likewise, in order to be "directed," "turned," and "subjected" to God as not only our natural but also as our supernatural ultimate end, and so as to be prepared for the reception of sanctifying grace and to be healed in our wounded nature, we depend on the same divine help [auxilium] of the first mover, the "gratuitous help of God who moves the soul inwardly or inspires the good wish [auxilium gratuitum Dei interius animam moventis sive inspirantis bonum propositum]."[62] Over and beyond habitual grace, which does not heal us completely in this world, we also need divine *auxilium,* the internal motion of the Holy Spirit, in order to be constantly "directed," "protected," and "preserved in the good" in moments of passion and ignorance, and thus to "persevere to the end of life."[63]

It is not only that the grace of divine motion—also called "actual grace" in the Thomist tradition—complements habitual grace by preparing the soul for it and protecting the soul against temptations because habitual grace does not heal completely in this world. Most importantly, as "actual" grace that moves us to movements and actions, divine motion "actualizes" habitual grace, as act actualizes potency. Habitual grace is the infused, intrinsic principle of all our supernatural virtues and actions operating in the manner of a formal, not an efficient, cause.[64] However, just as all virtues and powers remain only potential unless reduced to act, so habitual grace depends on the grace of divine motion (or actual grace) to actualize the habitual potencies or dispositions for meritorious acts. "No matter how perfect a corporeal or spiritual nature is supposed to be, it cannot proceed to its act unless it be moved by God."[65]

As the ultimate efficient and teleological power, divine motion not only moves all things to act but moves them to act precisely according to their form, natural or supernatural, and thus teleologically, that is, in view of their ultimate end. It is more than divine concurrence; it is the power whereby God executes the very "plan [ratio] of divine providence."[66] The grace of divine motion, therefore, is not one kind of grace alongside of habitual grace; it is the efficient and teleological foundation of habitual grace, while habitual grace is in fact a moment of divine motion itself.[67]

God does not simply move natural things to natural acts to acquire natural good, but also grants them certain intrinsic forms and virtues as principles of acts whereby they may be inclined to those acts of themselves [secundum seipsas], not merely extrinsically. Those acts whereby they are moved by God thus become "connatural" and "easy." For those whom he loves, God provides far more so that they may acquire supernatural good than he provides for creatures in acquiring natural good. Habitual grace refers to the supernatural "forms or qualities" infused into souls by God but also intrinsic to them as "principles" of supernatural acts whereby they are moved by God "sweetly and promptly" [suaviter et prompte] to acquire eternal supernatural good. As virtues mediate divine motion and particular natural acts, habitual grace mediates divine motion and particular supernatural acts.

As a quality of the soul, habitual grace is an accidental, not a substantial, form of the soul, and acts in the manner of a formal, not an efficient, cause.[68] It is not itself the same as virtue, the perfection of one of the powers of the soul, but is prior to virtue and thus also prior to the powers of the soul. It resides in the very nature of the soul and enables us in that very nature to participate in the divine nature after the manner of a certain *similitudo* through regeneration or recreation. As powers of the soul—the principles of acts—flow from the essence of the soul, so the virtues whereby the powers are moved to act flow into the powers of the soul from grace. Thus, "grace is the principle of meritorious works through the mediation of virtues, as the essence of the soul is the principle of works of life through the mediation of powers."[69] Habitual grace is "habitual" because it works as a certain disposition or *habitudo* which is presupposed by the infused virtues and their acts and makes them possible as their principle and source [*principium et radix*]. As natural virtues enable us to act according to the light of reason, so infused virtues enable us to act in accordance with the light of grace.[70]

As more than divine concursus, the grace of divine motion is God's efficient and teleological power that not only initiates but also sustains our orientation to God, and executes the plan of divine providence. It is an absolutely transcendental, a priori condition for doing and persevering in anything good, natural or supernatural.[71] Doing what we can and preparing ourselves for the reception of sanctifying grace is possible only because of this prevenient grace that empowers, motivates, directs, and sustains us to do so. One can prepare oneself for sanctifying grace precisely as empowered by this prevenient grace, but there is no preparation for this grace of divine motion as such which is not itself made possible by divine motion. "Doing what is in us to do" is itself possible only as we are "moved" by God.[72] "Even the good movement of the free will, whereby anyone is prepared for receiving the gift of grace, is an act of the free will moved by God. And thus a human being is said to prepare himself . . . ; yet it is principally from God, who moves the free will . . . [A] human being cannot prepare himself for grace unless God precedes him and moves him to good [nisi Deo eum praeveniente et movente ad bonum].[73]

This does not mean that there is no room for free will. "God does not justify us without ourselves [sine nobis], because while we are being justified we consent to God's justice by a movement of our free will. Nevertheless, this movement is not the cause of grace, but the effect; hence the whole operation pertains to grace."[74] Free will is indeed necessary, but not sufficient, and even its operation as a necessary condition is itself made possible and actual by God's prevenient grace. "God's motion to justice does not take place without a movement of the free will, but he so infuses the gift of justifying grace that at the same time he moves the free will to accept the gift of grace."[75] And for Aquinas, "when a human being by his free will, moved by God, strives to rise from sin, he receives the light of justifying grace."[76]

It is precisely from this perspective of grace—and the possibility of its rejection—already present in the operation of free will that Aquinas could define violation of nature as sin—a supernatural, theological category—and sin as violation of nature—a natural, philosophical category. "To sin is nothing else than to fail in the good which belongs to any being according to its nature"[77] or "nothing else than to stray from what is according to our nature."[78] One sins against oneself by violating the rule of reason, against one's neighbor by violating justice, and against God by violating the rule of the divine law, but "to sin against God is common to all sins, insofar as the order to God includes every human order" and should be followed in "all" things.[79] Thus, in order to avoid sin and to attain one's end, the supernatural vision of God to which humans are called by nature, human beings need habitual grace, which both heals by restoring the order of appetites to reason and the order of reason to God and elevates by justifying and giving us a share in God's own life.[80]

For Aquinas, there is no pure nature but only graced or sinful nature, a nature leading to sin when violated and an effect of grace when restored to its integrity and elevated to its ultimate end. "Although a human being before sinning may be without grace and without guilt, yet that the person is without guilt after sinning can only be because that person has grace."[81] There is no room for "the middle state of innocence in which a human being has neither grace nor guilt," a state of "pure" nature, so to speak.[82] The real contrast, therefore, is not between nature and grace but between sin and grace, between the sinner and the justified.[83]

There is no salvation, then, "outside nature," i.e., "outside *graced* nature" or "apart from the perfection of graced nature." Grace does not destroy but perfects nature, and human life is either the process of perfecting nature by grace or the violation of nature by sin. Nature and grace do not refer to two separate realities but to two distinct yet integrated aspects of one and the same reality. In Seckler's words, nature is the very "domain of operation [Wirkbereich] of grace."[84] Nature is not a "counterconcept [Gegenbegriff] to grace but the correlative of grace, created towards grace, that stands in the force field of grace [auf die Gnade hin geschaffenes Korrelat zur Gnade, das im Kraftfeld der Gnade steht]."[85]

There seems to be an inherent contradiction in Christian anthropology insofar as it sees human beings as called, by *nature,* to a *supernatural* vision of God's essence, which they cannot attain by their own nature but only through grace. Aquinas's way of resolving this apparent theological contradiction is to see divine grace as universal and nature as already graced so that living according to one's *nature* already involves the dialectic of grace and sin; nature is not a purely natural, empirical category, but rather a supernatural, theological category. One attains or loses one's ultimate end by acting according or contrary to nature.

As we saw in the first chapter, for Aquinas, the whole order of creation has been oriented from the very beginning toward grace and glory as part of the larger economic movement of the Trinity, in which the Father creates all things after the image of the Son and orders them to their ultimate end through the Holy Spirit. This intrinsic orientation of nature toward redemption and glorification has been based on the incorporation of all things into the body of Christ as head of the new creation, including redeemed humanity, and on the predestination of humanity to participate in the likeness of the natural Son. Furthermore, this supernatural destiny of nature, which the economic Trinity seeks to bring to eschatological completion, is itself rooted in the eternal processions of the immanent Trinity as such. In knowing himself in the Son, the Father already knows all things, and in loving himself and the Son in the Spirit, the Father already loves all things. The whole of creation is always already immersed in the teleological movement of divine grace. The grace of the triune God is the very element in which human beings live, move, and have their being.

The salvific grace of the triune God is universally available, and for Aquinas, it is given according to the distinctive nature, capacity, and situation of each person. God does not demand the unnatural or the impossible. One *cannot* expect all human beings to profess an explicit faith in Christ and the triune God revealed in him; this would depend on the accidents of one's birth. One *can* expect all human beings to affirm their orientation to their ultimate end in and through their moral acts by "doing what lies in them"; affirming their moral priorities is something common to all human beings, even if the conceptual content of such priorities certainly varies. In affirming one's commitment to the ultimate end, namely God, one implicitly professes faith in the ultimate end, hope in the possibility of attaining that end, and certainly charity toward it.

It is no wonder that Aquinas saw the operation of divine grace in the first and in all moral acts. It is in moral experience that faith in saving providence—the *prima credibilia* and substitute for explicit faith in Christ and the triune God—is most evident. The moral experience entails staking the totality of one's existence in a definitive choice against much objective uncertainty (Kierkegaard), and thus demands trust and hope that such a fundamental option will not lead to ultimate nothingness but to ultimate fulfillment through God's saving providence. The belief and hope that God would be "the liberator of humanity in ways of his own choosing and according as the Spirit would reveal to those who know the truth" is nowhere more urgent and appropriate than in the anguish of moral choice among competing ultimate ends.[86]

For Aquinas, conversion to God as "object of beatitude and cause of justification" requires "faith" going beyond natural knowledge.[87] Yet Cornelius *was* a believer—by virtue of "implicit" faith—even though he had not yet heard the Gospel, because his "works" [operatio] were found "acceptable" to God whom "none can please without faith."[88] Thus the preeminent space for such "works" must be our universal moral experience. Through the operation of divine grace and implicit faith our natural moral experience is supernaturalized.

In a perceptive and insightful analysis of the moral act, Seckler, following Jacques Maritain, has brought home the intrinsically theological or religious dimension of all moral experience. What is at stake in morality is the question of the ultimate meaning of life and thus also of salvation. In doing what is true and good for its own sake, in affirming value and truth that transcends the world of immanent utility, in the experience of an obligation and an authority that unconditionally imposes itself on us, in the intimations of an absolute being for whom we are willing to give up our human self-sufficiency and autonomy and to whom we entrust our entire being in hope, humility, and obedience, we necessarily affirm the ultimate meaning of life as well as experience something of the ultimate, absolute, and unconditional. What is involved is not so much a clear, conceptual affirmation of God as an existential affirmation of the source of that ultimate meaning, a connatural knowledge of God beyond the dichotomy of implicit and explicit, experienced more in the tendencies of the heart, the call of conscience, or the instinct of faith than in the conceptual clarity of the intellect. This existential experience of God in the moral act is an authentic experience of the God of faith, because "it is one and the same God who is the object of faith and the end of all longing."[89] In a similar way, for Rahner, every authentic act of freedom consists in the ultimate or definitive disposal of one's existence in its totality and implies acceptance or rejection of God as the transcendental horizon of such disposal.[90]

This moral way to faith is especially congenial to the perspective of Aquinas. As we saw, he defines sin as the violation of nature and its teleological orientation to the ultimate end. The role of grace is to heal the soul precisely by restoring order in the conflicting tendencies of its appetites and to elevate the soul to a share in God's triune life, its ultimate end. Aquinas's definition of sin and grace is thoroughly teleological and thus ultimately moral, insofar as morality has to do with the preservation and fulfillment of our teleologically ordered nature, just as moral life is intrinsically made possible by the sanctifying grace that heals nature so that it may function properly according to its nature. By opening up the moral way to faith under the teleological movement of the triune God, Aquinas has also placed Christian faith on the most universal ground. From its own perspective, Christianity can affirm the liberating presence of the triune God in our moral actions and try to discern the signs and forms of the healing and elevating work of divine grace in all of humanity. Grace is not limited to Christianity; it is as universal as the moral experience of humanity.

One may ask, however, whether seeing divine grace as universal and nature as already graced is not making a virtue of desperation and inconsistency. The solution proposed saves God from the unseemly appearance of sheer arbitrariness in creating humanity for an end which transcends their natural power and condemning them for not attaining it on their own. The solution appears rather formal, a demand of mere reasonableness. Many Thomist arguments for the unity of morality and faith tend to be formal arguments from the necessary identity of the God of faith and the God of nature, the God of revelation and the God of creation.[91] Does Aquinas also propose a material solution rooted in the history of salvation itself that does not merely postulate the necessity of universal grace as a matter of rational consistency and a consequence of the unity of creation and redemption, but also shows the *actuality* of divine grace operating in nature and demonstrating that unity? I think he does. We have already seen something of his attempt in his trinitarian theology of creation. Let us now turn to his trinitarian theology of salvation for more.

Chapter Three

A SACRAMENTAL THEOLOGY
OF RELIGIONS

The Religious Way to God

A Christological, Trinitarian Theology of Salvation

From a rather formal consideration of the necessity of faith, the
providential principle of nature and difference, and the soteriology
of the moral act in the preceding chapter, I now move to the theology of salvation as the material context for the discussion of the possibility of salvation of the non-Christian. In the first section I present
a trinitarian theology of salvation, which should complement the discussion of a trinitarian theology of creation in the first chapter. The
discussion includes the origin of salvation in the immanent Trinity,
the roles of the three divine persons in the economy of salvation, the
soteriological significance of the hypostatic union, the soteriological
solidarity of all humanity in Christ as head of the mystical body, and
the respective significance of Christ's passion and resurrection. In the
second section I discuss the roles of faith, charity, and the sacraments

as ways in which human beings are "incorporated" into the body of Christ and "configured" to the passion and resurrection of Christ the head, thus appropriating and participating in his saving power and merit. In the third section I try to develop, on the basis of preceding discussions, a pluralist sacramental theology of religions which considers each religion a sacrament in the same way that contemporary Catholic theology considers the church the "basic" sacrament out of which the particular sacraments flow. In the final section I discuss Aquinas's doctrine of predestination and reprobation, which may seem to put a damper on all his soteriological optimism, so evident in our preceding discussions, but which must nevertheless be squarely faced in order to get a complete picture of his theology of salvation.

For Aquinas, the economy of creation and salvation is rooted in the personal relations of the immanent Trinity. God is not a solitary being but a *consortium* of three persons.[1] As God the Father creates the world through his Word, the Son, and through his Love, the Holy Spirit, "the processions of the Persons are the *rationes* of the productions of creatures inasmuch as they include the essential attributes, knowledge and will."[2] As infinite goodness God creates, adopts, and redeems creatures so as to admit them into the mutual love of the Father and the Son in the Holy Spirit.[3]

God exists eternally as Father, whose essence is to generate the Son, a being exactly like himself in form, by communicating his numerically identical divine nature with him as a gift, which makes the Father and the Son respectively the primordial source and exemplar of all created paternity and filiation.[4] As the Word or self-knowledge of the Father, the Son is not only expressive of the Father but also expressive and operative of all creatures, which the Father creates after the image or example of his Son. The Son bears a relation to all creation within the immanence of God's knowledge and will, insofar as it is through him—word, image, and exemplar—that God will create and redeem any creature.[5] As the perfect likeness of the Father, the Son mediates the likeness of all creation to the Father in the fourfold similitudes of trace, image, grace, and glory.[6] For Aquinas, it is "in the same way and by the same eternal act" that "God predestinated us and Christ," Christ in his humanity to be personally united to the natural Son of God, and us to become God's adopted children. Christ's predestination serves as exemplar of our own in that it provides both the goal of our predestination, the adopted or participated likeness of his natural Sonship, and the means of attaining that goal, the fullness of his grace of which we have all received.[7]

If the role of the Son as Word is to represent the Father and all creatures in the order of form and exemplar, the role of the Holy Spirit as

Love, the mutual "unitive love" of the Father and the Son, is to inspire all creation, especially rational creatures, to achieve their ultimate end by imitating and loving God. The Holy Spirit is the "love of the primal goodness [amor bonitatis primae] whereby the Father loves himself and every creature."[8] The Spirit is the primordial divine movement and impulse directing all creatures to their teleological goal of imaging the Father by participating in the likeness of the Son, assimilating humanity to the "splendor of the eternal Son" by the "light of grace," "imprinting" on rational creatures the likeness of the Son in his union with the Father through grace and charity, and making them by adoption and participation what the Son is by nature.[9] The Spirit too bears an intrinsic relation to creation within the immanence of divine knowledge and will.[10]

Was it "fitting [conveniens]" for God to become incarnate? For Aquinas, what is fitting to a thing is what belongs to it according to the *ratio* of its proper nature. Reasoning befits a human being because she is rational according to her nature. God's very nature is goodness, and whatever belongs to the idea [ratio] of goodness is fitting to God. For Aquinas as for Bonaventure, and contrary to LaCugna, who exaggerates the difference between the two in this regard,[11] it is the very nature of goodness to communicate itself to others, and the nature of the supreme goodness to communicate itself to creatures in the supreme way, which occurs in uniting a created nature to itself so as to become one person.[12] God creates all things as their efficient, exemplary, and final cause "solely [tantum] in order to communicate her perfection, which is her own goodness," not, like a finite agent, in order to acquire a perfection, fill a need, or produce a benefit [utilitas] for herself, which makes God alone "the most generous one [maxime liberalis]."[13] Incarnation is fitting to God, as is creation.

It is worth noting here that the question for Aquinas is not, as it is for some contemporary pluralists such as John Hick, Paul Knitter, and Stanley Samartha, whether a *finite* being could represent and incarnate God, for no human flesh by its own nature is either capable of or "fitting" for personal union with God, but whether it is fitting for *God* in the infinite excellence of her goodness to empower a finite creature for that union through her grace for the sake of human salvation.[14] Aquinas answers that it is. The humanity of Jesus was united to the person of the Son of God not through his own merit but by the grace of hypostatic union, which far transcends all the finite modes of divine presence such as God's presence in all creatures by essence, presence, and power, or her presence in the saints by sanctifying grace and the moral harmony of intention and operation, all of which presuppose a relation between two distinct persons. In hypostatic union, which is proper to Christ alone, God the Son is so personally united to Christ's humanity that there exists only one person, the divine, although there exist two distinct natures, human and divine.[15]

For Aquinas, the incarnation of the Word was not strictly "necessary" for the restoration [reparatio] of the human race in the sense that such restoration could not have taken place without the incarnation; God in her omnipotence could have [poterat] restored human nature in many other ways, just as God could have become incarnate even without human sin.[16] Still, such incarnation was "necessary" in the sense that the end of human restoration could be attained better and more fittingly [convenientius] with it. In the latter sense of greater fittingness or suitability, Aquinas provides six positive and six negative reasons for the necessity of the incarnation. The positive reasons have to do with promoting our progress in good, the negative reasons with the removal of evil.

Regarding the positive reasons, the incarnation of the Word was necessary, first of all, to help us achieve certitude about the truths of faith by the God incarnate himself instructing us so that we might perceive divine teaching "in human fashion [secundum modum humanum]." Perfect beatitude, our ultimate end and salvation, consists in the vision of God that exceeds the capacity of every created intellect, and we need a certain "foretaste" of this vision in order to be able to orient ourselves to that end; this is done through faith. As the "principle" of all things ordered to the ultimate end, the knowledge that constitutes faith must be most certain. Things are most certain when they are either known "of themselves," like the first principles of demonstration, or at least reduced to things known of themselves, like the conclusions of demonstration. God's essence is not known "of itself" to us who lack the vision of his essence; nor, therefore, is it reducible to some other first principle from which we can conclude his essence. We can conclude his existence but not his essence from the first principle of causality applied to creatures. The first principle of our knowledge has to be God himself to whom the truths of faith are known of themselves. In order to achieve perfect certitude about faith, then, human beings had to be taught *in human fashion* and thus by the God incarnate himself.

The incarnation was necessary, second, to excite our hope for ultimate beatitude in the union of the beatific vision by demonstrating the real possibility of the union of humanity with God in the most compelling way. By uniting the divine and the human in the divine person of the Word, the incarnation helps overcome the temptation to despair of ever attaining our ultimate end, a temptation that is always there, given the infinite distance between God and humanity.

Third, it was necessary in order to strengthen our charity by showing how much God loves us by his willingness to join the "fellowship of our nature [naturae nostrae consortium]" in person. In order to orient ourselves to the ultimate end, the enjoyment of the divine in the beatific vision, it is necessary to dispose our love to a desire for that enjoyment. The desire to enjoy a thing is caused by love of the thing. In tending to perfect beatitude, therefore, we need an inducement to love God, and "nothing so induces us to love one as the experience of his love for us."[17] Nothing could be a more effective demonstration of God's love for us than his willingness to be personally united with our human nature to the point of "emptying himself," not in the sense of putting off his divine nature, which he cannot do, but in the sense of assuming a human nature in the form of a servant, sharing in its emptiness and defects, and filling it with grace and truth.[18] It is proper to love to unite the lover with the beloved as much as possible.

Fourth, the incarnation was necessary in order to present us an example of good behavior by showing us a divine model in word and example. As the reward for virtue, beatitude requires a virtuous disposition, and we are helped by words and examples to develop such a disposition. The more virtuous a person is, the more persuasive her words and examples become. No human being, however, is perfectly good and virtuous. In order to be solidly grounded in virtue, then, it is necessary for us to receive the teaching and example of virtue from the God made human himself.

Fifth, familiarity and friendship require a certain equality. In order for human beings to become more familiar with God, then, it was helpful for God to become the equal of human beings by becoming a human being. As Aristotle said, by nature a human being's friend is another human being. It was fitting that we are, in the words of the preface of the Christmas Mass, "born to the love of things invisible through God whom we know visibly [ut dum visibiliter Deum cognoscimus, per hunc in invisibilium amorem rapiamur]."

Finally, and most important, the incarnation was necessary in order to actually bestow on us through Christ's humanity the grace and possibility of full participation in the divine nature. As Augustine put it, "God became a human being so that human beings may become God." The divine nature infinitely exceeds the human, but human beings do have God herself as their end and have been born to be united to God by their intellect; the personal union of God with humanity in the incarnation is "an example and testimony of a sort" for this ultimate human vocation.[19] Christ is the Son by nature, and we become sons and daughters of the Father by conforming to and participating in his sonship, which makes him "the first born" of all humanity as the source and model of their divine filiation.[20]

As to the negative reasons, the incarnation was necessary, first, in order to teach human beings not to prefer the devil to themselves because human nature has been elevated above the devil by being personally united to God. Second, it was necessary in order to make us aware of our transcendent, supernatural dignity as beings called to the immediate vision of God as our ultimate end and beatitude, and to prevent us from seeking our beatitude in anything less than God, through idolatry. Through the incarnation God has manifested that dignity, which has now become a "partner of the divine nature [divinae consors naturae]." Third, it was necessary in order to take away our presumption, because the grace of God in Christ precedes all our merits. Fourth, it was necessary in order to condemn and cure human pride, the greatest barrier to our love of God, through a demonstration of humility.

Fifth, the incarnation was necessary in order to liberate us from the slavery of sin, the chief obstacle to beatitude, by offering a truly worthy or "condign" satisfaction for our sin which only Christ, both God and a human being, could have provided. This is so because the sin at stake has corrupted the whole of human nature, for which no human being can make up adequately, and because the sin committed against God incurs a certain infinity of offense, for which no finite being can satisfy. No mere human being can have the universal and transcendent significance necessary for reconciliation of all humanity with God; only a humanity indeed like our own but also elevated to that significance by the grace of hypostatic union and made "reformative of the entire human nature" [reformativa totius humanae naturae] and "the principle of merit [merendi principium]" can accomplish the task.[21] Finally, the incarnation was necessary in order to give us certainty about the remission of our sins through a visible sacrifice on the cross and actual forgiveness of sins on the part of the incarnate God himself.[22]

For Aquinas, then, the divine communication of goodness through the incarnation is fitting not only for God in his infinite goodness but also for human beings living here below. For all things regarding creatures, it is true that God's will is sufficient. Still, "divine wisdom requires that provision be made for the various classes of things in harmony with themselves [secundum earum congruentiam]." God could have effected by his will alone what he wanted to accomplish through his incarnation. Nevertheless, "it was in harmony with human nature [congruebat humanae naturae] to bring about these benefits through God made a human being."[23] In doing so, Christ was only fulfilling his role as the "way [via]" to beatitude, the ultimate end of the rational creature; all twelve reasons have to do either with promoting our progress on the way or with removing obstacles on it. In short, the incarnation was necessary in order for human beings to achieve their ultimate end or salvation in a way congruous with their human nature. The incarnation was the providential principle of nature applied to the situation of human salvation.[24]

Would God still have become incarnate even if human beings had not sinned? For Aquinas, this belongs among those things that spring solely from God's will beyond anything due a creature and can be known as such only through their revelation in Scripture. Since Scripture everywhere assigns the sin of the first human being as the reason for the incarnation, it is more appropriate [convenientius] to say that without sin the incarnation would not have occurred, although it is also true that God's power is not limited by this and that God could have [potuisset] become incarnate even without sin.[25]

For Aquinas, any one of the divine persons, not only the Son, could have assumed human nature. Assumption implies two things, the act of the one assuming and the term of the assumption. Now the principle of the act is divine power [virtus], and the term is a divine person. Divine power is indifferently common to all persons, as is the nature [ratio] of personhood, although personal properties are different. When a power is indifferently related to several things, it can terminate its action in any one of them, in the same way that rational powers, related to opposed things, can do any one of them. Divine power, therefore, could [potuit] have united human nature to either the person of the Father or the person of the Holy Spirit as it did to the person of the Son. Thus, the Father or the Holy Spirit *could* have assumed flesh, as did the Son, although it would not have been *fitting* for the Father to be sent in the technical sense of mission.[26]

Against the objection that the incarnation of any other person would tend to the confusion of the persons because incarnation means becoming the "son of man"—which would not be fitting [inconveniens] to either the Father or the Holy Spirit—Aquinas answers that it is not temporal but eternal filiation that constitutes the person of the Son and that temporal filiation is only a consequence of temporal nativity. Even if, therefore, temporal filiation were transferred to the Father or the Holy Spirit, it would not confuse the divine persons, who are constituted by eternal, not temporal, processions and relations.

However, if adoptive filiation is a participated likeness of natural filiation, and natural filiation does not belong to the Father or the Holy Spirit, would adoptive filiation still have been possible if someone other than the Son became incarnate? For Aquinas, adoptive filiation, which is indeed a participated likeness of natural filiation, is made possible through appropriation [appropriate] by the Father who is the principle of natural filiation and by the gift of the Holy Spirit who is the love of the Father and the Son. Thus, "God has sent the Spirit of his Son into your hearts crying, Abba, Father" (Galations 4:6). By the incarnation of the Son we have received adoptive filiation according to the likeness of his natural filiation, and we likewise would have received adoptive filiation by the incarnation of the Father as from the principle of natural filiation and by the incarnation of the Holy Spirit as from the common bond of the Father and the Son.

However, would the incarnation of the Father still be considered a mode of "being sent," since the Father is innascible and is from no one, which violates one condition of mission? (This issue will be discussed in detail in chapter 5.) For Aquinas innascibility regards eternal birth and is not destroyed by temporal birth. If, therefore, the Father became incarnate, it would still be genuine incarnation, although it would not be called mission. But since the Son is from the Father, the incarnation of the Son is also mission in the proper sense, mission according to the mode of incarnation.[27]

Nonetheless, even if it is true that any one of the persons, not necessarily the Son, "could" [potuit] have become incarnate by the divine power common to all three persons in their one divine nature, in Aquinas's view it is still "most fitting" [convenientissimum] for the Son to become incarnate. First, on the part of union, it is fitting that similar things should be united. Just as the word or concept of the craftsman bears an exemplary likeness of the things he makes, so the Son, as God's eternal Word and concept, bears the exemplary likeness of all creatures fashioned in his likeness as God's operative wisdom. Likewise, just as creatures are established in their proper species by participating in the likeness of the primordial divine exemplar albeit in their own mutable ways, so it is fitting that creatures should be restored in their ordination to their eternal and immutable perfection through the nonparticipative yet personal union of the Word with the creature. In a similar way, the craftsman restores a defective work by applying the form of his art according to which he originally fashioned it.[28]

The Word has not only a common agreement [convenientia] with all creatures but also a special agreement with human nature. For the Word is the concept of eternal wisdom from which all human wisdom is derived. As a rational creature, the perfection of the human being lies in wisdom, and human beings advance in wisdom only insofar as they participate in the Word of God, "the fountain of wisdom" according to Ecclesiasticus 1:5. There is a special kinship between the Word and human beings because both are related to *logos* or reason and called "images" of God. It is only fitting that the Word of God should himself be personally united to human nature and manifest the Father and the whole Trinity for the perfect fulfillment of human beings.[29]

Second, the reason of this fitness [congruentia] may be taken from the end of the union, which is the fulfillment of predestination and the bestowal of the heavenly inheritance, something possible only for the children of God. It is only fitting [congruum] that through him who is the natural Son, human beings should participate in the likeness of his filiation according to adoption (Romans 8:17 and 8:29). In order to lead us to this end of eternal glory Christ prepared the medicine of the sacraments as a means of wiping away the wound of sin that stands in the way of the end.

Third, the fittingness of the incarnation of the Son becomes clear from a consideration of the sin of our first parents. The first human beings sinned by seeking the knowledge of good and evil promised to them by the serpent. It is only fitting, therefore, that human beings, led astray from God through an inordinate thirst for knowledge, should be led back to God through the Word of true wisdom.

Both the first creation of all things and the second creation through redemption took place by the power of God the Father, and the power of creation is appropriated to the Father, but this does not make the incarnation of the Father more fitting. On the contrary, just as the Father by his power created all things *through* the Word, so it is fitting that the Father by his power should also recreate all things *through* the Word "so that restoration should correspond to creation" [ut recreatio creationi responderet]. Creation and recreation require not only divine power but also a divine model. Likewise, incarnation is geared towards the remission of sins, which is appropriated to the Holy Spirit. This, however, does not make the incarnation of the Holy Spirit any more fitting. It is proper to the Holy Spirit to be the gift of the Father and the Son, and the remission of sins is caused by the Holy Spirit precisely as the gift of God. Therefore, it is more fitting for our justification that the Son should become incarnate and send us the gift of the Holy Spirit.[30]

It is illuminating at this point to contrast Aquinas's position with that of Karl Rahner, who criticizes what he considers a common opinion since Augustine: that any one of the three persons could have become incarnate if that person simply wanted to. According to Rahner, this "common opinion" shows no awareness of any connection between the Word of God and humanity. To say that "the Word of God became incarnate" would simply be to say that one of the divine persons did. In order to understand the incarnation, we would not really need to know anything proper and exclusive to the Word of God. Rahner, by contrast, wants to see an intrinsic connection between the subject and the predicate, between the divine Logos and human nature, and thus a transcendental necessity for the incarnation. On his view, the Word of God and the incarnation can only be understood in light of each other.[31]

For Rahner, the human being is an "unlimited orientation toward the infinite mystery of fullness," and the incarnation is the culminating point of human existence "toward which it [human nature] is always moving by virtue of its essence," "the unique and highest instance of the actualization of the essence of human reality,"[32] that is, the human obediential potency for the hypostatic union with God. The incarnation is intrinsic, not merely accidental, to the meaning of human existence. The incarnation, however, has not only an anthropological meaning but also a theological meaning, that is, a meaning for God herself. In the incarnation God assumes the human reality as *her own* reality, thereby revealing herself as capable of change in an other although not subject to change in herself. In the "pure freedom of her infinite unrelatedness," which includes the primordial possibility of becoming "less" than she is, God can, out of love, empty herself, differentiating herself as a finite mutable reality from herself as the infinite, immutable one, and establishing an other as her own reality. The capacity to create—to establish an other without giving herself—is itself a possibility derived from the primordial possibility of incarnation. She is able to give herself to what is not God, and thereby really to have her own history in the other, but as her own history." The deepest meaning of creatures, then, is their capacity for being assumed by God, becoming "the material for a possible history of God," and serving as *"the grammar of God's possible self-expression."*[33]

From this perspective, Rahner claims that we can better understand "why precisely the *Logos* of God became a human being, and why he alone can become a human being." The possibility of creating an other, outside of God, presupposes otherness and distinction in God herself; a being without internal differentiation would simply cease to be itself when positing an other. In this sense, the possibility of creation has its "ontological condition" and its "ultimate ground" in the fact that God can express herself and establish an original distinction within herself and for herself. God's immanent self-expression is the condition for the possibility of God's outward self-expression and the guarantor of the identity of the immanent and outward expressions. Although creation is the work of God as creator without distinction of persons, its possibility is still grounded in the internal self-differentiation of God. If, therefore, God expresses her very own self into the emptiness of what is not God, this has to be the outward expression of the immanent Word, not something arbitrary or proper to some other divine person. The incarnation thus reveals that Christology is "the beginning and the end of anthropology, and this anthropology in its most radical actualization is for all eternity theology."[34]

This is no place for a full-scale comparison of Aquinas and Rahner on the theology of the Trinity and the Incarnation. The preceding discussion should, however, have indicated or at least suggested many areas of profound agreement, notably the eagerness of both to see an intimate, mutual connection between the incarnation of the Word and the ultimate theological vocation of the human being; the shared axiom that the eternal divine processions provide the *ratio* for creation and incarnation; and the affirmation by both that the incarnation was a free act, not compelled by any finite factor. Certainly, Aquinas does not share the "common opinion" mentioned above that showed no awareness of the intrinsic connection between the Word and humanity.

We can, however, still discern an important distinction between the two, which is ultimately derived from the difference between Aquinas's classical metaphysical and theocentric orientation and Rahner's modern transcendental, anthropocentric orientation. Aquinas is impressed by the incomprehensibility of the divine essence, to which we have no access, and he therefore limits theology to applying to humanity the general arguments from congruence and fittingness. For Aquinas, therefore, the incarnation of the Son was at best "most fitting," while the incarnation of another person was "possible," given divine omnipotence. For Rahner, however, who equally appreciates the divine incomprehensibility of the "absolute mystery," but who is eager, as a modern transcendental theologian, to overcome the dualistic extrinsecism of the divine and the human, the incarnation of the Son alone was a transcendental "necessity" whose intelligibility—"why precisely the *Logos* of God became a human being, and why he alone can become a human being"—can be shown by reflection on the inner connection between God and humanity as revealed in the incarnation.

Still, a brief further reflection on Aquinas's argument from "fittingness" [convenientia] should bring the two theologians even closer without ignoring their fundamental difference in orientation. This demonstration may start from the three characteristics that define Aquinas's conception of fittingness: its constitutive relation to nature or end, its function as an internal need, and its difference from external necessity.

First, given that God governs the world according to divine wisdom that provides for differing things according to their respective natures, what is fitting is not a matter of an arbitrary judgment but is measured by the "nature" or "end" of the thing to which it is fitting. What is fitting to a thing is "that which belongs to it according to the character of its own nature [illud quod competit sibi secundum rationem propriae naturae]."[35] Thus, incarnation is fitting to God, whose nature as goodness is to share herself, while being rational is fitting to a human being, whose nature is to be rational. The incarnation of the Son is fitting to the nature of the Son as the divine exemplar of all created things and as the natural Son of the Father, while the same incarnation is also fitting to the nature of human beings who can believe, hope, love, act, and be freed from the slavery of sin only in accordance with human nature corrupted by original sin.

Second, for Aquinas as for Aristotle, nature is always teleological or ordered to an intrinsic end that demands to be realized, which means that fittingness to a nature also implies an internal need or necessity of the nature. Thus, rationality as something fitting to human nature is not something to which human nature can remain indifferent, but is rather something that it requires for its own teleological completion. The incarnation of the Son is not an indifferent spectacle for human beings to behold and marvel at, but instead corresponds to the profound human need to be saved as human beings, not as angels, and therefore in ways that takes account of the human condition. Fittingness thus overcomes the extrinsecism that Rahner's transcendental theology seeks to overcome. The incarnation of the Word is not a purely external imposition on human beings who can have neither knowledge nor need for it, but answers the profound inner need of human nature in its most defining vocation. The reasons that Aquinas gives for the fittingness of the incarnation from the perspective of human nature do exemplify the "transcendental" necessity of Rahner's transcendental theology.

Third, Aquinas is careful to distinguish between what I would call "absolute" and "relative" necessity in the discussion of what is fitting. "Absolute" necessity refers to "that without which something cannot be [sine quo aliquid esse non potest]"; in this sense, food is necessary for survival. The incarnation of the Son and of the Son alone is not absolutely necessary because, just as another divine person could have become incarnate, God could have [potuit] saved human beings in many different ways. "Relative" necessity, on the other hand, refers to "that through which an end can be attained better and more fittingly [per quod melius et conventientius pervenitur ad finem]."[36] In this sense, a horse is necessary for a long journey and so is the incarnation for the salvation of human beings. For Aquinas, then, the incarnation of the Son, which is fitting in view of divine goodness but not absolutely necessary in view of divine omnipotence, becomes relatively necessary in view of the needs of human nature. Not everything that is fitting is necessary in the strict, absolute sense. Whether what is fitting is also necessary in the relative sense depends on the nature of the being involved. If human nature needed restoration in the human mode as in fact it did, the incarnation of the Son became necessary, but if human nature hypothetically did not need restoration because there was no human sin, the incarnation still could have occurred in view of divine power.

Aquinas's discussion of the incarnation, as of many other theological issues, is carried out in the multiple categories of absolute necessity, relative necessity, fittingness, and possibility, and always in consideration of the nature of the things at issue. What distinguishes Aquinas from modern transcendental theology is that the category of fittingness, so useful and important, is employed with a nuance and sensitivity to the different natures of the things involved. What is fitting to God in view of her divine goodness is not absolutely necessary in view of divine omnipotence. What is fitting to God in view of the needs of human nature is relatively necessary and could have been achieved in many different ways in view of divine power. The idea of divine omnipotence along with the insistence that we mortals do not have an intuition into the divine essence and the divine will protects Aquinas against the danger of turning what is humanly necessary into what is also necessary for God, i.e., the danger of anthropocentric anthropomorphism. Likewise, the idea of fittingness to human nature protects him against sheer extrinsecism. In short, the argument from fittingness is the most fitting form of theological argument for human beings who do not enjoy an intuition into God's inner life yet who have to make at least human sense out of the divine mysteries such as the Incarnation and the Trinity.[37]

For Aquinas, although the salvation of humanity is attainable in principle by the mere fact of incarnation, it is most fittingly attained by the incarnation at its most concrete, in the passion and resurrection of Christ. One of Aquinas's arguments against the fittingness of incarnation in all human beings is that such an incarnation involves the eliminating reduction of all *human* persons to the one divine *person* assuming the human nature in all and thus rules out the possibility of suffering and dying for us because there will be no human persons to suffer and die for. The divine person will be suffering and dying for himself, not for us, in all human beings. In Aquinas's view, however, it is in Christ's passion for us, not merely in the assumption of human nature, that God's love for us is particularly manifest.[38] God could have liberated humanity otherwise than by the passion of Christ. In fact, from the beginning of his conception Christ did merit our salvation, but given the many obstacles on our side hindering us from securing the effect of his merit, the way of passion was also the most "fitting"—and in this sense "necessary"—way of removing such hindrances.[39]

Christ's passion was necessary, for Aquinas, in order to provide a remedy for all the evils incurred by sin. First, it cleanses the sinner through the blood poured out in the passion and thereby removes the "stain" of sin that defiles a person when he sins. Second, it atones to God for the sin for which no human being can atone by himself, thereby removing the anger of God in a way that is fitting [conveniens] both to God's justice—because it made satisfaction for our sins—and to God's mercy—because God gave us his own Son to make a "condign" satisfaction which we could not make on our own.[40] Third, the passion loosens the power and hold of the sin that weakens us and inclines us more and more to itself. Fourth, it delivers us from the infinite debt of punishment by bearing our sins, i.e., the punishment due to our sins, in Christ's body, with an efficacy sufficient to expiate for all the sins of the world. Finally, by doing all these things, it reopens the gate of paradise and wins for us entry into the divine kingdom, meriting justifying grace and the glory of bliss for humanity.[41]

Christ's passion not only delivers us from sin but also produces changes in us that are appropriate and conducive to the integrity and perfection of human salvation. First, it impresses on us how much God loves us and stirs us to love God in return. Second, it gives us an example to follow in all circumstances of life as well as a model of all the virtues, such as charity, patience, humility, obedience, and justice, that are required for salvation. Third, the great price by which we have been delivered from sin motivates us all the more to refrain from sin. Fourth, it redounds to our greater dignity that a human being should overthrow the devil and vanquish death by dying.[42]

It is not only by his passion but also by his resurrection that Christ brought about our salvation. His resurrection is the cause of our resurrection because it is the "first" in the order of our resurrection, the "first fruits" of those who sleep. This is only reasonable given that the principle of human life-giving is the Word of God. It is part of the divinely established natural order that every cause operate first upon what is nearest to it and then through it upon others more remote. Thus, the Word first bestows immortal life upon "that body which is naturally united with himself" and through it upon all other bodies.[43] In this sense, the first or principal efficient cause of resurrection always remains God's life-giving power and her justice, from which Christ receives the power of passing judgment. Christ's resurrection is an instrumental and exemplary cause whose causality is derived from the divinity to which Christ is personally united and from which Christ's humanity in all its actions and passions derives its universal and transcendent salvific significance.[44]

Christ's resurrection is both the efficient and exemplary cause of our resurrection. It is "the efficient cause of ours through the divine power whose office it is to give life to the dead; and this power by its presence is in touch with all places and times; and such virtual contact suffices for its efficiency."[45] As judge of the living and the dead, this efficient power of Christ's resurrection extends to the good and the wicked, both of whom are subject to his judgment. Christ's resurrection is also the exemplar of our own. Just as it is "first" in time, so also is it first in dignity and perfection, through his personal union with the Word. Christ does not need an example, but we do. In order to be raised up, we must be "conformed" [conformes] to his resurrection. This is why the efficiency of his resurrection extends to both the good and the wicked, but his exemplarity extends only to the just, who are conformed to his sonship.[46]

Regarding the relation between Christ's passion and resurrection, Aquinas sees unity in their efficacy or efficiency of salvation, but distinction in their exemplarity corresponding to different aspects of the salvific process. His passion removes evils, but his resurrection is "the beginning and exemplar of all good things."[47] Justification involves forgiveness of sins and newness of life through grace. As regards "efficacy," which depends on divine power, both passion and resurrection are the causes of justification in both aspects; but as regards "exemplarity," passion is the cause of the forgiveness of sins, while resurrection is the cause of the newness of life through grace. That is, passion is the origin of justification, resurrection the goal of justification.[48] Again, regarding efficacy, both Christ's death and resurrection are the cause of both the destruction of death and the renewal of life. Regarding exemplarity, however, his death is the cause of the destruction of our death, while his resurrection is the cause of the renewal of our life.[49] At the same time, our sharing in his passion, our "conformity" to the suffering and dying Christ, is the condition for sharing in the "likeness" of his resurrection.[50] Likewise, both the passion and resurrection operate as efficient and exemplary causes, but only the passion also operates as a "meritorious" cause of our salvation.[51]

In all of these it is important to remember that God is the "principal" cause of our salvation while both Christ's passion and resurrection remain "instrumental" causes. For Aquinas, "the power of the principal cause is not restricted to one instrument determinately," which means that "God could deliver us in some other way than through Christ's passion and resurrection." However, "having once decreed to deliver us in this way," it is evident that the passion and resurrection become causes of our salvation. What Aquinas has done is to show, given such a decree and the human condition, how they are "fitting" instruments of human salvation.[52]

Mediation of Salvation through Solidarity, Ecclesiality, and Sacramentality

If Christ's incarnation, life, passion, and resurrection constitute the (instrumental) cause of our salvation, it is only fitting to ask how Christ can be the cause of *our* salvation and what this salvific causality presupposes by way of a theological relationship between Christ and humanity. Mediating God's salvation to humanity is not a purely ad hoc, contingent, individual event but presupposes two things: a general objective ontological relationship between Christ and humanity as a whole, for he mediates salvation for all humanity, not just for some individuals; and a particular subjective ontic relationship between Christ and individuals, for individuals still have to do their share in appropriating and making their own the fruits of salvation objectively made available through Christ. For Aquinas, the ontological relationship between Christ and humanity is manifested in the mystical solidarity of all with and in Christ as members of his "body," while the ontic relation between Christ and individuals is manifested in the appropriation of salvation through faith, charity, and sacraments.

Christ in his humanity is not divine by nature as are the Father and the Holy Spirit, or by adoption as are human beings, but rather by the grace of union between his humanity and the person of the Son.[53] Because of this grace of hypostatic union given in the incarnation, Christ in his humanity fulfills the role of the mediator between God and humanity and does so as the head of the church, which is his body and constitutes "one mystical person" [mystice una persona][54] with the head. The church here is not limited to the institutional church but embraces potentially all humanity from the beginning of the world to the end, including those already united to him by glory, those actually united to him by charity and by faith, those who will be united to him eventually by divine predestination, and those who are united to him in potentiality that may never be actualized because of divine reprobation and who will wholly cease to be members of Christ upon departure from this world.[55] For Aquinas, angels too are members of the mystical body or the church insofar as they too are ordained to one and the same end, the glory of divine fruition. The church as the mystical body of Christ is the totality of those reborn in and through Christ.[56]

Christ is the head of this church because of his hypostatic closeness to God, which confers the fullness of grace on him together with the power to confer grace on all members of the church, making him the principle or source of all grace as well as of all salvific virtue, an ontological as well as a moral exemplar of all salvation.[57] He is the head of the church in order, perfection, and power.[58] The merit of Christ appointed by God to be "the head of all humanity in regard to grace [caput omnium hominum quantum ad gratiam]" extends to all his members by spiritual regeneration, just as the sin of Adam appointed by God to be "the principle of the whole nature [principium totius naturae]" is transmitted to others by carnal propagation.[59] Because of the mystical unity of head and members, "Christ's satisfaction belongs to all the faithful as being his members, "[60] just as our sin to one another does injury to Christ himself.

In an age increasingly dominated by atomistic individualism, even in theological reflection, it is relevant here to remind ourselves of the profound degree to which Aquinas's soteriology is mediated by a conception of human solidarity constituted by the sharing of a common human nature. Without denying the individual character and responsibility of personal acts, whether sinful or meritorious, Aquinas insists that personal actions occur within the universal situation and context already corrupted by original sin in Adam as well as already renewed by redemption in Christ. We share both this primordial corruption and primordial regeneration precisely by virtue of our common human *nature,* the first because of our nature, the second because of saving grace. In both sin and grace we are in solidarity with one another as human beings. Neither our sins nor our merits are purely individual; we are dependent on one another for both. A purely individualist soteriology would not be Christian. As there is a mystical solidarity of all humanity in original sin, a sin of nature, by virtue of our sharing one common nature with Adam, the "principle" of corrupted human nature, so there is a mystical solidarity of all humanity—"one mystical person"—with and in Christ, the new Adam, the "principle" of renewed human nature, a solidarity of grace and life that circulates from the head to all his members.[61] In this solidarity— also called the "communion of saints"—the good of the head, his power, and his merit are shared by all members, just as the good of any one member is shared by all others, something best symbolized in the sacraments.[62] For Aquinas, as George Sabra points out, ultimately "humanity is one, not only because all are creatures of the one Creator, but also because all are members of the one Savior."[63] Here, common human "nature" does not remain an abstraction but is concretized in the unity of a "body" with an actual life of interdependence and sharing.

It is this ontological solidarity of all posited by God's salvific wisdom that makes it possible for Christ to suffer for all of humanity. For Aquinas, whoever suffers for the sake of justice in a state of grace thereby merits her salvation. Christ suffered for justice, meriting salvation not only for himself but also for all the members of his body.[64] We are delivered from our sins by the passion he suffered as our head, "in the same way as if a man by the good industry of his hands were to redeem himself from a sin committed with his feet."[65] His passion was an unsurpassable expression of solidarity with suffering and sinful members of his body: he died on our behalf, bearing all our sins, enduring "generically [secundum genus]" all types of human suffering,[66] making satisfaction for our sins by "bestowing what was of greatest price—himself—for us."[67] The passion of the head flows to and heals every baptized member "just as if he himself had suffered and died," and "just as if he himself had offered sufficient satisfaction for all his sins," healing both actual sins of individuals and the sin of nature or original sin in each and everyone.[68]

However, it is precisely Christ's personal union with the Godhead that makes him the head and source of universal human solidarity in his mystical body and confers universal, soteriological significance on his passion—as well as on everything he does—as a particular human being. The particular as particular cannot have a universal, transcendent significance, as Hick and Knitter rightly argue, but the passion of Christ is not just particular and human but also personally united to the divine person of the Son. Not every human being can suffer "vicariously" or "representatively" for all human beings; only Christ can. "Christ's passion, although corporeal, has yet a spiritual effect from the Godhead united: and therefore it secures its efficacy by spiritual contact—namely, by faith and the sacraments of faith."[69] Still, it is precisely in his humanity, not his divinity, that Christ performs the role of mediator. As divine, Christ does not differ from the Father or the Holy Spirit and has nothing to give them which they do not already have. As a human being, he is distinguished from God by nature and from other human beings by dignity of both grace and glory.[70] All grace of salvation comes to us from God *through* the humanity of Christ personally united to the Word and made the head of a new humanity by that union. There is, for Aquinas, no salvation apart from Christ and no salvation, therefore, outside incorporation into his body.

How, then, does an individual human being become a member of Christ's body? How do we share in the saving power and merit of his passion and resurrection? How is the effect and grace of his saving work "applied" to humanity? How is the objective salvation wrought by Christ's passion subjectively appropriated? For Aquinas, it is through faith, charity, and the sacraments. Sharing in the power and merit of Christ's passion requires incorporation into his body, which in turn requires "configuration" to Christ the head, which takes place precisely through faith, charity, and the sacraments.[71]

The humanity of Christ is corporeal and limited to a particular time and place, and its human causality is historically conditioned. Contact with that humanity on the part of human beings far removed from him in time and space will be contingent and fraught with the risks of uncertainty. As mentioned earlier, however, his humanity acquires not only universal and transcendent significance as the sole, universal cause of human salvation but also universal accessibility as the cause and exemplar of our salvation through its personal union with the Godhead. Through the divine power to which it is united and whose presence is not limited in time and space, the salvific causality of Christ's humanity extends as universally as God's own presence and is available for appropriation by spiritual contact.[72] The most fundamental mode of this spiritual contact is faith.

The ultimate happiness of a human being as a rational creature consists in a supernatural vision of God which we cannot attain by our natural power. Such a vision requires revelation, which we can only accept by faith—an intellectual assent whereby we believe in God and all other things in reference to God (*credere Deum*) on account of God as the First Truth (*credere Deo*) for the sake of God as our ultimate end (*credere in Deum*).[73] Christ dwells in us by faith, and it is by faith that we are united to Christ's passion and resurrection.[74] It is not, however, by lifeless [informis] faith, which can coexist with sin, but by faith living through charity [fides formata per caritatem] in the power of the Holy Spirit,[75] that Christ's passion is applied to us not only as to our intellects but also as to our hearts.[76] Charity is our friendship with God based on the fellowship of the Son to which all are called; it is a participation in divine love and the Holy Spirit, an orientation to our ultimate and principal good, the enjoyment of God, made possible only through the infusion of the Holy Spirit, the mutual love of the Father and the Son.[77] As such, charity is the "proper form" of faith because it "perfects" and "quickens" the act of faith in its orientation to the divine good as its ultimate end; likewise, it is the "form" and condition of all virtues in that it "directs the acts of all virtues to the last end."[78]

Another way of being incorporated into Christ's passion and resurrection and sharing in their salvific power is through the sacraments, which also presuppose living faith. As effective signs of grace, sacraments both signify and cause grace, the participated likeness of the divine nature. A sacrament is a "sign of a sacred thing insofar as it sanctifies a human being."[79] As a sensible sign of a spiritual reality, it signifies Christ's passion, which is the cause of our sanctification; grace and virtues, which are the form of our sanctification; and eternal life, which is the ultimate end of our sanctification. It also causes grace insofar as it incorporates us into Christ and makes us share in his saving power as members of his body. As an instrumental cause of grace, a sacrament does not work by the power of its own form but only by the motion of the principal cause, God; the effect is not likened [assimilatur] to the instrument but to the principal agent, who can ordain and empower a sensible instrument to both signify and produce a spiritual effect. Aquinas distinguishes two sorts of instruments here, a united instrument like a hand, and a separated one like a stick. The saving power of a sacrament as a separated instrument derives from Christ's divinity, the principal cause, through his humanity, a united instrument.[80]

Are the sacraments necessary for salvation? Aquinas says so, for three reasons. First, God in her wisdom "provides for each one according as its condition requires." The condition of human nature is such that human beings must be led by bodily and sensible things to spiritual and intelligible realities. "Fittingly [convenienter]," therefore, God provides human beings with means of salvation appropriate to the human condition, the corporeal and sensible signs called sacraments. Second, through sin human beings subjected themselves to corporeal things. It was "fitting" that God should provide us with a healing remedy, a spiritual medicine, precisely by means of corporeal signs. Sins committed through attachment to matter should be overcome through matter that points beyond itself to the spiritual. A human being cannot appreciate spiritual things if given without material mediation. Third, sacraments provide healthy bodily exercises to counteract the tendency of human action to be preoccupied with material things and engage in superstitious and sinful deeds. In short, sacraments are congruous with human nature [conveniens humanae naturae]: human beings are instructed through sensible things, humbled in confessing their subjection to them as well as receiving assistance through them, and preserved from bodily harms by salutary exercises.[81]

The necessity of sacraments for salvation does not mean that God's grace is not sufficient. It is, but "God gives grace to human beings in a way which is suitable to them [secundum modum eis convenientem]."[82] Sacraments are precisely a mode of receiving divine grace appropriate to human beings. Christ's passion is sufficient for salvation, and sacraments are ways of applying or distributing the merit of that passion to each person.[83]

Sacraments are necessary for salvation, then, "insofar as they are sensible signs of invisible things whereby a human being can be made holy."

After sin, "no human being can be made holy except through Christ."[84] "At no time, not even before the coming of Christ could human beings be saved unless they became members of Christ."[85] "Christ's grace reaches those only who became his members by spiritual regeneration, which does not apply to children dying in original sin."[86] Sacraments are means of saving incorporation into Christ. In order to secure the effects of his passion, we must become members of his body and "configured" [configurati] to him as our head, to his passion and death; this occurs sacramentally in baptism, where we share in his passion and death.[87] There is no salvation outside Christ, outside incorporation into his mystical body, and no salvation, therefore, outside the church as his mystical body. In this sense, the eucharist too is necessary for salvation insofar as its reality is none other than the unity of Christ's mystical body.[88]

The nature and necessity of the sacraments vary with the diversity in our soteriological situations. In the state of innocence prior to the fall, human beings enjoyed perfect integrity of nature where the higher rules the lower and in no way depends on it, and thus needed no assistance of corporeal signs to be perfected either in knowledge or in grace. Hence, there was no need for sacraments in the state of innocence. After sin, however, the perfection of the soul requires assistance from corporeal things and needs sacraments.[89] Even before the coming of Christ there was need for some visible signs to testify to our faith in the future coming of the savior. Because of sin human reason was clouded, and the precepts of the natural law were insufficient to make human beings live aright. They needed a written code of laws and certain sacraments in order to combat the overclouding of the natural law and to signify in a more determinate way their faith in the future coming of Christ. These sacraments of the Old Testament, such as sacrifices and circumcision, "foreshadow" Christ's passion.[90] As sacraments are "signs in protestation of the faith whereby a human being is justified,"[91] signs and sacraments should vary according as they signify the future, the past, or the present. The sacraments of the New Law are necessarily different from those of the Old. The ancient patriarchs were saved through their faith in Christ's future coming, whereas we are saved through faith in Christ's birth and passion. There is need for sacraments even after Christ came. In the state of glory, however, there will be no need for sacraments or sensible signs because all truth will be openly and perfectly revealed. As long as we know through a glass darkly in this world, we need such signs in order to reach spiritual realities.[92]

In elucidating the essential difference between the sacraments of the Old Law and those of the New, Aquinas points to an important distinction between faith and sacraments. Both indeed unite us to the power of Christ's passion, but in significantly different ways. The union through faith takes place in an internal act of the soul, the union through sacraments by means of external things. In the case of faith, an end whose actualization lies in the future—Christ's passion—can now preexist in the apprehension and desire of the soul and exercise its (final) causality. In the case of sacraments that use external things, the efficient cause can exercise its causality on external things only insofar as it first actually exists. Thus, the sacraments of the New Law do derive their power of justification from Christ's passion already accomplished, but those of the Old Law, existing prior to the passion, do not. Nevertheless, Old Testament patriarchs were justified by faith in Christ's passion "just as we are." They had faith in the future coming and passion of Christ, which, apprehended by the mind, could also justify them. Both faith and sacraments derive their justifying power from Christ's passion, which can exercise its final causality through faith retrogressively but its efficient causality through the sacraments only progressively.

In this sense, the sacraments of the Old Law could not confer sanctifying grace by their own power or derive the power of conferring such grace from Christ's passion. They were signs testifying to the faith in Christ's future passion without actually conferring justifying grace. They "merely signified" the faith by which human beings are justified. In short, they were "signs" of justifying faith but not "effective" signs conferring justifying grace. They "signified" but did not "cause" grace. If the patriarchs were saved by them, it was not because they were sacraments with their own instrumental causality but because they were signs of faith in Christ's passion. While grace is bestowed in baptism "by the very power of baptism itself, which power baptism has as the instrument of Christ's passion already consummated," circumcision bestowed grace "inasmuch as it was a sign of faith in Christ's future passion," the "seal" of that faith. What justified was "faith signified," not "circumcision signifying."[93]

The fact that the Old Testament patriarchs could be saved without access to the efficacious sacramental signs of the New Law by virtue of their faith in Christ's coming passion shows that the necessity of sacraments for salvation is relative, not absolute. The instrumental causality of the sacraments is an effect dependent on God's principal causality, but "since cause does not depend on effect, but rather conversely, . . . he [Christ] could bestow the sacramental effect without conferring the exterior sacrament."[94] In his sovereign freedom, "God did not bind his power to the sacraments, so as to be unable to bestow the effect of the sacraments without the sacraments."[95] God's power to confer grace is not bound to the sacraments or their ministers. The power to sanctify humanity is God's exclusive privilege, and it is for God alone to decide what means he will use for human sanctification.[96] What is absolutely necessary and what ultimately counts is faith quickened by charity, whereby we subjectively appropriate the source of our salvation, Christ's passion, and accept our saving incorporation into the body of Christ.

Thus, it is through faith—in Christ's future passion—that the Old Testament patriarchs were justified. Their laws and sacrifices were images and shadows of the reality to come, but the movement to an image as image and the movement to the reality are one and the same. By observing the legal sacraments the ancient Fathers "were borne to Christ by the same faith and love whereby we also are borne to him, and hence the ancient Fathers belong to the same church as we."[97] For Aquinas, the movement of faith and love affiliates them not only with the same church but also with the New Law. The New Law is the grace of the Holy Spirit, which is given to all with faith, "explicit or implicit," in Christ. The ancient Fathers had faith in Christ and thus the grace of the Holy Spirit as well, by which they belonged to the New Testament.[98]

Through the sufficiency of faith and charity, human beings can also find salvation apart from the sacraments of baptism and the eucharist. Baptism as a sacrament—the baptism of water—configures a human being to Christ's passion, from which it draws its efficacy in the power of the Holy Spirit. But a person can receive the same effect without the sacrament by being "conformed" [conformatur] through suffering for Christ and by believing in and loving God and repenting of her sins through the power of the Holy Spirit, that is, through the baptism of desire.[99] The baptism of blood is the most excellent of all because the passion and the Holy Spirit operate most excellently in it. The passion acts in the baptism of water through formal or figural representation, in the baptism of desire through a certain affection, but in the baptism of blood through the imitation of the work itself. Likewise, the Spirit acts in the baptism of water through a hidden power, in the baptism of desire through a movement of the heart, but in the baptism of blood through the most intense fervor of love and affection.[100]

For those, then, who die without an opportunity to receive the baptism of water, the baptisms of desire and blood suffice for salvation. Such desire and shedding of blood are the outcome of faith working through charity, whereby "God, whose power is not tied to visible sacraments, sanctifies a human being inwardly."[101] For the same reason, the eucharist of desire can substitute for the eucharist of bread and wine.[102] Before Christ's coming, human beings were incorporated into him by faith in his future coming sealed by circumcision. Before the institution of circumcision, they were incorporated by faith alone, along with sacrifices professing that faith. Thus, "although the sacrament itself of baptism was not always necessary for salvation, yet faith, of which baptism is the sacrament, was always necessary."[103] In short, salvation requires incorporation into Christ, which may be either sacramental or mental.[104]

Toward a Sacramental Theology of Religions

Our discussions in the preceding and present chapters should be sufficient to demonstrate that Aquinas is a most "reasonable" theologian regarding the possibility of salvation of the non-Christians. As an "orthodox" Christian theologian he insists that there is no salvation outside the church—the church in the sense of the mystical body of Christ, not in the institutional sense (although he is fully committed to this church, as well). No one can be saved unless he or she participates in the salvific power of the passion and resurrection of Christ, and no one can so participate except through incorporation into his body through faith. At the same time, as a "reasonable" theologian Aquinas does not demand what is contrary to the nature of things in all the diversity of their times, persons, and conditions. With full respect for this diversity, which often prevents the non-Christian's effective encounter with Christ, he requires only "implicit" faith and sound moral praxis as conditions for the salvation of the non-Christians. As discussed thus far, Aquinas can safely be regarded an inclusivist in his theology of the non-Christian. But is it possible to *develop* the implications of his position and draw a pluralistic inclusivist or even a straightforwardly pluralist position? This is what I shall now attempt.

Let me begin by restating certain fundamental principles that govern Aquinas's approach:

(1) God wants all human beings to be saved.

(2) All grace of salvation is mediated through the humanity of Christ, by our incorporation into his body: "At no time, not even before the coming of Christ could human beings be saved unless they became members of Christ."[105]

(3) The Holy Spirit is the Spirit of Christ, who orders the world to its teleological fulfilment by making all humans children of God in Christ by adoption. The healing and elevating grace of the Spirit is present wherever there is faith, even implicit faith in Christ.

(4) Given the universality of God's salvific will and the supreme imperative of salvation, God will provide the appropriate means of salvation to all. This may be called the principle of reason. It is a mark of reason to provide means appropriate to the gravity of the end, salvation, as well as to the nature of the provider, God's power and love. God will not demand the unnatural or the impossible, that beyond "what lies in one's power." As *De veritate*, 14, 11, put it, "it pertains to divine providence to furnish everyone with what is necessary for salvation, provided on his part there is no hindrance."

(5) This principle of reason becomes concrete through the principle of nature: God gives grace in a way suitable to human nature and the human condition. For example, as sensible beings human beings need the mediation of sacraments as the effective visible signs of invisible and spiritual realities. This sacramental principle, an application of the principle of nature to humanity, is a further concretization of the principle of reason.

(6) Another way of concretizing the principle of reason is the principle of reasonable accessibility, according to which the means of salvation must be available with reasonable ease. For example, an effective encounter with Christ is impossible for those who lived before the time of Christ or who live in cultural situations with no opportunities to hear the Christian message, and it is unreasonable to demand of them explicit faith in Christ as a condition of salvation. Implicit faith made effective through good moral praxis is sufficient. Likewise, given the importance of baptism, it is only fitting that the matter of baptism (water) be something easily available for all, and its minister, anyone.

(7) As the principal and sovereign cause of grace God is not bound to the sacraments or their ministers to confer grace. God alone determines

what means she will use for human salvation, as she alone determines what kinds of sensible things will be used as sacraments for different circumstances.

(8) The principle of reason also dictates the principle of difference, or, providential consideration of the differences in the nature of things and persons, requiring different things of different persons (Christians and pagans), times (before and after Christ), conditions, and places, and providing the means of salvation appropriate to each circumstance. Even the diversity of the moral conscience (e.g., that belief in Christ is evil) must be respected.

(9) On the basis of this principle of difference it is reasonable to believe that for non-Christians who have had no opportunity for a concrete encounter with Christ, the "implicit faith in divine providence" can substitute for the "explicit" faith in the Trinity and Christ the redeemer normally required of the adult Christian. Implicit faith means "believing that God was the liberator of humanity in ways of his own choosing and according as the Spirit would reveal to those who know the truth [credentes Deum esse liberatorem hominum secundum modos sibi placitos et secundum quod aliquibus veritatem cognoscentibus Spiritus revelasset]."[106] This implicit faith will have to become concrete through good moral praxis. The principle of difference also requires different forms of sacraments for different times (e.g., the Old Testament).

The above principles, then, already contain the possibility of the salvation of non-Christians as *individuals.* Can we go one step further and say that they can be saved not only as individuals but precisely as members of their religions, i.e., *through* their religions? Is it possible to recognize the salvific value of non-Christian religions as "ordinary ways of salvation"[107] for those who follow them? The question, it should be noted, is neither whether Aquinas ever advocated this position, which he clearly did not, nor whether he would were he alive today, which is simply impossible to answer, but whether such a position would be objectively coherent or "fitting" with the "logic" and "trajectory" of his principles. I think it would be.

We may begin the argument with the observation that for Aquinas, the Old Testament rituals such as circumcision and sacrifice were sacraments. They were not sacraments in the strict sense of effective signs of justifying and sanctifying grace with their own proper instrumental causality but only in the common sense of signs that do not cause but only signify justifying faith in Christ's future passion. In both cases, however, faith remains the essential condition for salvific grace, and sacraments remain meaningful only as sensible mediations of that faith. Whether they are merely "signs" of grace or "effective" signs of grace would not have been existentially relevant for those living in the Old Testament times, who could not know the technical difference as long as they had the saving faith and expressed this faith through their appropriate rituals. As far as they were concerned, these rituals were the necessary sensible mediations of their saving faith. They were not sacraments in Aquinas's technical sense because the efficient causality of Christ's saving passion does not work retrogressively on external things, but they were "implicit" sacraments in the sense that they were the necessary sensible mediations empowered by the Holy Spirit through which they not only "signified," in the sense of expressing, but also "caused," in the sense of actualizing, the salvific faith of the patriarchs. As long as they were not purely external formalities without content, they did serve as genuine sacramental mediations of saving grace for those who practiced them.

For all the difference in the theological situation of those living in Old Testament times and those living outside the effective sphere of Christian faith, the same logic should apply to the latter as well. As we saw, Aquinas defines the condition of salvation so broadly and minimally as to apply to every human being and every religion: "implicit faith in divine providence"—which means "believing that God was the liberator of humanity in ways of his own choosing and according as the Spirit would reveal to those who know the truth"—and the appropriate moral praxis of preserving one's ordination to the ultimate end in the pursuit of relative ends. What is required is faith in saving providence, the hope of ultimate liberation and fulfillment in ways known only to God, and even then implicit, not explicit faith. In this form, one can say, faith is indeed common to all human beings and religions. Brihadaranyaka Upanishad I.3.28 is one of the most eloquent expressions of that faith and hope: "From the unreal to the Real! From darkness to the light! From death lead me to immortality!"

The principle of nature and the sacramental principle now require that believers concretize their implicit faith and hope in the possibility of salvation through appropriate rituals of their own. The principle of difference requires that these rituals of different peoples will obviously differ among themselves as well as from the Christian and Hebrew sacraments. The principle of reasonable accessibility will require that these rituals will be precisely those available in the already existing religions of the particular regions. These rituals, however, are meaningful only as part of a concrete, organized totality of symbols such as rituals, beliefs, and practices that constitute a living religion. Likewise, we cannot expect human beings to acquire moral education simply on their own, in complete isolation from their religions and cultures. Just as their implicit faith is mediated through the very religions in their own cultures, so is their moral praxis necessarily mediated through their religions, which remain the dominant moral teachers for all humanity with the exception of contemporary, largely Western intellectuals alienated from all religions.

It is imperative here to concretize Aquinas's notion of the sensible mediation of the spiritual and to unpack the implications of the sacramental principle. As an embodied soul, it is the very nature of the human being to have access to spiritual realities only through the mediation of the material. The material, the sensible, the visible can serve as signs of the spiritual, the intellectual, and the invisible. The whole universe as such can serve as a sign or sacrament of God's presence and activity. The sensible sign, however, does not exist in isolation. Our sight never operates by itself but always in the context of our socio-historical existence: what we see is not an abstraction such as a "visible thing" but an already historically mediated "car," "house," "sky," or "sun." Likewise, sensible signs are meaningful only in the context of the interconnected, historically conditioned, and culturally differentiated totality of signs. It is important not to isolate or reify our senses and the sensible but to historicize, socialize, and thus concretize them by reinscribing them in the context of our socio-historical existence. In this sense, it is imperative to see non-Christian rituals always as part of the concrete totality that constitutes a particular religion, culture, or society. The mediation of faith and grace through the sensible is precisely mediation through the sensible made concrete in its socio-historical objectification, i.e., a particular, organized religion, usually the religion into which one is born.

Recent Catholic theology has taken notice of this relation of the particular sacraments and the church as a whole, proposing the church as the basic sacrament of which the particular sacraments are concrete expressions for existentially definitive, particular situations. If the church as such, as the categorically necessary socio-historical objectification of God's saving will, is a sacrament, so too by analogy are other religions as religions, which are the historically necessary embodiments of the implicit faith that saves. As embodied human beings, non-Christians too require the assistance of sensible signs to express and deepen their saving faith and do so precisely in a form appropriate to their concrete existence, i.e., as part of a living religion. Non-Christian religions, therefore, can be regarded as basic sacraments for non-Christians.[108] In this sense, both historically concrete and theologically sensitive to "the diversity of times and persons," Aquinas could say that "diverse sacraments suit different times."[109] At least such seems to be "fitting" to the culturally differentiated nature of the concrete social objectifications of the sensible mediations of invisible saving faith. There is a *religious* way to saving faith for all humanity, as there is a *moral* way and a *rational* way to God for all.

It goes without saying that from Aquinas's perspective, such sacraments mediate only the grace of Christ as head of his mystical body to which all human beings are called, and do so only in the power of the Holy Spirit, the universal, teleological power and the "soul" and "heart" of that body. To this extent his position would be inclusivist. Although different religions evince an irreducible difference, and we do not *now* know *how* they serve as mediations of the grace of Christ, Christians nevertheless believe and hope that the Holy Spirit, precisely as the Spirit of Christ, will provide for an ultimate convergence of different religions in Christ if not in historical Christianity. This position could be called "pluralistic inclusivism."[110]

Can we go further in the direction of a genuine pluralism? Many Christian inclusivists subordinate other religions to the Christian trinitarian dynamics and criterion or, like John Hick, reduce the particularity of religions to a common essence or measure. Is it possible instead to accept each religion as an (as yet) irreducibly different totality?[111] Here two factors can be brought into play. The first is the mutual irreducibility of cultures or religions as generally recognized today by cultural anthropology; the second is the idea of "light" as the epistemological horizon for the possibility of knowledge quite prominent in Aquinas's theology.

Multiculturalist anthropology has been insisting for some time that particular ideas, rituals, and customs make sense only within the totality of a culture, while that totality is not itself reducible to anything external to itself. Each religion or culture has its own horizon incommensurable to that of any other. There is neither a common essence of religion nor a common conception of an ultimate end. There is no superhorizon from which we can understand, compare, and relate the many different cultures and religions. Given the mutual dialectic of cultures and religions which constantly bring them together into common space and introduce all sorts of theoretical and practical changes into them and their mutual relations, it is premature to say that this mutual incommensurability is something permanent. I am inclined to think not. It is clear, however, as

Charles Taylor points out, that at the present time "we are far away from that ultimate horizon from which the relative worth of different cultures might be evident,"[112] a situation likely to last for the foreseeable future.

The sensible mediation of faith, then, means not only mediation by means of sensible signs or symbols or religions as totalities of such symbols, but also mediation by such totalities precisely with their irreducibly particular, historically differentiated contents. As a totality of sensible signs each religion "signifies" in its own unique way. Christianity is one such totality with its own horizon. Rahner argues, on the basis of the incarnational dynamic of grace, that the grace of the supernatural existential seeks embodiment in concrete socio-historical objectifications called religions. It must be added that such objectifications are also irreducibly particular in content. Without this addition the incarnational dynamism of grace remains abstract and formal.[113]

Is there anything in Aquinas himself that would justify this pluralism of religions as mutually incommensurable ultimate totalities? I think there is. The key notion in this regard is the notion of "light," especially the "light" of faith and grace. Light is not something seen itself *(id quod)* but that by which *(id quo)* other things are seen. It is the a priori horizon for the possibility of seeing particular things in a certain way. The "light" of faith makes faith possible in its very specificity as faith, which consists in its adherence to the "formal" object, the First Truth as both end and ground of faith. Faith can be directed to many material objects. In fact, all things can become material objects of faith, but only insofar as faith considers them from the perspective of its formal object, i.e., in relation to God [in ordine ad Deum] and on account of the divine truth [propter divinam veritatem], "on account of the First Truth proposed to us in the Scriptures, according to the teaching of the Church who has the right understanding of them."[114] Ultimately we believe in God only because of God, and in all other things only in relation to God and only because of the authority of divine revelation. No finite object as such can be either the object or ground of faith.[115] The light of faith makes it possible to "see" the credibility, although not the intrinsic intelligibility, of an object, to distinguish between what is appropriate [conveniens] and what is contrary to right faith, and to adhere to right faith with inclination and affection.[116]

Those who have this "light" and habit of faith and those who don't look at the world in two different ways. They live in two different worlds each with its own light or horizon. The articles of faith, the first principles of theology "are not known to those who do not have the light of faith, since not even naturally instilled principles would be instilled in us without the light of the agent intellect."[117] Unbelievers cannot be said to "truly" [vere] believe in God because they lack the formal object and light of faith and "do not believe that God exists under the conditions that faith determines."[118] Heretics who disbelieve even one article of faith do not have faith even though they do hold many other articles of faith—not because of their own intellectual judgments, which may or may not see the intelligibility of the object, but because they lack the formal object of faith, the willingness or will to believe because of the First Truth manifested in Scripture and the teachings of the church. They may hold many of the articles of faith but do so by their own will, not by faith.[119] The difference of formal object, horizon, or light changes the significance of the same content, distinguishing theology as part of sacred doctrine *secundum genus* from theology as part of philosophy.[120] There is no way of arguing with or demonstrating some of the articles of faith to those who do not accept the authority of divine revelation as manifested in Scripture or the articles of faith established by the church. To those who lack faith in this sense we can only show that the truths of faith are not impossible.[121] In short, the light of faith, when shared, produces a church, a believing community with its own internal criteria and horizon, distinguishing it from all other communities who do not share that light. The light of faith makes the faith community see things differently.

It must be remembered, however, that Aquinas says all this in the context of the Christian community as a community of faith with its shared light of faith. His basic concern in using the terminology of light is not so much the sociological one of distinguishing one community from another in terms of their different horizons as the theological one of distinguishing faith, its light, and its *credenda* from reason, its light, and its *intelligenda* on the one hand and from unbelief and heresy, itself a species of unbelief, on the other. Even while, therefore, distinguishing the genuine faithful from philosophers, unbelievers, and heretics, Aquinas does not utilize the category of light to justify the existence of different religious groups each with its own light. Unbelievers and heretics become such because they lack the light of faith, not because they have their own light. Furthermore, they lack the light of faith because of their lack of "the will to believe unless induced by reasons" [voluntas credendi nisi propter rationem inductam],[122] by their obstinate "adherence to their own will,"[123] and by their "opposition to faith" and "pride."[124] Unbelief and heresy are products of sin, not simply different lights.

In a provocative and enlightening essay using the same data from Aquinas as I did above, Bruce Marshall argues that Aquinas was a co-herentist, cultural linguistic postliberal in the manner of George Lind-beck, regarding religions as self-enclosed, incommensurable webs of belief each with its own internal criteria. I think Marshall is right in describing the Christian community as a community of faith with its own "web of belief," light, and internal criteria. He is wrong, however, in implying that Aquinas was a cultural linguist ready to generalize his coherentist defini-tion of faith to all religions. This is precisely because Marshall fails to note the distinction between the "theological" and the "sociological" uses of the concept of the light of faith. Aquinas uses it as a universal theologi-cal category distinguishing the Christian faithful from the unbelieving pagans and heretics in their sinful resistance to the light of faith, not as a neutral, pluralist sociological category distinguishing one religious group from another in terms of its own light of faith. Refusing to accept other religions—in his case, Judaism and Islam—as incommensurable totalities, he does not mind evaluating them by external, Christian criteria.[125]

Still, if Aquinas himself did not make a sociological application of the concept, those who wish to retrieve his thought today may have to. Given the mutual incommensurability and irreducible particularity of cultures and religions, at least for the foreseeable future, and the necessity of socio-historical objectification of faith as appropriate to human nature, there is nothing to prevent us from considering each religion as distinctive by virtue of its own different light of faith. What is true of Christianity in the sociological sense as a group with its own internal criteria is also true of other religions. Aquinas expressed the confidence that for pagans God would provide the necessary means of salvation provided they followed the lead and light of natural reason in their moral praxis.[126] We know today that this "light" of reason exists only in differentiated cultural and religious forms. For the time being at least, we know that there is no com-mon light of faith for all religions, that each has its own.

Aquinas's perfect sensitivity to the "diversity of times and persons" as well as his respect for human nature in its concrete historical manifes-tations might lead him to accept religious pluralism as a factual reality to be accepted. It is not likely that he would acquiesce in religious pluralism as something *de jure*. He is too committed to the transcendental unity of all things, of God, the universe, humanity, and the church in all their sote-riological interdependence and destiny, to take the present *de facto* plu-ralism of religions in all their stark irreducibility and relativity as the last word. Ultimately, to abandon humanity to all their stark differences is not only to ignore the growing interdependence of the world and the growing convergence of human needs and concerns but also to despair of reconciliation and solidarity. Aquinas, therefore, would struggle to work out a sacramental theology of religions that would meet the contradictory demands of both legitimate diversity and necessary solidarity, a theology of the solidarity of Others. I need not, however, engage in any further speculation on the future of Aquinas's theology.[127]

Predestination, Reprobation, Justice

Thus far I have concentrated on the positive aspects of Aquinas's theology regarding the salvation of pagans. The doctrine of implicit faith in saving providence, the principle of nature and difference, the presence of grace in natural moral acts, the christological solidarity of all humanity and creation within the teleological economy of the Trinity, the possibilities of pluralistic inclusivism: all of these provide positive possibilities eminently worth further exploration. Alongside these possibilities, however, we also have to face what today must appear to be the dark side of Aquinas's doctrine if we are to complete our presentation of his position.

Since Joseph de Guibert, the opinion has been widespread that there was a radical shift in Aquinas's position from his early, rather naive optimism regarding the salvation of pagans to an Augustinian pessimism in his later works, especially *Summa Theologiae*.[128] Three questions are at issue here: Why and how did he change his position on whether it is reasonable to require what is humanly impossible in the matter of the content of faith? Why and how did he revise his doctrine of predestination and reprobation? And, are these doctrines in fact radically new developments, first presented in the *Summa*?

As we saw, in his early works—and in fact as late as his commentary on the Romans—Aquinas was confident about the possibility of God providing a preacher or a private revelation to the unevangelized pagan who otherwise leads a good moral life. This position came in response to the question of whether it was reasonable to require something humanly impossible, namely an explicit faith in Christ, of someone who had never heard the Gospel. In the *Summa Theologiae*, however, Aquinas's answer to essentially the same question altogether drops the suggestion about the preacher and private revelation and seems to introduce the Augustinian specter of *massa damnata*. "If we understand those things alone to be in a person's power, which we can do without the help of grace, then we are bound to do many things which we cannot do without the aid of healing grace, such as to love God and our neighbor, and likewise to believe the articles of faith. But with the help of grace we can do this. To whomever this help is given by God, it is indeed given in mercy; to whomever it is not given, it is not given out of justice [ex justitia], as a punishment for a previous, or at least, original, sin, as Augustine states."[129]

It is crucial, however, to balance this passage, upon which so much attention has been focused, with another passage already noted which Aquinas wrote some eight questions later. Addressing precisely the same issue, namely whether inculpable unbelief is by itself damning, Aquinas answers "no." Here he distinguishes between unbelief as resistance to faith, which is a sin, and unbelief as invincible ignorance of faith, which "bears the character [ratio], not of sin, but of punishment, because such like ignorance of divine things is a result of the sin of our first parent." Aquinas continues: "If such like unbelievers are damned, it is on account of *other* sins, which cannot be taken away without faith, but *not* on account of their sin of unbelief"[130] (my emphases). Unbelievers may be damned for their personal sins, but not for that unbelief which is itself already a form of punishment for original sin.

We have also seen that the faith required for these personal sins to be taken away could be implicit faith, as in the case of Cornelius. As to why Aquinas dropped the possibility of the preacher and a private revelation, I have already offered the suggestion that Aquinas could have found such devices too ad hoc and unnatural, and substituted implicit faith as a more "fitting" solution.

Aquinas, of course, did believe with Augustine in the eternal damnation of those—such as unbaptized children and pagans—who have never been united to Christ's saving passion through faith and charity and who therefore died in the state of unforgiven original sin.[131] This doctrine and the doctrine of reprobation seem to negate what appears to be a preeminently reasonable, positive, and universalist dynamic of saving grace so evident in Aquinas's theology. In speaking of the grace of Christ as head of humanity, we have already seen Aquinas referring to some whose potentiality for union with Christ would never become actual because they were not so predestined.[132]

For Aquinas, predestination and reprobation are two aspects of divine providence. The first preordains some to the attainment of their ultimate end; the second "permits" others to fall away from that end. The first includes the "will" to confer grace and glory; the second includes the "will" to deny grace and to "permit a person to fall into sin, and to impose the punishment of damnation on account of that sin." Predestination is the cause of grace and glory, but reprobation is not the cause of sin, although it is the cause of abandonment by God and thus also the cause of eternal punishment. The doctrine of reprobation is all the more serious because, as commonly understood, it seems to put into question all the positive soteriological dynamic of Aquinas's theology, as well as the very notions of divine goodness and justice: divine reprobation is not the punishment of the sinner for his or her conscious rejection of divine grace that has been offered but, so it seems, an eternal decision by God to deny saving grace to certain individuals *prior* to their merit or demerit.[133]

Aquinas discusses the doctrine of reprobation in the context of predestination, and the doctrine of predestination in the context of providence. Let me, therefore, begin with a discussion of his doctrine of divine providence. As the divine economy with regard to all created things, providence is the divine equivalent of prudence, right reason that properly orders actions toward appropriate ends. As God is the cause of all things by her intellect, there preexists the *ratio* of all her effects in the divine mind including the *ratio* or plan of the ordering of things to their end, especially their ultimate end [ratio ordinis rerum in finem] or of things to be ordered to an end [ratio ordinandorum in finem]. As a prudent person directs all her actions toward the ends of her life, so God directs all her creatures to her own end. There are two aspects to this ordering of all creation to an end; providence in the narrow sense, which refers to the eternal ordering of things to an end [ratio ordinis] in the divine mind; and government, which refers to the temporal execution of that ordering [executio ordinis] in the world. These two aspects together constitute divine providence in the larger sense.[134]

In the sense of the eternal ordering of things to an end, divine providence is immediate over all things insofar as the divine mind eternally contains the *ratio* of all causes and effects. In the sense of the temporal execution of that ordering, however, divine providence uses the intermediaries of finite, secondary causes, not because of any defect in its power but because of the abundance and willingness of divine goodness to "impart the dignity of causality even to creatures."[135] In divine providence immediacy and mediation are not mutually exclusive.

Regarding providence thus conceived, there are three things we may ask, namely: What is the ultimate finality or end that God seeks to achieve through her providence? How does the secondary, intermediary causality of finite creatures serve the primary, universal causality of God? And, what is the role of evil and sin in promoting God's ultimate purpose in and for the universe?

With regard to the first question, the ultimate end to be promoted is the divine goodness itself, which, however, remains one and undivided in God. It can be manifested and represented by creatures only in a diversity of grades of being that itself contributes to the harmony of parts and whole, to the "beauty of order" [ordinis pulchritudo] in the universe, and thus to its common good or the "good of the whole" [bonum totius]. Creatures cannot attain to divine simplicity, but can imitate God only in a multiplicity of ways. The whole universe can participate in and represent divine goodness more perfectly than can a single creature. Likewise, a multiplicity of different and therefore unequal grades [gradus] of being and perfection, some more perfect and nobler than others, makes for a more perfect universe and a better representation of divine goodness than does any single grade. Moreover, the best universe is one in which every part is not the best taken absolutely or in itself but the best in proportion to the whole, and therefore one which is "best as a whole," showing the beauty and unity of order in which all things are teleologically related to one another and to God. It is God's ordering wisdom [sapientia ordinans] that underlies this diversity, inequality, and order among things. Divine providence ensures that creatures manifest this divine goodness and wisdom by contributing to the ontological diversity and teleological harmony of the universe for the sake of its perfection and completion.[136]

With regard to the second question, all things are subject to divine providence. Both the universal or general features of things and their individualizing principles are included in the divine ordering of effects to God's own end because nothing can escape the divine causality as the first, universal agent and source of all being [esse]. Finite particular agents may cause effects outside their intention and foresight, which are, therefore, accidental as far as those agents are concerned. But no effect can lie outside the divine intention and foresight precisely because all things are what they are as universals and particulars only insofar as they are or participate in the actuality of being [esse], whose ultimate source is God. All things that are in any way whatsoever, therefore, and all particular causes and their effects are subject to the providence of the first universal cause whose causality extends to all beings [entia] in their very being [esse].[137]

In exercising causality over the secondary causes so as to serve the end of her providence God does not act violently or arbitrarily. Instead, God acts "according to the condition [conditio] of proximate causes," preparing necessary causes for some things and contingent causes for others so that some things are ordained to happen necessarily and others contingently. Things not only are done which God wills to be done, but they are also done "in the way that he wills. Now God wills some things to be done necessarily, some contingently, to the right ordering of things, for the building up of the universe."[138] Ultimately, some effects willed by God happen contingently not because proximate causes are contingent but because God has prepared contingent causes for them. The order of divine providence remains immutable and certain insofar as all things happen as they have been foreseen, whether from necessity or from contingency. Both necessity and contingency are modes of being and fall under the foresight of the universal cause who provides universally for all being [universalis provisor totius entis], although they may escape the foresight of particular causes.[139] Likewise, rational and irrational creatures are subject to divine providence in different ways. As creatures capable of free will and choice in action, rational creatures are subject to divine providence in such a way that they are also responsible for what they do in terms of fault and merit and therefore in some way are responsible for their own punishments and rewards.[140]

With regard to the third question, how do evil and sin contribute to the providential manifestation of divine goodness, the ultimate end of all things? For Aquinas, this is never a question of God willing the evil of sin, which she cannot do, for sin consists in "the privation of right order toward the divine good [ordo ad bonum divinum]."[141] The proper object of desire, including the divine will, is always the good, and evil is desired only accidentally, insofar as it accompanies a good and insofar as this good is greater than the evil. Evil, therefore, is sought only as an indispensable means to an end, secondarily and indirectly, never in itself. God wills no good more than her own goodness, but she does will one finite good more than another for the sake of her own goodness. If she wills the evil of natural defect or punishment—not the evil of sin as such—it is because she wills the good to which such evils are attached. Thus, in willing justice God also wills punishment; likewise, she wills the natural corruption of some things in willing the preservation of the natural order.

Strictly speaking, "God therefore neither wills evil to be done, nor wills it not to be done, but wills to permit evil to be done; and this is a good."[142]

Thus God only "permits" "some defect" so as to make different kinds of good possible and thus promote the perfection of the universe and the good of the order of the whole. A particular provider tries to exclude defects in his effect as much as possible, but the universal provider permits some defects—within the plan of universal nature—in order to promote the good of the whole insofar as the defect in one thing leads to the good in another. For instance, corruption of one thing is the condition for the generation of another in much of the universe. Furthermore, God has the power to draw good even out of evil. The prevention of all defect would mean the prevention of so much good. There would be no living lion without the killing of animals, as there would be no patience of martyrs without persecuting tyrants, and no exercise of justice without injustice.[143]

It is in this context of providence that Aquinas goes on to discuss predestination. As all things are subject to divine providence, so it is appropriate [conveniens] for God to predestine human beings. To provide means to ordain things to ends, of which there are two kinds. One kind of end is proportionate to created nature and can be attained by the power of that nature. The other kind of end, however, exceeds the proportion and power of created nature; the end of eternal life consisting in the divine vision is above the nature of all created things. Just as an arrow is sent to the target by the archer, a creature must be directed to an end by another if the creature cannot attain it by its own power. The rational creature is capable [capax] of eternal life but cannot activate that capacity and attain the vision of God by its own power. It must be delivered [transmittitur] to eternal life by God. As there exists in the divine mind the *ratio* of the ordering of all things to an end, so there preexists in God the *ratio* of this deliverance. Predestination, then, is the *ratio* of the deliverance of the rational creature to eternal life preexisting in the divine mind. As such, predestination is that part of providence dealing with the supernatural destiny of rational creatures, including angels. It does not apply either to irrational creatures or to the natural life of rational creatures.[144]

This predestination, according to Aquinas, is a result of God's prevenient love and election. The eternal predestination of some to salvation presupposes God's love insofar as she wills this good of eternal salvation for them, and God's election insofar as she wills this good to some in preference to others, whom she reprobates. In the human situation, we love someone by willing the good already preexisting in the person and election therefore precedes love; but in the case of predestination God's love precedes election by willing to create the very good for the person.[145] Again, Aquinas makes a distinction between communicating divine goodness in general and communicating this or that good in particular. The first occurs without election in that all things in some way share in divine goodness, the second only with election in that God gives certain goods to some which she does not give to others.[146]

Aquinas is as emphatic as anyone that we can in no way "merit" this predestination to glory through our own works independent of God's prevenient grace. There cannot be any cause of the act of the divine will external to the divine will itself, and it is "insane [insanae mentis]" to claim that merit, whether of the former life (Origen) or the present life (Pelagius), causes the divine will to predestine some to glory. Nothing begun in us can cause the effect of predestination. Nor can we say that God preordains that she will give grace to someone because she knows beforehand that the person will make good use of that grace; this foreseen merit, itself the effect of predestination, is not the cause of that predestination on the part of God. This view makes a distinction between what flows from grace and what flows from free will, as though the same thing could not come from both; ultimately it treats divine grace and human will as two separate things at the same level. What is of grace is itself an effect, not a cause, of predestination and is already contained in predestination. The primary causality of God operates precisely through the operation of secondary causes, making it illegitimate to separate what flows from free will and what flows from the grace of predestination, or what comes from secondary causes and what comes from the primary cause.[147]

How, then, should we conceive of the relation between grace and merit? Both grace and merit are effects of predestination, and there is no reason why one effect of predestination cannot be the cause of another in such a way that a subsequent effect becomes the (final) cause of a previous effect, which in turn may become the (meritorious) cause of the subsequent effect. For Aquinas, then, "we might say that God preordained to give glory on account of merit, and that he preordained to give grace to merit glory."[148] No purely independent human causality can be the cause of predestination. Whatever is in us disposing us toward salvation, including even the preparation for grace, is already an effect of predestination. "Grace is the principle of all our good works [principium cuius libet boni in nobis]."[149] The dialectic between salvific grace and human freedom is itself a dialectic within the overriding causality of predestination. Predestination in the general sense of the total effect of predestination has its *ratio* in the divine will and divine goodness, while predestination in the particular sense of this or that effect of predestination may have varying causal relations among different things in which one effect of predestination can serve as the cause of another effect.[150]

This also means that prayers and good works neither alter nor are superfluous to divine predestination, two errors that Aquinas would exclude. As far as the element of preordination in predestination is concerned, no human works can further predestination: it is not due to our prayers that we are predestined by God. With regard to the effect of predestination, however, prayers and good works can help predestination because providence operates through secondary causes. Just as God provides natural effects by means of natural causes, without which those effects cannot take place, so God predestines a person to be saved precisely through those prayers and good works, without which, therefore, the person would not be able to attain salvation. For Aquinas, predestination does not mean dispensing with human choices and human works as though God does all the work, leaving nothing for human beings to do. Rather, predestination includes empowering human beings to do their share in their own salvation in a way worthy of the dignity of the free rational creature.[151]

How many, then, are predestined to eternal salvation? Many? Few? Or all? Aquinas grants that the answer is known only to God, not only formally by reason of her foreknowledge but also materially by reason of her deliberate choice and determination.[152] Still, Aquinas speculates that only a minority will be saved. His argument: "The good that is proportionate to the common state of nature is to be found in the majority; and is wanting in the minority. The good that exceeds the common state of nature is to be found in the minority, and is wanting in the majority. Thus it is clear that the majority of human beings have sufficient knowledge for the guidance of life; and those who have not this knowledge are said to be half-witted or foolish; but they who attain to a profound knowledge of things intelligible are a very small minority in respect to the rest. Since their eternal happiness, consisting in the vision of God, exceeds the common state of nature, and especially insofar as this is deprived of grace through the corruption of original sin, those who are saved are in the minority [pauciores]." That some are saved at all when "very many" [plurimi] are not, for Aquinas, is itself a testimony to the triumph of divine mercy.[153]

In contrast to those whom God predestines to attain their ultimate end by willing them eternal life and empowering them through grace to lead a worthy life in this world, there are those whom God reprobates to eternal damnation by withholding healing grace from them and permitting them to fall into sin. "As predestination includes the will to confer grace and glory, so also reprobation includes the will to permit a person to fall into sin, and to impose the punishment of damnation on account of that sin."[154] Why, then, does God predestine some to glory and reprobate others to eternal damnation? Why does God even "permit" some to fall into sin and thus to incur eternal punishment? Just as predestination is the special case of providence applied to the ultimate destiny of the rational creature, so, one can say, reprobation is the special case of those "defects" God permits in order to preserve the possibility of goods which would have been prevented without those defects and which would contribute to the diversity of grades of being so essential to the manifestation of divine goodness in the universe. For Aquinas, the logic of reprobation is the logic of the necessity of defects for the sake of the greater manifestation of divine goodness in the world.

This doctrine of reprobation raises at least two issues concerning God, one about her goodness and the other about her justice. Is reprobation compatible with God's goodness and justice? Doesn't God love all human beings and want them to be saved? Is God still just in creating human beings for the ultimate end of eternal life yet withholding the essential condition for attaining that end, healing grace? Aquinas is quite sensitive to these issues and addresses them head on, but in order to accurately grasp Aquinas's argument for compatibility, it is crucial to place it in the broader context of his doctrine of God's will and love in general.

For Aquinas, God "wills both himself as the end, and other things as ordained to that end: inasmuch as it befits the divine goodness that others should be partakers therein."[155] That is, God wills herself or her own goodness as the end primarily and necessarily, but other things only insofar as they serve and manifest the divine goodness. Just as it is the very nature of perfection to share or communicate itself even in natural things, it pertains to the divine will all the more to communicate its own good to others by likeness; but this ontological principle of generosity, so characteristic of Aquinas, it must be noted, is always subject to the theological principle of divine sovereignty—the judgment of God according to her own goodness—which remains the ultimate end and criterion of all created things.[156]

How does this apply to God's will regarding the salvation of humanity? Does not God "want all human beings to be saved" according to 1 Timothy 2:4? Here Aquinas makes a distinction between "antecedent" and "consequent" will. Antecedently, i.e., prior to the consideration of particular circumstances and therefore taken in itself, a judge may want all human beings to live, but consequently, i.e., in the particular situation of murder and therefore taken in relation to other things [secundum rem], a judge may will the murderer to be hanged. The antecedent kind of willing is a conditional willing, i.e., willing on condition that subsequent events do not change the moral situation. The consequent kind of willing is a simple, absolute willing because concrete conditions have already been taken into account. Aquinas's answer, then, is that God wills all human beings to be saved according to her antecedent will, but also wills some to be damned according to the demand of her justice according to her consequent will. Simply speaking, then, God does not will all human beings to be saved. Or, in another way of putting it, God wishes all human beings to be saved, but does not mind damning some in case justice should so require.[157]

What does this make of God's love? Does not God love all things and all humanity? Again, for Aquinas, it is crucial to remember the absolute ontological priority of God the creator over the creature. Creatures cannot demand to be loved by God as though their lovability precedes God's love. Rather, creatures are lovable insofar as they exist and possess varying degrees of perfections, and this lovability or goodness is itself an effect of God's creative love, which "infuses and creates goodness."[158] It is God's love that renders creatures lovable; it is not their antecedent lovability that makes God love them. A thing is good only insofar as it is willed by God, and is better than another only because God wills a greater good for it. Insofar as things exist and are good in any way, and in the sense that these are gifts of God, God can be said to will "some good" [aliquod bonum] to all things and love them. God also loves all humanity inasmuch as God wishes them "some good [aliquod bonum]" according to her providential judgment. It is only that God does not wish them "just any good [quodcumque bonum]." Reprobation means that God does not wish them the "particular" good [hoc bonum] of salvation.[159] In this sense God also loves sinners insofar as they exist as certain kinds of beings and derive both their existence and nature from God. To say that God cares for all things does not mean that God deals out equal good to all things but that she administers all things with an equal wisdom and goodness [ex aequali sapientia et bonitate].[160]

What of God's justice? Is reprobation compatible with divine justice? Here, likewise, it is crucial to remember the transcendent difference between divine and human justice and not to try to measure divine by human justice. As for Plato, so for Aquinas justice means the harmony of order in which each is rendered what is due to each [unicuique suum]. In this sense divine justice is shown in the order of the universe in both natural and voluntary things. However, the source of divine justice is divine wisdom, the norm or law, as it were, of divine justice according to which God wills and which makes God's will right and just. We act justly in following the law, but, the law we follow is extrinsic to us and comes to us from a higher source, whereas divine wisdom, the law of divine justice, is intrinsic to and identical with the divine will. God is thus a law unto herself [sibi ipsi lex] in the most profound sense, and it is this law of divine wisdom that governs all the relations of justice that we enter into with God and one another.[161]

Basically there are two kinds of order: one in which creatures are ordered to one another as parts to a whole, accidents to substance, and means to ends; and another in which creatures are ordered to God. Accordingly, there are also two kinds of debt or what is due: things due to God and things due to creatures, and in each case, God renders the debt and fulfills justice. It is due to God that creatures fulfill the requirements of divine will and wisdom and manifest divine goodness. In paying this debt to herself God is only doing justice to herself. It is due to creatures that they should possess what is ordered to them, e.g., human beings having hands, and other animals serving human beings. In giving to each thing what is due to it by its nature and condition God pays the debt to creatures and does them justice. This debt and justice to creatures, however, is derived from the debt and justice to God herself: what is due to each created thing is due to it only because it is so ordered by divine wisdom. Thus, God is not a debtor to creatures: creatures are ordered to God but God is not ordered to them. God's justice to creatures is only a fitting result and accompaniment [condecentia] of her antecedent creative ordering goodness. It is God's antecedent justice to herself that "constitutes the order in things that conforms to the rule of her wisdom [constituit ordinem in rebus conformem rationi sapientiae suae]," and that also constitutes the ultimate measure and thus the final "truth" of things and thoughts.[162]

Is reprobation, then, compatible or incompatible with divine justice? For Aquinas, there are three considerations that make reprobation not only compatible with divine justice but also a strict requirement of such justice. The first consideration is that eternal salvation, itself an effect of predestination, should be regarded as a gift [gratia], not as a debt, and that in matters of gifts, "the person can give more or less, just as he pleases, provided he deprives nobody of his due, without any infringement of justice [potest aliquis pro libito suo dare cui vult, plus vel minus, dummodo nulli subtrahat debitum, absque praejudicio justitiae]."[163] God does not act unjustly but only within the *ratio* of her infinite freedom if she does not grant eternal life to all human beings. Nor do human beings, created as they are with an essential receptivity for grace and glory, have a strict right in justice to eternal life, which as such goes beyond their nature. Salvation and damnation are matters for divine goodness, wisdom, and justice to decide.

The second consideration is that reprobated persons are still free to sin or not to sin even in the absence of healing grace and are therefore capable of incurring guilt, which makes them in some sense responsible for their own damnation. For Aquinas, in the state of corrupt nature we cannot avoid all mortal sins without grace or all venial sins even with grace, but we *can* avoid particular acts of sin [singulos actus peccati] without healing grace and thus remain responsible for them and their consequences.[164] "Guilt proceeds from the free will of the person who is reprobated and deserted by grace. . . . Reprobation by God does not take anything away from the power of the person reprobated."[165]

In this regard Aquinas calls attention to the difference in causality between predestination and reprobation. Divine predestination is the cause of both grace in this world and glory in the beatific vision. It does not dispense with the necessity of free choice, but it is predestination and not the merit of our free choice that causes grace and glory and also whatever merit there is in the exercise of our free will. Divine reprobation, on the other hand, is the cause of the abandonment of the person and of his eternal punishment by God, but it is not the cause of the person's sin. The cause of sin remains the free will of the sinner, who cannot acquire grace but still enjoys the free will to fall into this or that sin and so the capacity for guilt and responsibility. Our free choice is not sufficient for meriting grace and glory as in the case of predestination, but it is sufficient for committing sin and incurring guilt and punishment as in reprobation. Thus, reprobation does not have the same relation to the reprobated as predestination has to the predestined. It is true that predestination is a matter of God's eternal decision to confer saving grace on certain individuals *prior* to any of their merits, while reprobation is a matter of God's eternal decision to deny saving grace to certain individuals *prior* to any of their sins, but it is also true that while predestination is the cause of their merits, reprobation is not the cause of their sin, which is rather due to their free will. The reprobated are still being punished for what they have done by way of sin, i.e., not gratuitously, while the predestined are being rewarded gratuitously, i.e., not for what they have done.[166]

Furthermore, in reprobation God does not incline the will to evil by directly and actively moving it to do evil but permits the will to fall into evil by not providing grace and withdrawing the necessary support; in the same way, someone for her own good judgment may refuse to lend help to a falling person and permit the person to fall. The sinner falling into sin through his own free will does not place himself outside divine providence. God still remains the cause of the free will as such, although the use of free will to turn away from God—the privation of right order to the divine good—is the fault of the sinner, just as the limping of the leg is not the fault of the motive power that moves the leg but the fault of the defective leg incapable of receiving the full influx of the motive power.

It is important to note here how Aquinas divides responsibilities between God and secondary causes in the case of defective and sinful actions. In every action there are always two kinds of causalities at work, the primary causality of God as the first mover, who gives existence, actuality, and teleology to all things that are, and the secondary causality of created things who can receive the ontological and teleological movement from the first mover only according to their own mode, disposition, and receptivity. Even defective, sinful actions are due to God insofar as they are *actions* and as such sustained by God's will to keep them in existence and actuality, but they are due to the sinner insofar as they are *defective* and *sinful* and imply deviation from true being, actuality, and order. As deviations from right order, defects and sins are modes of non-being and as such the fault of defective secondary causes, but as participations in being and actuality perfections are the effect of the first cause. This is why God loves sinners but hates sin: "Insofar as sinners are certain natures, they are, and are from God [sunt, et ab ipso sunt], but insofar as they are sinners, they are not and fall short of being, which cannot be from God [non sunt, sed ab esse deficiunt, et hoc in eis a Deo non est]." In short, "whatever there is of being and action in a bad action is reduced to God as cause; whereas whatever defect is in it is not caused by God, but by the deficient secondary cause."[167]

The third consideration that makes reprobation a requirement of divine justice is that punishment is necessary for the sake of divine justice, which is itself a way of manifesting divine goodness, the ultimate end of divine providence. Divine goodness requires many different grades of being in an ordered universe for its manifestation. In natural things this often means that some grades of being can only be maintained by the corruption of other things, which, therefore, is an evil that God allows for the sake of the good of the order of the universe. In human affairs God manifests her goodness by sparing and showing mercy to those predestined but also by punishing and showing justice to those reprobated. The grace not to impede the reception of grace is not given to "all" but only to "some, in whom God desires his mercy to appear, so that the order of justice may be manifested in others."[168] God does not will the death of human beings, temporal or eternal, for its own sake, as she does not will the evil of sin, but she does will the punishment of sinners for the sake of justice, which also belongs to the order of the universe.[169]

Aquinas stresses God's own active role in reprobation by contrasting the universality of the sun in enlightening the world with the universality of God in illuminating souls with the light of grace. The sun enlightens all bodies "by necessity of nature." If window shutters are closed, and darkness follows, it is not the fault of the sun but that of the one who closes the shutters. God works freely according to the order of her wisdom. It may be that "God is always working the justification of the human being, even as the sun is always lighting up the air,"[170] but this does not mean that all we have to do is just to turn to God as we turn to the sun. Whether we turn to God at all depends not only on our free will but most decisively on the prevenient grace of divine motion to turn us to God. If we fail to turn to God and remain spiritually blind and hard of heart, "the cause of the withholding of grace is not only he who poses [ponit] an obstacle to grace but also God who, by her own judgment, does *not* counterpose grace [suo judicio gratiam non *ap*ponit]."[171] As a form of punishment and a preamble to sin, this sort of blindness may be only temporary and ultimately directed toward healing through God's mercy, but such an outcome "is not vouchsafed to all those who are blinded, but only to the predestined." It may also be directed toward damnation as a consequence of reprobation "to the glory of God's justice."[172]

For all his attempts to justify God's ways in the matter of reprobation, however, Aquinas is fully sensitive to the limits of human explanation and ends up with an affirmation of the sovereignty of God's ultimately incomprehensible will. "Why he chooses some for glory, and reprobates others, has no reason, except the divine will," just as "why this particular part of matter is under this particular form, and that under another, depends upon the simple will of God." Predestination and election do not find their cause in any human merits, for divine grace precedes all merits. The divine will is the first cause of things that are done, but "there can be no cause of the divine will and providence."[173] It is as much God's sovereign freedom to give sight to the blind out of the abundance of his goodness as it is not to heal all the sick, to offer his help in mercy to those who impede grace as it is to allow others to impede grace and suffer the consequences as a matter of justice, just as it is the artisan's prerogative to "form some vessels for noble uses and others for ignoble purposes."[174] "Hath not the potter power over the clay, of the same lump to make one vessel unto honor and another unto dishonor" (Romans 9:21)?[175]

The doctrine of the absolute sovereignty of God's will and providence to elect some for glory and others for damnation puts to a radical providential, not an eschatological, proviso all the soteriological optimism we have seen in Aquinas. The possibility of implicit faith among the pagans, the presence of saving grace in moral acts, the constitutive teleological ordering of nature to grace, the call of all humanity to solidarity with Christ and his predestination as the Son of God, and the overriding movement of the triune God are all thrown into question. Whether pagans will actually acquire the implicit faith in saving providence, whether a person will direct his or her life to God or to some finite creature as the ultimate end of life, whether a person will indeed prepare herself for the reception of sanctifying grace, whether nature will indeed be perfected by grace for glory, whether anyone will actualize their union with Christ as head of his mystical body through faith and charity: all of these possibilities depend radically on God's eternal decision to grant or withhold the prevenient grace of divine motion. And as we saw, in Aquinas's opinion this radical form of grace is granted only to a minority.[176]

The prevenient motion of the First Mover, which is the a priori transcendental condition for the possibility of all good acts, natural and supernatural, is granted "according to the plan [ratio] of his providence, not according to a necessity of nature."[177] This is why this prevenient grace is *not* necessarily given to whoever prepare themselves for grace by doing what lies in them, but only conditionally given, i.e., if they are predestined, not reprobated. "A person cannot prepare himself for grace unless God precedes him and moves him to good."[178] If grace is in some sense "necessarily" given, this is because "it has a necessity—not indeed of coercion, but of infallibility—as regards what it is ordained to by God, since God's intention cannot fail." But does God intend to give grace? For Aquinas, the preparation for grace by means of free will is only conditionally successful: "*if* God intends, while moving, that the one whose heart he moves should attain to grace, he will infallibly attain to it."[179] All our optimism about human salvation seems to come to grief on the scandal of the doctrine of reprobation. It is not true, after all, that "God does not deny grace to whoever does what he or she can." Whether one does what one can, and in fact whether one can do anything at all, depends on God's prevenient grace, which is not up to us but to God's own sovereign freedom to provide.

This doctrine of reprobation, however, is not something new with the *Summa Theologiae*. Already in the *Summa contra Gentiles*, Aquinas put forth a doctrine of election and reprobation identical in all essentials to that of the later *Summa*, except that the latter proceeds to the speculation that only a "minority" would be saved. In SCG, 3, 159, Aquinas held that "it is reasonable to hold a man responsible if he does not turn toward God, even though he cannot do this without grace," because the person has the ability in free will to "impede or not to impede the reception of divine grace," which God is indeed "ready to give to all," like the sun which shines on the entire world whether individual eyes remain open or closed to it. However, Aquinas hurries on in chapter 160 to qualify this statement drastically by saying that such ability to impede or not to impede divine grace is available only in the state of original integrity. Contrary to Pelagius, in the state of sin we do not by ourselves have the power not to impede grace and avoid sin altogether. Even though we are still free not to commit this or that particular sin, the weight of sin is such that we are not free to avoid all sins. For this we need healing grace.

In chapter 161, Aquinas makes it clear that the offer of this healing grace is not universal but elective: "God does not assist with his help all who impede grace, so that they may be turned away from evil and toward the good, but only some in whom he desires his mercy to appear, so that the order of justice may be manifested in the other cases." This election, however, is not based as Origen thought on the works done in previous incarnations, but solely on the sovereign freedom of God who, preceding all such works, "has decided from eternity not to give his grace" to some.[180]

Aquinas's doctrine of reprobation certainly remains a hard saying if not a scandal to us today, with our changed sensibilities. We no longer seem to share the tradition of Augustine's teaching about the *massa damnata,* about the sovereign freedom of God to save some and reprobate others, and about God's justice in condemning to eternal damnation even those whose only guilt is that of original sin regardless of whether they are infants without the use of reason or pagans who have never heard the Gospel.[181] To be sure, Aquinas is not as pessimistic as Augustine in this regard, but it is clear that it is not easy to reconcile his doctrine of the reprobation of the majority of humanity with either contemporary moral sensibilities or his own optimistic view of the universal presence of grace in natural moral acts and in the implicit faith of good pagans, under the teleological movement of the economic Trinity.

Several observations are in order about Aquinas's doctrine of reprobation. Aquinas insists that God only "permits" those reprobated to fall away from saving grace and that it is their own fault and responsibility to do so. Given the presuppositions, however, that human beings are created for an ultimate end—the vision of God—which they cannot attain on their own but only through grace, that they may be able to avoid particular sins without grace but not all sins without grace, and that they need to be empowered and sustained by the grace of divine motion for both conversion and perseverance, as well as to be healed by the gift of habitual grace, it is not clear that their damnation is either solely or principally their own fault. Aquinas's doctrine of reprobation, like the more general problem of evil, certainly threatens to call into question either God's generosity, which permits the majority to be eternally lost, or God's power, which can save only a minority. With Pesch, we might ask, "How are we to understand that God does *not* will sin, when sin and above all the final persistence in sin with the consequence of rejection can occur only through the fact that God is withholding the grace which, had God conferred it, would have infallibly and certainly prevented the sin according to the explicit assumptions?"[182]

Aquinas's doctrine of reprobation, which Pesch calls "intellectual violence,"[183] clearly poses a serious challenge to the general trinitarian optimism otherwise so characteristic of his theology. In a universe where only a small minority are saved and attain their ultimate end, one is led to wonder how Aquinas could say that "all things tend through their movements and actions toward the divine likeness as toward their ultimate end."[184] It is not easy to be persuaded that the reprobation of the majority of humanity somehow manifests divine goodness. After a century of countless genocides and mass murders and horrendous destructions through wars, pogroms, and gulags, the idea of permitting evil like the imperial persecution of Christians in the Roman Empire in order to manifest divine goodness through the courage, faith, and patience of martyrs should sound nothing short of scandalous, an unconscionable theological justification of unredeemable historical evils. Can we truly say that such a doctrine takes seriously the good news of the New Testament about the gracious, forgiving, compassionate God, the God who is love?

Aquinas's doctrine of reprobation, like that of Augustine, is based on certain assumptions which we can perhaps no longer share. Out of a certain conception of the sovereignty of God's will and freedom, Aquinas does not seem to mind reducing even our eternal, ultimate fate to merely a form of multiplicity necessary to manifest divine goodness, begging the question of how divine goodness requires the damnation of the majority. This all the more so, since God would be acting mercifully but not unjustly, were she to forgive humanity without demanding satisfaction for their sins.[185] He also reduces the matter of our eternal destiny to the same level of the incomprehensible mystery of the inexplicable divine will as that of why "this" form is united to "this" matter.[186] Salvation is treated here as though it were one particular [hoc] good among others, "this or that good [istius vel illius boni]," or "every [quodcumque]" good that God is free to withhold from some while giving to others without being unjust.[187] Aquinas even places salvation on the same level as "a profound knowledge of things intelligible," which is accessible by nature only to an elite minority.[188] Aquinas seems here to apply an elistist criterion in a matter that is certainly of the most universal and ultimate concern to us, that is, the *final* success or failure of *all* human beings.

By taking eternal salvation and eternal damnation as among the things "a person can give more or less, just as he pleases [potest aliquis pro libito suo dare cui vult, plus vel minus],"[189] Aquinas often renders the gratuity of grace indistinguishable from the arbitrariness of caprice and the assertion of sheer power. A truly loving God would not take such a cavalier attitude toward human salvation, the very attainment—or the very frustration—of the ultimate destiny for which she has created us. From the human standpoint, salvation is not one mere good among others that can be given or withdrawn at will. It is the fundamental good without which there can be no other meaningful human good, as well as the ultimate good whose significance cannot be judged in terms of sheer gratuity and legalistic justice.[190]

Furthermore, what does the failure of the majority of humanity to attain their ultimate end, the vision of God, for which they were created, make of divine providence, God's very ability to preordain creatures to their ultimate ends? Can the notion of *massa damnata* do "justice" to the teleology of human nature? Against the objection that the loss of the vision of God due to original sin would have rendered human existence incapable of attaining its ultimate end and thus useless and vain, Aquinas replied that it was precisely in order to avoid this futility of existence that God proposed from the very beginning of the human race a mediator between God and humanity as a remedy and liberation from this futility. Does the coming of a liberator provide a significant remedy for this futility when the remedy is effective only in the case of a minority?[191]

These are deep reservations about Aquinas's doctrine of reprobation based on contemporary humanistic sensibilities. It is likewise appropriate, however, to appreciate his underlying assumptions over against our own so as to allow him to challenge us as well. There are three assumptions in particular that provide such a contrast. They concern our contemporary attitudes toward the ultimate wisdom and providence of God, the eschatological salvation of human existence, and divine justice in history.

First, Aquinas's theology as a whole is marked by a profound awe for the divine providence for all things as manifested in the cosmic order and human history. A characteristic of the classical theological tradition in general, that awe is rooted in the faith that the destiny of all creation is ultimately in the hands of God, who guides all things, and in the hope and trust that God takes care of her creation precisely through her love and wisdom. As created intellects we do not have an intuition into the divine mind, but out of our creaturely respect for God's transcendent power, which is always guided by love and wisdom, and for God's transcendent love and wisdom, which are always effective, we trust in divine providence and submit ourselves, without complaint although not without perplexity, to the ways of divine wisdom including its ultimate incomprehensibility.

In contrast, I wonder whether we today have a sense of the cosmos vast enough to inspire reflection on its ultimate destiny, and a sense of God transcendent enough to inspire awe and submission to her cosmic providence. In fact, have we not become so anthropocentric as to completely cease to wonder about the destiny of the larger universe of which our human history is only a small part? Do we not turn God into such a familiar and trivial figure that we either finitize God, reducing her to our human proportions, or simply deny her existence when we cannot reduce those indeed horrendous evils of history to the canons of our all too human rationality? We have made ourselves an uncompromising measure of all things including God. Theologians, too, share this anthropocentrism. What will it take for contemporary theology to recover something of the sense of God's transcendent otherness so characteristic of the classical tradition?

Second, Aquinas was also dominated by the profound sense shared by the classical tradition that salvation is an incomparably serious matter because it involves the ultimate destiny, the success or failure, of human existence in its totality. This serious matter was rendered doubly difficult because it did involve the hard work of free choice in leading a good moral life throughout a lifetime, demanding that we work out our salvation "with fear and trembling," and because it ultimately depended upon God's gracious admission of us into the vision of her glory, for which we were indeed created but which nothing we could do could ever merit for us. Salvation was a supernatural event, and as such, it did not come "naturally," as we would say today. It is no wonder that the classical tradition strongly felt that only a minority would be saved. The fear of mortal sin and damnation in hell—however exaggerated we today may find it—was the legitimate conclusion from this logic of salvation.

In contrast, it is to be wondered whether contemporary theology, along with secular culture in general, at least in the Western world, has not fallen into the general trivialization of life with a consequent loss of the sense of the ultimate and serious in life's many decisions. Is it not perhaps true that the ethical demoralization of culture that Kierkegaard warned us about in the mid-nineteenth century is now entrenched in the West and verging on global domination? Capitalist commercialization has eroded our sense of both the ethical and the ultimate, and worked in the direction of relativizing all human values into the purely contingent and aesthetic. I wonder whether theology can today claim exemption from this erosion. Does theology take salvation seriously? Do theologians reflect on salvation with fear and trembling? Does contemporary theology even entertain the possibility that human existence could be jeopardized not only in its earthly destiny as by a nuclear or ecological disaster but also in its eternal, eschatological finality before God? Is divine love so obvious that we can simply take our salvation for granted, or is our conception of salvation so trivial as to merit no serious reflection? Aquinas was profoundly impressed by divine love, and yet he was prevented from drawing an optimistic conclusion about human salvation because he took salvation so seriously.

Third, Aquinas also shared the sense of sin and of the need for justice with the entire classical tradition. Human beings do sin out of their free will and choice, and sins do merit condemnation and punishment. Eternal damnation, offensive as this might be to our contemporary, even Christian, ears bespeaks the seriousness of sin as a breach against God and one another of the teleological order, an order established by divine wisdom and concretized in the natures of things. Some sins break relationships in such minor ways as to be forgivable or "venial." Other sins, however, destroy relationships in such major ways as to merit the death of the soul and thus be called "mortal." And if there is justice in the world at all, it does require appropriate punishment of the evil doers. Aquinas did not live in a world where all sins were considered equally trivial or thought to carry no important consequences to the sinner.

In contrast, contemporary theology is quite ambivalent about sin and justice. After the experience of the twentieth century with its horrific, human-willed evils, theology cannot be indifferent to the problem of sin. Yet modern theology tends to turn the problem of sin not into the problem of the sinner, whether the sinner be Hitler, Stalin, Pol Pot, or the U.S. government, but rather into the problem of theodicy, which while a serious theological problem also evades the problem of the many human agents of sin. While, therefore, Aquinas did not hesitate to assign eternal damnation for the Roman tyrants even though their persecutions occasioned the manifestation of the courage and patience of the early Christian martyrs, contemporary theology does not know what to do about justice for the perpetrators of incalculable human suffering. Hell simply does not exist, and so the only consequential responsibility belongs to God, something the classical tradition would have found rather arrogant and sacrilegious.

Any Christian discussion of reprobation must bring into play these three concurrent assumptions about divine goodness and wisdom, our share of responsibility for our own salvation, and divine justice. Karl Rahner says that here we have to do with one of the most basic examples of our creaturely knowledge. Christian theology can neither fully reconcile these assumptions nor deny any one of them without ceasing to be Christian.[192] We can say that Aquinas's teaching on reprobation was one of the most sophisticated attempts to make sense of the three essential Christian assumptions without claiming to reconcile them perfectly and therefore without ceasing to be a thoroughly creaturely knowledge. For all the historical limitations and theoretical tensions it reveals, and for all the scandal it may pose to contemporary anthropocentric sensibilities, Aquinas's teaching still contains essential lessons and challenges that contemporary theology can only ignore at a great loss. Aquinas was clearly straining his resources of intellectual creativity and synthesis to the limit in order to come to grips with an urgent, emerging problem of his time—the salvation of pagans—in ways both consistent with his major assumptions and relevant to the issues.

Finally, it must also be acknowledged that along with the doctrine of reprobation already there in the early works and continuing in the *Summa Theologiae,* we also find, as we saw, the persistence of positive doctrines in the *Summa,* including those of the presence of justifying grace in the first moral act, the universal offer of grace to those who do what lies in them, the solidarity of all humanity in Christ, the source and exemplar of creation and redemption, and the saving economy of the triune God. Even the reference to God's universal salvific will (1 Timothy 2:4) is often made simply, without the restricting distinction between antecendent and consequent will.[193] The appropriate conclusion, then, it seems, is not that the later Aquinas turned pessimist from his early soteriological optimism but that the *Summa Theologiae* still bears the unresolved tension between the legacy of the Augustinian doctrine of sin and grace and the more positive directions Aquinas was creatively exploring, and ultimately between his own sense of the incomprehensible ultimate sovereignty of divine freedom and his appreciation of the absolute generosity of the divine offer of salvation to all in view of Christ's death and resurrection for all. It is not so much a question of a radical shift as one of a continuing tension between two antithetical strains equally constitutive of the Christian tradition.[194]

Chapter Four

THEOLOGY AS
CONTEMPLATIVE WISDOM

The Contemplative Way to God

The Debate on Theory and Praxis in Theology

The relation between theory and practice, contemplation and action, pursuit of universal truth as an end in itself and involvement in social transformation, has always been a central problem of human existence. Aristotle defined the issue by naming and analyzing the three spheres of human activity as *theoria* or contemplation of the intelligible [intelligibilia], *praxis* or action dealing with the doable [agibilia] and *poiesis* or the production of things to be made [factibilia]. In the modern age armed with both critical consciousness of the world and critical praxis of transforming the world, Hegel, Marx, and critical theory have sharpened the issue and introduced an almost revolutionary sophistication into the academic and popular understanding of the relation between theory and praxis. In theology, this spirit of critique gave rise in the late 1960s to political and liberation theologies, generating ever since a radical questioning of the status of theology as theory.[1]

It has been maintained that theories cannot pretend to deal with the universal and transcendent and yet be indifferent to the problem of human praxis in a particular society and history. For all their claims to universality and objectivity, theories are always more or less contaminated by the biases and interests of a particular group and age and loaded with practical consequences for the well-being of their societies. No theory is innocent. Theories must therefore be self-critical with regard to their own self-interests and ideologies. In this critical spirit, traditional theologies, including that of Aquinas, have been subjected to a hermeneutic of radical suspicion and have been found guilty of classism, sexism, racism, and logocentrism. No theology today can proceed on the assumption of freedom from interests and ideologies. The first order of business for any retrieval of tradition has been a critical hermeneutic of suspicion, just as the first order of business for all constructive theorizing has been self-clarification with regard to the author's own position on the dignity and well-being of human beings in history and the praxis worthy of that dignity. Historical conditions of praxis can distort theory: Orthopraxis does not merely follow but also conditions orthodoxy.[2]

The last thirty years have seen a proliferation of theologies more oriented toward praxis than toward theory (contemplation) and wisdom. To use Thomistic terminology, these theologies place their focus on (political) prudence in the classical sense of the right understanding of human action [recta ratio agibilium] in matters of the common good.[3] The chief concern of these theologies has been the liberation of specific groups from various historical oppressions and the theological justification of the praxis of social transformation required for such liberation. The dominant horizons of these theologies have been those of humanity and history, not of God and eternity. In this shift, the classical content of theology has been thoroughly overhauled in the interest of human liberation in history. A telling example of this change of horizon is the shift in the understanding of eschatology itself. Traditionally, the proper study of eschatology was the four "last things" that will follow death and the end of history: the general resurrection, judgment, heaven, and hell. By contrast, Jürgen Moltmann and liberation theologians after him have identified the significance of eschatology in terms of "its mobilizing, revolutionizing, and critical effects upon history."[4] This is to say that eschatology is meaningful not in itself, but only as the source of hope for liberating history. Moltmann's *Theology of Hope* offered precious little by way of meditation on the last things themselves.

Alongside of and often in critical reaction to liberation theologies we have also seen steady attempts on the part of more traditionally oriented theologians to maintain or retrieve the contemplative, aesthetic, sapiential, and doxological dimensions of classical theology. An outstanding representative of this group is Hans Urs von Balthasar, who devoted his entire career to the defense and concretization of such a theology, which he called "that fierce fire burning in the dark night of adoration and obedience, whose abysses it illuminates,"[5] and whose task is to liberate and enable the Christian "heart" to "experience the cosmos as the revelation of an infinity of grace and love."[6] In a similar vein Frans Jozef van Beeck identifies the essence of Christian faith as the worshipful participation in the transcendent mystery of God, to which all other things, including soteriology, are considered secondary. Theology is possible only as doxology, and Christianity fails for all its soteriological concern for human liberation and fellowship when it lacks this sense of the divine mystery.[7] For Geoffrey Wainwright this liturgical approach to theology is precisely the way to keep the focus of theology on God and God's ultimate purpose in all its elaborations.[8] For Dietrich Ritschl, theology has its origin in worship, and must maintain a "doxological margin" or openness which "tests all our ideas and arguments by the question whether they are not only useful to men and women but can also be offered to God as a gift."[9]

In a famous threefold typology of contemporary theologies, David Tracy tried to uphold a theology of manifestation along with theologies of proclamation and historical action and to mediate the pluralism of theologies through the "analogical imagination," which is itself a feature of the theology of manifestation. While both proclamation and historical action stress alienation and the prophetic, ethical task to overcome that alienation, manifestation stresses the disclosure of the power of the whole and the sense of participation in that whole, inspiring wonder, joy, and a sense of mystery of existence at the disclosure of the world as sacred and of creation as a gift, overflowing into gratitude for divine grace and glorification of God beyond all utilitarian concerns. Theologies of manifestation nourish the mystical, sacramental, metaphysical/cosmological, and aesthetic dimensions of religious experience and avoid the ethical homocentrism to which prophetic theologies are often prone.[10] Similarly, Matthew Fox tried to retrieve these very dimensions in the works of Aquinas himself as ingredients of a spirituality of creation, while A. N. Williams tried to interpret the whole of the *Summa Theologiae* as a mystical theology contemplating the conditions of union with God.[11]

In this regard Josef Pieper's work on leisure still remains a classic source of a contemplative, sapiential, doxological, and aesthetic approach to philosophy and theology. Theoria or contemplation is not aggressive or manipulative but is receptive to reality as it is in its wholeness, letting beings be in all their wonder and objectivity, and ready to celebrate the gift of creation with gratitude and to glorify the creator for her own sake. As a non-activity freed from the pressures of the social function and useful achievement, contemplation is liberated to celebrate the intrinsic value of creation and to meditate on the ultimate finality of human existence beyond all preoccupations with temporal relativities. Contemplation sees and celebrates life in its totality and in its transcendent depth. It seeks wisdom.[12]

Perhaps a most relevant case in point is the eventual shift in Moltmann's own theological perspective. In his revisitation of eschatology after some thirty years in his *The Coming of God: Christian Eschatology*[13] he not only subordinates history to cosmology but also provides a substantial discussion of the intrinsic content of eschatology without reducing its significance to its impact on history. Subjects of discussion include death and personal eschatology, the status of the dead before the general resurrection, historical eschatology, the last judgment, the possibility of universal salvation, the cosmic eschatology of a new heaven and a new earth, and the divine eschatology of eternal joy. Also not to be missed in this connection is his long-standing appreciation, since his *Theology of Joy* (1974), of the aesthetic, contemplative, and doxological dimension of theology, which does moderate, without eliminating, his ethical concern for human liberation.

For Moltmann, human beings need not only the political, external freedom of the Exodus but also the spiritual, internal freedom of the Sabbath, i.e., freedom *from* the external compulsions and necessities of the workaday world with its preoccupation for achievement, competition, and calculation, and freedom *for* leisurely appreciation of the wonder and beauty of existence issuing in peace, celebration and glorification. We need a balance between doing and being, ethics and aesthetics, extrinsic evaluation and intrinsic appreciation, action and contemplation. We also need a balance between the monarchical, historical, and eucharistic Trinity in which we relate to God as the source of our being and salvation, and the doxological or immanent Trinity whom we glorify in worship for her own sake. Through doxology and adoration we experience, however briefly, an interruption of time, a transcendence of our own contingency and transience, and participation in God's own eternal life.[14]

In an illuminating comparative study of Aquinas and Luther,[15] Otto H. Pesch argues that many of their theological differences—including disagreements on certainty of salvation, cooperation between God and human beings, Christology, sin and grace, faith and charity—are at root traceable to a fundamental difference in their very ways of doing theology. Behind the differences in the content of theology lie different orientations in basic concern and interest, different ways of thinking [Denkvollzugsformen] which operate a priori in all theological reflection, i.e., what we would today call paradigms. Luther's paradigm is "existential" theology, Aquinas's "sapiential" theology. As the deepest, prereflective orientations and fundamental options of thought, these paradigms generate contrasting structures of questions and differing dogmatic formulations, even about one and the same reality.

The existential theology of Luther looks at reality—God, the world, and humanity—from the subjective perspective of someone in the very act of a personal encounter with God in faith and prayer, and thus from within the act of faith itself, without objectifying it. Its statements are therefore prayerful self-descriptions of the sinner before the holy God, expressed in the modes of confession and proclamation and necessarily stressing the nothingness and sinfulness of human beings and their need for divine forgiveness. Existential theology naturally relies on categories of interpersonal relationship and concentrates on human salvation. (Existential theology in the manner of Luther is not to be confused with theological existentialism and introspective psychologizing.)

Faith is essential for sapiential theology, too, but there it serves as the presupposition of theology, which needs the "light" of faith but not as its explicit thematic focus. By presupposing faith, but not making it thematic in every reflection and statement, sapiential theology describes reality objectively, in the third person, from the perspective of God and the *ratio Dei*. Its basic interest lies in objective knowledge of the theological significance of all reality in terms of its relation to God, the ultimate end. What counts in sapiential theology, then, is God's perspective revealed in light of faith, and God's sovereignty in creation and redemption of the world; sin cannot play the dominant role here that it does in existential theology, where the basic interest lies in the salvation of the sinner by the merciful God. Interested in the fate of all creation in light of God's sovereign providence, sapiential theology necessarily uses ontological categories of nature which alone can apply universally, rather than the interpersonal categories of the I-Thou encounter of existential theology.

Given the systematic significance of this difference in paradigm, Pesch argues that such a difference should be regarded as an essential hermeneutic element in any comparative study of Luther and Aquinas. Furthermore, each way of doing theology represents an essential element in Christian faith, and each requires the critical service of the other in order to avoid falling into distortions. "The Church needs both theologies in order to live out all the tensions entailed in Christianity."[16]

In what follows I discuss in some detail the motives and characteristics of Aquinas's sapiential theology or theology as contemplative wisdom and go on to evaluate the strengths and weaknesses of that conception in the context of contemporary needs and concerns discussed above. I provide a fuller appreciation of Aquinas in the final chapter, where I place his contemplative theology into dialectical "tension" with prophetic, political theologies and argue that this dynamic approach befits the human condition better than either type of theology taken in isolation or even both types taken together in mutual "balance."

Theology as Wisdom

For Aquinas, theology is wisdom, theory, and science. As wisdom, it is concerned with the knowledge of the *ultimate* end of human existence, God, and all other things *sub ratione Dei.* As theory, it is concerned with the *knowledge* of truth as an end in itself. As science, it is the activity of reason striving for certain and necessary knowledge on the premises of divine revelation. I have already dealt with theology as science in chapter 1. In this section I will concentrate on theology as wisdom, and in the next on theology as theory, or contemplation.

In the Western classical tradition wisdom consists in knowing the highest cause, ordering things according to their teleological relations to such a cause, and judging them according to their hierarchical relations disclosed in such a teleology. The role of the wise is to place in ordered relationships and to judge [sapientis est ordinare et judicare]. Wisdom means knowing what is more important and what is less, what is an end and what is only a means, what is a cause and what is an effect, subordinating the latter to the former, and judging the latter in light of the former. It means knowing things in their mutual relations, introducing order among them, and relating them to their ultimate end. Some things are more important than others. Not everything is equally important. The intelligible are more important than the sensible, the necessary more important than the contingent, the universal more important than the particular. The higher, more intelligible, and more universal the object of knowledge, the wiser one becomes in knowing it.

For Aquinas, the object of theology is God, the first, highest and final cause of the universe, the causal origin and ultimate end of the totality of beings in the totality of their being, not only as known by means of creatures as in philosophy but also as known to God herself alone and revealed to us, not the highest and ultimate in a particular order but the absolutely highest and ultimate transcending all genera and species. Theology, therefore, is wisdom in the highest sense, above all human wisdom including metaphysics. Although a knowledge acquired through study, not infused as one of the gifts of the Holy Spirit, it is nonetheless knowledge of what is the highest, most universal, and most ultimate in all human experience. As the ultimate in wisdom, theology is "the head and principle and commander of all sciences,"[17] judging them and using them as vassals for its own sake: whatever is contrary to theology in other sciences must be condemned as false. It is higher than either "understanding," the habit of first principles, or "science," the drawing of necessary conclusions from principles.[18] It orders and judges all things—including prudence—according to divine rules.[19] As *human* wisdom, however, theology is possible only by sharing in the "light" of divine wisdom.

It is important in this regard to remember the trinitarian dimension of Aquinas's discussion of divine wisdom. As there is only one essence in God, so there is only one wisdom: the Father, Son, and Holy Spirit individually and collectively constitute one wisdom. Nevertheless, divine wisdom is especially appropriate to the Son because the "works" of wisdom are proper to the Son.[20] As the eternal Word of the Father and "the image of God in his essence,"[21] the Son alone can know and manifest the Father and the Trinity, the divine things hidden in God's perfect self-knowledge. As "the perfect conception" of the wisdom of God the Father," the Word as begotten "wholly" contains the wisdom of the Father as unbegotten.[22] As the eternal exemplar of all creation, and the "eternal law" from which all the laws of nature are derived, the Son contains not only God's speculative but also her operative wisdom: he is "only expressive of what is in God the Father, but is both expressive [expressivum] and operative [operativum] of creatures," constituting the "productive idea" [ratio factiva][23] and "exemplary likeness" [similitudo exemplaris][24] of all creatures. As exemplar, he is also the model for the restoration of all things to their original perfection through his incarnation and redemptive work. The proper perfection of a human being as a rational creature lies in wisdom, but all wisdom is derived from the Word, "the concept of eternal wisdom."[25] Human perfection, therefore, is possible only through participation in the Word. As the natural Son of God he also leads us to our ultimate end, the eternal glory of our inheritance as God's adopted children, which is again possible only through sharing in the likeness of his filiation. In sum, the Son embodies in himself all the wisdoms there can be—the economic wisdom of creation and redemption as well as the wisdom of the eternal mystery of the immanent Trinity.[26]

If the works of wisdom are proper to the Son, it belongs to the Holy Spirit as the teleological power to actualize the wisdom embodied in the Word by governing and guiding all creation to its ultimate end with divine "prudence."[27] As the power of the love whereby God seeks to share her own goodness, the Spirit motivates the creation of things, giving them life and movement, and directing them to their ultimate end.[28] With regard to rational creatures, the Spirit inspires them to imitate God's love, establishes them as friends of God, reveals divine mysteries to them, binds them in sharing and fellowship, remits their sins, renews them in their hearts, and "configures" them to God as her children, sending them on their road to beatitude. It is the Spirit who makes us lovers and friends of God and inspires all the movements of friendship: eager contemplation of God and conversation with her as between friends; a sense of joy, trust, and security in God in times of adversity; and willingness to obey her commandments "freely out of love, not slavishly out of fear," by "so inclining us to act that he makes us act voluntarily in that he makes us lovers of God."[29] The Spirit liberates and guides us in a way befitting intellectual creatures, i.e., in genuine freedom: "Since the Holy Spirit inclines the will by love toward the true good, to which the will is naturally ordered, he removes both that servitude in which the slave of passion infected by sin acts against the *order* of the will, and that servitude in which, against the movement of his will, a man acts according to the law; its slave, so to say, not its friend."[30]

The "principal" object of theology as wisdom is the absolutely highest cause, God, but this does not mean that Aquinas excludes the knowledge of creatures, human praxis, or proximate ends in history from the proper scope of theology. As we saw in chapter 1, all things other than God can become objects of theology *sub ratione Dei* or under the formality of *ordo* and *motus* to God, which provides for the unity of theology as a science despite the diversity of its material objects.[31] Indeed, God and creatures are not equal, and theology does "principally" [principaliter] deal with God; but it deals also with creatures "insofar as they are referred to God as to their origin or end."[32] Likewise, theology contains both the theoretical and the practical within itself, just as God knows both herself and the things she makes by one and the same knowledge.[33] Although theology is "more" [*magis*] theoretical than practical because it deals "more principally" [principalius] with divine things than with human acts, it does also deal with human acts "insofar as, through them, human beings are ordered to the perfect knowledge of God in which eternal happiness consists."[34]

Precisely because God is the ultimate end whose attainment constitutes "salvation" for humanity, the object *per se* of revelation, faith, and theology consists of "the things which we shall enjoy in eternal life, together with the means whereby we are brought to eternal life."[35] "That through which we attain to blessedness . . . properly and in itself [*proprie et per se*] belongs to the object of faith."[36] The necessity of theology as *sacra doctrina* is itself derived from the fact that our salvation and ultimate end lie beyond the capacity of natural reason and that they must first be *known* before we can pursue then.[37] But in addition to what is intrinsically beyond the capacity of natural reason, Aquinas includes among the objects of faith what is both knowable by reason and revealable by God (e.g., the existence and attributes of God).[38] Only the actual revelation of such *revelabilia* can ensure that all humans can come to a knowledge of their ultimate end, because not all can have the knowledge of God and her attributes prerequisite for the knowledge of revelation in the strict sense. Some may lack the neccessary natural intelligence, while the temporal occupations of others may not allow time for contemplative inquiry, and still others may be too indolent. Even the few who do attain this knowledge through the use of reason do so only after a long time and with a mixture of uncertainty and error.[39]

Thus, although the principal object of theological contemplation is divine truth, theological contemplation can include as its secondary object contemplation of divine effects insofar as through them we are led to the contemplation of God. Theological contemplation, therefore, can include moral virtues, other acts besides contemplation, and contemplation of divine effects as well as contemplation of divine truth.[40] Theology includes human praxis in its relation to eternal happiness, which constitutes the ultimate end of all other practical sciences themselves.[41] As wisdom, theology not only contemplates but also consults eternal divine things as rules for judging and directing human acts. "To sin against God is common to all sins, insofar as the order to God includes every human order."[42] As a virtue of ordering, wisdom is also the basis of peace, the tranquility of order; the wise are peacemakers and become children of God because they share in the sonship of the Son, the begotten Wisdom.[43]

The structure of the *Summa Theologiae* makes clear that theology, whose "principal" goal is to communicate the knowledge of God, deals first with God as the beginning and end of all things, her existence, attributes, and trinitarian essence, and with the *exitus* of the creature in creation and government of the universe (Part One). These subjects are followed by the *reditus* of the rational creature to God [motus in Deum] through the teleological dynamics and dysfunctions of human passions, habits, virtues, charisms of the Holy Spirit, sin, law, grace, theological and cardinal virtues (Part Two). Lastly, theology deals with Christ, whose humanity constitutes for us "the way of tending to God" [via tendendi in Deum], the exemplary source of both creation and redemption through the Incarnation, the grace of Christ, his predestination and mediatorship, his life, passion, death, resurrection, the sacraments, the means of salvation made possible through Christ, and eschatology (Part Three).[44] All human struggles in history possess supernatural theological significance because they are part of the trinitarian economy of salvation that involves the solidarity of all creation in Christ and the saving providence of the Holy Spirit in which "glory is the end of the operation of nature itself assisted by grace."[45]

As wisdom theology considers God as the ultimate origin and end of all things. As discussed in the first chapter, all things are effects and images of God and seek to attain to divine goodness as their ultimate end by imitating, representing, becoming like, and participating in God "each according to its measure."[46] Each thing tends toward the divine likeness not only according to its substantial act of being but also through a diversity of operations that actualize its proper goodness—the passions that perfect its being, the immanent activities of understanding, sensing, and willing, and above all those operations that exercise causality on other things, which makes each "a co-worker with God [Dei cooperator]." The higher and more perfect a thing is, the more open it is to beings beyond itself, desiring to diffuse its own goodness more widely after the likeness of God, "the archetype for all diffusers of goodness."[47]

In what way is God the ultimate end of humanity? How do human beings search for God? What are some of the obstacles on the path? How does theology fit into this teleological orientation of humanity to God? If theology is not only wisdom but also necessarily theoretical or contemplative wisdom, how is this contemplative character related to our search for God as our ultimate end? Why is theology more theoretical or contemplative than practical? How does theological contemplation of God come closest to the vision of God, the ultimate end of the rational creature, in this world?

Aquinas presents a quite systematic discussion of God as the ultimate end of humanity considered as an intellectual substance. He distinguishes between the subjective and objective dimensions of the ultimate end, goes through a number of candidates that have traditionally been presented as the ultimate end, and concludes, by elimination and argument, that only the intellectual vision of God in her essence constitutes the ultimate end of humanity. The objective dimension of the ultimate end has to do with the thing that we desire to attain, the source of our ultimate happiness; the subjective dimension with the mode of our use, attainment, or possession of the thing.[48] Under the first, objective heading Aquinas examines the many different kinds of goods—external goods, goods of the body, goods of the soul, separated substances, and God—that human beings have historically pursued as their highest good. Under the second, subjective heading he examines the different modes of approaching the ultimate end such as operation, intellect, will, contemplation, and action. I will discuss the objective dimension in this section and the subjective dimension in the next.

What constitutes the ultimate end of human existence, that which we desire as our own ultimate perfection, that for the sake of which we desire everything else and beyond which there is nothing more to be desired?

For Aquinas, to begin with, the ultimate end of human existence as an intellectual substance cannot consist in external goods, such as honors, glory, wealth, and power, essentially "goods of fortune." The ultimate end cannot consist in honors because these are something conferred on a person by another, not a result of her own operation or virtue. To be honored is good not of itself, but only when it is a sign and attestation of some excellence in a person; to be worthy of honor is better than to be honored, which even an evil person can be.[49] Nor can the ultimate end consist in glory in the sense of a good reputation because glory is sought for the sake of honor, not in itself; because it consists chiefly in praise, which is given to those well ordered to their end, not those who have already achieved their end; because it is nobler to know than to be (well) known, which is good not of itself but only because of the good things known about a person; and because glory is neither certain nor enduring.[50] Possession of riches does not qualify as our ultimate end because they are not desirable in themselves but only as means to something else, because they are meant to be spent and expended, because human beings are better than riches, and because riches are unstable, subject to fortune, beyond rational effort.[51] Worldly power as such does not constitute the highest good of humanity either because it too is subject to fortune and can accrue even to bad persons, because power as such is neither good nor bad, and because it is contingent on the wills and opinions of people notorious for their inconstancy. In sum, human happiness cannot consist in any exterior good.[52]

Human happiness cannot consist in any pleasure or good of the body either. First, it cannot consist in the pleasures of the flesh such as food and sex for a number of reasons. They accompany operations that only serve the preservation of the individual or the species, which are themselves relative, not ultimate ends. Being common to humans and brutes, such pleasures are not appropriate to human beings. They are derived from union with certain sensible objects, which are inferior to human beings, who are most properly human only as intellectual, i.e., as thinking and knowing entities. They are good not of themselves but only when moderated by something else. Finally, they are "the chief impediment to contemplation [of God], since they plunge the human being very deep into sensible things, consequently distracting her from intelligible objects."[53]

Nor, secondly, does ultimate happiness consist in the external goods of the body such as health, beauty, and strength. Such goods are unstable, beyond the human will, and indifferently possessed by both good and bad persons. The body is inferior to the soul, which alone makes it alive and for which it exists as for its end. The goods of the body are not proper to humanity but common to humans and animals alike, and animals can often surpass humans in possession of these goods.[54] Nor, thirdly, can human happiness consist in the satisfaction of the senses. They too are common to humans and animals, and inferior to the goods of the intellect, which has a certain "infinity" over the body. Moreover, the greatest sense pleasures are those of food and sex.[55]

In principle, no good of the soul can constitute our ultimate happiness either. Whatever exists in potentiality exists for the sake of act as for its fulfillment. The soul exists in potentiality and cannot be its own last end. Nor can anything that belongs to it, such as powers, habits, and acts.

The ultimate end must be a perfect good fulfilling the rational desire for the universal good, but whatever good inheres in the soul is a participated and therefore a particular good.[56]

Specifically, acts of moral virtues cannot constitute our ultimate happiness, however noble these might be. Aquinas provides a broad array of arguments to support this point. In the first place, all moral operations are ordered to something else, e.g., courage to victory and peace. The good of moral virtue is something produced by reason in things other than itself, not something immanent in reason which is proper to humanity. Moral acts also fall short of the mark because they can be attributed to God only metaphorically and do not make human beings most like God, the ultimate end of all things. Even animals can somewhat share in acts of moral virtue such as liberality and fortitude although no animal can participate in an intellectual operation.[57] Ultimate happiness does not consist in the act of prudence either. It is one of the moral virtues and subject to their common inadequacies. It deals with contingencies of human action. Again, even animals participate somewhat in prudence. Like all practical knowledge, prudence is ordered to action as its end, not to itself.[58] Ultimate happiness must rather be a function of the best human operation according to what is proper to humanity, i.e., understanding, and in relation to the most perfect object, the most perfect intelligible. Nor does ultimate happiness consist in the productive art because, like practical knowledge, it too is ordered to an end other than itself and because the artifacts, the end of productive activity, are made for human beings, who are the ends of all artificial things.[59]

In these ways, Aquinas demonstrates that no finite good in this world can constitute our ultimate end or happiness. An essential mark of the attainment of the ultimate end is stability and rest, but these are not possible in this world because illnesses and misfortunes can always hinder the operation by which the end is attained. No good in this world can be the perfect good which the ultimate end must be because it is always mixed with evil, either the evils of the body such as hunger, thirst, heat, and cold, or the evils of the soul such as unruly passions, mistaken judgments, ignorance of things, and uncertainties. Above all, no one can be free from death or from the anxiety about death. Ultimate happiness consists in an operation, not a habit, which exists for the sake of an operation, but it is not possible to perform any action continuously, without interruption, in this world. No good can be so secured in this world as to be free from sorrow about the prospect of its loss through sickness and death. To sum up, no finite good can constitute our ultimate end because its contingencies and limitations cannot satisfy the desire of the will for the universal good. Our ultimate end can only be found in the infinite, uncreated good or God. All created goodness is participated and limited goodness.[60]

Theology as Theory/Contemplation

By way of elimination, then, we see that our ultimate end can only be God. This is the objective side of the question of the ultimate end for humanity. How should humanity, then, approach the attainment of this end? Is it through the will, the intellect, or something else in the human subject? What is the side of human subjectivity most relevant and appropriate to the attainment of the end? How do we go about determining which dimension of human existence has this privileged role? If the attainment of the ultimate end, according to Aquinas, is a matter of an "intellectual" vision of the divine essence, we must ask why the intellect should be so privileged over all other dimensions of human existence. Let me dwell a little on this subjective dimension because it highlights Aquinas's "intellectualism" and his distinctive conception of theology as theory or contemplation.

Aquinas's decision in favor of contemplation as the privileged locus of our relation to God depends on his ontology of human existence and the elimination of alternatives. Human existence consists of myriad layers of acts and potencies in reciprocal relations. Existence is actual in relation to the potency of essence. The substantial form of soul, potential in relation to existence, is actual in relation to prime matter. Between the first act, existence, and the last act, operation, there exist many degrees of actuality and potentiality. In this scale of act and potency Aquinas locates our ultimate perfection and happiness, the subjective experience of the attainment of the ultimate end, in operation [operatio]. A thing is perfect insofar as it is actual, imperfect insofar as it is merely potential. As our ultimate perfection, happiness must consist in the last act, which is operation. Furthermore, it must consist in the immanent operation that perfects and remains in the agent, whose happiness is at stake, not in any transient operation that perfects the patient.[61] Happiness consists more in contemplation than in action because contemplation can be more continuous while action is busy with many things and vulnerable to interruptions.[62] Insofar as our ultimate happiness consists essentially in being united with the uncreated good, our happiness cannot be an operation of the sensitive part.[63]

With regard to the operations of the intellectual part, Aquinas locates the "essence" of happiness in the operation of the intellect, not in the operation of the will. Our ultimate end consists primarily in "knowing" God, not "desiring," "loving," or "enjoying" God. Aquinas's assertion may sound rather counterintuitive. Isn't the ultimate end, like all other ends, some kind of a good, precisely the proper object of the will, while the proper object of intellect is the true? Apart from the fact that the will as an appetite, even if a rational appetite, is not "peculiar" or "proper" to an intellectual being, as will be commented on later, Aquinas adduces a number of reasons why the ultimate end cannot primarily consist in operations of the will.

First, in the case of all powers moved by their objects, the object is prior to the act of a power since it is the object that moves the power. Thus, the object of the will moves the will to act and is prior to the act of the will. The object of the will, however, can move the will only insofar as it is known, i.e., presented to the will by the intellect. No act of the will can be the first thing that is willed, i.e., the ultimate end which is the first in intention. The will wills its object, happiness, not its own act. Second, the act of the will as such does not discriminate between the true and false highest good, which depends on the judgment of the intellect.

Third, desiring still implies lack of possession, while the perfection of loving depends on whether it loves something already possessed. Delight, too, is a consequence of possession, and the rightfulness of delight depends on the nature of the thing delight accompanies—its goodness or badness—which too depends on the judgment of the intellect. What is primary is the attainment or possession of the true good, not desiring, loving, or delighting in it. The will either desires and moves toward the end which is not yet present or delights and rests in the end which has been attained; it is not as such the attainment of the end. The attainment of an intelligible good—the "essence" of happiness—is an act of the intellect, which makes it present. The delight that results from happiness pertains to the will as the "proper accident" of happiness, but it is not the "essence" of happiness. We desire, love, and enjoy something only insofar as it is first known and attained.

Fourth, in the order of nature pleasure serves the end of preservation of either the individual or the species and cannot count as the ultimate end. Furthermore, as the repose of the will in some appropriate good, pleasure is a concomitant of the attainment of the end by our inclination, not repose or cessation of all inclinations regardless of whether their end has been attained. Finally, just as for those for whom money is the end, it is not the craving or loving of money that is essential but the actual possession of money, so for an intellectual substance whose ultimate end is God, what is essential is the operation whereby the ultimate end is primarily attained, and this operation is an act of understanding. We cannot will, desire, love, or delight in what we do not know or understand.[64]

For Aquinas, the intellect is higher than the will because of the greater nobility of its proper object and its causal priority. First, the object of the intellect is simpler and more absolute, i.e., freer from the complexity and particularity of matter, than that of the will. The object of the intellect is the very idea [ipsa ratio] of the appetible good in its universality, while that of the will is the appetible good in its concrete particularity. The simpler and more abstract something is, the nobler and higher it is in itself.[65] Second, the intellect moves the will *first* and *per se,* while the will moves the intellect *accidentally,* that is, only on condition that the act of understanding is itself *known* as a good. The will would not move the intellect to its activity unless the intellect first knew such an activity as desirable. In this sense, the intellect moves the will in the same way as an end moves; the good *known* is the end of the will and presupposed by the will. Thus, "the intellect is higher than the will *absolutely* [simpliciter], while the will is higher than the intellect accidentally and in a restricted sense [per accidens et secundum quid]."[66]

This is also why the end of the intellect defines the end of the *whole* person. In any series of mutually ordered agents and movers, the end of the "first" agent is the end of the whole series, just as the end of the commander-in-chief is the end of all the soldiers under him. Now, of all the parts of the person, the intellect is the first and highest mover because it moves the will by proposing an object for it, which in turn moves the sensitive appetite, which in turn moves the body. Thus, "the end of the intellect is the end of all human actions." Now, the end of the intellect is the true, and its last end, the first truth. "Therefore, the last end of the *whole* person, and of all her deeds and desires is to know the first truth, namely God."[67]

Further, ultimate happiness consists in an operation of the speculative or contemplative intellect rather than in an operation of the practical intellect. First, happiness must involve the highest operation of the human being, which involves the operation of the highest power with regard to the highest object, i.e., the intellect whose highest object is the divine good, which is the object of the speculative, not the practical intellect. Second, contemplation of truth or wisdom dealing with *intelligibilia* is an immanent activity and sought for its own sake, while the practical intellect dealing with *agibilia* through prudence or with *factibilia* through technical art is ordered to a good outside of itself, i.e., action or production, which in turn is ordered to some other end.[68] The last end, therefore, cannot lie in an operation of the practical intellect. Our search for happiness can only rest and terminate in an end that is so ultimate as to command all other ends and that is to be loved for its own sake, not as a means to something else. All practical and technical sciences, as they deal with human actions and operations, serve extrinsic ends and are subordinate to speculative sciences, which seek knowledge as such and which are in turn subordinate to the most architectonic science of all, the knowledge of God. Divine knowledge alone is both ultimate and to be loved for its own sake. Our ultimate end, therefore, can only be knowledge of God, not some action or production.[69] Third, contemplation has something in common with beings above such as God and angels, while action shares something with animals.[70]

Aquinas's argument is that the intellect is not only the "highest" but also the most "proper" power of humanity, whose operation therefore constitutes the ultimate end of human existence. "Since happiness is the *proper* good of the intellectual nature, it must needs become the intellectual nature according to that which is *proper* thereto."[71] The end of a thing is "the operation *proper* to a thing," and "understanding is the *proper* operation of the intellectual substance, and consequently is its end," while "whatever is most perfect in this operation is its last end."[72] The perfection of an operation, however, depends on the perfection of the object which specifies and fulfills it. Thus, "the more perfect the object of any such operation, the more perfect is the operation. Consequently, to understand the most perfect intelligible, namely, God, is the most perfect in the genus of the operation which consists in understanding. Therefore, to know God by an act of understanding is the last end of every intellectual substance."[73] Again, "since happiness must consist in an operation of the intellect in relation to the most noble intelligible objects, it follows then that the ultimate happiness of human beings consists in wisdom, based on the consideration of divine things."[74] Thus, the way that intellectual creatures participate in the divine likeness and attain union with God as their ultimate end is through understanding God.

We may ask why, among thinking, acting, and making, the three areas of human operation, thinking or contemplation is not only "the most excellent in a human being" (*optimum in ipso*) but also "more proper to a human being" (*magis proprium homini*) than the other two. For Aquinas, the intellect is most proper to human beings because it constitutes the specific difference between human beings and animals, that is, because it is what human beings have *as* human beings and what animals lack. "This operation alone is proper to a human being, and it is in it that none of the other animals communicates."[75] The appetite is not proper to a human being because it is found in other beings as well, just as the life of pleasure is common to human beings and beasts and thus properly the life of a beast, not of human beings.[76] Even the will or intellectual appetite, as an appetite, "is not *proper* to the intellectual nature, but only insofar as it is dependent on the intellect," whereas "the intellect is *in itself* proper to the intellectual nature."[77] Activities of practical life are not proper to human beings because "they involve also the lower powers, common to human beings and animals."[78] In short, all other powers and activities of human beings are human derivatively, i.e., only insofar as they are *made* human by the intellect that proposes the right object for desires and actions and distinguishes between good and evil. Thus, happiness consists "principally and essentially" in an act of the intellect.[79]

Our ultimate end can, therefore, only be the knowledge or contemplation of God. Such contemplation is the only operation of humanity that is proper to human beings and in no way shared by animals. It is an end in itself and not ordered to anything beyond itself. It unites human beings with beings superior to humanity. For contemplation we are sufficient unto ourselves, not dependent on external things. All other human actions serve this end: the artifacts of productive art serve contemplation by promoting soundness of body, moral virtues and prudence by producing freedom from disturbances of the passions, and good government by promoting freedom from external disorders.[80]

Our knowledge of God in this world, however, allows of many different degrees and types, not all of which can be said to constitute the ultimate end and happiness of human beings. The ultimate in human finality and happiness would be attained only when the natural desire intrinsic to the dynamism of the intellect could be totally fulfilled and terminated. The human intellect has the natural desire to know not only effects but also their causes; not only their relative causes but also their ultimate, first cause; not only *that* it is but also *what* it is; not only the first cause as known through its effects but also the first cause as it is in itself, "in its very essence." As Aquinas puts it, "so great is our innate desire for knowledge that, once we apprehend an effect, we seek to know its cause. Moreover, after we have gained some knowledge of the circumstances investing a thing, our thirst is not assuaged until we penetrate to its essence. Therefore our natural craving for knowledge cannot be satisfied until we know the first cause, and that not in any fashion, but in its very essence. This first cause is God. Consequently, the ultimate end of an intellectual creature is the vision of God in her essence."[81] In other words, only God in her very essence can be "the most perfect intelligible," that which activates and satisfies the "infinite" potentiality of the intellect for wonder and transcendence.[82]

In this sense, Aquinas disqualifies all modes of knowledge of God which are possible here below as the ultimate end of human beings. The general and confused knowledge of God possessed by ordinary people cannot be the ultimate end because it is subject to many errors and because it is only a general, still potential knowledge of God, not an actual knowledge of God in terms of what is proper to God.[83] Nor will the demonstrative knowledge of God possessed by the philosophers do. It gives us a negative knowledge of what God is not in relation to creatures but not an affirmative, proper knowledge of what God is. Furthermore, it is accessible only to a few, also subject to errors and uncertainties, and in any case still in potentiality to a further knowledge of God.[84] The knowledge of faith is not any better. To be sure, we know by faith what we cannot know by reason. Nevertheless, faith derives its knowledge and certainty from the assent of the will to the authority of God, not from the operation of the intellect which could "see" the intrinsic intelligibility of its object in which happiness would properly consist. Faith remains less than vision, apprehending more of things absent than of things present.[85]

For Aquinas, the natural desire of the human intellect remains unquenched in this world because no created intellect by its own natural power can see the essence of God. According to Aquinas's ontology of knowledge, knowledge means the presence of the thing known in the knower; this is possible only according to the mode of the knower's nature, which thus constitutes the limit of all knowledge. If, therefore, the mode of being [modus essendi] or nature of an object exceeds that of the knower, the knowledge of that object remains inaccessible to the knower. Now, corporeal things have their being or *esse* in individual matter. Angels subsist through themselves, not in some matter, although they are not their own *esse* but have it from another. To be its own subsisting esse [suum esse subsistens] is the proper mode of being of God alone. Insofar as our soul, by which we know, is the form of certain matter, it is connatural [connaturale] to us to know things who have their being only in individual matter. Thus, through sense, which is an act of a corporeal organ, we naturally know things as they are in individual matter and, therefore, only as singulars. Through the intellect, which is not the act of any corporeal organ, we naturally know natures who have their *esse* only in individual matter but not as they are in individual matter but as they are abstracted from the latter by the considerations of the intellect, and thus as universals. The human intellect, united as it is to a body in this world, cannot know natures that do not exist in matter, as can the angelic intellect. Since no creature is its own existence [esse], and all creatures have only participated existence [esse participatum], it follows that no created intellect has the natural power to know the subsistent existence itself [ipsum esse subsistens], which is connatural only to the divine intellect.[86]

Because of this ontological limit of human knowledge, "the knowledge of God that can be gathered from the human mind does not transcend the genus of the knowledge gathered from sensible things."[87] The human intellect remains dependent on the phantasm for the intelligible species by which it knows things, but no intelligible species abstracted from phantasms is sufficient to represent the essence of separated, spiritual substances, still less the divine essence, a fact that deprives the human intellect of any intuition into the divine essence. At best, we know God as we know the cause from its effects, from God's effects in nature as in the case of philosophical knowledge, or from God's effects in grace as in the case of faith.[88] These effects indeed bear traces of likeness to God, but such likeness is so imperfect as to be "altogether [omnino] inadequate to manifest God's substance."[89] In this life, "what God is not is clearer to us than what God is," for God is "above whatsoever we may say or think of him."[90] The divine essence "infinitely" surpasses all created substance.[91] God "infinitely" transcends all things according to "every mode of transcendence."[92] Neither natural knowledge nor knowledge by faith achieves the intellectual vision of God in her own trinitarian essence and subjectivity.

Although no created intellect can see the essence of God by its own natural power, it can be empowered to do so by God, who unites herself to it and raises it above its own nature through her grace and makes herself intelligible to it. The senses cannot be raised to the knowledge of immateriality because they are totally material, but the intellect can because it is not itself a material power. The human intellect can separate the universal form from the particular matter in which the form is found and consider the form by itself, as the angelic intellect can separate the *esse* from the concrete subject of that *esse* and consider the *esse* by itself. Since a created intellect by its nature can abstract form and existence from concrete entities and show its capacity for transcendence, it can also be raised above its nature by grace to know separated subsisting substance and separated subsisting existence.[93]

This supernatural elevation requires a supernatural disposition of the intellect towards that elevation. A created intellect can see the essence of God only when this essence itself becomes the intelligible form or species for the intellect; no created species or form can contain the likeness of God by which we can know her essence that "infinitely" transcends every created form.[94] A supernatural disposition must be added by divine grace to increase its power of understanding and raise it to this sublime height. That disposition consists in the illumination of the intellect which renders it deiform, or similar to God. This created light is necessary for seeing the essence of God not because it renders the essence of God intelligible—God's essence is intelligible *per se*—but because it renders the intellect more capable of understanding. This is so in the same way that a habit increases the operating power of a capacity, or that a corporeal light makes the medium actually transparent and susceptible of color, thus making external sight possible. This light, therefore, is not a similitude or species in which God is seen, a medium *in quo*, but a certain perfection of the intellect that strengthens it to see God, a medium *sub quo*. This created light is the light of glory [lumen gloriae].[95] One's share of this light of glory increases in proportion to one's charity: greater charity means greater desire, which in turn means greater aptness for receiving the object desired. Those who possess more charity, therefore, will see God more perfectly and be beatified more.[96]

"Seeing" the essence of God, however, does not mean "comprehending" God. To comprehend something means to know it perfectly, i.e., so far as it can be known. A thing can be known insofar as it is actual. God whose *esse* is infinite is infinitely knowable. Now, a finite intellect can know the divine essence only to the degree that it receives the light of glory. The light of glory received into a created intellect, however, is finite. It is impossible, therefore, for any created intellect to know God infinitely, that is, to "comprehend" God in the strict and proper sense. No finite, created being ceases to be finite and created even in the beatific vision, and can contain God infinitely in that vision. The essence of God is indeed "seen" but not seen as perfectly as it is capable of being seen. Those who see God's essence see in her that she exists infinitely and is infinitely knowable, but this infinite mode does not enable them to know infinitely, just as to have an opinion that a proposition is demonstrable is not to know it as demonstrated. If the incomprehensibility of God thus remains even in the beatific vision in the strict sense of comprehension, it is, nonetheless, the incomprehensibility of God whose essence has been "comprehended" in the broad sense of "attainment," of a God who has been attained and possessed as present, no longer an object of hope, seen, no longer an object of faith, and enjoyed, no longer an object of charity in the alienating sense in which God is here below.[97]

Likewise, not comprehending God in the strict sense also means not seeing in the divine essence all things that God does or can do as the cause of all things. This does not mean that the natural desire of the rational creature is frustrated. This desire is to know everything that belongs to the perfection of the intellect, i.e., the species and genera of things and their meanings [rationes], which are also seen in the vision of the divine essence. To know singulars, their thoughts and facts, however, does not belong either to the perfection of the created intellect or to its natural desire. Moreover, "even if God alone were seen who is the fount and principle of all being and all truth [fons et principium totius esse et veritatis], he would so fill the natural desire to know that nothing else would be sought and the seer would be happy."[98]

In this beatific vision the divine essence does not cease to be infinite nor the created intellect to be finite, which keeps the vision eternally fresh and original, never satiating, tiresome, or dull—it never ceases to stimulate desire and wonder at the divine reality a finite intellect can never totally comprehend. It is our participation in eternity,[99] the highest form of our "assimilation" to God.[100] It is this vision alone that will fulfill and terminate the restlessness of the human heart, the "restless heart" [cor inquietum] of Augustine. In this union with God, the reward and end of all our labors that constitutes eternal life, there is the perfect vision of God, the perfect praise of God, and that perfect fulfilment in which God alone "satisfies and infinitely surpasses" our desire. In the perfect security of freedom from all fear, needs, and sorrow, we join the joyful company of all the blessed that is the perfect realization of the communion of saints. Here "the joy and gladness of one will be as great as the joy of all" because they participate in the perichoresis of the triune God in which the three persons are totally in one another.[101] As Aquinas put it in his famous hymn on the eucharist, *Panis Angelicus,* it is to this vision to which we ask God to lead us through his paths—*per tuas semitas*—the final goal to which we tend by the whole dynamics of graced existence—*duc nos quo tendimus*—which is the light in which God dwells—*ad lucem quam inhabitas.*[102]

According to Aquinas, beatitude or perfect happiness is "natural" only to God because beatitude and existence are identical in God. It is not "of the nature" of any created being, although beatitude does constitute "its ultimate end." Now everything attains its ultimate end through its own operation, which may be either "productive" [factiva] of the end when this end does not exceed the power of the agent, as in medicine producing health, or "deserving" [meritoria] of the end when this is beyond the power of the agent, as in a created being striving for beatitude, in which case the end is expected "from the gift of another" [ex dono alterius].[103] It is remarkable here how, using different terminology, Aquinas's theology of ultimate beatitude or salvation more than anticipates Karl Rahner's theology of the supernatural existential. For Rahner as well, beatitude is not "of the nature" of any created being or, in his own phrase, "constitutive" of a finite being. Still, by virtue of God's teleological ordination given with creation called the supernatural existential, beatitude is the ultimate end "of" humanity or, in his phrase, "intrinsic" to human existence. A supernatural destiny can be *intrinsic* to, without being *constitutive* of, the human being through the grace of God, which is not the result but the "principle" of good works.[104]

Now, theology is not itself the intellectual vision of the divine essence; it is only our human knowledge of the essence as revealed through the medium of the finite and as known in light of faith which accepts that revelation. Nevertheless, the proper object of theology still remains the theoretical or contemplative *knowledge* of this God precisely as our *ultimate* end and as knowable through revelation and faith. As such, theology comes closer to the ultimate *beatitudo* than anything else in this world, reaching its perfection in *patria,* while active and civic life are limited to this world.[105] As the highest wisdom contemplating the *altissimum intelligibile,* God, it is the most architectonic of all human sciences, judging all things. As such it is "a certain beginning or participation

of future happiness [quaedam inchoatio seu participatio futurae felici-
tatis],"[106] "a certain participation in true and perfect beatitude [quaedam
participatio verae et perfectae beatitudinis]."[107]

In his commentary on the Prologue of John's Gospel Aquinas describes John's meditation on the Word as a contemplation that is high,
full, and perfect. It is a "high" contemplation in the sense of lifting up
one's eyes on high and contemplating the creator of all things in his
authority as the ultimate end to whom all things are ordered and who
comes, therefore, to the world as "his own," in his eternity "in the beginning," in his dignity as a being who exists by his own essence and therefore as the summit of all things that exist only by participation in him,
i.e., as the Word that was God, and in the incomprehensibility of his truth
as the first and ultimate truth that surpasses all finite intellects, i.e., as the
God whom "no one has ever seen." John's contemplation is "full" in the
sense that he considers not only the cause but also all its effects, not only
the essence of the cause but also its power, i.e., how "through him all
things came into being." John's contemplation is also "perfect" in the
sense that "the one contemplating is led and raised to the height of the
thing contemplated," which is the end of contemplation, i.e., "adhering
and assenting by affection and understanding to the truth contemplated."
John not only teaches how the Word is God, raised above all things, and
how all things were made through him, but also that we are sanctified by
him and adhere to him by grace "of whose fullness we have all received,"
through "the sacraments of his humanity."

According to Aquinas, these characteristics of contemplation belong
to the different sciences in different ways. Moral science evinces the perfection of contemplation because it deals with the way of attaining the
ultimate end of things. Natural science or science of nature demonstrates
the fullness of contemplation because it considers all things as proceeding from God. The height of contemplation is found in metaphysics, that
is, in theology as it deals with God as the summit of all things. John's
Gospel, however, "contains all together what the sciences have in a
divided way, and so it is most perfect."[108] My discussion thus far, as well
as my coming discussion of the immanent Trinity in the next chapter,
should make it quite evident that what Aquinas says about John's Gospel
is equally a commentary on his own theology as sapiential contemplation
of God. Moreover, it is safe to say without further elaboration that his
two *Summas* are among the best exemplifications of the "high," "full,"
and "perfect" contemplation of God ever attempted by a theologian.

As theoretical, speculative, or contemplative knowledge of God, theology belongs to the contemplative life in general, and it is important to dwell a little on the relation between contemplation and action, a problem that was controversial enough in Aquinas's own times and that has become compelling in our own.

It is a well-known part of Aquinas's "intellectualism" that contemplation is "superior" to action, which is only a corollary of the superiority of the intellect to all other dimensions of human existence. Contemplation is superior to action for the many, essentially Aristotelian reasons we spoke of earlier: Contemplation suits human beings according to what is *best* in them, their intellect, and its proper object—*intelligibilia* and divine things—while action is occupied with external, human concerns and involves lower powers common to humans and beasts. Contemplation is sufficient unto itself and free from external, temporal necessity, whereas action and production are essentially dependent on external, material things and thus exposed to the frustrations of contingent existence in the world of time and matter. Thus, contemplation can be more continuous than action which is always vulnerable to interruptions. Contemplation affords greater delight [delectatio], rest [vacatio], and quiet [quies] than does action, for it offers not only its own inherent delight—the exercise of one's most proper and noblest power, the intellect—but also the delight which comes from contemplating what one loves, God. The ultimate perfection of contemplation is not only to "see" but also to "love" divine truth, which inflames us to gaze on God's beauty. As Gregory the Great says, "contemplative life tramples on all cares and longs to see the face of its Creator."[109]

Thus, the contemplative life is a life of "freedom" with its "liberty of soul [animi libertas]"; the active life a life of "servitude."[110] Contemplation embodies the ideal of the free person, his autonomy, self-sufficiency, and liberation from external necessity, and to that extent contemplation of *intelligibilia* is an end in itself whereas action on *agibilia* or production of *factibilia* is always instrumental and desirable only for the sake of something else. Action is ultimately a means to the end of contemplation. Aristotle put it thus: "As the man is free, we say, who exists for his own sake and not for another, so we pursue this as the only free science, for it alone exists for its own sake."[111] For these reasons Aquinas, in agreement with Aristotle, finds contemplation *in itself* and *simpliciter* more excellent than action, whereas action may be preferable only in a qualified sense or in a special case, that is, "because of the necessity of present life."[112] As he quotes Aristotle: "It is better to philosophize than to seek riches, but for him who is in need, it is better to seek riches."[113]

The ideal for Aquinas, then, as for the entire Greek tradition, is to pursue the contemplative life rather than the active. As a concession to "the necessities of present life," the contemplative life may be interrupted, but such a concession is always a burden to be borne according to the demand of charity, which as the ultimate source of merit (*radix merendi*) may redeem the active life. The intrinsic and ideal superiority of the contemplative life, however, emerges equally clearly within the order of charity itself. While charity embraces both the love of God and the love of neighbor, nevertheless, "to love God in himself (*secundum se*) is more meritorious than to love one's neighbor." That which pertains "more directly" to the love of God is more meritorious *ex suo genere* than what pertains "directly" to the love of neighbor even when it is motivated by the love of God. The contemplative life belongs directly and immediately to the love of God, whereas the active life is more directly concerned with the love of neighbor. The former, therefore, is more meritorious than the latter.[114]

It may "happen" [*contingere*] that someone merits more in the works of the active life than in those of the contemplative, if, for example, she accepts "temporary" separation from the "sweetness" of divine contemplation out of an abundance of divine love in order to fulfill God's will for her glory. But such merit is "accidental" because external labor for God is valuable only as a "sign" of charity, which alone is "essentially" meritorious. A much greater sign of this charity would be to renounce all things belonging to this life and enjoy giving oneself *only* to divine contemplation. Even the apostolic "zeal for souls" is more meritorious when it means seeking to unite one's own and others' souls to God in contemplation than when it means offering something external to God by means of action. Of all the human goods, the soul is the most pleasing to God.[115] Likewise, the act of faith is *per se* the activity of the speculative intellect because its object is the true (*verum*), the *prima veritas*. If faith works through charity, it is not because faith *per se* is ordered to it but because the first truth is "the end of all our desires and actions" and because the speculative intellect, through the mediation of the ultimate end, "becomes practical by extension," to use the words of Aristotle.[116]

What, then, is the relation between contemplation and action, between theory and praxis? Are they merely different as the superior from the inferior, or are they also related to each other in the sense of interaction? According to Aquinas, they are indeed mutually related—not essentially, but dispositionally, i.e., accidentally. Contemplation properly consists in the activity of the intellect, but this activity can be impeded by the vehemence of passions and the disturbances arising from quarrels with others. The moral virtues, especially temperance and justice, which properly belong to the active life, "dispose" one to the contemplative life by removing such impediments and causing peace and purity of mind. Thus, the moral virtues pertain to the contemplative life dispositionally but not "essentially," any more than does the love of God and neighbor, which is also required for but not essential to the contemplative life. The causes which move, affect, or dispose a thing "do not enter into the essence of a thing, though they prepare for and complete it."[117] The moral virtues contribute to contemplation accidentally in the sense of securing the *external* conditions of its integrity, not essentially in the sense of determining or influencing the *internal* content of its activity.

What about external actions as such? Do they in any way, even dispositionally, contribute to contemplation? For Aquinas, they do not. In fact, the active life, which as such consists in external activities concerned with *sensibilia,* "impedes" contemplation because one cannot be engaged in both contemplation and action at the same time, because the mind is less free when occupied with corporeal things, and because external occupation decreases our ability to comprehend the *intelligibilia* separated from the *sensibilia.* What the activities of the active life do is to enable us to see more clearly in judging *agibilia.* Both experience and the attention of the mind contribute to the knowledge of *prudence,* whose end lies in the activity of the appetitive power and which belongs to the active life. They do not in any way contribute to the knowledge of *wisdom,* whose end lies in the knowledge of truth as such.

Ambiguity of Theological Intellectualism

There is something uplifting, broadening, and refreshing about Aquinas's vision of theology as contemplative wisdom. This is so especially for those who have been concerned over the increasing fragmentation of contemporary theology into special interests and regional issues, its increasing preoccupation with the relativities of history, and its constant syndrome of hope and despair over the fluctuating fortunes of various liberation projects. Beyond such fragmentation, preoccupation, and syndrome, Aquinas calls our attention to what ultimately counts—the triune God who creates, redeems, and invites us into her own eternal life. Aquinas keeps our vision open to the totality, including the whole of creation and all of humanity united in their graced origin, fallen nature, and redeeming return to their ultimate end. He constantly reminds us of perspective and hierarchy lest we should lose ourselves in the transient relativities of history and forget our ultimate destination to the eternal homeland where we shall "see" God face to face. Things historical are important, but they are important only *sub ratione Dei.*

In order to appreciate the ultimacy of God and the proper, transcendent significance of all things in their relation to God, we must learn to step back from the immediate urgencies and compulsions of human action, even liberating action, learn to open our hearts and minds to God, and thus contemplate all reality in its enduring, eternal significance in the providential economy of the triune God. Through contemplation we come to liberate ourselves from the confining anxieties and compulsions of our historical productions and projects and learn to appreciate all creation as a gift of God, valuable beyond their human utility, a joy to behold, a sacrament of God. Contemplation of all things, not only my own ethnicity, gender, status, region, and religion, *sub ratione Dei,* liberates us from ourselves, even from our worthy, liberating concerns, and restores to us both a rightly ordered vision and a rightly ordered will. We recover a true sense of perspective and acquire an openness to let things be and show themselves in their truth and value. We acquire wisdom.

It is regrettable that this sense of the ultimate and the whole and our search for meaning in that ultimate and whole have largely been suppressed as a theological topic in most mainstream progressive theologies. The result of this default and neglect is that people hear about the ultimate and the whole only during homilies at funerals or search for that liberating sense of the ultimate and the whole only in movements of "spirituality" often based on simplistic theology. Compelling as is liberation from various types of historical oppressions, contemporary theology must recover a contemplative vision of the ultimate and the whole and reintegrate its many partial and relative concerns into that vision. Without the centrality of God as the ultimate origin and end of all things and without a vision of all things *sub ratione Dei,* we simply have no "theology," the *logos* of and about *theos;* at best we have sociology in theological guise. Aquinas's classical vision of theology as contemplative wisdom is a refreshing relief from the deliberately cultivated partialities and compulsions of contemporary theology and provides at least one model for restoring the theological sense of the ultimate and the whole to theology today.

However, before I go on to retrieve the positive possibilities of Aquinas's theological vision for contemporary theology in the final chapter, it is essential, in the remainder of this chapter, to pass many of the assumptions and implications of that vision through a hermeneutic of suspicion. The preceding exposition should have made it clear that Aquinas's concept of theology was largely determined by his anthropology. His intellectualism, which regards the activity of the intellect as the most proper and noblest dimension of human existence, posits the superiority of theory to praxis, which leads to his intellectualist determination of and emphasis on our ultimate end, in turn determining the scope of theology. It also determines the function of theological reason, which is to provide an *intellectual* defense and clarification of the content of faith itself conceived basically as an act of the intellect. Given Aquinas's— fundamentally Aristotelian—anthropological assumptions, it seems difficult to deny either the coherence of his arguments or the consistency of his position as a whole.

For Aquinas, the relation between theology and praxis is largely extrinsic and negative. The practical moral virtues "dispose" one to contemplation by removing the hindrances of inward passions and social disruptions; they do not contribute to the *content* of contemplation itself. There is no positive and intrinsic mediation between wisdom and the moral virtues.[118] As to the practical activities themselves, they only "impede" the theological activity of contemplation. They may have a positive, intrinsic relation to the knowledge of *prudence,* which depends on such experience, but their relation to theology as wisdom is only negative. The practical and productive occupation with things external and sensible is detrimental to the theoretical occupation with things internal and intelligible. The only positive relation of praxis to theory is the instrumental relation: it serves theory as means serves its end, the proximate the ultimate, the body the soul. At worst, praxis is detrimental to theory as the external is to the internal, the sensible to the intelligible, the body to the soul. In either case, the mediation is extrinsic, not intrinsic. The dualism of categories cannot be more explicit.

To put the consequences of this relation in contemporary terms, the economic sphere of production (*factibilia*) and the socio-political sphere of human praxis (*agibilia*) serve the *act* of theologizing by providing "the necessities of present life" and the social, moral conditions for undisturbed contemplation. In themselves such activities are detrimental and distracting to the act of contemplation. In either case, our economic, social and political experiences do not have an intrinsic relation to contemplation; the content of praxis does not enter into the *content* of our knowledge of God. Theology as theory is not affected, in its very content, by the ideas and values, the ideologies and intellectual trends, the signs and crises, the perspectives generated and horizons acquired precisely in the process of human praxis and production. For Aquinas, praxis neither challenges nor transforms the content of theology by posing new questions, forcing crises, or revolutionizing the traditional content of theology.

Underlying this separation of theory from praxis, of theology from the practical and productive sciences, is the conscious value judgment of the superiority of theory to praxis, a judgment based on the Platonist superiority of *intelligibilia* to *sensibilia.* In theory the intellect considers intelligible necessities abstracted or freed from the contingencies of the actual world. It deals with its own ideal creations or ideas of things as they exist in the mind, and whatever conflicts it suffers are generated and resolved within the circle of immanence, untouched by the actual conflicts of the external, material, social world of praxis. The world of praxis, on the other hand, is intrinsically mediated by *sensibilia* and subject to their contingency, vulnerability, and frustration. Natural disasters, contradictions between intention and consequence, mutual misunderstanding, struggle for power: all of these are inherent in the world of praxis. To put it in Hegelian terms, the world of theory is ruled by the principle of *identity,* the identity of the intellect with itself. Whatever otherness emerges in theory is conquered within the immanence and identity of theory itself. The world of praxis is ruled by the principle of *otherness,* externality, and opposition, which can never be completely sublated [aufgehoben] in this world. If freedom means self-determination and liberation from external necessity, theory promises it. In contrast, praxis only promises struggle with external necessity and at best temporary liberation.[119]

Furthermore, Aquinas takes intellect and will, thought and action as already *given* each in its distinctness from the other according to its own formal intelligibility. This formal, analytic approach loses sight of the *whole* person as a concrete totality and ultimately leads to a truncated conception of theology. I am not, of course, denying either the reality of formal distinctions or the necessity of formal abstraction for the sake

of greater intelligibility; such formal procedures are essential to the operation of the human intellect. The question is whether, in analyzing and
distinguishing the various powers and activities of the human subject,
Aquinas also preserves the very conditions which alone make and keep
them possible precisely as *human* powers and activities in all their concreteness. There are, I think, two such conditions: the concrete unity of
the subject and the mutual internal mediation of such powers and activities within that unity.

First, let us see how Aquinas accounts—or fails to account—for the
concrete unity of the subject. The human subject is not a collection of
independent powers and activities (atomistic empiricism) but an ontologically prior unity which is indeed expressed and actualized by means
of such diverse powers and activities but which, precisely as their subject,
lends unity and human specificity to them. The human intellect is human,
not angelic, not primarily, as Aquinas says, because it is limited by the
materiality of the senses, but because human existence as a concrete
totality of intellect and sense is human, not angelic. By the same token,
human senses and appetites are human, not brute, as Aristotle and Aquinas
tend to argue when they say that human beings and animals have them in
common. Even when they are degraded into vices, they remain human,
not brute; degraded humanity is still humanity, not animality. We often
blame human beings for acting like animals, although we do not blame
animals for doing so; we blame them because they are human beings who
act *like* animals, not because they *are* animals. Rationality and sensibility
are indeed two distinct dimensions of human existence, but they also
remain expressions of the one human subject, whose unity and humanity
are ontologically prior to such dimensions. They are not a subsequent
collection of angelic rationality on the one hand and animal sensibility on
the other, each already constituted and given in its proper reality.

Aquinas, of course, is well known for his insistence on the *essential*
unity *(per se unum)* of the human composite (this is why and how he
could also argue for the rationality of resurrection), and this distinguishes
his hylomorphism from the dualism of Plato and Descartes. He also
insists that the subject of action is not the powers but the whole being in
its unity, the supposit. This unity, however, remains formal, not concrete.
When it comes to characterizing the concrete content of that unity, he
reverts to the formal notion of what is proper and unique to human existence, defined as what is not shared with animals, i.e., the intellect; he fails
to grasp what is proper and specific to human existence precisely as a

concrete totality, that which pervades all the distinct powers, activities, and dimensions and renders all of them the *human* expressions of the *one* subject.

Second, we must ask whether Aquinas can accommodate the mutual mediation of diverse powers and activities within the unity of human existence. As distinct dimensions of the *one* concrete subject, such powers and activities are not separate or independent of one another but interact among themselves. This interaction is not merely factual, like two cars colliding in an accident, but constitutive in the sense that the operation of each, precisely in its formal distinction *from* the other, is made possible and mediated by an a priori relation *to* the other, a relation which is in this sense mutually internal. Thought is not sensation; as the power and activity of transcendence, it is directed to the universal, while sensation is limited to the particular. *Human* thought, however, is not the *pure* thought of an angel. It is internally mediated by the conditions of sensibility which generate the need for thought to transcend such conditions, which make its content concrete, and which in any case limit its range and scope. No one has perhaps been more aware of this mediation than has Aquinas, but, I am afraid, without drawing from it the appropriate anthropological conclusions about the concrete, not abstract, totality that a human being is. Likewise, *human* sensation is never the pure, brute sensation devoid of and unmediated by thought; the recognition of the particular *as* particular is possible only through the presence of thought *in* sensation.[120]

In each case it is always the concrete unified totality of the person, not intellect or sense by itself, which remains the subject of the experience and in which the formally distinct powers and activities each contribute its share only through the mediation of the other. To take a thing "concretely" is to take it precisely as a totality of *all* such mediating relations which constitute it as what it really is and apart from which it becomes a reified abstraction. For the purpose of limited consideration it is indeed necessary to abstract from certain relations, but by the same token it is also necessary to recognize it for what it is, an abstraction, to ask whether one is taking into account all the relations relevant even to one's limited consideration, and in any case to maintain a vision of the whole in all its concrete, constitutive relations.

Consider the relation of theory and praxis, where we can see clearly Aquinas's analytic approach and the consequences of his failure to maintain such a vision of the whole with an internal dialectic of mediation. For Aquinas, theory consists in the contemplation of *intelligibilia* either abstracted from *sensibilia* or subsisting in themselves, such as angels and God, for the purpose of understanding as such. It is the activity of intellectual transcendence pursued for its own sake. Theology as theory consists in such transcendence towards God as the ultimate end and origin of all things. As mentioned earlier, it has no positive, internal relation to the realm of *sensibilia* in which human beings engage in the socio-political praxis of liberation and the production of material necessities, even though these political and economic activities, as moral actions dealing with proximate ends, preserve their salvific significance in their ordination to God, their ultimate end, in some abstract way. Theology as theory is distinct from praxis and production in both its formal object and end. In Aquinas, then, theory and praxis remain two *coordinate* or coequal and distinct dimensions of human existence, side by side with each other, only negatively and extrinsically related. The question remains, however, whether this formal, analytic approach is adequate either to the respective nature of theory and praxis precisely as *human* activities or to the concrete unified and unifying reality of the human subject involved in both precisely as manifestations of his or her concrete subjectivity.

The glory of theory lies indeed in its capacity for intellectual transcendence. It is this transcendence that makes possible the religious quest for the transcendent as it also makes God's self-revelation possible and intelligible to human beings (Rahner and Tillich). It furthermore underlies advances and originality in the philosophical and artistic search for universal meaning beyond the immediacy of present fact. As human theory, however, it is not simply autonomous or independent of human praxis and production under conditions of concrete history. Our intellectual transcendence is dependent on our historical existence in at least two ways that affect the very goal, content, and limit of such transcendence and which are in this sense essential and intrinsic, not accidental or extrinsic, to theory as *human* theory.

First, the very goal of theory is the attainment of truth for its own sake, an attainment in which the intellect enjoys its liberation from all external necessity in a secure possession of intrinsic *intelligibilia*. What, however, motivates the human intellect to engage in theory in the first place? Is it the purely theoretical "wonder" about the first cause of things with which Aristotle begins his *Metaphysics,* as Aquinas notes? Perhaps not quite. Even Aquinas admits that such a wonder is part of the desire for happiness, a desire which cannot be completely satisfied in this world because of its contingency, sinfulness, and mortality. Thus, Aquinas limits theoretical activity to the pursuit of intelligible necessities either abstracted or separated from the contingencies of history. He also limits the goal of theory to the liberation of the intellect by locating such liberation either in the contemplation of *intelligibilia* external to the realm of praxis and production or in the beatific vision. Implicit in this procedure is the experience of the contingencies of concrete historical existence as the starting point for the search for happiness. It is the experience of contingencies such as accidents, sickness, hunger, oppression, death, and vulnerability to sin in all its concrete historical manifestations, which motivates the search for happiness.[121] It is precisely this experience of historical alienation in all its material and social content—theologically interpreted as "sin"—which we seek to transcend when we search for happiness. As Marx put it long ago, our religious yearnings for salvation are both "an *expression* of real suffering and a *protest* against real suffering."[122] Without this experience, there would be no search for happiness, at least for us human beings. The search for happiness is motivated, implicitly at least, by a dissatisfaction with and a protest against historical evils, by the judgment that these evils ought not to be, by the desire for the liberation and transcendence of concrete historical existence from its alienating oppressiveness, sinfulness, and mortality. Without this desire for concrete historical liberation, the search for happiness, even for the beatific vision, would be impossible.

The contradiction in Aquinas lies in the fact that on the one hand, the search for happiness begins with the desire for liberation of concrete historical existence, which remains—at least implicitly—the a priori condition for all the stages of the search for happiness, while on the other, the theoretical life does not locate happiness in the concrete liberation *of* historical existence and its eschatological transformation but only in the theoretical liberation *from* historical existence in the form of contemplation and its extension in the beatific vision. The problem of happiness is not only the problem of absolute eschatological fulfillment but also that of liberation from the relative alienations *in* history, the realm of praxis and production, while the solution Aquinas proposes is theoretical abstraction *from* history and supernatural transcendence of history. The problem is solved only abstractly, not concretely; or, more accurately, it is dissolved as a concrete historical problem even while it remains the a priori motivating and sustaining condition for the very search for happiness.[123]

Second, our intellectual transcendence in theory is mediated not only by the desire for the liberation of historical existence but also by the assumptions, perspectives and horizons generated and acquired through that existence. If the demand of concrete history for liberation and reconciliation provides the challenging and motivating origin and context of theory, concrete history also enters into the very content of theory by providing it with the concepts, languages, symbols, and the very perspective and horizon with which to operate and which are generated in the social process of producing material necessities and relating to others at various levels of common life. Human theory in its content is never pure but is intrinsically affected by the concerns, preoccupations, and ethos prevailing in the social, political, and economic world, simply for the reasons that the subject of theory is also the subject of praxis and production directly or indirectly, and that theory and praxis are never separate but always found concretely united—not necessarily harmoniously—within the historical unity of the personal subject. Human theory is a theory not only for the sake of liberating the conditions of praxis but is also a theory of praxis and within praxis, of praxis in the sense that it implies an interpretation and evaluation of praxis, and within praxis in the sense that it operates within the cultural perspectives and assumptions of a particular history of human praxis.[124]

This is not to deny the freedom and transcendence of thought, in the fashion of mechanistic determinism, but only to point out the inevitable limitations of reason *as* finite human reason, which is always reason *in* history. Human reason is not born free and transcendent except as an abstract potentiality; it becomes so in a complex process of socialization, and its freedom and transcendence is always a matter of degrees, never an absolute freedom from history or an absolute transcendence over history. Such freedom and transcendence belong only to God and angels.

Aquinas's failure to see this dialectical mediation of theory and praxis is not without important consequences for the character of his theology. On one hand, theology becomes a form of theory dealing with *intelligibilia* either abstracted or separated from history, formally distinguished from praxis in the realm of *sensibilia,* and without the benefit of substantive material mediation by praxis. When, therefore, theology is called upon to judge human praxis in its function as wisdom, its practical instructions tend to be abstract generalities perhaps uplifting but also without the power to effectively address the central issues of the day. On the other hand, praxis remains an extrinsic tool of theory, only a means to be ordered to the ultimate, supernatural, suprahistorical finality of human existence, but without the capacity to stimulate rethinking of the traditional content of theology such as the trinitarian doctrine, Christology, salvation, and justification. Proud of rising above the contingencies of history, theology suffers from the incapacity to provide compelling reflections appropriate to the changing human situation as well as from the tendency to uncritically accept the prejudices and ideologies of the times. This lack of historical sensibility, adaptability, and effectiveness, I am afraid, has been the story of Thomism in the modern world.

Underlying these problems is the more fundamental problem of Aquinas's philosophical and theological method, which as such infects the whole corpus of his system. The method consists in "distinguishing" things and their aspects according to their "proper" intelligibility or *ratio.* Thus, Aquinas distinguishes between intellect and will, theory and praxis, wisdom and prudence, ultimate and proximate ends, ends and means, God and creatures, intelligible and sensible, each according to its proper object. As both Maritain and Gilson never ceased to point out with evident admiration, Aquinas is a master of the art of intellectual ordering, of "putting everything in its proper place. Each thing in its own place, a place for each thing."[125]

This penchant for distinguishing according to the criteria of formal intelligibility contributes to the admirable clarity of Aquinas's thought and accounts, at least partially, for its strength and enduring popularity among some. I am afraid, however, that this search for distinct, formal intelligibility is also its basic flaw. Such a search often remains blind to the concrete unity and internal mediation among the elements so distinguished, a unity and mediation prior to the constitution of each in its formal intelligibility and operative throughout the process of its concrete becoming. The human person is not a collection of mutually extrinsic powers and activities but a totality which shapes and conditions each of them, which such powers and activities at once express and concretize, and within which they interact with one another in an internally constitutive relation. What is true of the diverse powers and activities of the person is also true of the relation among persons, who are also internally constituted by their mutual historical relations—political, economic, and cultural—in a concrete community. And the same is true of the relation between God and creatures, who form a concrete totality in which God and creatures mediate one another. The concrete modalities of actual relations differ in each case, and certainly the mediation between God and creatures is qualitatively different from the mediations among the creatures themselves. Nevertheless, antecedent unity, its concretion in terms of diversity, the mutual relation among the diverse elements expressed in and through their conflicts and the struggle to overcome such conflicts, and the concrete totality in which the antecedent unity becomes concrete through the mediation of its parts precisely in their relations of alienation and reconciliation: these dialectical categories, I think, are essential for an understanding of reality in its historical concreteness.

In contrast, Aquinas focuses on the different powers and activities as already *given* precisely in their formal difference, and remains blind to both the presence of the whole *in* the parts and of the parts *in* the whole as well as to the mutual constitutive mediation among the parts themselves. The only unity he recognizes is the formal unity of a common subject: reason and faith, for example, cannot contradict each other because two contrary opinions cannot co-exist in the same subject. As to the unity of all beings, he locates it in God, the common source and end, and in the formal structures they individually share (e.g., act and potency, various causalities, and *convenientia*). The community of being, in short, is constituted by the community of ultimate finality and similarity of structure. It does not include the dynamic ontological relation among the entities themselves, although it does include the moral necessity of right order among them for the good of the whole. Aquinas's search for formal intelligibility, therefore, cannot escape the charge of the fallacy of "misplaced concreteness" (Whitehead) and "reification" (Hegel and Marx). His intention is to make things intelligible by keeping them "distinct," but precisely by neglecting the totality of concrete relations which alone make them intelligible as what they really are, not merely as ideas, he ends up by keeping them "separate." The dualism of theory and praxis, intellect and will, ends and means, transcendence and history, is only formally overcome; in reality, he reduces the concrete totality to a purely formal and extrinsic synthesis of abstractions, each taken in its distinctness from the other.[126]

For all these inadequacies, however, it remains to Aquinas's credit that he never lost his focus on the contemplative and eschatological dimensions of theology without which theology ceases to be theology and of which we contemporary theologians, for all our historical preoccupations, continue to need a large dose of reminder. For all of Aquinas's one-sided ahistoricity, it still remains true that it is by virtue of our intellectuality and the transcendence it implies that we human beings possess a theological and contemplative vocation. In the final chapter I provide a dialectic of Aquinas's sapiential theology and contemporary political theologies.

Chapter Five

CONTEMPLATING THE TRIUNE GOD

The Beginning and End of All Things

Human Knowledge of the Triune God

The principal object of theology as contemplative wisdom is God who is the beginning and end of all things, and this God, for Aquinas, is a Trinity. I have already dealt with the triune God in her dealings with the world or her economic mission in the first and third chapters. I devote this chapter to Aquinas's discussion of the triune God in herself or in her immanent reality. In the course of the twentieth century many issues have been raised about the trinitarian doctrine as the center of Christian faith and about Aquinas's formulation of it in particular. I shall present the doctrine in Aquinas in some detail with an eye to its subtlety and complexity. Already two generations of theologians have been brought up completely cut off from the classical tradition, its vocabulary, insights, and assumptions. Retrieving an accurate understanding of the classical doctrine of the Trinity in its fullness has become a crucial necessity. In the next chapter I shall go on to address some of the substantive contemporary issues raised about Aquinas's trinitarian theology.

In treating of Aquinas's discussion of the Trinity, largely based on the *Summa Theologiae*, I would like to make one change in the order of discussion. Just as he places the discussion of our knowledge of God in question 12 of the First Part, not in question 1 or even question 2, as we today would be inclined to, he also places the discussion of our knowledge of the Trinity not at the beginning but at the end of the general discussion of the Trinity (question 32) prior to the discussion of particular persons. He does so perhaps in fidelity to his theocentric, deductive method that follows the absolute order of reality rather than the relative order of its manifestation to us and hence moves from causes to effects, from the existence and nature of God to our knowledge of God, since the extent of our knowledge depends on who God is and subsequently on who we are as created by God. There is a profound logic to this method of theology that regards itself as wisdom and concerns itself primarily with God as the beginning and end of all things and secondarily with all created things *sub ratione Dei.* As William J. Hill points out, Aquinas's way is that of teaching [via doctrinae], not that of discovery [via inventionis] or history, and is determined more by the nature of the thing to be known than by the needs of the knower.[1] Today, however, we are more used to approaching the question of God with an epistemological, anthropological, existentialist, or liberationist prolegomenon. For this reason I begin with Aquinas's discussion of the human knowledge of the Trinity as a brief introduction to his discussion of the immanent Trinity.

What, then, is the necessity or relevance of the knowledge of the triune God? Why do we have to bother to know God in her Trinity? Is not the knowledge of the one God sufficient? Aquinas gives two reasons, one dealing with creation, the other with salvation. The first reason is that the trinitarian doctrine helps avoid both the false, pantheistic idea that creation was a necessity of divine nature and the false, finitist idea that God created things out of some extrinsic need or because of some external cause. That there is a procession of intellect in God and that God made all things by her Word, not by necessity of nature, mean that God created things through free choice, just as human beings prove their freedom by acting according to their concept of things. That there is also a procession of will or love in God and that God created all things through the Holy Spirit mean that God did not create them because God lacked anything external or was moved to do so by some external cause but on account of the love of her own goodness that she also wanted to share with others. In addition to providing the right idea of creation, there is a second, and more important [principalius] reason for the doctrine of the Trinity, providing the right idea of salvation. Salvation is not simply the work of the one God. It is the fruit of the Father's primordial decision to send the Son and the Spirit, the incarnation of the Son, and the gift of the Holy Spirit. The doctrine of the immanent Trinity is essential to the doctrine of the economic Trinity.[2]

Necessary as it is to know the Trinity, however, such knowledge is not accessible to natural reason but only through revelation and faith. Knowledge of God by natural reason is limited to what we can necessarily infer about God as cause from her effects in the world, i.e., the knowledge of God as the creative principle of all things. This creative power, however, is common to all three persons in their divine nature, a matter of the unity of the divine essence, not a matter of the differential function of three distinct persons within that unity. The properties of persons are relations through which they are related to one another, not to creatures. To know God as the one creative source of all things is not yet to know God as three persons.[3]

In fact, for Aquinas, trying to prove the Trinity of persons by natural reason derogates from faith in two ways. Such rationalism offends the dignity of faith insofar as it is concerned with invisible realities that exceed human reason. It also needlessly subjects faith to the ridicule of the unbeliever by trying to prove faith with less than cogent reasons, since there cannot be any cogent or necessary reasons for it. We should not try to prove what is of faith except by appeal to the authority of revelation alone, and we should do so only for the benefit of those who accept that authority, i.e., believers. To those who do not believe, all that can be done is to prove that what faith teaches is not impossible, that it is not opposed to natural reason.

Historically, attempts have been made to explain or provide a rationale for the Trinity by arguing from the nature of God's infinite goodness as communicating herself infinitely through the procession of divine persons; from the very nature of goodness, which cannot be enjoyed apart from being shared with another (Richard of St. Victor); or from the procession of the word and love in the mind (Augustine). Aren't these attempts ways of "proving" the Trinity?[4] Isn't this also what Aquinas himself does? Here Aquinas distinguishes two uses of reason. One is to "prove" [probare] in the strict sense of providing necessary reasons. The other is to "show" [ostendere], once a principle is established as true on other grounds, that certain consequences are "congruent" [congruere] with it. "Proving" in the strict sense applies to the existence and various attributes of God, such as unity, simplicity, and infinity, but it cannot apply to the Trinity. What avails with regard to the Trinity, once it is posited on the ground of revelation, is to "show" or "manifest" [manifestare] the Trinity by means of certain congruent reasons, i.e., not reasons that make the Trinity necessary but reasons that make it fitting, appropriate, and plausible to human reason. As we saw in chapter 3, "fittingness" does not imply strict necessity, although it does not imply pure contingency either. The failure to appreciate this difference between "proving" and "manifesting" has led some—John Milbank and Catherine Pickstock, for instance—to claim wrongly that Aquinas "in fact argues for the Trinity in much the same way that he argues for the divine attributes."[5]

The lack of univocity between the divine intellect and the human, between the infinite goodness of God and finite goodness rules out the latter as an adequate basis of proving anything about the Trinity as such. It is indeed an act of infinite power to produce from nothing, and to this extent, creation necessarily points to the infinite goodness of God. Insofar as it is not necessary that an infinite effect follow from God's communication of herself by her infinite goodness but only that each effect receive that goodness according to its own measure, the finite created world does not allow a vision of God's infinite, inner life. Richard of St. Victor's argument that the perfection of love requires another person to love and a third person with whom to share that love applies to the created, finite world where no one person possesses perfect goodness, but not to God, a response that equally applies to Richard Swinburne's recent revival of that argument.[6] If Aquinas, along with Augustine, uses the analogy of the procession of word and love in our minds as the closest created likeness of the divine mind, it is not because we can really "know" the Trinity by natural reason. The intellect does not exist in God and in us univocally, and no finite likeness can be a sufficient basis of strict proof. Aquinas, therefore, agrees with Augustine that we arrive at knowledge by faith, not conversely. What Aquinas does in his treatise on the Trinity, then, is precisely to provide "congruent" reasons for making the Trinity, which we know through divine revelation, fitting and plausible on the basis of human concepts; in Walter Kasper's language, to "illustrate," not to "demonstrate," the truth of the Trinity.[7] The treatise is not a claim to have an intuition into the divine essence or the intrinsic necessity of the Trinity. It is a pure misunderstanding, therefore, to charge Aquinas, as does Catherine Mowry LaCugna, with an attempt to know the Trinity "in itself," apart from both the analogies of created experience and salvation history, after the manner of the Kantian "thing in itself."[8]

In using human concepts to make the Trinity plausible to us, Aquinas is aware of the fact that Scripture may not contain words such as "person," "relation," "notion," and other technical terms as such or as applied to God. The task of the theologian, however, is not to repeat the terms or words of Scripture but to explicate or manifest the "sense" or "meaning" [sensus] of Scripture. The terms may not be found in Scripture, but as long as what they signify is there, at least implicitly, theologians should feel free to use them in exploring the depth of meaning in it. If we were to use only the terms of Scripture, we would have to speak in its original languages. Such a linguistic fundamentalism is indifferent to the urgency of responding to the issues raised by heresy with new words that also express the ancient faith about God.[9]

In predicating names of the triune God, as in predicating names of the one God, the theologian works with analogy. We are limited to knowing God only on the basis of sensible creatures, which poses a quandary. Because of the infinite distance between God and creatures, knowledge of creatures does not enable us to see the essence of God through her effects, thus ruling out any univocal knowledge of God. On the other hand, a purely equivocal knowledge is no knowledge. Aquinas's way out of this dilemma is the analogical way of predication, in its three steps. Insofar as God is the cause of material things, there is some similarity between them as between cause and effect, which enables us to know not indeed what God is but at least whether God exists, along with what must necessarily belong to God as cause of all things. This is the way of causality. Insofar, however, as there is an infinite inequality between God and creatures, we can predicate of God what we know from creatures only after removing from the perfections predicated any finite characteristics that properly belong to created beings in their "mode of signification [modus significandi]." This is the way of negation. We can then elevate the perfections to the supereminent mode of infinity worthy of God in whom essence and existence coincide and affirm them of God properly and "literally." This is the way of eminence. This predicability applies only to those "pure" perfections whose "signified content" [res significata] or intelligible meaning [ratio] implies no intrinsic materiality or finitude. In fact, these pure perfections—such as being, goodness, beauty, wisdom, life—belong to God more properly and are predicated of God with greater priority [per prius] than of creatures.

Whatever perfection we attribute to creatures "pre-exists in God, and in a more excellent and higher way."[10]

This also means that those perfections whose very meaning [ratio] or "signified content" implies intrinsic materiality or finitude can apply to God only "metaphorically." God can be, for example, a "rock" or a "lion" only in the metaphorical sense, while only a rock is a rock in the literal sense. Aquinas, therefore, distinguishes between "analogy" and "metaphor." Analogy has to do with the "proper" and "literal" application of the "signified content" or meaning of a perfection to God after negation of its finite "mode of signification" and its elevation to infinity. Metaphor has to do with transfer of a meaning properly found only in a material being to a non-material being, with a correspondingly changed *ratio* or content. Thus the solidity of a rock, properly found only in a rock, is applied to God in the changed sense of spiritual, not material, solidity. In short, the "signified content" of an analogically predicated perfection such as wisdom or goodness applies to God literally, not metaphorically, albeit still analogically, that is, after negation and elevation. The "signified content" of a metaphor applies literally only to a being whose perfection it originally constitutes, and to all other beings only metaphorically, i.e., with a changed content. The difference between an analogy and a metaphor, then, is that the intelligible content of meaning remains identical in an analogy but changes in a metaphor. It is important to remember this distinction, given our contemporary tendencies to reduce all analogies to the metaphor and then treat metaphors as "only" metaphors without intrinsic reference to God.[11]

We not only know God only as she is known through creatures, but also name divine things not as they really are in God where they exist "united and simple" but only according to our human mode of signification taken from created things where they exist "divided and multiplied."[12] If we are to express ourselves correctly, we have to consider not only the content signified but also the mode of its signification. For example, God and Godhead are really the same because of divine simplicity, yet the mode of signification is different in each case. Since "God" signifies the divine essence in her who possesses it, it can, from its mode of signification, of its own nature, stand for the person. Thus, things which properly belong to the persons can be predicated of "God," as we can say, for example, "God is begotten" or "begetter." "God" can also stand for the essence, as we can say that "God creates." The divine essence, however, in its mode of signification, cannot stand for person because it signifies the essence as an abstract form. What properly belongs to the persons whereby they are distinguished from each other cannot be attributed to the divine essence. This is how Joachim of Fiore went wrong in saying that "essence begot essence" in the same way that we can say "God begot God." He was guilty of violating the grammar of divine predication. God and the divine essence are really the same, but (human) religious language must respect the difference in their respective mode of signification.[13]

This also raises a methodological problem for the theology of the Trinity. If we cannot know God as she is in her essence in this world, and we are structurally dependent on analogies from creatures in order to know anything about God, what created models or paradigms should be our starting point for the knowledge of the Trinity? For Aquinas, the answer is the highest creatures—intellectual substances—although these too fail to represent the divine objects in an adequate way. One should be careful to understand God not according to the mode of the lowest creatures, i.e., material things, but only according to that of the highest, i.e., intellectual beings.[14] Aquinas's trinitarian theology will thus be framed in terms of the immanent operations and characteristics of an intellectual being, its intellect and will, its proper processions, relations, persons, and notions. This is an important point to remember. Aquinas's trinitarian doctrine, like that of Augustine, is often called a "psychological" doctrine as opposed to the presumably "social" doctrine of the Cappadocians. This is not quite accurate. Aquinas's interest in the immanent activities of an intellectual being is not so much psychological as ontological. He is interested in an intellectualist understanding of the Trinity because intellectuality denotes the mode of being on the part of creatures that (as far as we know) "approaches nearest to a likeness to God,"[15] not because he is interested in the immanent operations of the mind as such, and certainly not because he is interested in any empirical "psychology" of the divine mind.

As we launch into Aquinas's theology of the Trinity, it is essential to keep in mind the cautions and reservations he builds into his theology as the human mode of speaking about the triune God. As far as the Trinity is concerned, human theology is a "persuasive" or "illustrative," not a "demonstrative," reasoning, resorting to congruent reasons and analogies rather than "proofs"; and it is restricted to the human mode of signification that will be pursued, to its human limit, according to the rules of analogical—never univocal—predication with its affirmation, negation, and supereminence. Aquinas himself will remind us occasionally of these limitations.

An Ontology of the Triune God

Aquinas begins his treatise on the Trinity in the First Part of *Summa Theologiae* with a discussion of how plurality is possible in God without prejudice to her unity and simplicity (questions 27–32), goes on to discuss the particularity of each divine person (questions 33–38), and concludes with a discussion of the persons in relation to the divine essence, relations, notional acts, one another, and their respective mission to creatures (questions 39–43).

Processions

The first logical question about the Trinity, it is fitting to say, is how plurality is possible in God. What constitutes differentiation in a being marked by essential simplicity and unity? This is not only the first but also one of the central questions in trinitarian theology, and as such, it can also only be answered gradually, receiving a substantial discussion in the section on relations and persons. As a start, we can say that for Aquinas, differentiation in God cannot arise from anything in the divine nature itself, which is one and simple, but only, to speak humanly, from the non-essential dimension of divine being. A material being has nine categories of accidents that describe its non-essential dimension—quality, quantity, action, passion, relation, place, time, posture, and state—but God is not a material being. In God, such a non-essential dimension is reducible to action and the relation it brings about, which in turn is confined to the action of "proceeding" and the relations it contains. Aquinas takes procession in the widest possible sense as any act and relation of origination in which one thing comes forth from another.[16] We cannot, however, use a material model of procession in which an effect proceeds from its cause or in which a cause proceeds to its effect. In a material entity such a procession is always a transient, external act between cause and effect considered as two different [diversi] entities, which is inappropriate to God, who is not dependent on anything external to herself or really related to creatures.

The model must therefore be taken from the intellectual life, in which cause and effect are mutually internal and which is therefore closer to the divine. An intellectual act is an immanent, not a transient, act and as such remains within the agent. When the intellect understands something, such an act generates a conception of the object understood, that *in which* it understands the nature of the object, as distinct from the species *by which* it understands the object. Both the act and the conception, both the cause and effect, remain within the person understanding. This conception is the mental, internal word or "word of the heart," the word in the most proper sense of the term, of which the spoken word or word of the voice is only an external expression. It is this intellectual emanation of the word proceeding from the speaker yet remaining in her that is the model for understanding the procession in God. To understand something means that the intellect in act becomes one with the intelligible in act. The more a thing is understood, the more the intellectual conception becomes intimate and united with the intellectual agent. In an intelligible procession, then, the more perfectly a thing proceeds, the more closely it is one with the source whence it proceeds. In a human being the concept or internal word is an accident distinct from her essence, but in God it is the same as God herself, "since there is nothing in God that is not the divine essence."[17] Since God is supremely perfect, the divine Word is necessarily perfectly one with the source from which it proceeds without any diversity [diversitas]. Thus—and in other ways yet to be explained—divine processions are compatible with divine simplicity.[18]

How many processions, then, are there in God? For Aquinas, there are two, and only two, processions; one is called "generation," the procession of the Son, while the other is "procession" in the technical sense, the procession of the Holy Spirit. Divine processions are immanent activities proper to an intellectual agent, and there are only two such actions, that of the intellect, in which the object understood is in the knower, and that of the will or love, in which the object loved is in the lover. The emotions and sensible appetites that also constitute part of human nature imply materiality and external dependence and, therefore, do not exist in God. While there are many more processions in us, as there are many acts of the intellect and many acts of the will in us, in God there are only two such acts or processions, that of the intellect and that of the will, because "God understands all things by one simple act, and by one act also she wills all things."[19] We understand different things through separate concepts and words; there is no one word or concept in which we understand all things. God, however, "understands both herself and everything else through her essence, by one act," and thus "the single divine Word is expressive of all that is in God, not only of the persons but also of creatures."[20] There is only one perfect Word and only one perfect Love in God.

Of course, in God intellect and will are not two different things [aliud]. Still, their very nature [ratio] requires a certain ordered relationship between them, insofar as nothing can be loved by the will unless it is first known and conceived in the intellect. Just as there is a certain order of the Word to its divine principle from which it proceeds, although in God there is an identity between the substance of the intellect and its concept, so there is at least a distinction of order [distinctio ordinis] between the processions of intellect and will, insofar as love by its nature can proceed only from the concept of the intellect whereby the object loved is known, although in God they are the same. No object can be loved unless it is first known.[21]

The first procession in God, then, is the generation of the Son. This generation is not to be taken in the human or finite mode of change from non-existence to existence or from potentiality to act, or of origination of a living being from a conjoined living principle like hair emerging from a body or even a worm emerging from animals with generic similitude. Like all generation, it signifies the origination of a living being with the similitude of the same specific nature from a conjoined living principle, but as divine generation it occurs in a mode that does not involve change from potentiality to act. The concept of the intellect is a likeness of the object conceived and exists in the same nature as the intellect because in God the act of understanding and the act of existence are the same. Thus the Word in God proceeds by way of intellectual action, an activity of a living being, from a conjoined principle, the Father, with the similitude of the same specific nature.

In us, the act of understanding is not the same as the substance itself of the intellect, and our words are not of the same nature as the source from which they proceed. The idea of generation, therefore, does not apply—except metaphorically—to the intelligible emanation that occurs in us. We too use the language of "conception" to convey the similitude between concepts and things understood, but there is no identity of nature between them, which makes it a metaphor. The divine act of intellect, however, is the very substance of the one who understands. The Word proceeds as subsisting in the same divine nature and can, therefore, "properly" be called begotten and Son. The use of organic expressions like "conception" and "birth" in Scripture in reference to the origination of divine wisdom must be understood in this way. In a supereminent sense, then, there is a generation of the Son in God.[22]

The second procession is the procession of the Holy Spirit. The difference between the procession of the Word and that of the Holy Spirit is the difference between intellect and will. "The intellect is made actual by the object understood residing according to its own likeness in the intellect; whereas the will is made actual, not by any similitude of the object willed within it, but by its having a certain inclination to the thing willed."[23] The procession of the intellect is by way of similitude and is called generation, and that of the will is by way of impulse and movement towards an object [secundum rationem impellentis et moventis in aliquid]. What proceeds in God by way of love, therefore, does not proceed as Son but as Spirit, which designates a certain vital movement and impulse [vitalis motio et impulsio], as we are moved or impelled by love to perform an action.

Why is the procession of the Holy Spirit not also called generation? Is it not true that all that exists in God is God and is one with the divine nature? Does not the Father express himself, i.e., his divine nature, in understanding and loving himself? Does not all procession, therefore, involve communication of the divine nature? If there is a likeness of nature involved in every procession, why is the procession of the Spirit not also called generation? For Aquinas, in God there is more than one way of communicating nature, whereas there is only one way of doing so, i.e., generation, in all created things. Because of the identity of the divine nature and divine operation, every immanent operation or procession does communicate the divine nature. Depending on the difference of the operations involved, however, the divine nature can be communicated in different ways. This is also where the difference of persons must be located: in the order of relationship between the different processions. This order is based on the nature of intellect and will and names each procession accordingly; it is not derived from the divine essence, which is one and common to all persons.[24]

Thus, the Holy Spirit that proceeds as love receives the divine nature, as does the Son, but the Holy Spirit is not said to be born. Similitude belongs to the very nature of word as a likeness of the object understood, but it does not belong to the very nature of love as though love itself were a likeness. Rather, if similitude also belongs to love in some way, it does so not because similitude constitutes the essence of love but because it is the principle or cause of loving: similitude induces love. Likeness is the very essence of word, but love as such does not proceed as a likeness of that whence it proceeds. What, then, do we call this procession of love? As we can name God only from creatures, the procession of the Word is called generation because generation is the only principle of communication of nature available to us from created beings. There is no other form of procession that involves communication of nature in created beings, and thus no appropriate name for the procession of the Spirit. The procession of the Spirit may, however, be called spiration.[25]

Relations

Essential to the classical doctrine of the Trinity is the notion that persons are subsisting relations. By means of relations based on processions, the tradition seeks to introduce plurality into the unity of the divine nature without impairing its simplicity. As Boethius put it, "in God the substance contains the unity; and relation multiplies the trinity."[26] It is crucial, therefore, to have an accurate understanding of the metaphysics of relation in understanding the Trinity.

Relations in God are based only on immanent actions, which are also actions of origination, and not on extrinsic or transient actions toward creatures because these are not, for Aquinas, real relations in God. There are only two actions or processions of this kind, that of the Word derived from the action of the intellect, and that of Love derived from the action of the will. Each of these processions implies two opposed relations. The procession of the generation of the Word implies paternity, the relation of the principle of generation to the generated, and filiation, the relation of the one proceeding from the principle to the principle itself. Likewise, the procession or spiration of the Spirit implies, for lack of better words, "spiration," the relation of the principle of spiration to the one proceeding, and "procession," the relation of the one proceeding from the principle to the principle. Thus, there are four and only four relations in God. God may understand and will many created things, but this does not add to the four relations because God understands and wills all created things by understanding and willing herself, and because in God there is perfect identity both between the creative intellect and its object and between the creative will and its object, which rules out any change in God and therefore of any real relation of God to creatures.[27]

Are the persons distinguished only by relations, as Boethius claimed? What is the principle of distinction and plurality among the persons who share the same divine nature? There are two such principles, origin and relation. These do not differ in reality, but they do in the mode of signification. Origin is signified in the mode of act such as generation, relation in the mode of form such as paternity. Since relation follows upon act, some have argued that the divine persons are distinguished by origin, not by relation. The Father is distinguished from the Son insofar as the Father begets and the Son is begotten, relations only manifesting the distinction of persons already made by the act of origination.

Aquinas, however, disagrees, for two reasons. First, distinction must be based on something intrinsic to the things that are distinguished. In created things it is based on either matter or form. Origin, however, does not designate anything intrinsic but only the way from something to something, e.g., from the generator to the generated. Thus the generator and the generated cannot be distinguished by generation alone, which remains extrinsic, but require something intrinsic to both by which one is distinguished from the other. In a divine person there is nothing to presuppose but essence and relation. Since the persons agree or are united in essence, they can only be distinguished from one another by relations. The divine persons are not distinguished as regards being [esse] in which they subsist or in anything absolute but only as regards something relative.

Second, the distinction of the divine persons is not to be so understood as to divide the indivisible divine essence common to them. The distinguishing principles themselves must "constitute" the things that are distinct. Now relations or properties do distinguish and constitute the persons insofar as they are themselves subsisting persons; paternity is the Father, filiation the Son, because of the real identity in God between the abstract and the concrete. It is, however, against the very *ratio* of origin to constitute a person. In an active sense origin means proceeding from a subsisting person, which it presupposes as its subject, while in a passive sense—as nativity—it means the way to a subsisting person not yet existing, therefore not yet constituting the person. Relations also presuppose the distinction of the subjects when it is only an accident as in the case of relations among material substances, but they do not presuppose but bring about distinction when they are subsistent as in the case of divine relations.

For Aquinas, then, both origin and relation distinguish the persons, yet it is better to say that persons are distinguished principally by relation because in our mode of understanding, the act of origination remains extrinsic to the things to be distinguished and presupposes their existence without, therefore, really constituting them, while relation is intrinsic to the things distinguished and constitutes them in their distinction. Thus, "Father" or "Son" signifies not only a property but also a person because it means the relation that is distinctive and constitutive of the person, while "Begetter" or "Begotten" signifies only a property because it means the origin which as such is not distinctive or constitutive of the person. For the same reason it will not do to substitute active verbal terms of origination such as "initiation, fruition, and emergence," as David Cunningham suggests, for relational terms such as Father, Son, and the Holy Spirit.[28]

The only source of distinction in God, however, is not just any relation but the particular kind of relation called "relative opposition." Things that are not opposed but merely different can belong to the same thing, as wisdom, goodness, and simplicity all belong to the same divine nature. If divine persons are really distinct, then, such distinction must be based on some sort of opposition among them. There are many kinds of distinctions that will not apply to God, such as the distinction of being from non-being, from which follows the opposition of affirmation and negation; the distinction of the perfect from the imperfect, from which follows the opposition of habit and privation; or the distinction of diversity of form, from which follows the opposition of contrariety. The only source of distinction in God, therefore, can be "relative" opposition or the opposition of relation as the respect of one towards another, such as begetter and begotten, spirating and spirated.

Relative opposition may be based on quantity, which in turn may be based on diversity of quantity (such as the double and the half, the greater or the lesser) or on unity itself (such as identity of one substance, equality of quantity, and similarity of quality). Neither of these two modes of opposition would apply to God: the diversity of quantity would take away the equality of three persons, while unity allows no distinction. Relative opposition may also be founded on action and passion, as in the case of master and slave, mover and moved, or parent and child; but this mode of opposition stems from transient action always involving difference of power and does not apply to God. *The only source of distinction which posits a distinction without also positing difference in nature and power is that of origin in which one thing produces another similar and equal to itself in nature and power. Persons in God are distinguished only by relations of relative opposition based on origin, that is, by the divine processions discussed above.*[29]

It is important to note here, however, that it is not the relative opposition as such but the presence of such opposition in the divine nature in which there cannot be any accident that makes the relation subsistent. Being parents and children among human beings involves relative opposition, but this does not make parenthood or childhood subsistent. Both remain accidents in human beings. It is a real misunderstanding, therefore, for David Cunningham to say that a relation is subsistent whenever there is relative opposition, and to argue that "motherhood, childhood, and mediating," one of his alternative trinitarian formulas, are, therefore, subsistent relations.[30]

Are the relations among the Father, Son, and Holy Spirit, then, real or only logical? For Aquinas, we have a "real" relation when it is rooted in the very nature of things as between two things that are mutually ordered and inclined by their very nature, like a heavy body inclined to fall to earth, while we have a "logical" relation when it exists only in the apprehension of reason comparing one thing to another, like the relation of species to genus, of being to non-being, or of the known to the knower. The distinction between real and logical relations is not, as LaCugna misconstrues it, a distinction between "nature" and "accidents," but between "reality" and "reason" as sources of that distinction.[31] When something proceeds from a principle of the same nature, and what proceeds and that from which it proceeds agree in the same order, their relation is considered real. Since divine processions occur in an identity of nature, their relations are necessarily real relations. As both the divine intellect and the concept proceeding from that intellect are real, so is their relation. Paternity and filiation are real relations in God.[32]

By saying that the divine relations are real, not just logical, and that God is truly Father, Son, and Holy Spirit, not just in our manner of understanding, we avoid the Sabellian heresy; but by saying that such relations are real because they are really rooted in the divine nature, are we not also introducing a composition of essence and accidents into the divine nature and destroying divine simplicity? For Aquinas, the fact that relations are real and distinct from one another in God does not violate divine simplicity because of the unique character of relation among accidents.

Aquinas distinguishes two aspects in the nature of accidents and relation. One aspect is the existential aspect regarding the mode of existence or *esse* common to all accidents as accidents, whose *esse* is to inhere in a subject [accidentis esse est inesse subjecto]. Considered as an accident, relation, like any other accident, has accidental existence [esse accidentale], i.e., inherence in a subject. The other aspect is the formal aspect concerning the specific nature or proper meaning [propria ratio] of each category of accidents. Here the category of relation shows itself to be unique among all the categories of accidents. In all other categories, such as quality and quantity, even the specific nature of the categories is derived from their respect or reference to the subject [comparatio ad sub-jectum] in which they inhere; thus quantity means precisely the measure of substance, and quality the disposition of substance. The proper mean-ing of relation, however, is derived from its reference not to the subject in which it inheres but to something other than the subject [respectus ad aliud]. Relation is not something internally determined by the subject in which it inheres, although in material things it does necessarily inhere in a subject. Rather, its unique meaning lies in pure referentiality to an other, a respect, reference, or tendency from the subject to something other, assisting or standing toward [ad-sistens] something else.

Aquinas applies this twofold aspect of relation in created things to God with appropriate negation and eminence. Regarding its existential aspect, whatever has only accidental existence in creatures has substantial existence [esse substantiale] in God because whatever exists in God, by virtue of her simplicity, is her essence and there is no accident inhering in her as in a subject. The really existing relation in God, therefore, has the existence [esse] of the divine essence itself and is altogether identical with it [idem omnino ei]. Relations that remain accidental and distinct from the essence in creatures are identified with the essence and become sub-sisting relations in God. Regarding its formal aspect, however, relation signifies a reference [habitudo] to something else, to its opposite term, not to the essence. The "Father" signifies a reference to the "Son," and the "Son" signifies a reference to the "Father," but neither as such signi-fies a reference to the divine essence. Thus, in God relation is "really" [secundum rem] the same as essence insofar as there is no real difference between the *esse* of relation and the *esse* of essence, and relation differs from essence only in "the mode of intelligibility" [secundum intelligen-tiae rationem] insofar as relation implies the respect to its opposite that is not implied in the term "essence," which, in creatures, does mean two different things (as, for example, being a father, a relation, and being a human being, an essence).[33]

It is crucial to take account of both aspects of relation. If we ignore the existential aspect and attend only to the formal, we fall into the error of Gilbert de la Porree who made the claim, later revoked, that relations in God are assistant or externally determined, which denies the divinity of God and turns her into a creature. If we ignore the formal aspect and attend only to the existential, we deny the reality of divine relations and affirm only a unitarian God far from the Trinity of Christian faith. It is by maintaining both the existential and formal aspects of relation that we can do justice both to the simplicity of God and to the reality of the divine, trinitarian relations; the former because of the existential aspect that identifies the divine essence and the divine relations in their *esse* or existence and avoids composition and multiplicity in God; the latter because of the formal aspect that relates the divine relations not to the divine essence but to one another precisely in their pure relationality and referentiality. Likewise, not only the reality of divine relations but also a multiplicity of divine relations truly distinguished from one another are possible because of this purely referential character of relation. There cannot be multiplicity and distinction in the "absolute" reality of the divine essence which by its very nature allows only unity and simplicity, but there can be and must be in the "relative" reality of relations whose very nature lies in the regard of one to another [respectus unius ad alterum], which implies distinction and multiplicity. This distinction is based on real relative opposition in God.

It is primarily this uniqueness of relation among accidents, not, as Cunningham claims, the biblical insight that the character of persons becomes apparent only through relations, that leads Aquinas to introduce relations into the account of the immanent Trinity.[34] In fact, for Aquinas, the simpler a thing is, the more relations it can have because the power to cause effects and generate relations of effects to itself is proportionate to the ontological simplicity of the agent. The supreme simplicity of God can generate "infinite" relations between God and creatures, insofar as she produces creatures different from her but also in some way like her.[35]

One ancient objection against the identification of the divine relations or persons with the divine essence, repeated recently in exactly the same words by social trinitarians such as Cornelius Plantinga, Jr., is that if two things are the same as some third thing, it must follow that the two things are identical with each other, and that, likewise, if the divine persons are identical with the divine essence, it must follow that the persons are identical with one another, that is to say, that there is only one person in God.[36] Following Aristotle, Aquinas answers that two things (e.g., relations), each identical with the same third thing (e.g., the essence), will be identical with each other only if the first identity (e.g., relation and essence) is both real and logical, but not if they still differ logically [ratione]. For Aquinas, as we just saw, there is a "real" identity between essence and relation insofar as the *esse* of relation is the same as the *esse* of essence, but there is also a "logical" difference or difference in meaning [ratio] between them insofar as the *ratio* of relation indicates pure referentiality to another which is not implied in the *ratio* of essence. As Aristotle says, action and passion are really the same as motion. Still, it does not follow that action is the same as passion. Action implies reference as of something *from* which there is motion in the thing moved, while passion implies reference as of something which is from another. Similarly, paternity is the same as the divine essence in reality, as is filiation. Still, in their proper meaning paternity and filiation imply respects that are mutually opposed and which are not implied in the name of essence, which do distinguish one relation or person from the other.[37]

Persons

As important for an accurate understanding of the classical trinitarian doctrine as are "procession" and "relation" is the terminology of "person" and other related metaphysical terms such as "substance," "hypostasis," "subsistence," "essence," and "nature." According to the hallowed Boethian definition, which Aquinas accepts, a person is "an individual substance of a rational nature" [rationalis naturae individua substantia]. It is important to note that this is a metaphysical, not a psychological or a phenomenological, definition and is therefore not to be confused with our contemporary conception of "personality" as a "center of consciousness."

The "person" is first of all a "substance," a word which has itself two different meanings that must be distinguished, designated by Aristotle as "first substance" and "second substance." As "second substance" it signifies the essence, quiddity, or nature of a thing as covered by its definition, for which the Greeks use the term *ousia,* translated as "essence." It is not itself a thing, like a human being, a horse, or God, but only a constitutive principle of a being by which a being is the kind of being it is. It is in this sense of essence that the trinitarian tradition speaks of the Son as being born of the "substance" of the Father, of his being "consubstantial [homoousion]" with the Father, and of God being three persons in one "substance."

The person is not a substance in this sense but in the sense of "first substance," which refers to the whole concrete entity, not to a principle of being. It exists in itself and is individualized by itself, unlike accidents that can exist only by inhering in a first substance and are individualized only by the subjects in which they inhere. First substances refer to individual entities in the category of substance as opposed to the categories of accidents in Aristotle. As such, they exclude both pure universality like "humanity" and parts like a hand or even a soul, neither of which is a (first) substance. As individuals substances have particular modes of subsistence and cannot be assumed by others, as can "nature," e.g., the human nature of Christ assumed by the Word. They cannot be either predicated of or made present in another subject, as accidents can. Depending on the different aspects of substantiality to be highlighted, a first substance has been called by many different names, a "supposit" insofar as it is the ultimate subject of being and action, a "thing of nature [res naturae]" insofar it underlies some common nature, "subsistence" insofar as it exists in itself, not in another thing, and a "hypostasis" or "substance" insofar as it underlies the accidents.

Not every first substance, however, is a person. The person is a first substance of a certain kind, an individual substance of a "rational" nature, i.e., an individual substance who has dominion over her own actions through reason and whose individuality, therefore, is a result of rational decision and action. "Individual substance," then, signifies the singular in the genus of substance, and "rational nature" signifies the singular in rational substances. This is not an attempt to define this or that singularity precisely in its singularity but only the common *ratio* of singularity. It is crucial here, however, to note some confusing differences between East and West in the usage of the term "hypostasis." In the strict sense, "hypostasis" refers to any individual in the category of first substance, e.g., a tree or a dog, but the Greeks usually apply it to persons, i.e., individual substances of a rational nature. Furthermore, it corresponds etymologically to the Latin "substantia" with its twofold confusing meanings as first substance (subsistence) and second substance (essence). Therefore, when the Greeks use "three hypostases" for the Latin terminology of "three persons" and "three subsistences," it can be misinterpreted as "three substances" in the sense of second substance, meaning "three essences or natures." It is far preferable, therefore, to use "subsistence" rather than "substance" for "hypostasis."[38]

Can we, then, predicate personhood of God? For Aquinas, the person as a subsistent individual of a rational nature is what is most perfect in all creation and must be attributed to God whose essence contains all perfections. It is fitting [conveniens] that we apply the name *person* to God but must do so in a more excellent way [excellentiori modo]. In its objective meaning—or "content of signification"—"person" belongs to God preeminently [maxime], far more to God than to creatures. In its "mode of signification," however, it is essential to purify the concept of any finite characteristics before applying it to God by way of eminence. Thus, "rational" for God does not mean discursive reason as in the case of human reason but perfect and pure intuition. Nor is God an "individual" in the sense of singularity that is materially conditioned and therefore separated from other individuals but only in the sense of incommunicability. God is a substance in the sense of self-subsistence, not in the sense of something underlying accidents.[39]

If the "person" in God means a (first) "substance," however, does it exclude the signification of "relation"? Does the "person" express the divine nature absolutely and the three persons relatively? If it means only the divine essence, how can we predicate it of three persons in their respective distinctiveness? Can we say, then, that it means both the essence and the relation, the essence directly and the relation indirectly, or vice versa? In order to escape from this quandary, Aquinas begins, as usual, by making distinctions. Just as it makes sense to distinguish between asking the meaning of "animal" in general and asking its meaning as it applies to "human beings," so it is necessary to distinguish between the meaning of "person" in general and its meaning as applied to God, all the more so in view of the qualitative difference between God and creatures. Person in general means an individual substance of a rational nature. An individual, however, is an entity that is undivided in itself yet is distinguished from others. The person, therefore, signifies what is distinct in any nature. In human beings it refers to "this" flesh, "these" bones, and "this" soul, the individuating principles of a human being, which belongs to the particular meaning of the human person, although not to the general meaning of all persons.

Once more, then, what is the individuating principle in God? As we have seen, all distinction in God is solely through the relations of origin. Now, relation in God is not an accident inhering in a subject as are relations of material things; it is the divine essence itself and thus subsistent. As divinity or the divine essence is God, a subsisting subject, so divine paternity, a relation, is God the Father, a subsisting person. Thus, a divine person signifies a relation as subsisting, as (first) substance— a hypostasis subsisting in the divine nature. Person signifies relation directly and the essence indirectly. Insofar as the divine essence is the same as the hypostasis, it is also true to say that person signifies the essence directly and the relation indirectly. In God the hypostasis is expressed and distinguished by the relation, which is to say that relation as such enters into the notion of the person indirectly. Heretics who attacked the use of the term "person" failed to clearly perceive this *relational* meaning of person and used it absolutely like any other substantive term.[40]

If there are several real relations in God in their respective distinctiveness, and if these relations subsist in the divine nature, then there are several persons in God. One might ask, however, why it is only relations, and not other properties as well, that constitute persons in God. Here Aquinas distinguishes between "absolute" properties such as goodness and wisdom, i.e., properties that can be taken in themselves, and "relative" properties such as paternity and filiation, i.e., properties that necessarily entail regard to an other. Absolute properties are not mutually opposed and thus not really distinguished from one another. They subsist, but not as several subsistent realities. The absolute properties in creatures do not subsist, although they are really distinguished from one another, like whiteness and sweetness. The relative properties in God do subsist and are really distinguished from one another. Hence the plurality of persons in God. The supreme unity and simplicity of the divine nature excludes every kind of plurality of things taken absolutely, but not the plurality of relations. Relations are predicated relatively and do not introduce composition into the thing of which they are predicated.[41]

Why only three persons in God, however, when there are four relations in her? Divine persons are subsisting relations really distinct from one another. A real distinction can come only from relative opposition. Two opposite relations must then refer to two persons, but if a relation is not opposed, it must belong to the same person. Thus, paternity and filiation, as opposed relations, necessarily belong to two persons. The subsisting paternity is the person of the Father, the subsisting filiation the person of the Son. The other two relations, spiration and procession, are not opposed to either paternity or filiation, but they are opposed to each other and cannot belong to one person. Either one of them must belong to both the Father and Son, or one must belong to one person and the other to another person. Procession cannot belong to both the Father and the Son or to either of them because this would make generation, the procession of the intellect, issue from the procession of love, from which spiration and procession are derived. Thus spiration must belong to both the Father and the Son because it has no relative opposition either to paternity or to filiation. Spiration is a relation but not a property in the sense of belonging to only one person. Procession belongs to the Holy Spirit who proceeds by way of love. There are three relations, paternity, filiation, and procession, that are also three personal properties, constituting three persons. Thus only three persons in God.[42]

What, then, do unity, plurality, and numeral terms in general signify in God? Do they denote anything real in God? Do they have any positive meaning or only a negative meaning? According to Aquinas, plurality is a result of division, which may be of two kinds. One kind of division is material, from which result quantity and number. The other kind of division is formal, which occurs through opposite and diverse forms and from which result a multitude that do not belong to a genus but are transcendental in the sense in which being is divided by one and by many. This kind of multitude is found only in immaterial things. Numerical terms in God are not derived from number, a species of quantity that denotes an accident added to being. Numerical terms of this kind, like other bodily properties such as length and breadth, can apply to God only in a metaphorical sense. Properly, numerical terms in God derive from multitude in the transcendental sense, in which the term "one" is convertible with being and adds nothing to being except a negation of division, or in other words, where "one" signifies undivided being. "One human being" thus means the undivided nature or substance of a human being; "many things" means many things each of which is undivided in itself. Thus "one divine essence" means the essence undivided, "one person" the person undivided, and "many persons" those persons and their individual undividedness.[43]

We must next ask whether the term "person" is common to the three divine persons, since only the divine essence is common and "person" denotes something incommunicable. The term "person" is indeed common to the three, but not in the sense of the common possession of a thing by three, as in the case of the one divine essence commonly possessed by the three; this would reduce three persons to one person. Now, even in human affairs the name "person" is common by a community of meaning [ratio], not as a genus or species (such as "animal" or "human being," respectively) that signifies the common nature itself, but as an unspecified individual (in the sense of "some man") that signifies the common nature with the determinate mode of existence of singular things, i.e., something self-subsisting as distinct from others. "Person" does not signify an individual on the part of a nature but a reality subsisting in that nature. What is common to the three persons in idea [ratio] is that each subsists distinctly from the others in the divine nature. Thus the name "person" is common to the three in idea. The personal reality of the person is indeed incommunicable, but the mode of incommunicable existence as such can be common to many.[44]

The doctrine of the Trinity, which in its etymological sense seems to signify the one essence of the three persons or tri-unity, but in its strict sense rather signifies the number of persons of one essence according to Aquinas,[45] is beset with many heretical possibilities. The most notable are those of Arius, who together with the trinity of persons posited a trinity of substances or essences, and Sabellius, who together with the unity of essence posited a unity of person. Avoiding these errors and observing the grammar of trinitarian language requires great linguistic care and sophisticated metaphysical sensibility. In order to avoid Arian errors, Aquinas suggests that we do not use for God terms like "diversity" and "difference," which imply difference of essence, lest we take away the unity of essence, but instead use the term "distinction," which can accommodate the relative opposition among persons without denying the unity of essence. We should likewise avoid the terms "separation" and "division" (which refer to parts of a whole and risk denying the simplicity and singleness of the divine essence), "disparity" (lest we take away equality), and "alien" and "discrepant" (lest we remove similitude).

As for Sabellian errors, we must avoid the term "only" [unicus] or use it with extreme care, lest we take away the plurality of persons. For instance, we must not speak of the "only" God when deity is common to several persons; however, to refer to the "only" Son is fine because there is no plurality of Sons. Other terms to avoid in this connection are "singularity" (lest we deny the communicability of the divine essence), "confused" (lest we remove the order of their nature from the persons), and "solitary" (lest we take away the society [consortium] of three persons). We can say that the Son is "other" than the Father in the masculine sense of *alius,* which implies difference of supposit or person, but not that the Son is "other" than the Father in the neuter sense of *aliud,* which implies difference of essence.[46]

Finally, how does the term "alone" [solus] properly apply to essential terms in God? As a categorematical term that ascribes its meaning to a given supposit absolutely, like a "white" man, the term "alone" cannot be applied to God because it would imply that God was solitary. A syncategorematical term, however, imports and qualifies the order of the predicate to the subject, as in "Socrates alone writes," which does not mean that Socrates is solitary but rather that although others may be with him, he is the only one writing. As syncategorematical, the term "alone" can be joined to any "essential" term in God (i.e., a term that expresses or refers to the divine essence) as excluding the predicate from all things but God, as when we say, "God alone is eternal," because nothing but God is eternal.[47]

As whatever is known is known according to the mode of the knower, so we also name a thing as we understand it. Our human intellect cannot attain to the absolute simplicity of the divine essence considered in itself and must, therefore, apprehend and name divine things according to its own human mode, i.e., insofar as they are found in the sensible things from which it derives its knowledge. Now, in sensible things we use abstract terms such as "animality" and "maleness" to signify simple forms, and concrete terms such as "animal" and "male" to signify subsistent things. Similarly, with regard to divine things, we have to use abstract terms, such as deity, wisdom, paternity, and filiation to express their formal simplicity, and concrete terms, such as God, the wise, Father, and Son to express their subsistence and completeness.

Aquinas mentions two motives for this differential use of abstract and concrete names for God. One is apologetic: In the confession of the trinitarian faith we are often asked to answer whereby [quo] the three persons are one God and whereby they are three persons. Here, just as we have to use abstract terms to answer that they are one in "essence" or "deity," so we must be able to use abstract terms to signify the properties or notions whereby the persons are noted and distinguished from one another. The divine essence is signified as "what" [quid], the person as "who" [quis], and the property or notion as "whereby" [quo]. The other motive is clarificatory. One person in God, i.e., the Father, is related to two persons, the Son and the Holy Spirit, and is related to them by two relations, paternity and spiration, not by one relation, which, since "relation alone multiplies the trinity," would make one person out of the two. There are as many relations as there are relative oppositions. Since there is only one person in the Father but two relations in him whereby he is respectively related to the Son and to the Holy Spirit, it is necessary to signify each of the two relations and notions separately, which entails the use of abstract terms.[48]

Notions

According to Aquinas, there are in God one divine essence, two processions, three persons, four relations, and five "notions." A notion is the proper idea [propria ratio] whereby we know and characterize a divine person. As we have seen, the only source of distinction in God is that of origin, which includes both the idea of someone from whom another comes and that of someone that comes from another. This is how a person is known. As the Father is from no one, he is known by innascibility. As the source of the Son and the Holy Spirit, he is also known by paternity and common spiration. The Son comes from the Father and is known by filiation. As source of the Holy Spirit along with the Father, he is also known, as is the Father, by common spiration. The Holy Spirit is from the Father and the Son and is known by procession, not by the fact that another proceeds from her. Thus, there are five notions— innascibility, paternity, filiation, common spiration, and procession. Of these five notions, only four are relations; innascibility is not a relation because it is not a relative opposition between two terms. Only four notions are properties; common spiration is not a property [proprietas] because it belongs to two persons. Only three notions are personal notions or notions constituting [constituentes] persons: paternity, filiation, and procession. The other two, innascibility and common spiration, are notions of persons in the sense that they help characterize a person, but not personal notions in the sense that they involve those relative oppositions constitutive of persons in their mutual distinction. The five notions in God are not realities or things [res] in God like the one essence and three persons; they are "proper marks" [propriae rationes] that make the persons known but without making God quinary.[49]

Notions are not subjects of existence and action, as are persons. Therefore, we cannot predicate actions, essential or personal, of these notions by saying, for example, that "paternity begets," that "paternity is wise." Essential perfections, however, that are not ordered to any act but only remove creaturely imperfections from God, can be predicated of notions. We can say, for example, that "paternity is eternal." Because of real identity we can also predicate substantive terms, both personal and essential, and say that "paternity is God" or that "paternity is the Father."[50]

Father, Son, and Holy Spirit

The Father

After an analysis of the ontological constitution of the Trinity, its processions, relations, persons, and notions, we now move on to an individual consideration of the three persons. We begin with the person of the Father. Contrary to LaCugna's claim that the Father in Aquinas is only one of the three persons who share equally the divine essence, not, as in the Greek tradition, the source of divinity [fons divinitatis],[51] the most important characteristic of the Father, for Aquinas, is precisely that he is "the principle of the whole Godhead [principium totius deitatis], not as generating or spirating it, but as communicating it by generation and spiration."[52] He is the "principle" in the sense of something from which another proceeds in some way. A "principle" is wider than a "cause," which implies diversity of substance and dependence of one on another as well as a distance of perfection and power between cause and effect. None of these is implied in "principle," which implies only a certain order of one thing to another, as when we say that a point is the principle of a line or that the first part of a line is the principle of a line.[53] In this sense, the Father is the principle of the whole deity, thus also of the Son and the Spirit, without implying the subjection or inferiority of the two persons proceeding from him. He is not, as Leonardo Boff alleges, the source of divinity in the sense of "cause."[54] By derivation, the word "principle" has a primary meaning not of priority but of origin.[55] How it is possible for there to be a procession in God without a relation of subjection or inferiority will be considered later on. For now, let us continue our treatment of the Father himself.

Aquinas asks how proper and appropriate the term "father" is to a divine person. For Aquinas the proper name of a person is what distinguishes the person from all other persons. Since it is paternity that distinguishes the person of the Father from the other persons, the name "father" is the proper name of the person of the Father. Among us human beings relation is not a subsisting person, and "father," a relation, does not signify a person as such but an accident of a person. But in God "person" signifies precisely a relation subsisting in the divine nature. Likewise, with human beings the word is not a subsistence and cannot properly be called begotten or son, but the divine Word is something subsistent in the divine nature and is properly called Son, just as his principle is also properly called Father.

For Aquinas, the terms "generation" and "paternity," like other terms properly applied to God, are said of God *before* [per prius] they can be said of creatures, as regards the thing signified although not as regards the mode of signification. As Ephesians 3:14 says, all paternity in heaven and on earth is named from the Father of Jesus Christ. It is of the essence [ratio] of the generator to generate what is like itself in form. A generation is the truer and more perfect, the nearer is the generated to the form of the generator. Now, in the divine generation the form of the begetter and begotten, i.e., the divine essence, is numerically the same; the only distinction is relational. In creatures, by contrast, the form, i.e., human nature, is not numerically but only specifically the same; it is accompanied by many distinguishing and individuating factors in addition to relation. Generation and paternity, then, in their proper *rationes,* apply more properly to God than to creatures.[56] "True" paternity is "the divine paternity by which the Father communicates his whole nature [totam naturam] to the Son without any imperfection," and from which we also derive our own capacity to procreate.[57] It is worth noting that Aquinas locates the essence of paternity in the communication of the same nature and the love that motivates the communication, rather than in some moral qualities such as love and care which are *per se* independent of the communication, as do John D. Zizioulas and Thomas F. Torrance, who also remain agnostic about the meaning of divine generation and fatherhood.[58] In the sense of the communication of the same nature, Aquinas holds that the first person of the Trinity is truly and properly although analogically "father," not metaphorically, as some misinterpret him, ignoring the distinction between analogy and metaphor established above.[59]

Is "father" primarily [per prius] a personal name applied to the Father or primarily an essential name applied to the whole Trinity? A name is applied primarily to that which preserves the whole meaning [ratio] of the word perfectly, and secondarily to that which does so in a limited way. The latter bears the name only by reason of its similitude to the essential meaning of the word contained in the former. Thus, the name "lion" applies first to the animal and secondarily to a human being who shows something of a lion's nature. Now, the perfect *ratio* of paternity and filiation is found in God the Father and God the Son because of the oneness of the nature and glory that belong to them. In the creature's relation to the triune God as Father, however, filiation is not perfect because creator and creature do not share the same nature but only a certain likeness that is the more perfect the nearer we approach the true idea [ratio] of filiation—that of the Son—and thus the more we are "conformed [conformes] to him."[60] This does not deny that we can only acquire the concepts of father and son from created things, but we are concerned here with the question of priority in the matter of the reality of the thing named, not with how we first acquire the concepts.[61]

The Word proceeding from the Father proceeds as the principle of the production of creatures, as the word conceived in the mind of the artist is first understood to proceed from the artist before the thing designed, which is produced in likeness to the word conceived in her mind. The Son proceeds from the Father before the creature, having what he receives by nature while creatures receive it only by grace. The name of filiation only applies to the creature insofar as it participates in the likeness of the Son (Romans 8:29). Unlike Pannenberg, who limits paternity to the Father and forbids any application to the whole Trinity, Aquinas insists that paternity is applied first to the personal relation of the Father to the Son but also admits its analogical applicability to the relation of God or the whole Trinity to creatures.[62] Thus God is called the Father of irrational creatures by reason of a trace or vestige; of rational creatures by reason of the likeness of his image; of adoptive children ordained to the heritage of eternal glory by reason of the similitude of grace; and of those already enjoying the vision of glory by reason of glory.

The Father is the first principle not only in the sense of being related to what proceeds from himself, the Son and the Holy Spirit, and thus known by paternity and common spiration, but also in the sense of "a principle not from a principle" [principium non de principio], of not being from another, and thus known by innascibility signified by the word "unbegotten" [ingenitus]. "Unbegotten" as a property of the Father does not mean mere negation of generation, which would also apply to the Holy Spirit, who is not begotten either, but spirated. It means not being derived from another in any way whatsoever including generation and spiration, while also being the principle or origin of everything else. In this sense it belongs neither to the Holy Spirit nor even to the divine essence, in which at least the Son and the Holy Spirit derive from another, but to the Father alone.[63]

The Son

If Aquinas emphasizes the Father as the unbegotten principle of both the whole deity, sharing his numerically identical divine essence with the Son and the Holy Spirit, and of all created paternity, he emphasizes the Son as the Word and Image of the Father. Taking the Son as Word,[64] the first question is whether the Word can be a personal name in God. Is not the divine Word a metaphor, as Origen said? If knowledge and thought are essential terms in God, how can word, so closely associated with them, be a personal term? Furthermore, don't all three persons "speak"? For Aquinas, however, the Word in God, taken in its proper sense, is only a personal name, not an essential name.

The human word, in its proper sense, has three aspects: the word that is spoken by the voice, or the exterior word; the interior word, or concept of the mind that is expressed by the spoken word; and the exterior word as it is imagined. Insofar as both the spoken and imagined sounds are words only when they express an interior concept of the mind, words primarily and principally refer to these interior concepts. In God, who needs neither voice nor imagination, word means strictly the concept of the intellect. The concept has to proceed from something other than itself, namely, from the knowledge of the one conceiving. Thus the Word in God strictly signifies something proceeding from another and a relation of origin, which in God distinguishes and constitutes a person. In this sense, the Word in God is said personally, not essentially, while the intellect itself and the act of understanding are said essentially or absolutely, not relationally or personally. Only the word, which the intellect forms in its conception, signifies a relational reality, i.e., that of emanating from another. Knowledge, too, in the strict sense, stands for what the intellect conceives by knowing.[65]

As the Word is not common to the three persons, so it is not true that the Father, Son, and Holy Spirit are one speaker. As only the Son is the Word, so only the Father is the speaker of the Word. As it belongs only to the Son to be spoken as a word is spoken, so it belongs to each person, the whole Trinity, and indeed all creation to be spoken as a thing is said to be spoken when it is understood in the word. "For the Father, by understanding himself, the Son, and the Holy Spirit, and all other things comprised in his knowledge, conceives the Word; so that thus the whole Trinity is spoken in the Word; and likewise also all creatures: as the intellect of a man, by the word he conceives in the act of understanding a stone, speaks a stone."[66]

To be and to understand are not the same in us, and what has intelligible being in us does not belong to our nature. In us the word is an accident, not a subsistent being and therefore not a person. In God, however, to be and to understand are one and the same because of divine simplicity. Thus the Word of God is not an accident in her but belongs to her very nature. It must be something subsistent, as whatever is in the nature of God subsists. As the Word proceeds by way of emanation of the intellect in God that produces a concept of the same nature as the intellect itself, the procession of the Word is called generation, and in this sense the Word is a proper name of the person of the Son.[67]

Does not whoever understands conceive a word in the act of understanding, and does not the Son also understand, as in fact also do the Father and the Spirit, and if so, don't words proceed from the Son and the Holy Spirit as well as from the Father? What, then, is so particular about the Word that constitutes the Son? Aquinas's answer here, as elsewhere, depends on an important distinction between the essential and the personal in God. To understand is said of God essentially, i.e., as a reference to an act of the divine essence common to the three persons. As an essential name, understanding belongs to the Son as well as to the other two, as does being God. However, the Son is God begotten, not God begetting. He understands, therefore, not as producing a Word but as the Word proceeding. In God the Word proceeding does not differ really from the divine intellect except by relation. The same must be said of the Holy Spirit, who also understands, not as producing a Word or as the Word proceeding, but precisely as Love proceeding.[68]

For Aquinas, the Word implies relation to creatures. The word conceived in the mind represents all that is understood in the concept. Human beings, therefore, have and need different words for the different things they understand and conceive. God, however, understands himself and all things by one act. His one and only Word, therefore, expresses not only the Father but also all creatures. God's knowledge is only cognitive as regards God but both cognitive and productive [factiva] as regards creatures; thus the Word of God is only expressive of what is in God the Father but both expressive and operative of creatures. As Psalm 32:9 puts it, "He spoke, and they were made." The Word of God contains the productive speech [fatio factiva] of what God makes, "the intelligibility [ratio] of things made by him,"[69] the eternal law that governs the created world. All things preexist in the Word as in their exemplar before they exist in their own proper nature. The divine Word thus constitutes the one absolute truth—truth by essence—in which finite truths must participate if they are to be true. The Word is the one absolute wisdom in which we must participate if we are to be wise, the one absolute Word in which we must participate if we are to speak authentic words. As the knowledge of the divine intellect from which all intellectual cognition is derived, and as the exemplar and pattern of all forms through which things are understood and made known, the Word is the "light" that manifests the truth to human beings. Salvation and sanctity consist in participating in the Word who is this "light" by his very essence.[70] It is impossible that God should make or redeem anything except through his Word and Son. In this sense, then, the Word contains (logical) relation to creatures.

However, is not relation to creatures a matter of the unity of the divine essence, not of a particular divine person? For Aquinas, the essence or nature is indirectly included in the name of the person, which is, after all, "an individual substance of a rational *nature.*" The name of a divine person, precisely as a personal relation, does not imply relation to the creature, but such a relation is implied in what belongs to the divine nature. As long as the divine essence or nature is included in the meaning of person, there is nothing to prevent the divine person from implying a relation to creatures. As it properly belongs to the Son to be the Son, so it properly belongs to him to be God begotten or the creator begotten, and in this sense the name Word imports relation to creatures.

What exactly is the nature of this relation to creatures? Relations follow from actions. Some of God's actions, such as creating and governing, are transient actions, that is, actions that pass over into some exterior effect. Names of relations following on these transient or economic actions are applied in time. Some relations follow upon immanent actions that abide in God, such as knowing and willing. Names of these relations are not applied to God in time. It is this kind of relation to creatures that is implied in the name of the Word. Not all relations to creatures are applied in time, but only those following upon transient actions that produce an exterior effect in the world. This still does not make the relation to the creature a "real" relation in God in the sense of God having a real dependence on the creature. God does not derive her knowledge of creatures from the creatures but from her own essence. The Word is expressive of creatures because it is the word or concept of the divine knowledge that knows all things by knowing itself, not because it is derived from creatures as are human words. There is only one personal Word of God, not many words, because God understands every creature in the single act of understanding herself.[71]

Aquinas asks the same questions about "Image." Is Image a personal, not an essential, name in God? If it is a personal name, is it a proper name of the Son as distinct from the Spirit? For Aquinas, similitude constitutes one aspect of the proper meaning [ratio] of image; here he refers to similitude in the species or form of things or at least in some sign of species, such as the figure—but not for instance the color—of an animal in the case of corporeal things. Similitude alone, however, is not sufficient to constitute the *ratio* of image. Origin, also, is required. One egg is not the image of another egg, because it is not derived from it. True image requires that from something proceeds another similar to it either in species or in some sign of species. Now, whatever imports procession or origin in God belongs to the persons. Thus, Image is a personal name. Image is derived from imitation of an exemplar and implies "before" and "after" in created things, but in God imitation signifies not posterity but only assimilation.[72] Insofar as Image in God imports procession, then, it is a personal name. And because it implies procession with similitude of form or species, it is the proper name of the person of the Son, whom Scripture calls "the Image of the invisible God" (Colossians 1:15) and "the brightness of his glory and the figure of his substance" (Hebrews 1:3).

Against the Greek tendency to predicate "image" of the Holy Spirit, Aquinas insists on the Latin tradition of predicating it only of the Son. He is concerned, however, to identify the correct reason for not predicating "image" of the Holy Spirit. Therefore he considers and rejects two mistaken arguments. Against those who argue that the Holy Spirit cannot be the image of the Father and the Son because there cannot be an image of two, Aquinas answers that as long as the Father and the Son are one principle of the Holy Spirit, there is nothing to prevent the Holy Spirit being the one image of the two, just as even a human being is one image of the whole Trinity. Others have argued that the Holy Spirit cannot be the image of the Son because there cannot be an image of an image, nor the image of the Father because the image must be related directly to its exemplar (which the Spirit cannot be because she is related to the Father through the Son). These arguments do not hold. A human being is called an image of God, although it is mediated through the Son and thus an image of an image. Rather, Aquinas locates the true argument in the difference between word and love. Both the Spirit and the Word receive the divine nature of the Father through their respective processions, and to that extent the Holy Spirit too receives the likeness of the Father. Nonetheless, the Holy Spirit is not said to be born and is therefore not called Image. The Son proceeds as word whose essence lies in similitude of species to the source from which it proceeds, which, however, is not the *ratio* of love, the inclination or movement toward an object, however appropriate this may be to the love which is the Holy Spirit insofar as she is divine love.[73]

The fact that human beings are also called the image of God does not prevent the Image being the proper personal name of the Son. An image of an exemplar may be found in something in two ways, in something of the same specific nature, as the image of the king is found in his son, and in something of a different nature, as the image of the king is found in a coin.[74] The Son is the Image of the Father in the first sense, human beings are images of God in the second. In order to show the imperfect character of the divine image in human beings, they are not simply called the image but are said to be made "to the image" [ad imaginem], implying a certain movement of tendency to perfection. The Son cannot be said to be "to the image" because he is the perfect image of the Father. Paternity is, first of all, the personal name of the Father in whom fatherhood—the communication of the same nature—is actualized in a supereminent way because it is the communication of a "numerically identical" divine nature, and from which all created paternity is derived as the communication of a "specifically identical" nature. Just so, the Image is the personal name of the Son in whom the similitude of specific form, the divine nature of the Father, is actualized in a supereminent way because he is of the numerically identical nature, and from which all creaturely imaging is derived as a reflection of the divine nature in a created nature.[75] Precisely because the Son is the perfect Image of the Father, he is also the divine Exemplar of all created things, and can be called, in the words of Charles Andre Bernard, "the principle of all objective manifestation of the Father."[76]

For Aquinas, the truth of the Son cannot be expressed by any one name and requires many different names, each highlighting a particular dimension of that truth. Some names are better suited to express certain dimensions than other names. Thus, he is called "Son" to express the fact that he is "connatural" [connaturalis] with the Father, "Splendor" to show that he is "coeternal," "Image" to show that he is "altogether similar" [omnino similis], and "Word" to show that he is "immaterially begotten." According to Aquinas, John the Evangelist used "Word," not "Son," in his prologue because "the idea of manifesting [the Father] is implied better in the name 'Word' than in the name 'Son.' " "Word" [verbum] is also a better translation of "Logos" than is "notion" [ratio]: whereas "notion" only names a conception of the mind precisely as in the mind, "word" signifies a reference to something exterior as well and is better suited to convey a reference not only to the Son's existence in the

Father but also to the operative power of the Son through which all things were made. Notwithstanding these differences, however, the three personal names—Son, Word, and Image—have a key aspect in common. Aquinas says that Paul used "form" instead of "nature" in the famous kenosis passage in his letter to the Philippians (2:6)—"though he was in the form of God"—because "form" is constitutive of all three names. The Son, as begotten by the Father, has the form of the Father perfectly since the end of begetting is the form. As the Word of the Father, the Son also shares the form of the Father because he "receives perfectly the entire nature of the Father [totam naturam patris] through eternal generation" and leads us to a knowledge of his nature.[77] As Image of the Father the Son necessarily has the form of that of which he is the image. Aquinas's conception of the Son, one can say, is thoroughly "formal."[78]

The Holy Spirit

Aquinas's discussion of the Holy Spirit asks first: Is the "Holy Spirit" the proper name of a divine person? Here we hit immediately upon a signal peculiarity of the Holy Spirit that we first encountered above. With regard to the procession, relation, and person of the Son, we have readily available relational names or names that imply relative opposition, such as generation, filiation, and Word or Son. With regard to those of the Holy Spirit, however, we have no such ready names and have to accommodate certain linguistically contrived usages, such as "procession" for procession (the same word used in the specific and the generic senses of the term, respectively) and "spiration" for relation. With regard to the name of the person, however, we have been making do with biblical and ecclesiastical usage, and say "Holy Spirit."

Aquinas defends the appropriateness of this name and usage in two ways. First, as the Spirit of both the Father and the Son, it is appropriate that the Holy Spirit should be called by a name common to both, namely, the Holy Spirit, since both are holy and spirits. Second, "spirit" signifies, in corporeal things, impulse and motion, like breath and wind, corresponding to the property of love, which is to move and impel the will of the lover towards the object loved.[79] Likewise, insofar as holiness is attributed to whatever is ordered to God, and insofar as the third person proceeds by way of the love whereby God is loved, the person is appropriately called the Holy Spirit. Although the name, unlike Father and Son, does not of itself indicate a relation, it still takes the place of a relative or relational term inasmuch as it is accommodated to refer to a person distinct from others only by relation. It could also be understood as including a relation if we understand the Holy Spirit as being "breathed" or "spirated."[80]

We have earlier discussed how the Holy Spirit proceeds from the Father by way of the will. Does the Holy Spirit also proceed from the Son? Touching upon an ecumenically sensitive issue, Aquinas provides seven reasons why the Spirit does proceed from the Father *and* the Son. First, as sharers of the numerically identical divine nature, the three persons are not distinguished from one another absolutely but only by relational oppositions, which are possible only through processions or originations, i.e., the way in which each originates in relation to the other. In order to produce a personal distinction between the Son and the Spirit, then, either the Son proceeds from the Spirit, or the Spirit proceeds from the Son. Since we cannot say the first, the second must be true.[81] Second, the Son proceeds by way of the intellect as Word, and the Holy Spirit by way of the will as Love. Since we cannot love something that we do not know, love must proceed from word. The Holy Spirit must therefore proceed from the Son.[82] Third, the beauty of divine wisdom requires order. If two persons proceed from the one person of the Father, there must be some order between the Son and the Holy Spirit. There cannot be any other order than that of their origin whereby one is from the other.[83] Fourth, precisely because the Holy Spirit proceeds from the Father perfectly, it is also altogether necessary to say that the Spirit also proceeds from the Son. One power belongs to the Father and the Son, who are one except in the relation of filiation. Whatever is from the Father, therefore, must also be from the Son unless it is opposed to the property of filiation. Since there is no relative opposition between the Father and the Son as the principle of the Holy Spirit, they are one principle of the Holy Spirit.[84]

Fifth, the personal distinction between the Son and the Holy Spirit is based on the difference of origin between the two, but this difference comes from the fact that the Son is only from the Father, while the Holy Spirit is from both the Father and the Son. Otherwise, the processions cannot be distinguished from each other. Differences of origin in general depend on the subject, term, or principle. Differences in subject apply when the nature of the species is received in diverse matters, which is not the case with God who is immaterial. Differences of term do not apply to God, either, because one and the same divine nature, numerically identical, is received by the Son by generation and by the Holy Spirit by procession. Both generation and procession terminate in the same divine nature. The distinction of origin, therefore, can only be on the part of the principle. The principle of the origin of the Son is the Father alone. If the Holy Spirit too were from the Father alone, she would not be different from the Son. In order to be really distinct from the Son, then, the Holy Spirit must be from both the Father and the Son.[85]

Sixth, in order to indicate a real distinction it is not enough to say that the Son proceeds from the Father by way of intellect and the Holy Spirit by way of will. Will and intellect in God are distinguished only in reason, not in reality, which would enable us to say that the divine intellect is the divine will, and conversely, because both are identical with the divine essence, and that the Son is the Holy Spirit, and conversely. This, however, is the "Sabellian impiety." We must therefore remember the note of relative opposition in origin by saying that the Holy Spirit is from the Son, as the Son with the Father is the single principle for the spiration of the Holy Spirit.[86]

Seventh and last, as Love, the Holy Spirit is the bond of the Father and the Son. The Father loves himself and the Son with one Love, which expresses the relation of the Father to the Son, as of the lover to the beloved. Insofar as the Father and the Son love each other, this mutual love, the Holy Spirit, proceeds from both as their "unitive love."[87]

Can we also say that the Holy Spirit proceeds from the Father "through" the Son? Insofar as the Spirit does proceed from the Son, and insofar as such procession is itself granted by the Father in the sense that the Son receives from the Father that the Spirit proceed from the Son, we can say that the Holy Spirit proceeds from the Father through the Son, that the Father spirates the Holy Spirit through the Son, as a king may work through a bailiff, or that the Holy Spirit proceeds from the Father immediately and from the Son indirectly. If the power of the Son to spirate the Spirit were numerically distinct from the power of the Father, the Son would be a secondary and instrumental cause, in which case the Spirit would proceed more from the Father than from the Son. However, the same spirative power belongs to both the Father and the Son, and the Holy Spirit proceeds equally from both, although sometimes we might say that the Spirit proceeds principally or properly from the Father because the Son's power is derivative from that of the Father.

These considerations make it clear that Aquinas does accept the "Filioque" but does so for reasons other than those feared by its opponent. With Jürgen Moltmann, he too would reject the idea that "the Spirit could proceed 'from the Father and the Son' in the sense of the Son's being a 'second origin' of the divinity of the Holy Spirit, in competition with the Father." Aquinas holds, quite clearly, that the Son is not a second origin of the divinity of the Holy Spirit that is distinct from and competes with the Father, and does so precisely for the same reason that Moltmann adduces, namely that "the Father is the 'origin' of the Son and communicates to him his whole essence, with the sole exception of the capacity for being himself the 'origin' or 'source' of the Godhead."[88]

Aquinas differs from Moltmann in teaching that precisely because there is the communication of the numerically identical divine nature from the Father to the Son, one identical nature and power belong to both except in the relation of filiation. Wherever the relation of filiation is not involved, as in the case of the spiration of the Spirit, both possess the same divine power to spirate the Spirit, except that the Father does so as Father, the underived source of divinity, while the Son does so as Son, the derived one. Without denying the primordial ontological dependence of the Son on the Father, Aquinas, unlike Moltmann, also draws the implication of the sharing of the numerically identical divine nature between the Father and the Son for all things except where relative opposition is involved, and therefore with respect to the spiration of the Spirit. That the Father is the one, unoriginate origin of the divinity of the Son and the Spirit does not prevent the Son from sharing, as a derivative power, in the Father's activity of spirating the Spirit; rather, it entails that sharing because the Father generates the Son by communicating his numerically identical divine nature in an intimacy of unlimited, mutual union, which would in fact make it odd if the Son did not participate in the Father's spirating of the Holy Spirit who is meant to be the bond of love that unites both. The Filioque means that the Father and the Son are united in the very spiration of the Spirit.

The procession of the Holy Spirit through the Son does not mean that the Son was first begotten *before* the Holy Spirit was spirated. Both the generation of the Son and the spiration of the Holy Spirit are eternal operations. Contrary to Dionysius, Aquinas states that the Father did not exist before begetting the Son; rather, the generation of the Son is coeternal with the Father. Likewise, the procession of the Holy Spirit is coeternal with its principle, the Son, who was not begotten before the Spirit proceeded.[89]

Is Love the proper name of the Holy Spirit? Isn't it more an essential name applicable to all three persons, as all three are also called Wisdom? Moreover, love indicates an action, not a subsisting person, which the Holy Spirit is. Aquinas allows that love in God can be taken both essentially, as a reference to the divine essence, and personally, as the proper name of the Holy Spirit, as Word is the proper name of the Son. In the two processions in the modes of the intellect and the will, the procession of Word is better known to us and has been described by more appropriate names. As regards the procession of Love we have been obliged to use circumlocutions. The relations of Love have been described in terms of procession and spiration, but these are more expressive of origin than of relation in the strict sense of the terms.

Apart from linguistic usage, however, it is also necessary to consider the nature of each procession as such. When we understand something, there results in us a conception of the object understood, which we call "word." Likewise, when we love an object, there results in our affection a certain impression [impressio] of the object loved, by reason of which the object loved is said to be in the lover, as the thing understood is in the one who understands. When someone understands and loves herself, then, she is in herself, not only by real identity, but also as the object understood is in the one who understands and as the thing loved is in the lover. Now, as regards the intellect, we have found different suitable words for different purposes, e.g., "understand" to describe the mutual relation of the one who understands to the object understood, and "speak" and "word" to express the procession of the intellectual conception. In God, therefore, we apply "speak" and "word" to the personal relation of the Father as speaker to the Word as spoken because they directly imply the relation of the speaker to the word that proceeds from him; by contrast, we apply "understand" only to the essence because it does not imply a direct relation to the product of understanding, i.e., the Word that proceeds.

As regards the will, however, apart from "dilection" and "love," which express the relation of the lover to the object loved, there are no other terms to express the relation of what proceeds—the impression or affection of the object loved that is produced in the lover by the fact that she loves—to the source or principle of that impression, as do "speak" and "word" in the case of the procession of the intellect. Poverty of language thus compels us to use "love" and "dilection" for both essential and personal relations. This means that insofar as love means only the relation of the lover to the object loved, "love" and "to love" are said of the divine essence, as are "understanding" and "to understand." In this essential sense, the Holy Spirit loves, as do the Father and the Son, but the Holy Spirit does so precisely as Love proceeding, while the Father and the Son do so as spirating Love. However, insofar as "love" means the love proceeding, i.e., the impression of the beloved in the lover, and "to love" means the spiration of the love proceeding, "love" is the proper name of the third person, and "to love" is a notional term, as are "to speak" and "to beget."[90]

Can we say that the Father and the Son love each other "by" the Holy Spirit? If so, in what sense? What is the meaning of the ablative "by" in "by the Holy Spirit" [Spiritu Sancto]? Does it mean that the Holy Spirit is the "cause" or principle of love to the Father and the Son, which seems to contradict the procession of the Holy Spirit from them, and to be as false as to say that the Father is not wise except by Wisdom begotten, a proposition that Augustine is said to have retracted? Does it mean that the Holy Spirit is simply God's essential love appropriated to the Spirit, which would seem to deny the personal role of the Spirit in the mutual love of the Father and the Son as their bond [nexus]? Or, does it mean that the Holy Spirit is the "sign" that the Father loves the Son inso-far as the Spirit is the product of their love proceeding from both? Or, does it mean the relation of a "formal cause" in the sense that the Holy Spirit is the form of the love whereby the Father and the Son love each other? Or, does it mean only the relation of a "formal effect"?

Aquinas's answer is that the Holy Spirit is more the "formal effect" of the mutual love of the Father and the Son than its "cause," "sign," "formal cause," or the personal appropriation of God's love taken essen-tially. Names of things are commonly taken from their form, e.g., man from humanity, white from whiteness. Everything from which the name of a thing is taken, therefore, stands in the relation of form to the thing named. Now, in the case of naming a thing from its action, if the effect itself is included in the idea of the action, it may be named either from the action itself or from its effect. Thus we can say both that "fire warms by heating" although "heating" refers to the action of the fire, not to the heat, which is the form of the fire, and that "a tree flowers with the flower" although the flower is not the form of the tree but an effect pro-ceeding from the form. In either case, the ablative—"by"—introduces an effect that proceeds from the agent (e.g., the fire, the tree) and therefore bears the form of the agent in some way, whether in the form of an action such as "heating" or that of an effect such as "flower."

Aquinas applies this formal relation between a thing named and that from which it is named and between an agent and its effect to the example of love in God. Now, if we take love in the essential sense, we have to say that the Father and the Son love each other by their essence, not by the Holy Spirit. It is wrong in this case to say that the Father cannot love Himself or the Son or the Holy Spirit except by the Holy Spirit, just as it is wrong to say that the Father is not wise except by the Son or Wisdom begotten. If we take love in the notional sense, however, it means to spirate love, just as to speak is to produce a word, and to flower is to produce a flower. In this case, it makes perfect sense to say that the Father and the Son love each other and us by the Holy Spirit or by Love proceeding, or that the Father speaks himself and his creatures by the Word or Son proceeding, in the same way that it makes good sense to say that "a tree flowers by its flower." The ablative, "by," in these instances, then, introduces not so much the efficient cause, formal cause, or sign of the action of the agent as the "formal effect" of the agent. The Spirit proceeding is the formal effect of the Father and the Son loving each other in the same way that the Word proceeding is the formal effect of the Father speaking himself.

If, however, the idea of an action does not include a determinate effect distinct from the action, the principle of the action cannot be denominated from the effect but only from the action. We cannot say that "the tree produces the flower by the flower" but that "the tree produces the flower by the production of the flower." In a similar way, we cannot say that the Father spirates the Holy Spirit by the Holy Spirit, because the Holy Spirit is not a distinct effect of the action of spirating the Holy Spirit but is part of the action itself. Nor, for the same reason, can we say that the Father begets the Son by the Son. We can say, somewhat redundantly but correctly, that the Father spirates the Holy Spirit by spirating the Holy Spirit, and that the Father begets the Son by begetting the Son. If we cannot say that the Father spirates by the Holy Spirit or that the Father begets by the Son, we can say that the Father loves the Son by the Holy Spirit proceeding, a determinate effect of but also distinct from the action of the mutual love of the Father and the Son; likewise, we can say that the Father speaks by the Word, also a distinct effect of the Father speaking himself, which always produces a word.

For Aquinas, then, "as the Father speaks himself and every creature by his begotten Word, inasmuch as the Word begotten adequately represents the Father and every creature, so he loves himself and every creature by the Holy Spirit, inasmuch as the Holy Spirit proceeds as the love of the primordial goodness [amor primae bonitatis] whereby the Father loves himself and every creature."[91] According to Aquinas's trinitarian grammar the ablative, "by," in both instances of "by the Word" and "by the Holy Spirit" imports a relation of a "formal effect" to the agency of the Father.

Precisely as such formal effects of the Father's generation and spiration, the Word and Love also imply relation to the creature in a secondary way, inasmuch as the divine truth and goodness are a principle of understanding and loving all creatures. Just as the Word is the exemplary cause of wisdom by which we know God, so the Holy Spirit is the exemplary cause of love by which we love God.[92]

Is "Gift" the proper, personal name of the Holy Spirit as is Love? Again, there are many objections to this idea. A personal name in God implies a distinction, which the word "gift" does not seem to. The paradigmatic gift in God is the divine essence itself that the Father gives to the Son, but what belongs to the essence cannot be personal. Further, gift implies inequality between giver and recipient, which contradicts the equality of persons in God. Gift also implies a relation to the creature in time, whereas personal names are said of God from eternity.

For Aquinas, gift means aptitude for being given, and implies a relation both to the giver whose it is to give and to the recipient to whom it is given to be his. A divine person belongs to another either by origin, as the Son belongs to the Father, or as possessed by another. Possession implies free use or enjoyment and is possible only with rational creatures. In this sense a divine person cannot be possessed except by a rational creature joined to God. The rational creature often possesses the divine person in this sense when it becomes partaker [particeps] of the divine Word and the Love proceeding so as freely to know God truly and to love her rightly. The rational creature, however, cannot possess the divine person by its own power; it must be given to the creature from above. A thing is said to be given to us when we have it from another source. In this sense, a divine person can be given and be a gift.[93]

The word "gift" in this sense, then, implies a distinction insofar as it belongs to another by its origin. In the case of the Holy Spirit, we are, of course, talking about a gift which the Holy Spirit is. The Holy Spirit gives herself in as much as she is her own and can use or enjoy herself as a free person belongs to herself. Nothing belongs to us more than we ourselves. In this sense, a thing may belong to someone by real identity, in which case the gift is the same as the giver, as when the Holy Spirit gives herself as a gift, or when the Father gives the gift of the divine essence, which is himself, to the Son and the Holy Spirit in the processions of generation and spiration. In another sense, a thing may belong to someone as a possession or a slave, in which case the gift is essentially distinct from the giver. The gift of God in this sense is a created thing. In a third sense, a thing may belong to someone through its origin only, as the Son belongs to the Father, and the Holy Spirit to both. In this third sense, the gift, the Holy Spirit, is the possession of the givers, the Father and the Son, yet is personally distinguished from the givers and is constituted a personal name. As a personal name in God, the gift does not imply subjection but only origin.

Furthermore, something is not a gift because it is actually given but because of its "aptitude to be given" [aptitudo ut possit dari]. The Holy Spirit is called Gift from eternity for this reason, although actually given in time. The name does include a relation to the creature, but such a relation does not make the name essential but keeps it personal, in the same way that the name Word remains a personal, not an essential, name, although it implies a relation to the creature as the divine operative *ratio* of creation. In both instances, the idea of the divine nature is indirectly included in the name of person as "an individual substance of a rational *nature.*" As it properly belongs to the Holy Spirit to be Holy Spirit, and as it belongs to the Father and the Son to be Father and Son respectively, so it also properly belongs to the Holy Spirit to be God spirated or the creator spirated, as it also belongs to the Father and the Son to be respectively God and creator unbegotten and God and creator begotten. As creator spirated, whose gift enables creatures to love God, Gift indirectly imports a relation to creation, as does Word as creator begotten.[94]

Gift is not only a personal name in God but also the proper name of the Holy Spirit. Properly understood, gift implies unreturnable giving and contains the idea of gratuitous donation. The reason for this gratuitous donation is love by which we wish someone well. What we first give someone, then, is love. Love has the *ratio* of the first or primordial gift [primum donum] because it inspires and enables the giving of all free gifts. Insofar as the Holy Spirit proceeds as Love, then, he does proceed as the first gift. That the Son too is given to us does not prevent the Gift being the proper name of the Holy Spirit, any more than the fact that the Spirit too is like to the Father whose essence it receives prevents the Word being the proper name of the Son. In each case, what is at stake is the respective *ratio* of its procession. As the Son is called the Image because he proceeds in the mode of word, whose very *ratio* is to be the similitude of its principle, so the Spirit is properly called the Gift because he proceeds from the Father as love, whose *ratio* is to give oneself to others. The Son too is given to us precisely from the Father's love.[95]

Three Persons in Relation

The consideration of the ontological constitution of the Trinity and each of the three persons in herself does not exhaust Aquinas's reflection on the Trinity. There still remain for discussion the intricate relation of the three persons to the divine essence, their properties, and their notional acts, their mutual likeness and equality, and their economic mission. The preceding discussion should have acquainted us by now with the basic terminology, metaphysical ideas, and guiding principles of his trinitarian theology, and prepared us well for the discussion that follows.

Persons and the Divine Essence

The first question here has to do with the relation of the person to the divine essence. In God the essence is the same as the person because of divine simplicity. All created beings are composed of a multiplicity of distinct intrinsic principles of being: at least act and potency in the form of existence and essence in the case of angels or substances separated from matter; and in addition substance and accidents, substantial form and prime matter, in the case of material beings including the human. God, on the other hand, is a pure act unmixed with potentiality, whose very essence is identical with her existence, the very act of existing subsisting through itself [ipsum esse per se subsistens].

Because of this intrinsic simplicity in God, essence is the same as the supposit, which in intellectual substances is called person, in a way that is not true of created beings; for example, human nature is not identical with "this" particular individual. The problem here is that in God there are three persons multiplied by relation while there is only one essence, which has led some to think that person and essence are not identical in God, and to consider the relations in their references to another only as accidents but not as realities. In creatures relations are accidents, but in God they are the divine essence itself. Hence in God essence is not really distinct from relation and person, although the persons are *really* distinguished from one another. The person signifies relation as subsisting in the divine nature, but relation does not differ really [re] from essence except in our way of thinking [ratione], while, as referred to an opposite relation, relation has a real distinction by reason of that opposition. There is a real identity—with only a logical distinction—between person and essence in God, but a real distinction among the three persons themselves. The relations and persons are really distinguished from one another insofar as they are relationally opposed to one another, but not insofar as they are identified with the essence. Thus, there are one essence and three persons, one God and the Father, Son, and Holy Spirit. Insofar as they differ in our way of thinking, although not in reality, it is legitimate to deny something of one—that there are three Gods—and affirm it of the other—that there are three persons.[96]

Can we predicate the one essence of the three persons? Again, we name divine things not as they are in themselves, which we cannot know, but only in a way that belongs to created things. Now, in sensible things from which we derive our knowledge, the nature of the species is individuated by matter, and nature is as the form, while the individual is the supposit of the form. Likewise, in God the essence is taken as the form of the three persons, according to our mode of signification. Now, in creatures we say that every form belongs to the subject of which it is the form; e.g., the health and beauty of a man belongs to the man. We do not say that the subject belongs to the form unless some adjective qualifies the form; e.g., "that woman is of a handsome figure." Similarly, in God where the persons, but not the essence, are multiplied, we speak of the one essence of the three persons and three persons of one essence, where the genitives are understood as designating the form.[97]

Should we predicate essential names in the singular or in the plural of the three persons? Some essential names—e.g., God—signify the essence after the manner of substantives, others—e.g, wise, eternal—after the manner of adjectives. Substantive names are predicated in the singular only, not in the plural, because they signify something by way of substance, while adjectival names are predicated in the plural, because these signify something by way of accident inhering in a subject or supposit. The singularity or plurality of a substantive name depends on the nature of the form signified by the name, while that of an adjectival name depends on the number of supposits in which they inhere. Now, in God the essence is signified by way of a form. Thus, substantive names for the divine essence, which is one by nature, are predicated of the three persons in the singular; e.g., "the Father, Son, and Holy Spirit are one God," not "three Gods." By contrast, substantive names for the human essence, which is intrinsically multiplied in a plurality of human supposits of that essence, are predicated of human persons in the plural; e.g., "Mary, Martha, and Magdalene are three human beings," not "one human being." However, adjectival names for the divine essence are predicated of the three persons in the plural because of the plurality of supposits or persons, e.g., as in "three wise beings." When these are used in a substantive sense, however, they are to be predicated in the singular, e.g., "one wise being."[98]

Personal Appropriation of Essential Names

Perhaps the theologically most fruitful aspect of the relation between the divine essence and the three persons is the question of "appropriation," i.e., whether the essential names should be appropriated to the persons and, if so, how. In what Karl Barth calls "the clearest and most complete definition of the concept of appropriation," Aquinas says that "to appropriate is nothing else than to apply what is common to what is proper . . . not because it is more fitting to one person than to another but because that which is common has a greater similitude to that which is proper to one person than to what is proper to another."[99] The underlying issue is whether we can say, for example, with Paul, that Christ is "the power of God and the wisdom of God" (1 Corinthians 1:24), when both the "power" and "wisdom" are essential names belonging to the shared divine essence, not to a particular person. If we can say so, on what ground is this possible? For Aquinas, personal appropriation of essential names is fitting [conveniens] for the elucidation of faith. It is impossible to prove the trinity of persons by strict demonstration, but it is possible and fitting to clarify and make it plausible by things better known to us. Now, the essential attributes are clearer [magis manifesta] to us according to reason than are the personal properties, because we can know such attributes with certitude from creatures, the source of all our knowledge. It is quite fitting, therefore, to make use of the essential attributes for the manifestation of the divine persons, just as we use the likeness of the vestige or image found in creatures for the same purpose. This manifestation of the divine persons through the essential attributes is precisely what is meant by "appropriation."

This manifestation or elucidation can occur in two ways: First, by similitude, that is, by appropriating things that belong to the intellect to the Son, who proceeds in the mode of the intellect as Word; second, by dissimilitude, that is, by appropriating power to the Father lest we should imagine God as feeble, as are human fathers in their old age. The point of appropriation is not to apply essential attributes exclusively to a particular person, which would be dangerous to faith, but to manifest or clarify the truth about a person by means of similitude or dissimilitude. As Augustine showed, appropriating wisdom to the Son does not mean that he alone is wise in such a way that the Father too is wise only by the wisdom begotten, as though the Father alone would not be wise. The Son is called the wisdom of the Father because he is wisdom from the Father who is wisdom. As the Word and concept of the Father's self-understanding, the Son is wisdom begotten and manifests the wisdom of the Father who understands himself. Each of them is of himself wisdom, and both together are one wisdom. The Father is not wise by the wisdom begotten by him but by the wisdom which is his own essence.[100]

Aquinas now surveys the traditional appropriations made by the doctors of the church to ask if they are fitting. Hilary appropriated eternity to the Father, species to the Son, and use to the Holy Spirit, while Augustine appropriated unity, power, and "from him" to the Father, equality, wisdom, and "by him" to the Son, and concord, goodness, and "in him" to the Holy Spirit. Here again, Aquinas's answer follows the way of analogy with creatures. Just as we know God only from creatures, so we can consider her only according to the mode derived from them. Now, there are four essential points to consider in any creature: its being, taken in itself or absolutely; its unity; its intrinsic power of operation and causality; and its relation to its effects.

Hilary's appropriation applies to God taken absolutely in her own being. "Eternity" means a being without a principle and has a likeness to the property of the Father as the "principle without a principle" [principium non de principio]. "Species" or "beauty" includes three conditions—integrity or perfection, due proportion or harmony, and brightness or clarity—and bears a likeness to the property of the Son in that the Son has truly and perfectly the nature of the Father, is the expressed image of the Father, and is the Word which is the light and splendor of the intellect. "Use" in the wide sense that includes enjoyment is similar to the property of the Holy Spirit as Love, whereby the Father and the Son enjoy each other, as well as to the property of the Holy Spirit as Gift, whereby we enjoy God. It is important to note here that eternity, species, and use are appropriated to the persons but that essence and operation are not because these are common to the persons and there is nothing in their concept that likens them to the properties of the persons.

Augustine's appropriation of unity, equality, and concord applies to God considered as one. All three attributes imply unity, in different ways. Unity said absolutely without presupposing anything is appropriate to the Father because, as the principle without a principle, he does not presuppose any other person in the sense of being dependent on the person. Equality implies unity in relation to another and is appropriated to the Son who is "the principle from a principle" [principium de principio]. Union or concord implies unity of two and is appropriated to the Holy Spirit who proceeds from the two as their mutual love. Aquinas also accepts Augustine's extension of these appropriations to the whole Trinity in the sense that the three persons are one by reason of the Father, equal by reason of the Son, and united by reason of the Holy Spirit. For Aquinas, unity is first perceived in the Father, from whom other persons derive their unity. Without the Son equal to the Father, the Father cannot be called equal—not because the Son is the principle of equality in the Father but simply because the equality of the Son to the Father is the very meaning of that equality, although the Father is the first instance of equality in God, from which is also derived the equality of the Spirit to the Father. Likewise, we cannot understand the oneness of the union between the Father and the Son without the Holy Spirit; not, again, because the Holy Spirit is the principle of their union but because the Holy Spirit as their mutual love constitutes the very meaning of that oneness.

With regard to the third area, God's intrinsic power of operation and external causality, Aquinas says that power, wisdom, and goodness are appropriated both by reason of similitude as regards what exists in the divine persons and by reason of dissimilitude as regards what exists in creatures. Power has the nature of a principle and has a likeness to the Father, who is "the principle of the whole Godhead, not as generating or spirating it, but as communicating it by generation and spiration,"[101] but is dissimilar to human fathers who often lack power because of old age. Wisdom is similar to the Son because the Word is nothing other than the concept of wisdom, but wisdom is often lacking in human sons because of their lack of years. Goodness as the nature and object of love has likeness to the Holy Spirit, who is Love, although it is often repugnant to earthly spirits who are carried away by violent impulses.[102]

Finally, with regard to the fourth area, God's relation to her effects in creation, "from whom" [ex quo] is appropriated to the Father in the same way as power is appropriated to him, in the sense that he is the efficient cause of creation by reason of his active power, although by no means a material cause. "By whom" [per quem] implies an intermediate cause, as a smith works "by" a hammer, and belongs to the Son properly and strictly, as "all things are made by him" (John 1:3), not in the sense of an instrumental cause but in the sense of a principle from a principle. Sometimes "by" designates the habitude of a form by which an agent works, as a craftsman works "by" his art. Similarly, as wisdom and art are appropriated to the Son, so also is "by whom," in the sense of an exemplary cause of all creation. "In" implies the habitude of one containing other things. God contains things in two ways: first, in her knowledge by virtue of their similarity to God, in which case "in" belongs properly to the Son; and second, in her goodness whereby she preserves and governs them, guiding them to a fitting end, in which sense "in" is appropriated to the Holy Spirit, as is also goodness. Aquinas notes here that goodness as the final cause need not be appropriated to the Father because, although the Father is the principle of the other two persons, these do not, as Leonardo Boff misinterprets the classical position, proceed from the Father as towards an end, each of them being the last end.[103]

Again, creation in the sense of the production of the being [esse] of things pertains to God according to her *esse,* which as her essence is common to the three persons. Creation, therefore, is not proper to any one person but belongs to the whole Trinity. This does not mean, however, that creation is related to the three persons as to God in general, in indeterminate ways. Just as the one God exists in three personally differentiated ways in an order of nature based on origin, so creation is related to each of the persons in a different way according to the nature [ratio] of their respective processions. As God is the cause of things through her intellect and will, and as the craftsman produces things through the word conceived in his mind and through the love of his will for the objects to be made, so the Father creates things "through" his Word, the Son, and "through" his Love, the Holy Spirit. "The processions of the Persons are the models [rationes] for the production of creatures insofar as they include essential attributes which are knowledge and will," as well as "a cause for creation [causa creationis]." The economy of creation and redemption is rooted in the eternal processions of the immanent Trinity.[104]

As the divine nature belongs to each of the persons in a kind of order, so the power of creation, common to them, still belongs to each in a differentiated way. The Son receives the numerically identical power from the Father, and the Holy Spirit receives it from both. Thus, to be creator is attributed to the Father as to someone who does not receive the power from another; being someone "through whom all things were created" is attributed to the Son as to someone who has the same power from another; and we attribute to the Holy Spirit, who has the power from both, the government and vivification of things created by the Father through the Son. This is in line with the doctrine of appropriation discussed above, which assigns power to the Father as the efficient cause, wisdom to the Son as the formal cause, and goodness to the Holy Spirit as the final cause. Government in the sense of bringing things to their proper end and the giving of life in the sense of a certain interior movement belong to goodness as the final cause of things and thus properly to the Holy Spirit.[105]

Creatures themselves reflect and image the trinitarian exemplar according to the logic of the divine processions. Insofar as every creature subsists in its own being and exercises its own causality, it represents the Father as cause and principle. Insofar as it has a specific form, it represents the Son as the primordial divine model. And insofar as it has an ordered relation to something else, it represents the Holy Spirit as love because the order of the effect to another thing is from the will of the creator.[106]

In criticism of Aquinas's doctrine of appropriation and his assignment of the work of creation to the whole Trinity, LaCugna claims that "by virtue of the doctrine of appropriation, creation is *attributed* to the Father because the Father proceeds from nothing, but the Trinity creates," and that such a position is "inconsistent with the biblical and credal statements that God the Father creates *through* the Son. Thomas's position also depersonalizes the creative act of God by linking it generically with the divine nature rather than identifying it as the *proprium* of a particular person."[107] Likewise, Robert W. Jenson interprets the idea that the works of God *ad extra* are the works of the whole Trinity to mean that "the saving works are *indifferently* the work of each person and all," and to deny that "each work is the joint work of Father, Son, and Spirit, in which each identity plays a distinct role."[108] In light of the whole preceding presentation of Aquinas's position it is rather patent that these criticisms are both false to what Aquinas actually argues for and unfair to the problems Aquinas—and in fact any trinitarian theology—has to grapple with. It is well to recall that for Aquinas, the knowledge of the triune God is necessary precisely for the sake of the "correct" conception of creation and redemption in the sense that these two operations are those of the three divine persons in their distinctiveness, not simply those of the one God.[109]

In Aquinas the doctrine of appropriation is based on two ideas. As appropriation of *essential* attributes, it is based on the idea that essential attributes are clearer to us than the personal properties because we can know such attributes with certitude from creatures, which we cannot say about personal properties, and that creation is a common act of the whole Trinity by virtue of their divine essence. The essential attributes, therefore, are common to all three persons, and it would be heretical to apply them exclusively to a particular person. As *appropriation* of essential attributes, however, the doctrine is also based on the idea that the three persons do have distinctive roles to play in creation and salvation that must be manifested and highlighted, not depersonalized, precisely by virtue of their distinctive properties in the immanent Trinity according to the *ratio* or logic of divine processions where the monarchy of the Father is clearly preserved.

To summarize, Aquinas's doctrine of appropriation is motivated by four concerns, all of which I believe are legitimate and compelling for any trinitarian theology. It is concerned, first, to maintain the divinity of all three persons, for creation is indeed the prerogative of a divine being; second, to allow for differentiation among persons in the work of creation, as Scripture tells us; third, to do so by deriving such differentiation not arbitrarily or extrinsically but from the personal differentiation within the immanent Trinity; and, fourth, to make such differentiation plausible to us in humanly intelligible language. The aim is to maintain balance between the unity of the divine essence and the distinctiveness of the three persons, not to sacrifice one for the other, which would end up destroying both by falling into either modalism or tritheism, either Sabellianism or Arianism.

Persons and Relations

After a consideration of the relation of persons to the divine essence, we now move on to the relation of persons to relations or properties. First of all, is person the same as relation? Relation, considered as a reality in God and not just as the regard of one towards another, is the same as the divine essence itself, which is the same as person. Relation therefore must necessarily be identical with person. The relational properties, which distinguish the persons although not the essence, are like the forms of the persons and are designated by abstract terms such as paternity and filiation; since a form exists in the thing of which it is a form, the properties are in the persons and also are the persons, as the divine essence is in God and is God herself. Persons and properties are really the same but they also differ in concept, which means that multiplication of one does not entail multiplication of the other. "Three" persons does not dictate "three" relations or properties; "three" persons in fact involves "four" relations.

We must remember, however, that in God divine simplicity requires a twofold real identity as regards what in creatures are distinct. First, it excludes the composition of form and matter, which entails the identity of the abstract and the concrete, e.g., of Godhead and God. Second, it also excludes the composition of subject and accident, which entails that whatever is attributed to God is the same as her essence itself; divine wisdom and power are identical with the divine essence and thus with each other. According to this twofold identity, then, property in God is the same as person. Personal properties are the same as the persons because of the identity of the abstract and the concrete; they are the subsisting persons themselves, as paternity is the Father himself, filiation the Son, and procession the Holy Spirit. Non-personal properties, i.e., innascibility and common spiration, are the same as the persons according to the identity of whatever is attributed to God and the divine essence. Thus common spiration is the same as the person of the Father and that of the Son, not in the sense that it is one self-subsisting person but in the sense that it is one property in the two persons as there is one essence in the two persons.[110]

Persons and Notional Acts

Let us move now to the relation of persons to notional acts or acts proper to each person. Should we attribute notional acts to the persons? In the divine persons distinction is based on origin, which can be properly designated only by certain acts. To signify the order of origin in the divine persons, therefore, we must attribute notional acts to the persons. In God there is a twofold order of origin, the procession of creatures from God, which is common to all three persons and in which therefore the divine actions belong to her essence, and the procession of person from person in God, in which the divine actions that designate the order of this origin are called notional because notions are the mutual relations of the persons.

The notional acts differ from the relations of persons only in their mode of signification, for these are altogether identical in reality. Generation and nativity as notional acts are identical with paternity and filiation as relations. Origin of one thing from another is first inferred from movement. Action in its primary sense means origin of movement. If we remove movement from action, however, as we should do in the case of God, action implies nothing more than the order of origin insofar as action proceeds *from* some cause or principle *to* what is from that principle. Since there exists no movement in God, the personal action of the one producing a person is only the habitude of the principle to the person who is from the principle, which habitudes are the relations or notions. Since we have to speak of divine things after the manner of sensible things, in which actions and passions, as movement, differ from the relations which result from action and passion, it was necessary to signify the habitudes of the persons separately in the mode of act and in the mode of relations. Thus acts and relations are really the same but differ only in their mode of signification.[111]

Are the notional acts voluntary or necessary? As usual, Aquinas begins by making a distinction, here between two ways of being voluntary or being made by the will. In one sense, the ablative "by" means only concomitance, as when I say that I am a man by my will, i.e., I will to be a man. In this sense, the Father begot the Son by will, as God is God by will, because she wills to be God and wills to beget the Son. In the other sense, the ablative imports the habitude of a principle, as when we say that the workman works by his will in the sense that the will is the principle or source of his work. In this sense, we cannot say that the Father begot the Son by his will, although we can say that God produces the creature by his will.

Here we have to distinguish between will and nature as principles and as sources of causation. Nature is determined to one effect, while the will is not determined to one but open to many effects. This is because the effect is assimilated to the form of the agent, the intrinsic principle of her action. Now, there is only one natural form of each thing whereby it exists and operates. Thus, as it is itself, such also is its work. The form whereby the will acts, however, is not only one but many, depending on the number of ideas understood from which the action proceeds. Hence the quality of the will's action does not depend on the quality of the agent but on her will and understanding. In this sense, the will is the principle of things which are contingent and which may be this way or that way, e.g., becoming a doctor or a theologian, whereas nature is the principle of those things which can be only in one way, e.g., human parents giving birth to a human being, not a cat.

Now, God is of herself a necessary being, whereas a creature is contingent because made from nothing. Arius insisted that the Father begot the Son by will in order to turn the Son into a contingent, created being. Aquinas rejects this view, stating that the Father begot the Son not by will as a principle of operation, but by nature, although with the concomitance of the will. God naturally understands herself, and the conception of the Word is natural, as God naturally wills and loves herself; thus the Holy Spirit proceeds by nature as Love, although she proceeds precisely according to the mode of the will. With regard to all things other than herself, however, God's will is undetermined in itself or free. To be natural, however, is not the same as to be simply necessary. A thing may be necessary of itself or by reason of another. The latter, extrinsic sense of necessity in turn has a twofold meaning, as a necessary effect of an efficient and compelling cause, or as a necessary means to an end. The divine generation is not necessary in any of these extrinsic senses since God is neither subject to compulsion nor a means to an end. God is necessary of herself because she cannot but be, because her essence is to exist. In this sense of intrinsic necessity, it is necessary for God to be, and for the Father to beget the Son and spirate the Spirit. All the notional acts are necessary in this intrinsic sense with the necessity of the divine nature.[112]

Do notional acts proceed from something? Is the Son, for example, begotten from something, and if so, from what? Here. Aquinas appeals to the classic distinction between making, creating, and generating. Making something always presupposes external matter out of which it is made. Creation means the production of the whole substance of a thing out of nothing, i.e., without presupposing anything else whatsoever. Generation means the production of something of a like nature neither from nothing nor from external matter, but from the nature of the parents themselves. We have to distinguish, however, between human and divine generation. When a human being is born of human parents, a part of the human substance of the parents passes into the substance of the one begotten. When the divine Son is begotten from the substance or essence of the Father, it is not part of the substance of the Father, which cannot be divided, but "the whole nature" of the Father or "the essence of the Father as such [ipsa essentia patris]" [113] that the Father communicates to the Son, only the distinction of origin remaining. The Son was neither made nor cre-

ated, but was begotten from the Father in the sense that he proceeds neither from nothing nor from external matter but from the substance of the
Father. If the Son were simply created or made, he would not be a Son.
The divine essence is not changeable or susceptible of another form;
that is, divine generation is necessarily "consubstantial" or "homoousia."
"The Son is begotten *of* the essence of the Father, inasmuch as the essence
of the Father, communicated by generation, subsists in the Son." It is
of the essence of generation that the generated receives the "nature" of
the generator, always implying a unity of nature between the Father and
the Son, whereas in creation the created do not receive the nature of the
creator.[114]

Does the power of begetting signify a relation? For Aquinas, it cannot. Power means that by which an agent acts. Every agent that produces
something by her action produces something like herself as to the form
by which she acts. A man begotten is like his parents in the human nature
in virtue of which the parents also have the power to beget a human
being. In every begetting, then, the power of begetting is precisely the
nature in which the begotten is like the begetter. The Son is like the
Father in the divine nature, which is, therefore, the power of begetting in
the Father. The power of begetting, therefore, principally signifies the
divine essence, as Peter Lombard said; it signifies neither the relation
only nor the essence identified with the relation so as to signify both
equally. Paternity is taken as the form of the Father, but it is a personal
property and individual form of the Father, which does constitute the
person begetting but is not that by which the begetter begets. Otherwise,
Socrates would beget Socrates, and the Father beget the Father. "That by
which the Father begets is the divine nature, in which the Son is like to
him." Thus the power of begetting signifies the divine nature directly and
the relation indirectly.[115]

Power is that by which an agent acts. The agent is distinct from that
which it makes, and the generator is distinct from the generated, but the
nature—that by which the generator generates—is common to generator
and generated, and is the more perfectly and intimately common to them
in proportion to the perfection of generation. In the most perfect case,
that of the divine generation, then, the divine essence, that by which the
begetter begets, is common to the begetter and begotten by a community
of numerical identity, not only by specific identity as in created things.
Because of divine simplicity, of course, there is real identity with only a
distinction of reason between the power of begetting, the act of begetting,

the divine essence, and paternity. The power of begetting, insofar as it is identical with the divine essence, is common to the three persons, but insofar as it connotes a notion, it is proper to the person of the Father.[116]

Can several persons be the term of one notional act, i.e., can there be several Sons and Holy Spirits in God? Aquinas gives four reasons why there is only one Father, one Son, and one Holy Spirit in God. First, this is so from the nature of relations in God. Persons in God are distinguished by relations alone and are the relations themselves as subsistent. These relations serve as forms of the persons. Since forms of a species are not multiplied except in respect of matter, and since there is no matter in God, there can be only one subsistent paternity, filiation, and procession.[117] Second, this is so from the manner of processions in God. In the "one, simple, and perfect" act of understanding herself, she also understands all other things, just as in the likewise one, simple, and perfect act of loving herself, she also loves all other things. God does not have to posit many different acts of understanding and willing. There can be, therefore, only one person—the Son—proceeding in the mode of word, only one person—the Holy Spirit—proceeding in the mode of love, and only one person—the Father—who does not proceed.[118] Third, this is so from the manner of processions in God. Persons proceed naturally, that is, from the nature of God, with the concomitance of the Father's will, but not from the divine will as a principle of operation, and nature is determined to one, not many. Fourth, this is so from the perfection of the divine persons. The perfection of the Son contains "the entire divine filiation," as the perfection of the Holy Spirit contains the entire divine common spiration.

Aquinas now asks whether the Son, as God, does not have the same power to beget as the Father. And if he does, could he not beget, if not himself, at least his own son? Moreover, if created parents can beget many sons and daughters, why cannot the divine Father? And as the final step in this connection, if the Father in his infinite goodness communicates himself infinitely and produces a person, the Son, why could not the Holy Spirit in her infinite goodness also communicate herself infinitely and produce a person, who in turn could produce another, and so on infinitely? Here also, the answer requires a careful distinction between the one divine nature and the three distinct persons of that nature. Just as the Father and the Son have the same being [idem esse] and same essence to which the power belongs yet differ from each other as Father and Son, so the Son has the same power as the Father yet also differs from the Father in that the power of the Son is not the power of begetting but the power of receiving the divine nature and being begotten, while the Father's power is the power of communicating the divine nature and begetting.

Similarly, the infinite goodness of the Holy Spirit is not different from that of the Father but is exactly the same goodness that belongs to the divine essence, existing in the Father as the principle of its communication and the spiration of the Spirit, and in the Spirit as derived and received from another. If the infinite goodness of the Spirit were different from that of the Father, the Spirit would also be her own principle of self-communication and production of a person. The opposition of relation within the same divine nature does not allow the relation of the Spirit, procession, to be one with the relation of the principle of another divine person, the Father.[119]

The question of multiples within the persons of the Trinity can be phrased somewhat differently. In God the power to beget is the power to understand himself. If the Word is a product of the self-understanding of the Father, why can't we say that the Word also understands himself and thereby produces a concept or word of himself, which in turn may understand himself and produces another word, and so on *ad infinitum?* The answer is similarly that the Word does not have a separate power and act of understanding himself whereby to produce a word of his own. Just as the Word is not a God other than the God whose Word he is, so he is not another intellect with a separate act of understanding. Just as there is only one act of understanding himself in God, so there is only one intellect or power of understanding himself, which is identical with the act of understanding, which in turn is identical with the divine essence. The knowledge, power, and operation of God are her essence. As belonging to the one divine essence, the power of understanding is common to all three persons but exercised in personally differentiated ways. It is from the same power that the Word is conceived, as it is from the same power that the Father conceives the Word.

The ultimate reason, then, that there is only one Son and only one Spirit, and that the Son and the Spirit cannot respectively generate and spirate other persons of their own, is not any lack in the power of any one of the persons but rather the unity of the divine essence and the divine power shared by the three persons in three different ways. In the perfection of the divine power, the Father communicates his entire divine nature and begets a Son, who by himself contains "the entire filiation," and spirates a Spirit, who by herself contains "the entire spiration."[120]

The unity of the divine essence assures the identity of all that belongs to the essence, such as the power to generate, to understand oneself, and to communicate onself, while divine simplicity and infinity assure the unicity of each of the divine acts as "one, simple, and perfect" act such as generating, spirating, and creating, preventing what Hegel would call the "bad infinity" of created things.[121]

It is quite appropriate to consider in this context a typically modern question that Aquinas never asked as such, namely, whether the three persons constitute three distinct centers of consciousness. In light of the preceding considerations about self-understanding in God, of which the question of self-consciousness of each person is a natural extension, it is clear that consciousness, like understanding, belongs to the one divine essence. Power, understanding, wisdom, love: these depend on the kind of being or essence their subject belongs to, and in God, therefore, they are attributes of the one divine essence and as such are common to all three persons. Just as there is only one power to beget, only one act of self-understanding, only one wisdom, and only one love in God, so there is only one divine consciousness, not three separate consciousnesses. However, just as wisdom, understanding, the power to beget, and other attributes of the one divine essence are shared by the three persons in their different ways according to the logic of the immanent processions, we can likewise say that the one divine consciousness subsists in three personally differentiated ways or three distinct subjects, all of whom are conscious of themselves in their personal difference by means of the one divine consciousness. The Father understands and is conscious of himself as Father, as the unoriginate origin of all things including the Son and the Holy Spirit. The Son understands and is conscious of himself precisely as the Word begotten, the self-concept and image of the Father. The Holy Spirit understands and is conscious of herself as the Love proceeding from the Father and the Son. In each case it is the same divine consciousness shared by the three persons but shared by each according to the personal properties of each.[122]

The Mutual Relation of Persons

How, finally, are the persons mutually related? Are they truly equal despite the order of procession? Given the ever present possibility of subordinationism throughout history, this is perhaps one of the most critical questions to ask in any trinitarian theology. Aquinas's answer is framed in terms of the indivisibility of the divine essence. Equality, according to Aristotle, signifies the negation of greater or lesser or quantitative difference. Quantity is twofold, encompassing both the quantity of bulk or dimension found only in corporeal things, which has no place in God, and the quantity of virtue or power, which is measured according to either the perfection of the form or nature or the effects of the form in terms of being and operation. Quantity in God is quantity of virtue, which is nothing else than her essence. Now, if there were any inequality in the divine persons in the perfection of their respective forms, being, and operation, they would not have the same essence, in which case the three persons would not be one God, which is impossible.

In matters of virtual quantity, equality includes likeness but also something more. Whatever things have a common form may be said to be alike, but they are not equal if they do not participate in the form equally perfectly. The Father and the Son not only share the same divine nature and are like each other, contrary to Eunomius, but share it in perfect equality so that the Son is equal to the Father, contrary to Arius. In God equality and likeness are mutual. The Son is both equal and like to the Father. The divine essence is no more the Father's than the Son's. As the Son has the greatness of the Father and is equal to the Father, so the Father has the greatness of the Son and is equal to the Son. In created things, however, equality and likeness are not mutual. Effects are like to their causes insofar as they have the form of the latter, but the form is principally in the cause and secondarily in the effect.[123]

The Son is, therefore, necessarily equal to the Father in greatness, which in God means the perfection of her nature. It is of "the very nature [ratio] of paternity and filiation that the Son by generation should attain to the possession of the perfection of the nature which is in the Father, in the same way as it is in the Father himself."[124] The Father and the Son have the same essence and dignity, which, however, exists in the Father according to the relation of giver and in the Son according to the relation of receiver. This perfect sharing of the same divine nature among the persons rules out any application of the logic of part and whole to the Trinity. Relation in God is not a universal whole, although it is predicated of each of the relations; all the relations are one in essence and being [esse], which contradicts the idea of a universal consisting of parts each of which is distinguished in being [esse]. Nor is person, for the same reason, a universal term in God. All these truths point to the profound, incomprehensible mystery of the triune communion: "All the relations together are not greater than only one; nor are all the persons something greater than only one; because the whole perfection [tota perfectio] of the divine nature exists in each person."[125] Thus also: "The Father is of the same magnitude as the whole Trinity."[126] The same holds true of the Son and the Holy Spirit respectively.

Are the Son and the Holy Spirit coeternal with the Father? A thing proceeding from a principle may be posterior to the principle for two reasons, one on the part of the agent, and one on the part of the action. On the part of the agent, this occurs differently depending on whether the agent is free or natural. Free agents can choose both the form and the time in which to produce their effect. Natural agents do not have the perfection of their natural power from the first but obtain it after a certain time, as a human being is not able to generate from the very first. On the part of action, there is no simultaneity between agent and effect whenever the action is successive, as it must be in all actions that involve material change, in which case the effect would exist only in the instant of the action's termination.

None of these applies to God. The Father does not beget the Son by will but by nature, the Father is perfect from eternity, and the act of begetting is not material and therefore not successive either. The intellectual word is not posterior to its source except in an intellect that has to pass from potentiality to act, and the divine intellect is always in act. For Aquinas, eternity excludes the principle of duration but not that of origin. Every corruption is change from existence to non-existence. Divine generation does not involve change. The Son is ever being begotten, and the Father is always begetting, not in time but in the "now" of eternity, the *nunc semper stans*. There never was a time when the Son was not, contrary to Arius. The Son, therefore, is coeternal with the Father, as also is the Holy Spirit.[127]

Is there an order of nature in the divine persons? Order is based on some principle, and there are as many different kinds of order as there are many different principles. In God a principle exists solely according to origin, without priority. There is, therefore, an order according to origin without priority in God, which is the order of nature whereby one is from [ex] another without being posterior to another. One is "from" another but not "after" another. In created things the principle, formally considered as principle, comes first in the order of both nature and reason, even when what is derived from a principle is coeval in duration with its principle. However, in the case of the relation between cause and effect or between the principle and the thing proceeding from the principle, the things so related can be simultaneous in the order of nature and reason if the one enters into the definition or essence of the other; this is true in God. The relations themselves are the persons subsisting in one nature. The Son as proceeding from the Father is included in the very divine nature of the Father as principle, and vice versa. No person can be prior to another either on the part of the nature or on the part of the relations, i.e., according to either nature or reason. The Son, therefore, is *from* the Father but not *after* the Father. The same should be said of the Holy Spirit.[128]

Are the divine persons in one another in mutual circumincession or "perichoresis," and if so, what makes such mutual presence necessary? For Aquinas, considerations of the essence, relation, and origin dictate the mutual inherence of the three persons. As regards the essence, "the Father is in the Son by his essence, forasmuch as the Father is his own essence, and communicates his essence to the Son not by any change on his part."[129] Thus, as the Father's essence is in the Son, the Father himself is in the Son, and likewise, as the Son is his own essence, he himself is in the Father in whom is his essence. As regards the relation, the Father and the Son are relatively opposed, not essentially or absolutely, and each of two relative opposites is in the concept of the other, as the concept of "begetter" exists in that of "begotten," and vice versa. As regards origin as an immanent act, the procession of the intelligible word is not outside the intellect but remains in the utterer of the word. The same considerations also apply to the Holy Spirit. None of the finite modes of mutual presence is adequate to represent the mutual presence of the three divine persons. The closest analogy is the presence of something in the principle from which it originates, as in the case of immanent acts whose effects remain in the agent. The qualitative difference, however, will always persist between the mutual inherence of the three divine persons and any mutual presence of finite things, because the numerical unity of essence between the principle and those which proceed from it is found only in God, never in created relations.[130]

Thomas F. Torrance on Being and Person

Before I conclude the presentation of Aquinas's doctrine of the immanent Trinity, I think it is relevant to dwell briefly on an important systematic issue raised by Thomas F. Torrance and to consider how Aquinas might respond. The issue is whether we should derive the unity of the Godhead from the *person* or the *being*—meaning "ousia"—of the Father, whether we should understand monarchy in terms of the monarchy of the Father or the monarchy of the whole Trinity, and how we are to understand the order of relations in the Trinity, especially the priority of the Father. Torrance raises the issue in the context of the trinitarian developments from Athanasius to the Cappadocians, which as such is not my concern, but engaging the issue can further clarify Aquinas's position and illuminate the significance of his contribution to trinitarian theology.

According to Torrance, the Father, as Father of the Son, does enjoy a priority in order, a certain monarchy, among the divine persons. But this priority only means priority in the order of trinitarian relations within the one indivisible being of the triune God and the ontological equality of the three persons, not priority in being or deity; it is a priority in "position," not "status," in "form," not "being," in "sequence," not "power." It is wrong, therefore, to consider the Father as the "deifier" of the Son; the Father is Father only as Father of the Son, who is no less divine than the Father.[131] Torrance is responding to a problem that arose when Basil and Gregory of Nyssa shifted the emphasis from the homoousial identity of being of Athanasius and the Nicene confession to the differentiating particularities of the three persons. They tried to avoid tritheism by anchoring the unity of God in the Father as the one origin, principle, or cause of deity and by deriving the being and deity of the Son and the Holy Spirit not from the being or ousia but from the *person* of the Father, who now, according to Torrance, "causes, deifies, and personalises the Being of the Son and of the Spirit and even the existence of the Godhead."[132] By conflating the sense of "Father" taken absolutely in its reference to the Godhead and the one ousia of God, and the sense of "Father" taken relatively in its reference to the Father of the Son, the Cappadocians derived the unity of God from the latter—the person of the Father—not from the former—the ousia of the Father. The generation of the Son and the procession of the Spirit were then taken as causations of their being rather than as modes of their personal differentiation within the one being of the Godhead.

This derivation of the divine unity and the deity of the Son and the Spirit from the person of the Father, with the untenable distinction between the underived deity of the Father and the derived deity of the Son and the Spirit, introduced for subsequent trinitarian theologies the danger of subordinationism and hierarchical thinking. This danger was countered only through the doctrine of perichoresis, which affirms the coinherence of the persons in one another in an equality and wholeness that excludes all surbordination and degrees of deity.

The Father is the principle [arche] of deity only in the sense of his being unoriginate or Father, i.e., not being a Son, rather than in the sense of his being the principle or cause of the divine being of the Son and the Spirit. The Nicene "homoousion" means the perfect unity and identity of being among the three persons: the Son is begotten not of the person but of the being or ousia of the Father, which as such is totally and equally shared by the three persons. As begetter of the Son the Father is the principle of the Son but he is not so apart from the Son, without whom he cannot be the Father. Insofar as the being or Godhead of the Father is common to the other two, the one principle or monarchy belongs to the Trinity as a whole, not to the Father alone.

For Torrance, restoring the language of the homoousion not only eliminates the lingering Origenist subordinationism but also resolves the question of the Filioque: insofar as the Spirit proceeds from the being of the Father, and insofar as this being belongs to all three indivisibly and equally, the Spirit proceeds not only from the being of the Father but also from that of the Son. As long as the monarchy is understood as the monarchy of the divine being or ousia that belongs to the whole Trinity, and not as the personal prerogative of the Father, both formulations, "from the Father and the Son" and "from the Father through the Son," are equally in order.[133]

It is clear that Torrance's position is based on a sharp opposition between essence and person and is motivated by the desire to avoid subordinationism. From his standpoint, any attempt to derive the deity of the Son and the Spirit from the person of the Father seems to lead to subordinationism and difficulties with the Filioque. Torrance's view seems to treat person and essence as though they are separable in God, allowing the Father to relate himself to the Son and the Spirit in some other way than according to the kind of being he is, i.e., according to his divine essence, and treating the Father's own essence as though it were simply that of the being common to all three without personal differentiation. This is the definition of modalism. By the same token, on Torrance's view the priority of the Father as a person has nothing to do with the origin of the deity or divine being of the Son and the Spirit, but only with the origin of their persons, as though the Father could be the Father of the Son without also fathering the person of the Son precisely in his divine being. Yet what would it mean to beget the Son only as a person and not also in his divinity, a person therefore separated from his divine essence?

Consequently, when we ask wherein consists the relational priority or monarchy of the Father traditionally indicated by the words "fatherhood," "sonship," "generation," and "spiration" or "procession," Torrance must plead agnosticism based on their incomprehensibility: "As divinely given they are irreplaceable ultimate terms which we cannot but use and which are always to be used only with godliness, reverence, and fidelity. They denote ineffable relations and refer to ineffable realities." We are to "suspend our thought before the altogether inexpressible, incomprehensible Nature of God."[134] It is inconsistent for Torrance, who elsewhere argues for the differential use of "being" and "person," the monarchy of the Trinity over against the monarchy of the Father, and the mutual indwelling of the three persons in the undivided being of the Godhead, to plead ignorance when it comes to the further specification of the relational priority of the Father. On the face of it, "being," "person," "monarchy," and "perichoresis" in the life of the triune God should be no less incomprehensible than "paternity," "filiation," "generation," and "spiration," but Torrance does not justify any distinction. Nor does he utilize the metaphysics of divine generation, an idea consistently prevalent among the Fathers East and West, central to the Nicene confession itself, and testifying precisely to the Son "begotten" from the substance of the Father. Torrance's appeal to incomprehensibility does not convince.

As the whole discussion in this chapter should have made clear, Aquinas's sophisticated metaphysics makes it possible to guarantee the ontological equality of the three persons and their perichoresis without separating essence and person, without sacrificing the traditional monarchy of the Father in favor of the monarchy of the Trinity, and without claiming to reduce the essential incomprehensibility of the mystery of the triune God. It is crucial here to recall some of the salient features of Aquinas's metaphysics of divine generation, though without repeating in great detail all that we have seen above.

Contrary to Torrance's attempt to reduce divine generation to a relational, personal reality separated from the divine essence, Aquinas points out that a person can only act according to the kind of being she is, that is, only according to her own essence or nature, and that this is especially true of the act of generation. As already discussed, a person begets according to her own nature in the double senses that the power to beget belongs to one's nature, not to one's personal peculiarities, and that what is begotten is like the begetter precisely in her nature, not in her individual personality. The relation between begetter and begotten does constitute the person of the begetter and the begotten, but the power of begetting is rooted not in the relation but in the nature. Socrates, as a human being, begets another human being; he does not, as an individual, beget another Socrates. In every begetting the power of begetting is the nature in which the begotten is like the begetter. Insofar as one begets according to one's nature, the power of begetting signifies the nature or essence directly. Insofar as the power of begetting, nevertheless, does belong to a person as begetter, it also signifies the person and relation indirectly. The Son is like the Father in the divine nature, which is, therefore, the power of begetting in the Father. "That by which the Father begets is the divine nature, in which the Son is like to him."[135] Every offspring is not only begotten from the father but also precisely from the nature, essence, or substance of the father. It is not possible to separate person and essence in any act, certainly not in the act of generation.

It is the peculiarity of generation that it communicates the nature of the begetter to the begotten and establishes a community of nature or essence between them; this is not true of either making or creating, neither of which establishes a community of essence between the agent and the product. "The Son is begotten *of* the essence of the Father, inasmuch as the essence of the Father, communicated by generation, subsists in the Son."[136] Furthermore, the community of nature and mutual intimacy between begetter and begotten increases in direct proportion to the perfection of generation. Thus, in the case of divine generation the divine nature or essence is indivisible and can only be communicated in its indivisible totality or not at all. Divine generation, therefore, necessarily involves the communication of the numerically—not just specifically—identical divine nature or essence of the Father to the Son. It is the peculiarity of *divine* generation, then, that it cancels not only the exteriority of begetter and begotten but also the hierarchy of superiority and inferiority, priority and posteriority, that mark all human and other biological generation. It is precisely the communication of the entire, undivided, numerically identical divine nature of the Father that makes the complete mutual indwelling of the three persons both possible and necessary: the undivided essence of the Father—and therefore the Father himself—is in the Son and the Spirit, and vice versa, sharing everything except their respective relationally constituted personhood. It is also the communication of the undivided divine nature that cancels any inequality in terms of superiority or inferiority, priority and posteriority.

This is why Aquinas insists that divine generation does posit an order of relation between the principle and that which proceeds from the principle but only an order according to origin, not priority of time or superiority of power. In created things, if we consider the principle formally *as principle,* the principle does come first in the order of both nature and reason even when what is derived from a principle is coeval in duration with its principle. However, if we consider the *relation* between cause and effect or between the principle and the thing proceeding from the principle, the things so related can be simultaneous in the order of nature and reason if the one enters into the definition of the other, which is true in God. The relations themselves are the persons subsisting in one nature. The Son as proceeding from the Father is included in the very divine nature of the Father as principle, and vice versa. No person can be prior to another either on the part of the nature or on the part of the relations. The Son, therefore, is *from* the Father but not *after* the Father. The same should be said of the Holy Spirit.[137]

It is true, then, that the Father alone is ungenerate and that the Son and the Spirit do derive their divine nature or essence from the Father, but there are two things to note here. First, without separating person and essence as does Torrance, but also sensitive to his concern, Aquinas does deny that the Father begets (or spirates) the Godhead or divine nature of the Son (or the Holy Spirit). Rather, the Father is "the principle of the whole Godhead, not as generating or spirating it, but as communicating it by generation and spiration."[138] The Father begets the Son in his divine nature not by begetting the divine nature of the Son, as though the divine nature needed begetting—which does sound odd, as Torrance points out—but by communicating or sharing his own numerically identical divine nature with the Son and thereby constituting himself as Father and the Son as son.

Second, it is the peculiarity of divine generation that this "derivation" also cancels itself into an affirmation of equality in which the three persons share one another and dwell in one another. Divine generation is the mystery of sharing in which the giver, the Father, so totally shares himself (except his being Father) as to cancel the very superiority of the giver—and the inferiority of the recipient—and in which the recipient is so totally constituted by the gift, the divinity of the Father, the Father himself in his very being, as to be what the Father is without ceasing to be Son. It is the mystery of being that remains thoroughly identical despite relational differences, and the mystery of relation that remains thoroughly distinct despite ontological identity.

The Father, then, does remain the one *arche* of the divinity of the Son and the Spirit, but it is a monarchy that also cancels its own superiority in the very exercise of its power. It is, therefore, not necessary to appeal to the monarchy of the Trinity as a whole for fear of subordinationism; it is the privilege of the monarchy of the *divine* Father to generate the Son and spirate the Spirit, both numerically identical in nature to himself, and thereby make genuine equality both possible and necessary. The inherent order in the origination of the persons also means that the numerically identical divine nature exists in each person in a differentiated way proper to its place in that order, as unoriginate in the Father, as communicated in the Son and in the Spirit. In contrast, the idea of the monarchy of the Trinity may make sense in relation to creation, of which the undivided Trinity remains the one *arche*, but applied to the trinitarian relations, it either makes no sense at all—the trinitarian persons as the "one *arche*" of themselves?—or reduces itself to the modalism of the one divine undifferentiated ousia separated from the persons whose mutual relations—"fatherhood," "sonship," "generation," and "spiration"—simply remain unexplained in a premature appeal to incomprehensibility.

It is this peculiarity of the idea of generation—the identity of nature and relational difference between begetter and begotten—that made the analogy of generation so essential to the trinitarian speculations of the Fathers from Origen through Athanasius to the Cappadocians, Augustine, and Aquinas.[139] The analogy is so rich as to be able to do justice to the monarchy of the Father, the real distinction among persons, and their ontological equality and mutual indwelling, requirements of any "orthodox" trinitarian theology. It is a real loss that Torrance, along with other contemporary trinitarian theologians such as Moltmann and Pannenberg, simply ignores the rich metaphysics of divine generation so central to the classical tradition.[140]

Furthermore, in Aquinas, this trinitarian metaphysics of divine generation does not deny the ultimate incomprehensibility of the triune God. As pointed out in chapter 1 and earlier in this chapter, theological speculations about the triune God are human attempts to elucidate according to human modes of speaking and understanding what we believe about the Father, the Son, and the Holy Spirit, based on congruent reasons and finite analogies and affirmed only analogically by way of causality, negation, and eminence. We can in no way claim to have attained a vision of the immanent life of the triune God, which will remain only partially comprehended even in the beatific vision. No one is more sensitive to this human limit of theological predication than Aquinas, who, as we have seen, reminds us of the human character of all theological assertions at every important juncture. By the same token, not many have his courage to go as far as they can in providing this human attempt without prematurely pleading divine incomprehensibility.

This is well illustrated in his discussion of divine generation. In our human mode of speaking we have to distinguish among the act of begetting, the power of begetting, the divine essence, and fatherhood, as we have likewise been distinguishing between essence and existence, essence and supposit, person and essence, in this chapter. Aquinas reminds us, however, of the utter transcendence of God by always telling us that what exist multiple and divided among finite beings exist in God united and undivided, i.e., simple. By appeal to divine simplicity, which many analytic philosophers resent, Aquinas also points to the limit of human predication: there is a real identity, only a distinction of reason, among the act of begetting, the power of begetting, the divine essence, and paternity, which we can only affirm without being able to "see." In our human mode, however, we can only say that the power of begetting, insofar as it is identical with the divine essence, is common to the three persons, but that insofar as it connotes a notion, it is proper to the person of the Father.[141]

The Missions of the Triune God

We now come to the last question in the treatise on the triune God, the mission of the three persons in the economy of creation and redemption. I have already treated of the concrete content of this divine mission in terms of creation and redemption in the first and third chapters respectively, and will confine myself here to the fundamentals of that mission as they bear on the logic of the immanent Trinity.

For Aquinas, the *ratio* of mission includes two things: the relation of the one sent to the sender, which implies a certain kind of procession of the one sent from the sender, according to command, counsel, or origin; and the relation of the one sent to the term to which she is sent, to be present there either for the first time or in a new way. The mission of a divine person is fitting [conveniens] if we consider it as a procession of origin according to equality from the sender, not according to command or counsel, which implies inequality, and as a new way of existing in another, not as local motion, which applies only to material beings. Thus the Son is sent by the Father into the world inasmuch as he begins to exist in a new way, i.e., visibly, by taking our nature, in the world where he was never absent before.[142]

Is the divine mission eternal or temporal? Among the many words that express the origin of the divine persons, some, such as "procession" and "going forth," express only the relation to the principle; others express both the principle and the term of the procession, of which some, such as "generation" and "spiration," express the eternal term, and some, such as "mission" and "giving," express the temporal term. A thing is sent so that it may be in something else, and is given so that it may be possessed. For a divine person to be possessed by any creature or to exist in it in a new mode is temporal. In this sense, mission and giving are only temporal, while generation and spiration are only eternal. Procession and giving, on the other hand, are both eternal and temporal. The Son proceeds eternally as God, but also temporally, by becoming a human being according to his visible mission, or by dwelling in human beings according to his invisible mission. This new mode of existence in a creature or being possessed by a creature in time does not entail any change in God but only in the creature, just as God is called "lord" temporally because of a change in the creature's real relation to God.[143]

The divine mission whereby one of the divine persons exists in a new mode in a creature or is possessed by a creature occurs only by sanctifying grace [gratia gratum faciens]. Prior to the mission, God already exists in all things, not as part of their essence or their accident, but as the cause exists in its effects, by her essence as the cause of their very being [causa essendi], by her power to which all things are subject, and by her presence to which all things are naked and open, thus most intimately.[144] This is a mode of divine presence common to all creatures. Above and beyond this common mode, however, there is a special mode characterizing God's presence in the rational creature, in which God is present as the known is present in the knower, and the beloved in the lover. The rational creature, through knowledge and love, attains to God herself, who, therefore, not only exists in the rational creature but also "dwells" therein as in her own temple. This presence of God in the rational creature in this new mode is none other than sanctifying grace, which perfects, enables, and disposes the rational creature not only to freely use the created gifts of God but also to possess and enjoy the divine person herself. Thus, the divine person is sent and proceeds temporally only according to sanctifying grace. The Holy Spirit is possessed by a human being and dwells within her, in the very gift of sanctifying grace; that is, the Holy Spirit herself is given and sent.[145]

Is it fitting [conveniens] for the Father to be sent on an economic mission? For Aquinas, the answer is no because God's economic mission reflects the personal relations and differences of the immanent Trinity. The very idea of mission means procession from another, which in God means procession according to origin. The Father, as "the principle not from a principle," is not from another, so it is not fitting for the Father to be sent, but it is fitting for the Son and the Holy Spirit to be sent because it belongs to them to be from another. Of course, the Father, too, freely gives himself to be enjoyed by the creature and dwells in it by grace, but mission in the sense of being given, which implies the authority of the giver, belongs only to the person who is from another.[146]

If it is fitting, therefore, for the Son to be sent visibly through the Incarnation, is it also fitting for him to be sent invisibly, i.e., according to the gift of grace? It is, of course, the whole Trinity that dwells in us by (sanctifying) grace, but the sending of a divine person by invisible grace means both that the person has his origin from another and that he dwells in the creature in a new way. Both of these belong to the Son and the Holy Spirit, and it is fitting, therefore, for them to be invisibly sent, as it is not fitting for the Father to be sent—visibly or invisibly—because it does not belong to him to be from another even though he does dwell in us by grace. Now, the soul is con-form-ed [conformatur] to God by grace. If a divine person is to be sent through grace, there must be a likening of the soul [assimilatio] to that person by some gift of grace. Because the Holy Spirit is Love whereby God loves herself and us and whereby we are enabled to love God, the soul is likened to the Spirit by the gift of charity, whereas the soul is likened to the Son, who is not just any word but the Word that breathes forth Love, by the illumination of the intellect which breaks forth into the affection of love, a sweet knowledge, or wisdom. Thus, the mission of the Holy Spirit is according to the mode of charity, that of the Word according to that of wisdom. The two missions are distinguished according to origin, as are generation and procession, and according to the indwelling by grace in the effects of grace, which are the illumination of the intellect in the one case and the kindling of the affection in the other. Although the two missions are distinct in these ways, they are united in the root [radix] of grace. It is clear, moreover, that one mission cannot take place without the other, because both presuppose sanctifying grace and the persons are inseparably united.[147]

On the part of the creature, mission means a new mode of divine presence in the form of the indwelling of grace and a certain renewal [innovatio] by grace.[148] Whenever these two conditions are present, we can say that an invisible mission takes place. This means that an invisible mission is operative in all human beings who participate in grace and its renewal, in those who receive grace through the sacraments as well as those who lived before the time of the visible missions of the Son and the Holy Spirit, for example, in the patriarchs of the Old Testament. Likewise, the invisible mission takes place with regard to progress in virtue or increase of grace, but especially in order to promote proficiency in the performance of a new act or in the acquisition of a new state of grace, as evidenced in miracles, prophecy, and fervor of charity leading one to expose oneself to the danger of martyrdom, to renounce one's possessions, or to undertake any difficult work.[149]

If it is fitting for the Holy Spirit to be sent invisibly, is it also fitting for the Holy Spirit to be sent visibly in the form of a dove, wind, or tongues, perhaps? Here Aquinas begins with the fundamental principle discussed in the second chapter, that God provides for all things according to the nature of each thing. Human nature requires that human beings be led to the invisible by means of visible things, and therefore that the invisible things of God should be made manifest to human beings by things that are visible, and therefore that the invisible missions be made manifest by some visible creatures. As we would expect, the mode of manifestation applies differently to the different persons. As it belongs to the Holy Spirit, who proceeds as Love, to be the gift of sanctification, so it belongs to the Son, from whom the Spirit also proceeds, to be the author of sanctification. Thus, the Son was sent visibly as the author of sanctification, and the Holy Spirit as the sign [indicium] of sanctification. The Holy Spirit is sent visibly wherever she shows herself in created things that serve as signs of her presence.[150]

An important consequence follows from this difference. The Son assumed the visible creature in which he appeared into the unity of his person; hence, whatever can be said of the creature can be said of the Son of God. The Holy Spirit, however, did not assume the visible creatures in which she appeared into the unity of her person; hence, what is said of the creatures cannot be predicated of the Holy Spirit. The Holy Spirit, therefore, cannot be called less than the Father by reason of any visible creature, as the Son can by reason of the nature assumed. It was necessary [oportuit] for the visible mission of the Son to take place according to a rational nature capable of acting and sanctifying and to assume it into a personal unity because the Son was the author of sanctification and needed to act. For the visible mission of the Holy Spirit as the gift of sanctification, however, any visible creature could serve without needing to be assumed into personal unity because it was used not for the purpose of action but only for the purpose of a sign and without also, therefore, needing to last beyond such use. These differences, however, should not be understood as in any way denying the fundamental unity of the divine missions and their goal: "The Holy Spirit manifests the Son, as the Son manifests the Father," so that "others might be regenerated to the likeness of the only Begotten."[151]

Chapter Six

CONTEMPORARY TRINITARIAN DISCUSSIONS IN LIGHT OF AQUINAS

In the preceding chapter I presented Aquinas's theology of the immanent Trinity in some detail. It is certainly one of the most systematic, most comprehensive, and most sophisticated accounts of the doctrine of the Trinity ever attempted, a most profound, creative, and coherent synthesis of the biblical teachings about the Father, the Son, and the Holy Spirit, the patristic heritage of both East and West, and the best available philosophical insights of the day.[1] Even those who disagree with the doctrine will have to acknowledge it as a most daring human attempt to come to grips with what Kasper calls "the grammar and summation of the entire Christian mystery of salvation" or what Nicholas Lash calls "'the summary grammar' of the Christian account of the mystery of salvation and creation."[2] Aquinas accomplished all this without lapsing into either the hubris of reducing it to pure human intelligibility or the despair of a fideism that simply repeats the letter of the Bible.

In recent decades, however, Aquinas's doctrine of the Trinity has come under severe criticism, first from Protestant theologians preoccupied with the theology of revelation in Scripture, then from Catholic theologians following their Protestant colleagues, and finally from both as they made the modern turn to the human subject and human history. Challenges have been made to the abstractness of the metaphysical language (as opposed to the concrete narratives of Scripture), the sexism of the trinitarian formula, the inadequacy of the psychological model of one subject and one substance, the isolation of the doctrine of God from the doctrine of salvation, the practical irrelevance of the traditional doctrine, the separation of the treatise on the one God from the treatise on the triune God, and the undue emphasis on the unity of the divine essence at the expense of the trinity of persons.[3] In this chapter I will try to respond to these issues from the perspective of Aquinas, often also subjecting their underlying contemporary assumptions to a critique in light of Aquinas's insights.

The Problem of Metaphysical Language

One of the most common criticisms of Aquinas's trinitarian theology is that it is expressed in abstract and abstruse metaphysical language. This criticism is understandable for various reasons. To contemporary readers, who are generally cut off from the classical tradition—and this includes many professional theologians—Aquinas's terminologies must be abstruse enough: substance, accident, form, matter, essence, existence, procession, spiration, relative opposition, notion, formal effect, hypostatic union, personal and essential names. These concepts are not easily comprehensible today in terms of our own empiricist, phenomenalist, and descriptive language. To many contemporary readers and theologians, who have been nurtured on existentialist, personalist, liberationist, feminist, and political theologies with their "concrete" human, historical content, Aquinas's theology must indeed appear abstract. It is more ontological and cosmological than personalist or homocentric. It is no wonder that contemporary readers tend to be put off by the very language of Aquinas's theology.

It is important to remember, however, that Aquinas's ontological language was quite appropriate to theology conceived as *sapientia* or wisdom, which seeks to contemplate God and all created things *sub ratione Dei*. For Aquinas, the principal purpose of theology was not so much to arouse Christians to immediate action or to produce reflections relevant to a particular generation as it was to reflect on God as the origin and end of all things and on the place of all other things including but not limited to human beings in reference to God; from there he also drew ethical principles for human praxis. Despite the ideological contamination and historical conditioning of some of his ideas, which is true of all theologies, his sapiential theology was cosmological, not anthropocentric, and universalist, not intentionally confined to the needs of a particular time. A universal theology that deals with God and all other things with reference to God, however, and does so not narratively but in a comprehensive, systematic way will have to reckon with the language of ontology, that is, the language of being in its intrinsic unity and plurality as well as in its absolute universality, however abstract and abstruse it may sound. After all, there is nothing that is not contained in *being,* which is necessarily more comprehensive than any other category that can be thought, be it process, becoming, evolution, relationality, intersubjectivity, existence, narrative, praxis, liberation, or hope. A sapiential theology is necessarily a theology of being, however this being may be interpreted, a reflection on God as the source and end of all beings and on all finite beings in reference to God.

With the increasing recognition of the problems of homocentrism or anthropocentrism today and thus with the necessity of rethinking the place of humanity in the larger scheme of the universe, it is becoming increasingly relevant to retrieve something of the ontological, cosmological dimension of Aquinas's sapiential theology and its vision of the whole. The point is not to return to the Middle Ages but to reappropriate its universalist, cosmological ontology for our time, with appropriate modification and as one among other types of theology, so as to provide a counterpoint to the dominant anthropocentrism of contemporary theologies. This would introduce a tension between historicist anthropocentrism and cosmological ontocentrism, a tension we need to maintain insofar as we cannot remain indifferent either to the challenge of historical human problems or to the need for relativizing anthropocentric claims in light of universal being.

If we approach Aquinas in this light, and cultivate a little more understanding of classical metaphysical terminologies and a little more patience with its abstract language, I think there is plenty that we can appreciate in Aquinas today, in terms of both his style and content.

In terms of his style, anyone who comes to Aquinas after a heavy immersion in contemporary theology and philosophy is immediately struck by a certain self-withdrawing impersonality, ahistorical serenity, and contemplative acceptance of reality. In contrast to the personal, often autobiographical style of much contemporary theology in which the reader is never allowed to ignore the dominating presence of the author with his or her personal backgrounds and concerns, Aquinas never asserts his own personality or subjectivity. He withdraws himself totally before the objective content of the matter at issue. As one observer put it, Aquinas "disappears from sight as an individual," becoming "only the expression of a point of view."[4]

Likewise, in contrast to the historical anguish and frustration and the cry for relief so characteristic of much recent theology, Aquinas seems to rise above the preoccupations and crises peculiar to his own age, showing a certain freedom from overwhelming historical concerns. Not that he is not concerned with the problems of his age: he is, as we see in his involvement with such contemporary problems as the challenge of Aristotle, the defense of the faith against non-Christians, the salvation of the non-believer, and the status of theology in the academy. But he is not so emotionally *pre*-occupied with them as to inject his historical anguish into his writings. There is no overriding sense of the particular historical context which twentieth-century theology uses as a justification for concentrating on certain issues, be it unbelief, otherworldliness, or oppression, and expressing itself with varying types and intensities of emotion such as indignation, outrage, *han,* or despair. In Aquinas there is none of this concentration of the whole of theology on a particular theme, none of the screaming, crying, yelling, or protesting that we are used to in recent theologies. There is only a quiet, serene, confident acceptance of reality that comes from the contemplation of God and all other things with reference to God, indeed concerned over evil and injustice in the human world but leaving their ultimate resolution, beyond what human beings can and should do on their own, to God's incomprehensible providence, and integrating particular historical, contextual concerns into the universal ontological context of the fundamental relation between finite and infinite mediated through the universal experience of contingency, death, sin, and the need for salvation. The stylistic difference between Aquinas and contemporary theology stems from the difference between sapiential and prophetic theology, which I will take up in some detail in the next, final chapter.

In terms of content, I can simply point to certain examples of profundity and insight that we might appreciate in Aquinas's approach if we are able to overcome our resistance to the abstract and abstruse language of his metaphysics and make ourselves willing to penetrate, beneath the language, into the content which is his real concern and which he puts in a matter-of-fact way, quietly, simply, without exaggerating, absolutizing, screaming, or trying to provoke. Aquinas's treatments of the Son and the Holy Spirit provide examples of how brilliantly he synthesizes the often disparate elements contained in the respective traditional doctrines by means of his metaphysical concepts and insights.

The New Testament refers to Christ as the Son, the Word, the Image, the mediator through whom and for whom the universe was created and through whom human beings receive adoption as children of the Father. Likewise, the New Testament refers to the Holy Spirit as the Spirit of love and fellowship as well as the Gift of the Father. It is not at all clear, however, how these terms are so coherently related to one another as to refer to one being in each case without denying the diversity of functions they do indicate. Nor is it not obvious why the Father should create the world through the Son but govern it through the Holy Spirit, why the Father's Son and Word should be the same being, why the Holy Spirit should be Spirit, Love, and Gift, and why the generation of the Word and the spiration of the Holy Spirit should be mutually distinct when both involve the same communication of the divine nature. In a similar vein, Moltmann pointed to the problem of integrating the logic of the Father and the Son and the logic of the Word and the Spirit as a real issue in the theology of the immanent Trinity. The concept of the Spirit has "no organic connection" with the doctrine of the Father and the Son with its language of generation, which tends to reduce the Spirit to an appendix, but it does cohere with the doctrine of the Word where the "uttering" of the Word and the "breathing out" of the Spirit seem to belong together indissolubly and simultaneously, rendering the Spirit the equal of the Word. How, then, integrate these two logics and find coherence between the Son and the Word, generation and spiration?[5] Questions of this kind can be multiplied in trinitarian theology.

It is clear that Aquinas is using certain basic metaphysical principles and insights in his trinitarian theology in a way that is both consistent and insightful. Some of these basic principles and concepts include divine simplicity, the distinction between intellect and will, formal and final causality, and participation. Because of divine simplicity all processions in God communicate the numerically identical divine nature of the Father, but they do so each in a different way according to the respective nature of the processions. The Son proceeds by way of the intellect and therefore as the Word or Concept of the Father's self-knowledge, bearing the likeness of the Father, while the Holy Spirit proceeds by way of the will and therefore as the Love of the Father's self-love, bearing the impulse and inclination of the movement toward the Father. Insofar as the Word or Concept of the Father is of the numerically same nature as the Father, the Word is also called the Son, in which sense generation applies to the Father most properly and in an eminent way. Insofar as the Word bears the perfect likeness of the Father, it is also the Image of the Father. Thus the numerical identity of the divine nature communicated from the Father to the Son provides consistency among the names of Son, Word, and Image, while the difference in the mode of that communication provides coherence in explaining the difference between the Son and the Holy Spirit.

It is the same idea of the communication of the numerically identical divine nature that also accounts for consistency in the analysis of the Son's role of mediating between God and the world as its creator and redeemer. As the Father understands himself and all other things in one and the same act, the Son is not only the concept or word of the Father but also of all other things the Father understands in the same act. In this sense the Son is the Father's wisdom not only regarding himself but also regarding all creation, thus the expressive and operative *logos, ratio,* exemplar, blueprint, or eternal law of all created things and therefore also the model of what redeemed creatures should be. As the perfect Image of the Father the Son is also the perfect exemplar of all creation and salvation. One can say that the Son is the proper formal effect of the Father and the transcendent formal cause of all created and redeemed things, to use the language of causality.

Likewise, Aquinas sees consistency in the three names of Spirit, Love, and Gift as names of the Holy Spirit because the Holy Spirit proceeds by way of the will, as the impression of the Father's self-willing, implying impulse and movement like a spirit, inclination to the object willed like love, and thus the first or primordial gift which love is as the principle of all gratuitous donation. The concept of will provides coherence for the three functions of the Holy Spirit. Just as the logic of the procession of the Son as the Father's Word is reflected in the relation of the Son to the world, so this logic of the procession of the Holy Spirit as the Father's Love in the immanent Trinity is likewise reflected in the economic relation of the Spirit to creation, where the Spirit serves as the transcendent cause that enables and disposes all creatures to love and return to God as their ultimate end by giving themselves to one another and participating in the exemplary likeness of the Son to the Father.

As I have already indicated in preceding chapters, I do not mean to endorse the whole of Aquinas's metaphysics, but I am raising the challenge that any comprehensive sapiential theology today has to employ some sort of ontology or metaphysics and that any such metaphysics must be profound, subtle, and broad enough in its conceptuality to do justice to the different doctrines of Christian theology both in themselves and in their relation to one another as parts of a systematic whole.

The Grammar of Trinitarian Language

Before going on to other issues, I think it is quite relevant and necessary to summarize the essentials of trinitarian theology discussed in the preceding chapter for what might be called "the grammar of trinitarian language." Aquinas's theology of the triune God integrates the essential elements of Cappadocian and Augustinian theologies, and a grammar of trinitarian language based on Aquinas represents the basics of classical trinitarianism. In dealing with various issues of contemporary trinitarian theology, especially its attempts to reformulate the doctrine in ways that are not sexist and that are more social and biblical, it is quite relevant to have at hand a grammar of classical trinitarian language, not as an absolute standard for evaluating and dismissing contemporary attempts that deviate from it but as a source of fundamental and determining insights that must be taken into serious consideration in any discussion and that can be dismissed only for the gravest reasons.

There are two parts to this grammar. The first has to do with the rules for the predication of divine names, the second with the essentials of trinitarian theology that must be preserved in any reformulation. The first has to do with the form, the second with the content, of the trinitarian faith. The rules for theological predication are given in Aquinas's discussion of analogical predication and can be summarized in the following theses.

(1) Insofar as effects are similar to their cause and express something of the perfections of their cause, we *can* predicate created perfections of God as their cause, in whom they preexist. Since we do not have an intuition into the essence of God, this is also the only way of theological predication. This is the way of causality.

(2) Insofar as there is an infinite distance between God and creatures, created perfections must be purified of such imperfections as are

intrinsically incompatible with God before they can be applied to God. There are two kinds of such imperfections. Qualities of material things in their materiality—e.g., God as rock, lion, heavenly—cannot properly apply to God as a spiritual being and must be treated as "metaphors." Non-material or "pure" perfections, which do not imply any intrinsic limitation—e.g., being, goodness, wisdom, vitality, beauty—must be purified of the limitations accruing to them by virtue of their "mode of signification" in the human context, where they exist in a state of division and multiplicity, before they apply properly to God in whom they exist simple and united. This is the way of negation, which separates analogical predication from all mythological and ideological projections of human desires and ideals. Just as no human ideal should be attributed to God without negation of its human limitations, neither should a genuine human ideal be denied application to God by way of causality because of its human limitations, which any truly analogical predication would seek to remove. The first denies the necessity of negation directly, the second does the same indirectly.

(3) Once purified of their finite limitations in their "mode of signification," pure perfections in their *ratio* or content of signification can properly and must be predicated of God in "a more excellent and higher way." This is the way of eminence.

(4) Analogical predication involves all three ways or stages of predication. It is an intellectual process or *movement* of ascending from the finite to the infinite by way of affirmation, negation, and eminence. Without negation and eminence it is confused with univocity, where analogy is reduced to simple similarity. Without affirmation and eminence it is confused with equivocity. It is also important to note here that some identify "univocal" with "literal" and divide all predication into "literal" and "metaphorical" predication, identifying the analogical sometimes with the literal, sometimes with the metaphorical. For Aquinas, analogical predication is "proper" predication in the sense that the proper *ratio* or meaning of a term is affirmed as predicable of God, although in an eminent way, and is in this sense "literal" predication. Analogical predication is literal without being univocal because it does apply the same *ratio* or meaning to different things but with due respect for the differences in the *mode* of its signification or realization and requiring negation and eminence. It is not metaphorical because it is not an application of a quality to a being to whom it cannot intrinsically apply. A human being is neither a pig nor an angel, and it is purely metaphorical to call a human

being a pig or an angel. The proper meaning of fatherhood lies in the communication of the same nature to another, and it is literal and proper to call both the divine Father and a human father "father," although it is more—or infinitely more—proper to call the former "father" because divine fatherhood requires the negation of the limitations of finite fatherhood and elevation to the infinite mode in which the *ratio* of fatherhood is completely fulfilled in the communication of the "numerically identical" divine nature.[6]

What one considers the essential content of the trinitarian faith that must be preserved in any reformulation will certainly depend on the numerous assumptions one makes about the nature of Christian faith, scriptural authority, the tradition of Christian self-understanding in theology and ecclesial praxis, the demands of history, and so on. I will thus simply present the following theses taken from the discussions of the preceding chapter as essential to any trinitarian faith that takes the classical tradition seriously.

(1) The doctrine of the Trinity is known only through Scripture. Any new formulation of the doctrine of the immanent Trinity, then, must be a coherent deduction from reflection on Scripture. It certainly cannot be indifferent to or incompatible with Scripture. I call this the "scriptural" principle.

(2) It is precisely in the economy of salvation that the Trinity of God was revealed, and it is precisely for the sake of that economy that the economic Trinity was traced back to and grounded in the immanent Trinity. The God revealed in the economy is identical with God in her own eternal being. The economic Trinity is salvific because it expresses the logic of the immanent Trinity. The new formulation, therefore, must in some way preserve this logic and not reduce the triune God to economic functions without roots in her eternal triune being. All personal appropriations of essential names must reflect the logic of the immanent processions. I call this the "immanent logic" principle.

(3) Insofar as only the communication of the numerically identical divine nature makes possible the unity of God, equality of the three persons, and their mutual inherence or perichoresis, the very process of origination of the persons in their very distinctness must be understood as a process of the communication of the divine nature. Any new formulation must embody the notion of the communication of the numerically

identical divine nature explicitly or implicitly. I call this the "identical nature" principle.

(4) The three persons revealed in the economy of salvation must be considered as truly distinct in their eternal being and therefore in the immanent Trinity. No reformulation can ignore this intrinsic ontological distinction of persons by reducing them to merely functional distinctions of the one God without internal self-distinction. I call this the "real distinction" principle.

(5) Christian trinitarianism serves, among other things, the purpose of guarding Christianity against the pantheistic identification of God and the world by preserving God's freedom and transcendence over the world. It does this by defining the persons of the Trinity in "personal" terms expressive of knowledge and will. Insofar as the Trinity is also invoked as center of prayer and worship, and only a person can be so invoked, Christianity has referred to the triune God in personal terms. Any reformulation must recognize the centrality of personal terms in naming the triune God even if it may also complement them with other non-personal terms. I call this the "personalist" principle.

(6) The numerically identical divine nature being shared by all three persons, the persons can be distinguished from one another only by relative opposition in the process of origination. Persons, therefore, must be understood as essentially relational realities. I call this the "constitutive relationality" principle.

(7) Insofar as Scripture so clearly presents the Father as the source, sender, and end of the Son and the Holy Spirit, the monarchy of the Father as the principle of the whole divinity must be preserved in any reformulation. I call this the "monarchical" principle.

(8) Insofar as the Son is the perfect Word and Image of the Father, the Son also serves as the mediating exemplar for both creation and redemption, as the principle of all objective manifestation of the Father. Any new formulation must preserve this exemplary status of the Son in both the immanent and the economic Trinity. I call this the "formal exemplar" principle.

(9) Insofar as the Holy Spirit is the perfect Love and Gift of the Father, the Holy Spirit also serves as the uniting and reconciling power whereby the Father loves creatures and creatures are empowered to love God and others in union with the Son. Any new formulation must preserve this reconciling function of the Holy Spirit. I call this the "reconciliation" principle.

(10) While we cannot say that there is only one conceptual system capable of serving as the philosophical mediation of the trinitarian faith, any system employed to render the trinitarian doctrine humanly plausible must be versatile enough to meet as many of the above principles as possible. These principles, it must be noted, defend the trinitarian faith against traditional heresies such as tritheism, modalism, Arianism, subordinationism, and pantheism as well as relate to the most important conceptual issues. I call this the "versatility" principle.

(11) In addition to the problem of form and content, any reformulation of the trinitarian formula must attend to the ease and gracefulness of its literary expression. The formula is used by the whole church, not only by theologians and intellectuals, for all occasions, public and private, official liturgies and private prayers, doctrinal formulations and religious education, not only in theological discourse. It must, therefore, avoid sheer neologisms, convoluted expressions, and awkward idiosyncracies. I call this the "felicity" principle.

The Problem of Sexist Language

A criticism of the traditional formula of the Trinity as such and therefore also applicable to Aquinas is the charge of sexism. The formula of "Father, Son, and Holy Spirit" applies the masculine gender to two of the three persons and excludes the feminine. This exclusion is not just a matter of linguistic expression. As contained in the formulation of the central Christian dogma and most frequently repeated and reinforced in baptism and the official liturgy of the churches, such exclusion hides, nurtures, and justifies patriarchy, a most serious kind of exploitation and alienation of women in all areas of life. A non-sexist revision of the trinitarian formula, therefore, appears to be a most compelling task of contemporary theology. For this purpose, a wide-ranging set of proposals have been made with far-reaching implications, generating a passionate debate among proponents of different positions.[7] For Robert W. Jenson, such feminist critiques and proposals are tantamount to "an invasion of an antagonistic religious discourse" and represent "a true crisis of the faith" equivalent to the crisis of Gnosticism and Enlightenment rationalism.[8] Perhaps no one has put the revolutionary potential of the current feminist critique more aptly than does Alvin F. Kimel, Jr.:

A revolution is now taking place in the worship and discourse of English-speaking Christianity. Fads in theology come and go, of course, and rarely do they impact the parochial discourse directly and formatively. Not so, however, with the new feminist theology. Not only does the new thinking present a powerful critique of traditional theology and faith—as well as offering an attractive and, for many, compelling religious substitute in the name of Christ—but also it embodies this critique in very practical directives that alter the church's speech and prayer: the triune name is suppressed, prayer to the Father is asserted to be exclusive of women believers and therefore discountenanced, the appropriation of feminine images of God in worship and meditation is encouraged, and the use of the masculine pronoun for the deity is proscribed. This is one theological revolution that truly seeks to alter permanently the fact and constitution of Christian faith.[9]

In light of the above grammar of trinitarian language, what can we say about the feminist critique of the masculine language of the traditional formula? Thomas F. Torrance defends the traditional formula by an appeal to the absolute authority of God's self-revelation in Jesus Christ, in whom God has named himself "Father, Son, and Holy Spirit" "once and for all."[10] For Elizabeth Achtemeier and Robert W. Jenson, "God is the one whom Jesus reveals as his Father."[11] And God reveals himself as Father and in the masculine language as a way of preserving divine freedom and transcendence over against the identification of God and nature in the ancient pagan cults (and recent feminist attempts to naturalize God as the "Primal Matrix" (Ruether).[12] For Wolfhart Pannenberg too, the idea of God as "Father" is not just a projection of the prevailing social conditions of the ancient world. "On the lips of Jesus, 'Father' became a proper name for God. It thus ceased to be simply one designation among others. It embraces every feature in the understanding of God which comes to light in the message of Jesus."[13] J. A. DiNoia and Robert W. Jenson have tried to defend the traditional formula by simply denying that the language of "Father" and "Son" is sexist at all precisely on the Thomist ground of analogical predication: these terms apply to God only after excluding their finite, sexual limitations.[14]

Leaving aside the larger question of the authority of Scripture and the issue of the patriarchal vs. matriarchal determination of the scriptural conception of God, let me specifically pursue the question of whether the grammar of analogical predication can save Aquinas from the charge of sexism. As we saw, it is true that for Aquinas "Father" (or "Son") is a literal, not metaphorical, although analogical, name of God because the essential meaning or *ratio* of fatherhood lies in the communication of the same nature and applies in a preeminent way to the divine Father because he communicates not the "specifically" but the "numerically" identical divine nature in the generation of the Son. It is from the fatherhood of the Father that all finite fatherhood is derived. It must be asked, however, why Aquinas attributes the function of generation in the sense of communicating the same nature to the father, not to the mother. Aquinas presents a very clear answer:

> One should, of course, note carefully that the fleshly generation of animals is perfected by an active power and by a passive power; and it is from the active power that one is named "father," and from the passive power that one is named "mother." Hence, in what is required for the generation of offspring, some things belong to the father, some things belong to the mother: to give the nature and species to the offspring belong to the father, and to conceive and bring forth belong to the mother as patient and recipient. Since, however, the procession of the Word has been said to be in this: that God understands Himself; and the divine act of understanding is not through a passive power, but, so to say, an active one; because the divine intellect is not in potency but is only actual; in the generation of the Word of God the notion of mother does not enter, but only that of father. Hence, the things which belong distinctly to the father or to the mother in fleshly generation, in the generation of the Word are all attributed to the Father by Sacred Scripture; for the Father is said not only to "give life to the Son" (cf. John 5:26), but also "to conceive" and to "bring forth."[15]

The preceding passage is more than revealing. It makes clear, first, that the Father combines the function of both father and mother, not just that of the father, in human generation; the Father also evinces a maternal side. It makes clear, second, that the reason why the Father, not Mother, assumes both the paternal and maternal functions is that in the generation of the Son through the act of self-understanding, the divine intellect is only actual, not potential, which, therefore, involves only the notion of the father as the active principle of generation, not the mother as its passive principle. It makes clear, third and finally, that it is the role of the active principle to "give the nature and species to the offspring," while it is the role of the passive principle to "conceive and bring forth."

It must be remembered here, of course, that Aquinas is not giving an independent reason for using the masculine language for the triune God but only trying to provide a humanly plausible or appropriate [conveniens] reason for such usage already there in Scripture and tradition.

Still, it is also quite clear that his contemporary knowledge of the biology of generation, which assigns the function of communicating the same nature to the father alone, did play a decisive role in his theological justification of the masculine language, to the point of arguing that if only Eve, not Adam, had sinned, original sin would not have been transmitted.[16] To this extent, and by the standard of *our* biological knowledge of generation, it seems difficult to exculpate Aquinas—or for that matter any of his contemporaries—from the charge of sexism. It will not do to say that "Father" is not sexist because analogical predication requires that we purify the concept of fatherhood of all finite, sexual dimensions before we apply it to God. The evident fact is that it is still "Father," not "Mother," that is chosen for such analogical purification and predication precisely because of a certain differential and invidiously prejudicial conception of human fatherhood and motherhood. It will not do to say, as does Jenson, that such analogical predication says "thereby nothing whatever about the relative worth of fatherhood and motherhood."[17] Analogically predicated, "Mother" too could be applied to God without its finite, sexual dimension, which inevitably raises the issue, why only "Father," and not also "Mother?" One cannot say, as does DiNoia, that "Father" is a personal name of the first person, whereas "Mother" can only be a metaphor.[18] Nor can one say, with Jenson, that "Father" is appropriate but not "Father and Mother" because it connotes divine androgyny.[19] As long as the dominant concern in the language of "generation" is the communication of the same nature, and as long as both father and mother have essential roles in the communication of human nature, it seems difficult to justify the exclusive use of masculine language in referring to the first divine person.

As ways of overcoming the sexism of the trinitarian language, many substitutes or alternative formulations have been proposed. The issue here, it must be remembered, is not whether these substitutes can also serve as complementary formulations. The trinitarian tradition is full of alternative or complementary formulations which are also used in different contexts and under different situations. The issue is whether these can also serve as the "primary" formulation in the way that "Father, Son, and Holy Spirit" has in terms of its historical dominance in the New Testament, doctrinal formulations, church's public worship, administration of the sacraments, especially baptism, and private prayer and spirituality. Historically, speaking of the Trinity means speaking of "Father, Son, and Holy Spirit." No other formula comes remotely close to it in terms of biblical authenticity, historical venerability, doctrinal implication, and devotional familiarity. Jenson rightly points out that the traditional formula has been indeed the proper name of the Christian God, as it "immediately summarizes the primal Christian interpretation of God."[20] The question is whether the proposed alternatives are appropriate to serve as "primary" formulations in place of the traditional formula. Let me examine some of the proposed alternatives.

One of the most commonly proposed alternatives has been "Creator, Redeemer, Sustainer/Sanctifier." It is clear that by virtue of the doctrine of appropriation, this formula has been frequently used in traditional designations of the triune God. As long as it also affirms the logic of the immanent processions that underlies such appropriation, this formula would be a good complementary one. The problem is that the formula is proposed as a primary formula independent of the logic of the immanent Trinity and as a self-sufficient one. For Peter van Inwagen, it is in danger of suggesting that the Father alone was involved in creation, the Son alone in redemption, and the Spirit alone in sanctification.[21] Jenson regards the proposed formula as an assemblage of theological abstractions that do not and cannot name or identify in the same way that in the traditional formula "Father" refers to the Father of the Son, Jesus Christ, and the Holy Spirit to the common Spirit of Father and Son. Any deity must claim to "create," "redeem," and "sanctify," and the nature of creation, redemption, and sanctification can only be specified in terms of the nature of the divinity. The predicates demand prior specification of the subject. Predicates alone do not sufficiently identify. For Thomas F. Torrance, apart from God as Father, Son, and Holy Spirit, the nature of the activities, primarily correlated with what we are, is reducible to a symbolic expression of human religious consciousness.[22]

Furthermore, the formula is crypto-modalist. For Donald Bloesch as well as for many others, it does not exhibit anything of the internal personal differentiation of the triune God and merely names the economic functions of God without internal differentiation. For Torrance, the formula only expresses a unitarian conception of God characterized by three different modes or operations, which, moreover, cannot coinhere in one another because this would mean God creating, redeeming, and sustaining himself. This in effect identifies God's functional relations with creatures with God's immanent being, which would amount to a gross form of anthropomorphism.[23] For DiNoia, speaking from the Thomist perspective, the formula uses essential names that describe God's relation to creation and cannot substitute as personal names that describe the mutual relations among the persons themselves.[24] The same critique would also apply to any formula that uses God's essential functions in relation to creation, such as "Creator, Savior, Healer" and "Creator, Liberator, Comforter." In short, these formulas seem to violate the "immanent logic" principle.

The formula, "God, Christ, Spirit," also suffers from serious defects. In distinguishing "Christ" and "Spirit" from "God" it is in danger of subordinating the second and third persons to the first, while "Christ" fails to name the personal relation of the second person to the first and the third. The formula, "Source, Word, and Spirit," which combines one essential name ("Source") referring to God in her relation to creation, and two personal names ("Word" and "Spirit"), likewise tends to subordinate the second and third persons to the first, while leaving the personal relation of the first to the second and third persons ambiguous.[25] These two formulas seem to violate both the "immanent logic" principle and the "identical nature" principle. The formula, "Father/Mother, Child, and Spirit," does use personal names for all three persons, but "Father/Mother" is an awkward doublet, a violation of the "felicity" principle, while "Child" connotes essential immaturity, a violation of the moment of negation in analogical predication. "Parent, Child, Spirit" removes all sexism, but calls disturbing attention to the bisexuality of the first person, likewise violating the moment of negation in analogical predication, in addition to the application of immaturity to the second person.

Ruth C. Duck suggests "God the Source, the fountain of life, Christ, the offspring of God, the liberating Spirit of God, the wellspring of new life," especially for use in the form of questions during baptism, such as, "do you believe in God, the Source, the fountain of life," "in Christ, the offspring of God," and "in the liberating Spirit of God, the wellspring of new life?"[26] Duck argues that all three are here named God, using personal, not essential, names that also suggest inner relationships ("fountain of life," "offspring," and "wellspring") without falling into subordinationism. I do not doubt that this can be used as one of the complementary formulas during baptism; as Duck claims, it is biblical, accessible to people, and a good summary of Christian faith. However, for use as a primary formula for liturgical use in general, I do not find it quite appropriate. In addition to the above criticism of "God, Christ, Spirit," which constitutes the basic structure of Duck's proposed formula, it is open to three criticisms. It uses terms that are both metaphorical and impersonal, which are not quite suitable for invocation and doxology. It seems to violate the "personalist" principle. The mutual relations among "fountain of life," "offspring," and "wellspring" are not clear. There seems to be an underlying metaphor of "spring" common to all three terms, but there is no clear relationship of origination among the three, while "fountain" and "offspring" are mixed metaphors. It seems to violate the "constitutive relationality" principle. Nor does the formula really avoid the risk of subordinationism. Is the "offspring of God" a "natural" or an "adoptive" offspring? It seems to violate the "identical nature" principle.

In light of the grammar of trinitarian language and the problems inherent in many of the recent proposals for alternatives to the traditional formula, I propose to preserve the traditional formula of "Father, Son, and Holy Spirit" as the primary formula for referring to the triune God while referring to the one God in the feminine. I find this the theologically most acceptable, ethically most just, stylistically most graceful, and overall practically simplest, solution there is.

Theologically, according to the grammar of trinitarian language, the formula of "Father, Son, and Holy Spirit" best satisfies the rules of that grammar. It is not only thoroughly scriptural but also enjoys twenty centuries of uninterrupted ecumenical support as the primary formula for the triune God, a fact not lightly to be dismissed. It expressly embodies the logic of the immanent processions, clearly indicates the identity of the divine nature which makes possible the unity of the triune God, the equality of the three persons, and their mutual inherence—the theologically most crucial condition of an acceptable formula—as well as making the real distinction of persons unambiguous, referring to the persons in personalist and mutually relational terms without denying the monarchy of the first person, and manifesting both the exemplarity of the Son for all created beings and the reconciling activity of the Holy Spirit in creation as the Spirit of both Father and Son. (Whether the language of "Son" necessarily makes the formula subordinationist[27] was discussed in the preceding chapter and will be more fully discussed later in this chapter.) It goes without saying that all these functions of the formula have been made possible not because of any self-evident validity and persuasiveness of the formula taken in isolation, but only because so much usage and tradition, theological, liturgical, educational, and devotional have been invested in it. It must also be admitted, however, that not every formula lends itself to such communal investment, and that the traditional formula, because of its biblical roots and multiple connotations derived from the human experience of generation, best lends itself to such investment. The family analogy does have a privileged status in the trinitarian discourse.

In this connection feminists may argue that "Mother, Daughter, and the Holy Spirit" fulfills the above rules of trinitarian language just as well and that it should be adopted as an alternate primary formula. I have two reservations about this argument. One is that the proposal introduces a dissonance into the way we refer to the second person of the Trinity. The second person was hypostatically united with the human nature of Jesus, which in turn makes possible the *communicatio idiomatum* or exchange of attributes in such a way that the attributes of one can be predicated of the other. For example, when Jesus was born in the manger and talked to women, we can also say that the second person of the Trinity was born in the manger and talked to women. The proposed formula would express this by saying that the divine Daughter was born in the manger and talked to women when we are fully conscious that Jesus was a male. There is a dissonance between the femininity of the reference to the second person of the Trinity and the masculinity of the human nature assumed by that person in history. This is not a theological dissonance: the divine Daughter is not literally feminine and can assume the human nature of any gender. It does remain a linguistic dissonance based on a historical dissonance and violates a certain human sense of fittingness [convenientia]. The second reservation is that the Christian communities, so long accustomed to the scriptural, liturgical, and theological usage in the matter, will find this dissonance too disturbing and the innovation too radical.

I propose instead, therefore, to balance the masculine language of the traditional trinitarian formula by using the feminine whenever the reference is to the one God except where the context dictates otherwise. This may occur by way of adding to the traditional formula the phrase, "one God, Mother of us all," as is the practice of the Riverside Church in New York City,[28] and/or referring to the one God with feminine pronouns. I do not have any empirical data to show a concrete parity in the use of feminine and masculine genders according to my proposal, but I do believe there might be if we consider all the references to the one and the triune God in theological discourse, religious education, official liturgies, private prayers, and common Christian discourse.

There are two provisos to my proposal to retain the names Father, Son, and Holy Spirit. First, this would constitute only the primary formula of the triune God, which not only does not entail that it be the only formula used, but also encourages the use of complementary formulas as has been the case with the trinitarian tradition all along. The other proviso is that along with the practice of any new proposal including mine, the Christian communities must undergo an education in the appreciation of analogical predication, which applies to all proposals about divine names. We begin with the human experience at once most elementary, most common, and most generous, the experience of the gift of life in the same nature from parents to children. We apply, therefore, the reality of generation and the relations it involves to the divine persons by way of causality. We do so, however, by way of negation and eminence at the same time, purifying the relations of generation of all their finite limitations and affirming them of God in an infinitely higher mode. This purification applies equally to the masculine and the feminine names of God: God is neither father nor mother in human fashion. What applies to God is neither the gender nor the sexuality of human parenthood but the gift and sharing of life in the same nature in the mode proper to God's infinite, eternal being.

It is irrelevant, therefore, whether our personal experience of our own fathers and mothers has been fulfilling or abusive. To say that we can attribute fatherly or motherly qualities to God because we have a positive experience of them is just as mistaken as to say that we should not do so because we have a negative experience.[29] Both are guilty of the violation of the moment of negation in analogical predication—negation of a univocal projection of human qualities, good or bad, into the divine. Regardless of the quality of empirical relationships between parents and children, the moral imperative is that generosity or love should mark the relationship that is at once so elementary, so common, and so profound because what is at stake is the transmission of life in the same nature. If abusive relations are so pervasive as to make it undesirable to refer to God either as Father or as Mother, this not only indicates a real social crisis but also makes all the more urgent the theological reflection on the fatherhood or motherhood of God, who generates precisely by giving and sharing herself in the totality of her undivided divine nature, and the pastoral elucidation of human parenthood from the divine source of all finite fatherhood or motherhood. Abusive parental relations as such do not argue for doing away with the predication of fatherhood or motherhood of God, any more than negative experiences of "God" argue for doing away with the name of God.

The moment of negation in analogical predication also invalidates all concern about reinforcing certain gender roles and stereotypes through gender attribution of God. It makes no more sense to worry that we might reinforce the limitation of the role of women to that of the mother by calling God Mother than to worry that we might limit the role of men either to that of the father or son by calling God Father or Son. It makes no more sense to be concerned that attribution of maternal compassion to God might result in reinforcing the stereotyping of women as compassionate but powerless, than to be concerned that attribution of paternal authority might reinforce the stereotyping of men as powerful but heartless.[30] Analogy should make it clear that God is Father, Son, or Mother in not the empirical but the transcendent sense, of which Christians should be reminded at every opportunity for religious education.

Under these two provisos, my proposal is not only the theologically most acceptable and ethically most just but also the practically simplest solution to the problem of sexist language. All I propose to do is to preserve the traditional formula and simply add "one God, Mother of us all" and/or refer to the one God in the feminine to provide a balance in the frequency of references to God. This formulation would circumvent the stylistic idiosyncracies and infelicities that have been creeping into theological language in the name of gender justice, such as ungrammatical neologisms like "Godself" and awkward repetitions like "himself or herself" and "he or she." According to my proposal, "God" will be consistently referred to as "she," "her," and "herself."

Social Trinitarianism on the Unity and Trinity in God

One of the perennial questions of trinitarian theology has been how to provide a balance between the threeness of persons and their unity as one God, without reducing each to the other. Many contemporary theologians have accused the Western tradition of reducing the threeness of persons either to the monarchy of the Father as the origin of the one divine substance or to three modes of being of the one absolute subject in its self-differentiation and self-identification, reducing Christian trinitarianism to abstract monotheism and incurring subordinationism in the first case and modalism in the second. For various reasons, political, biblical, and philosophical, the demand has recently been made to revive what is sometimes called "social" trinitarianism and to begin with the three divine persons in their distinction, rather than with the one divine substance or one absolute subject. This approach seeks to account for their unity itself in trinitarian terms, not in terms of the same divine essence or identical divine subject.

Jürgen Moltmann: The Perichoretic Unity of the Triune God

Jürgen Moltmann, who has done so much to restore the Trinity as a central theme in theology in recent decades, has been a most vocal advocate of "a social doctrine of the Trinity."[31] Moltmann is critical of both the classical notion of God as "supreme substance" and the modern notion of God as "absolute subject," the former because its underlying cosmology is no longer convincing today, the latter because it is a projection of the modern anthropocentric preoccupation with the human subject in its individual selfhood. Neither is acceptable as a "specifically" Christian doctrine of God, which is essentially trinitarian. The classical trinitarianism of substance places the unity of the three persons in the common possession of the one, indivisible, homogeneous, divine substance; it does so with a full complement of Greek metaphysical presuppositions about divine immutability and substantiality, which puts an undue stress on the unity of the triune God, does not accommodate the possibility of the Son suffering on the cross, and ends up by reducing the concrete tri-unity of God to abstract monotheism. The modern trinitarianism of subject—from Hegel to Barth and Rahner—reduces the three persons to three modes of being in which the one identical divine subject reflects on itself and communicates itself or to the triadic structure of the self-relation and self-mediation on the part of the one absolute subject. Both of these views dispense with the notion of "person" as subject of acts and relationships in its own right. Here, too, the stress on the unity of the divine subject reduces persons to "mere aspects" of the one subject as in modalism and ultimately reduces the doctrine of the Trinity to monotheism.[32]

The recovery of a genuinely Christian doctrine of the Trinity must begin with the biblical tradition of the history of Jesus the Son and develop the doctrine from there without presupposing the unity of God either as homogeneous substance or as identical subject. Instead of beginning with the unity of God and asking about the Trinity later, we must reverse the procedure to begin with the trinity of persons and inquire later about their unity, which must itself be conceived in trinitarian, relational terms. What Moltmann proposes, then, is a "social" doctrine of the Trinity and a trinitarian hermeneutic which thinks in terms of relationships and communities, not isolated substances and subjects. Such a doctrine and hermeneutic will also be conducive to the promotion of human fellowship and interdependence between humanity and all creation so urgent in the contemporary world.[33]

For Moltmann, the Bible does not speak of God, a single subject, revealing himself, but of three divine subjects in relationships. It is not God who reveals himself, but the Son who reveals the Father, and the Father who reveals the Son. The history of Jesus in the Bible is the "history of the reciprocal, changing, and hence living relationship between the Father, the Son, and the Spirit," which are *relationships of fellowship and open to the world.*[34] The mission of the Son takes the "form of the Trinity" in that "the Father sends the Son through the Spirit, the Son comes from the Father in the power of the Spirt, and the Spirit brings people into the fellowship of the Son with the Father."[35] The passion of the Son shows the same trinitarian form in that "the Father gives up his own Son to death in its most absolute sense, for us; the Son gives himself up, for us, and the common sacrifice of the Father and the Son comes about through the Holy Spirit, who joins and unites the Son in his forsakenness with the Father."[36] Finally, the resurrection of the Son is not only an eschatological event but also a trinitarian event in that "the Father raises the Son through the Spirit; the Father reveals the Son through the Spirit; and the Son is enthroned as Lord of God's kingdom through the Spirit."[37] In the sending of the Spirit by the risen Son from the Father for the eschatological renewal of the world, the Trinity opens itself to fellowship with humanity and all creation.

The history of Jesus in the Bible, then, does not reveal the self-relation and self-communication of the single divine subject, but reveals instead the form of the Trinity in that it tells of the joint operations and relations of three divine subjects. Moreover, there is no single fixed pattern to this form of the trinity. In the mission, passion and resurrection of Christ we find the pattern: Father → Spirit → Son, where the Father takes the initiative, the Son remains the recipient, and the Spirit is the means whereby the Father acts on the Son and the Son receives the Father. In the lordship of Christ and the sending of the Spirit we find another pattern: Father → Son → Spirit, where the Son and the Father take the initiative, a pattern which has been dominant in the Western dogmatic tradition. In the eschatological consummation and glorification, however, we find the opposite pattern: Spirit → Son → Father, where the Father receives the kingdom from the Son and glory from the Spirit.[38]

If this is the biblical norm for the doctrine of the Trinity, what are its implications for the unity of the three divine subjects? For Moltmann, it cannot be a monadic unity based on the numerical unity of either substance or subject. It can only lie in the *union* or fellowship of the Father, the Son, and the Spirit as three distinct subjects. The Father and the Spirit are "one [hen]" but not "one and the same [heis]." Furthermore, it cannot be a closed union but must be a union open to fellowship with all creation. A Christian doctrine of the Trinity must be essentially open to this soteriological and eschatological dimension.[39] The union of the three persons, therefore, must be communicable, open, inviting to and capable of integrating creatures. Neither the homogeneity of the divine substance nor the sameness and identity of the absolute subject can accommodate this openness to created others without negating itself.

Moltmann finds such a communicable and open concept of unity in the concept of "unitedness or the at-oneness [Einigkeit] of the three persons with one another." The one God is a God "at one with himself [einiger]" in three "personally," not "modally," self-differentiated ways; only persons—neither modes of being nor modes of subsistence—can be at one with one another. This union is not presupposed by the three persons as their single substance or their identical subjectivity. Instead, it is "already given with the fellowship [Gemeinschaft] of the Father, the Son and the Spirit. It therefore does not need to be additionally secured by a particular doctrine about the unity of the divine substance, or by the special doctrine of the one divine lordship."[40] The Father, the Son, and the Holy Spirit are not only distinguished from one another but are also just as much united with one another and in one another: their "personal" and "social" characters are only two aspects of the same thing. The concept of person must contain both distinction and union in itself. This union of three divine persons, therefore, can be fitted into neither the homogeneity of the one divine substance, nor the identity of the absolute subject, nor into one of the three persons, e.g., the Father. It can be perceived only in their eternal perichoresis. Unless the unity of God is understood as this perichoretic unity, we remain liable to the dangers of Arianism and Sabellianism.[41]

This eternal perichoresis among the Father, the Son, and the Spirit makes them intrinsically open to the creation of finite creatures and to fellowship with them, and provides the basis for the joint operations of the three persons in the economy. Their perichoresis in love grounds the identity of the immanent and economic Trinity, and provides the divine model for human life characterized by mutual respect, acceptance, participation, and solidarity, without privilege and domination. The unity of the triune God does not correspond either to the solitary human subject in its relation to itself or to the human subject in its claim to lordship over the world. "It only corresponds to a human fellowship of people without privileges and without subordinances. . . . The more open-mindedly people live with one another, for one another and in one another in the fellowship of the Spirit, the more they will become one with the Son and the Father, and one in the Son and the Father."[42]

In affirming the eternal at-oneness or perichoresis among the three divine persons Moltmann does not deny the traditional monarchy of the Father. After all, the almighty Father, without origin himself, is the origin of the Son and the Spirit. For Moltmann, "if one does not want God to disappear into Sabellian obscurity, then one must see the eternal origin of the Trinity in the Father."[43] He is both the origin of the Godhead and the source of the Son and the Spirit. This intra-trinitarian monarchy of the Father "only defines the inner-trinitarian constitution of God, not the world monarchy of a universal Father."[44] This thinking of the Father as the "origin" of the Godhead, however, is a product of metaphysical, cosmological thinking, which we can only apply to the Trinity "haltingly." "It can only be used appropriately if the logical compulsion to monarchical reduction and the non-trinitarian notion of the single origin (both of which are inherent in it) are overcome."[45] For all their origin in the Father, the Son and the Spirit are equally primordial. When predicating "origin" of the Trinity we must underline its incomparable uniqueness and difference from anything cosmological.

As the eternal Son of the Father, the Son proceeds from the "substance" of the Father, who communicates to the Son his divinity, his power, and his glory, in fact everything except his personal characteristic as Father. The Son receives his divinity and his being as person from the Father, and cannot, therefore, be a second Father or second origin of the Godhead. Moltmann is opposed to the Filioque because it seems to imply that the Son is a second origin of the divinity of the Holy Spirit distinct from and in competition with the one origin, the Father. Eternally generated by the Father from his nature, out of the necessity of his being, not from his will, the Son belongs to the eternal constitution of the triune God. The Father loves the Son with "engendering, fatherly love," while the Son loves the Father with "responsive, self-giving love." The Father's engendering love is thus "open for further response through creations which correspond to the Son."[46]

The Holy Spirit is neither without origin like the Father nor generated like the Son but proceeds from the Father in a relation peculiar to herself. Moltmann seems uneasy about the Western tradition since Augustine that regards the Holy Spirit as the mutual love of the Father and the Son, a person that both distinguishes and unites the Father and the Son in their mutual relationship; this tradition can tend to reduce the Spirit to an aspect of the relation between Father and Son. Moltmann finds no organic relationship between the concept of the Holy Spirit and the doctrine of the Father and the Son, but he does find coherence between the concept of the Holy Spirit and the doctrine of the Word or Logos in the relationship of utterance, which seems to take the Spirit more seriously. Because the Father "utters" his eternal Word in the eternal "breathing out" of his Spirit, the Word and the Spirit are inseparable in God. The uttering of the Word and the issuing of the Spirit belong together without the priority of the Word. "Word and Spirit, Spirit and Word issue together and simultaneously from the Father, for they mutually condition one another."[47] The Spirit, like the Word, issues from the Father out of the necessity of his being and is of the same essence as the Father and the Son. "In experiencing the Holy Spirit we experience God himself; we experience the Spirit of the Father, who unites us with the Son; the Spirit of the Son, whom the Father gives; and the Spirit who glorifies us through the Son and the Father."[48]

This, then, is the "constitution" of the Trinity according to Moltmann, which seems to share so much with the classical tradition. He differentiates this "constitution," however, from the "life" of the Trinity. In this trinitarian "life" there is a reciprocal relation between "person" and "relation" itself. Moltmann cannot say, as Aquinas seems to, that the person "is" relation or that relation "constitutes" the person. For Moltmann, relation "presupposes" but does not "constitute" the person. The Father is indeed "defined" by his fatherhood to the Son, but this "does not constitute his existence; it presupposes it." Fatherhood is a relation, a mode of being, but also more, being or existence in itself. To be sure, "there are no persons without relations; but there are no relations without persons either. The reduction of the concept 'person' to the concept 'relation' is basically modalistic, because it suggests the further reduction of the concept of relation to a self-relation on God's part."[49] For Moltmann, however, we can no more say that "the relations only *manifest* the persons" than that they are or constitute the persons. Manifestation "presupposes the constitution of the persons simply in themselves, and without their relations. Then the relations would only express the difference in kind of the persons but not their association or fellowship."[50]

If relations neither "constitute" persons, which would reduce persons to relations, nor "manifest" persons, which would reduce persons to isolated substances without mutual internal relations, how does Moltmann propose to get us out of this dilemma? His way is to distinguish two aspects of divine personhood, the "substantial" aspect (i.e., the subsistence in the "common divine nature," which makes each independent and is irreducible to relations) and the "relational" aspect (i.e., their mutual relationship that determines their "particular individual nature"),[51] *and* to see a "genetic" connection between the two: "If, as we are maintaining here, personality and relationships are *genetically connected,* then the two arise simultaneously and together. The constitution of the persons and their manifestation through their relations are two sides of the same thing. The concept of substance reflects the relations of the person to the common divine nature. The concept of relation reflects the relationship of the persons to one another. These are two aspects which have to be distinguished from one another. The trinitarian persons *subsist* [subsistieren] in the common divine nature; they *exist* [existieren] in their relations to one another."[52]

Furthermore, this "existence" means, as for Richard of St. Victor, existence "in the light of the other and in the other [ein Bestehen von einem anderen her]." It means a deepening of relation. In this sense of "existence" a divine person is "a non-interchangeable existence of the divine nature." By virtue of their mutual love the divine persons "ex-ist [ek-sistiert] totally in the other: the Father ex-ists, by virtue of his love, as himself entirely in the Son; the Son, by virtue of his self-surrender, ex-ists as himself totally in the Father; and so on."[53] To the substantial (Boethius) and relational (Augustine and Richard of St. Victor) understanding of person Hegel added the historical understanding of person. Persons do not merely "exist" in their relations but also "realize" themselves in and through one another by virtue of their self-surrendering love in history. For Moltmann, a doctrine interested in depicting the Trinity as a dynamic eternal life needs not only the concepts of person and relation but also the concept of history, a history of God in which living changes occur in the divine persons and relations through the revelation, the self-emptying, and the glorification of the triune God. We have to learn to think persons, relations, and changes in the relations *together* for a dynamic concept of the Trinity.

This brings us back to the topic of perichoresis, the key to Moltmann's way of reconceiving the unity of the Trinity. For him, as for John Damascene, by virtue of their eternal love for one another the divine persons live and dwell in one another with such a perfect and intense empathy that they are one. In this perichoretic circulation of divine life, "precisely through the personal characteristics that distinguish them from one another, the Father, the Son and the Spirit dwell in one another and communicate eternal life to one another. . . . [T]he very thing that divides them becomes that which binds them together."[54] It is this perichoretic unity of the three persons that prevents the "social" conception of the Trinity from falling into "tritheism." Although the persons are three distinct *subjects* of their own actions and relationships, they are not three different *individuals* who are first constituted as separate individuals and only subsequently enter into mutual relationships: "The unity of the triunity lies in the eternal perichoresis of the trinitarian persons. Interpreted perichoretically, the trinitarian persons form their own unity by themselves in the circulation of the divine life." It is exclusively in terms of this perichoretic life fulfilled in their mutual relations that Moltmann locates the unity of the trinitarian persons: "The unity of the triune God *cannot* and *must not* be seen in a general concept of divine substance. That would abolish the personal differences." By the same token, their very differences as persons lie in their relational, perichoretic life, which means they cannot be reduced to the modes of being of one and the same divine subject. In this sense, "the persons themselves constitute both their differences and their unity."[55] For Moltmann, the doctrine of perichoresis provides for a perfect balance between oneness and threeness without reducing one to the other.

This perichoretic understanding of the unity of the three persons also helps to avoid subordinationism. Divine life cannot be consummated by any one subject but requires the living fellowship among the three. Their unity does not lie in the one lordship of God but only in the unity of their tri-unity. For Moltmann, to be sure, as the origin of the Godhead the Father is the starting point for the constitution of the Trinity, but this monarchy belongs only to the "constitution" of the Trinity and not to its "life." The monarchy "has no validity within the eternal circulation of the divine life, and none in the perichoretic unity of the Trinity. Here the three Persons are equal; they live and are manifested in one another and through one another."[56]

To conclude, then, Moltmann speaks of the unity of the triune God in three ways. First, there is the unity at the level of "constitution" provided by the monarchy of the Father as the unoriginate origin of the divinity of the Son and the Spirit. This is the monarchical unity of the Trinity in its constitution. Second, with respect to the inner life of the trinity, the three persons form their own unity by virtue of their perichoretic, mutual relation of love. This perichoretic unity of the Trinity is concentrated around the eternal Son. Third, the mutual transfigurations of the Trinity in the divine glory in uniting mutuality and community come from the Holy Spirit. As Moltmann sums it up, "the unity of the Trinity is constituted by the Father, concentrated around the Son, and illumined through the Holy Spirit."[57] In short, the unity of the Trinity must itself be conceived in trinitarian, not monadic terms. Neither the classical Trinity of substance nor the modern Trinity of subject will do.[58]

Wolfhart Pannenberg: The Unity of Essence and Persons as Dialectic of Divine Love

Likewise, Wolfhart Pannenberg, whose theology is also one of the most sophisticated contemporary attempts to fundamentally rethink on a more biblical basis the entire trinitarian tradition, both classical and modern, finds plenty to criticize in that tradition. He too finds subordinationism in the classical attempt to derive the Trinity from the monarchy of the Father as the origin of deity, which reduces the Son and the Spirit to derivative modes of the Father, and modalism in both the classical attempt to derive it from the unity of the divine nature in its self-knowledge and self-love and the modern attempt to derive it from the self-development of the one absolute subject or from the triadic structure of the concept of self-consciousness, love, and revelation; both attempts reduce the three persons to three modes of the one God taken either as one divine nature or one divine subject.[59] For Pannenberg, the divine essence cannot be an ontologically prior source from which the divine persons are to be derived. "As forms of the eternal God, Father, Son, and Spirit cannot be derived from anything else. They have no genesis from anything different from themselves."[60] The three persons are three "separate centers of action and not just modes of being of the one divine subject."[61]

If we cannot derive the unity of the triune persons from the monarchy of the Father, the unity of the divine essence, or the unity of the absolute subject, nor can we, in the view of Pannenberg, locate the unity of the persons in their joint operations in the world (the Cappadocians) or in their eternal perichoresis (Moltmann). The joint operations of the persons in the economy only presuppose and express the unity of the divine essence; they do not provide the basis for that unity. Likewise, in itself the doctrine of perichoresis begins with three distinct persons and only affirms the de facto unity among them; it too presupposes and can "only manifest" this unity without providing a foundation for it.[62]

How, then, do we account for the unity of the three divine persons without deriving them from the unity of the monarchical Father, the divine essence, or the divine subject? Here, in a significantly new approach taken by an orthodox Christian theologian, Pannenberg introduces Hegel's constitutive notion of mediation and relation into all the important areas of trinitarian theology in an explicit and systematic way and sees the polarities of the triune persons and the one divine essence and of the divine essence and its manifestations in the world as intrinsically mutually mediating and mutually related on the "force field" of the divine life by virtue of the dynamic of divine love with which Pannenberg, along with the author of 1 John, identifies the one God and the divine essence. There are many innovative steps he takes in executing this thoroughly relational approach to trinitarian theology, of which I propose to highlight six.

First, Pannenberg moves away from the exclusive classical emphasis on the relation of origin as the only distinguishing factor among the persons, an emphasis still left intact at least in the "constitution" of the Trinity in Moltmann, and insists on recognizing a thoroughgoing mutual mediation and reciprocity among the persons as constitutive of both their personal identity and their very divine nature. The Son not only comes from the Father and bears witness to his reign; the Father also bears witness to the Son and depends on the Son for the execution of that reign. Not only does the Son subject himself to the lordship of the Father, but the Father also hands over his reign to the Son. The Spirit not only proceeds from the Father but also completes the revelation of the Father by the Son, glorifying the Father and the Son precisely in their mutual fellowship as the love that unites them. Relations among the persons are not reducible to the relations of origin in terms of generation and procession, which cast the Son and the Spirit in purely passive roles. Contrary to Moltmann, persons are indeed constituted by relations, which both distinguish and unite them, but they cannot be reduced to any one relation; each person is a catalyst of many relations. As long as we emphasize the derivation of the deity of the Son and the Spirit from the deity of the Father in an exclusive, "simplistic"[63] emphasis on the relations of origin and fail to recognize the dependence of the deity of the Father on the Son and the Spirit, we cannot escape subordinationism. For Pannenberg, relations are constitutive not only of their personal distinctions but also of their respective deity or divine nature as such. We must find a way of affirming the equal deity and reciprocity among the three divine persons.[64]

For Pannenberg, however, this mutual dependence of the persons does not entail the simple removal of the monarchy of the Father. In the work of creation, the Son and the Spirit serve the monarchy of the Father by respectively establishing and consummating his kingdom, while the Father in turn can have his kingdom only through them. This is also true of the personal relations in the immanent Trinity. Without being ontologically inferior, the Son subjects himself to the Father as the eternal locus of the Father's monarchy, where he is united with the Father by the Holy Spirit. Thus, the monarchy of the Father is not simply removed but understood as a thoroughly mediated reality: it is "not the presupposition but the *result* of the common operation of the three persons. It is thus the seal of their unity."[65]

This also means that it is wrong to distinguish, as does Moltmann, between the "constitution" of the Trinity from the Father as the unoriginate origin of deity and the "life" of the Trinity in which personal relations are lived in perichoretic mutuality. If, as Moltmann himself insists, persons constitute not only their distinction but also their unity, then we have to learn to see the monarchy of the Father and the life of the Trinity not as mutually competitive but as mutually mediating so that the monarchy of the Father "has its reality precisely *in* the life of the Son and the Spirit."[66] The communion of the persons finds its content in the monarchy of the Father as a result of their cooperation, which makes it possible to say that the trinitarian God is precisely "the one God" whom the Son proclaimed and the Spirit glorified, i.e., the heavenly Father known as the one God by the Son in the Spirit. The unity of the divine essence is not solely the function of the monarchy of the Father but also intrinsically mediated by the Son and the Holy Spirit. "The essence of the Father's monarchy acquires its *material* definition through this mediation."[67]

The second innovative step Pannenberg takes is to introduce an equally thoroughgoing mediation and relation between the divine essence and the three persons. It is not only that the three persons are constituted by their mutual relations as in the classical tradition but also that in contrast to the classical tradition, the divine essence is likewise regarded as "internal," not external, to the divine relations, which means that "the unity of the essence may be found only in their concrete life relations."[68] Unlike Moltmann, who restricts the relevance of the category of divine substance or essence to the "constitution" of the Trinity and sees no use for it as a principle of the unity of the persons except as a negative example to be avoided, Pannenberg takes full advantage of the classifical unifying function of the category of the divine essence by making it, in full Hegelian fashion, dialectical, self-differentiating, and self-manifesting. The divine essence is not a static self-identity but is intrinsically differentiated into three persons and expresses itself through their self-distinguishing and self-uniting movement of relations. By the same token, the three persons are thoroughly mediated by the uniting dynamic of the one divine essence, which guarantees their intrinsic mutuality in the immanent Trinity and the unity of their joint operations in the economy. The three divine persons are indeed three "separate centers of action" yet also so bound together by the relational unity of the divine essence as to form one God. The real distinction of persons prevents them from being just modes of being of the one divine subject. The unity of the divine essence inherent in the mutual unifying relations of the persons prevents them from becoming members of a mere collection bound by a common genus as the Cappadocian solution tends to reduce them.[69] The mutually constituting dialectic of the one divine essence and the three persons thus renders the trinitarian doctrine a "concrete" monotheism while also keeping it from the threat of both modalism and tritheism.[70]

Pannenberg's third step is to introduce a metaphysics of self-manifestation or self-expression into the concept of essence, of which the preceding self-manifestation of the divine essence in the relations of the three persons is a primordial source and example. It is of the essence of the divine essence to manifest and express itself and to consist of the sum total of such self-manifestations. The essence has its existence [Dasein] in the persons. The essence of the one God is manifested in the three persons, which are "three forms of the existence of God [Gestalten des Daseins Gottes]—in the world, yet also, transcending the world, in eternity."[71] The Father has his existence [Dasein] in the Son, who reveals the one God and the divine essence by revealing the Father, who also reveals his essence by sending the Son. "The essence of the one God is revealed by both Father and Son, and by their communion in a third, the Spirit, who proceeds from the Father and is received by the Son and given to his people. The Spirit is not just identical with the commonality of the divine essence which Father and Son share. He also mediates the fellowship of the Father and the Son as he proceeds from the Father and is received by the Son. In this function the Spirit is a third form of the existence [Gestalt des Daseins] of the one divine essence alongside the Father and the Son."[72]

The fourth innovation Pannenberg makes is to introduce a dynamic, almost revolutionary paradigm into the relation between the divine essence and its manifestations, especially the divine persons. He compares the relation between the divine essence and the divine persons to the relation between a "force field" and the particular objects that play out their identities, relations, and motions in the field. A force field is a field that manifests its power in the pushes and pulls of particular things while also remaining universal and autonomous in relation to concrete material objects that are its secondary manifestations; it implies no necessary ordering to anything in particular. Pannenberg compares the deity or divine essence to this force field because it can find equal manifestation in all three persons, just as a common spirit can bring a number of persons together in living fellowship. At the same time he also identifies the divine essence as a force field with the Spirit because it represents the creative and life-giving dynamic of God. The divine persons are bound to each other by the Spirit of love on the force field which is the Spirit itself. The divine persons are "simply manifestations and forms [nur Manifestationen und Gestalten]—but eternal forms—of the one divine essence," which "comes to expression in the living fellowship of Father, Son, and Holy Spirit."[73] Thus the one God is also a "living" God.

Pannenberg's fifth innovation, then, is his identification of the Holy Spirit with the divine essence as a force field manifested in the three divine persons while also preserving the Holy Spirit as a distinct, hypostatic person. In a reversal of the classical doctrine which identifies the Father both as the divine nature and as a distinct person, Pannenberg identifies the Holy Spirit as both the divine nature and a distinct personal manifestation or existence [Dasein] of that nature. He does so because he sees the "essence" of both the divine essence and the Holy Spirit as uniting love. As he puts it:

> The idea of the divine life as a dynamic field sees the divine Spirit who unites the three persons as proceeding from the Father, received by the Son, and common to both, so that precisely in this way he is the force field of their fellowship that is distinct from them both. . . . As a field, of course, the Spirit would be impersonal. The Spirit as

person can be thought of only as a concrete form of the one deity like the Father and the Son. But the Spirit is not just the divine life that is common to both the Father and the Son. He also stands over against the Father and the Son as his own center of action. This makes sense if the Father and the Son have fellowship in the unity of the divine life only as they stand over against the person of the Spirit. Precisely because the common essence of the deity stands over against both—in different ways—in the form of the Spirit, they are related to one another by the unity of the Spirit. If the union is to include the Spirit as person, it must be assumed that the personal Spirit, as he glorified the Son in his relation to the Father and the Father through the Son, knows that he is united thereby to both. A self-relation is proper in different ways to the persons of the Father and the Son as well.[74]

The Spirit unites the Father and the Son as the divine essence common to both yet distinguishes himself as a person from both as the uniting agent distinguishes himself from the things he unites.

What does this do to the notion of divine agency or God as an acting subject? Pannenberg refuses to assign that agency either to the Holy Spirit as one of the three persons or to the divine essence as such, which cannot itself be a subject alongside the three persons, without reducing the persons to mere aspects of divine subjectivity. Only and all three persons precisely in their relations and fellowship are the subject of divine action. The field theory helps us "understand trinitarian persons, *without derivation* from a divine essence that differs from them, as centers of action of the one movement which embraces and permeates all of them."[75] The divine essence is constituted by the one movement of the divine Spirit, who has his existence only in the three persons. "The persons are not first constituted in their distinction, by derivation from the Father, and only then united in perichoresis and common action. As modes of being [Daseinsweisen] of the one divine life they are always permeated by its dynamic through their mutual relations."[76] The common action of the persons *ad extra* can be only a manifestation of the unity of life and essence by which they are always already bound to one another.

Pannenberg's sixth (and for us, last) innovative step is to meditate on the Johannine assertion that God is love and systematically apply the dynamics and structure of divine love to the relation between the one divine essence and the three divine persons as well as to the relation between the immanent and the economic Trinity. God does not just love us but is love. Loving is not an activity among others in God but constitutes God's essence. As Feuerbach observed, love is not a predicate but the very substance of God. God does not primarily know and love himself, generating the Son and spirating the Spirit in the process, as the classical position has it. From all eternity the Father loves the Son, the Son loves the Father, and the Spirit loves the Father in the Son and the Son in the Father. Each person loves the other as other and fulfills himself thereby. One does not love oneself in the other. Love means fully giving oneself to the other and receiving oneself afresh in the responsive love of the other who is loved. Love is a "power" over persons who love one another, "glowing through them like fire," turning, relating, and uniting them with one another, and confirming and constituting their selfhood through such mutual self-giving, the mystery between persons responsible for all forms of fellowship.[77]

Now, 1 John 4:8 and 16 ("God is love") identifies the mutual love among the three divine persons with the divine essence. Love is the materially concrete form of "Spirit" as the characteristic of God's essence. The two statements that "God is Spirit" (John 4:24) and that "God is love" are different ways of denoting the same unity of essence by which Father, Son, and Spirit are united in the fellowship of the one God. For Pannenberg, the Spirit is the dynamic force field of love, "the power and fire of love glowing through the divine persons, uniting them, and radiating from them as the light of the glory of God."[78] It is the power at work in the reciprocity of the three persons as each lets the others be what they are. It is the power of love that "lets the other be" and as such also grants existence to creatures in their otherness. However, love is not a separate subject apart from the three persons. "As the one and only essence of God it has its existence in the Father, Son, and Holy Spirit. But it is the eternal power and deity which lives in the Father, Son, and Spirit through their relations and which constitutes the unity of the one God in the communion of these three persons."[79]

In this love each person is related ec-statically to one or both of the others and has his personal identity or selfhood in this relation. The Father is Father only in relation to the Son whom he generates and sends, as the Son is Son only in obedience to the sending of the Father, while the Spirit exists hypostatically only as he glorifies the Father in the Son and the Son as sent by the Father. As the classical tradition recognized, relation is constitutive of divine personhood. Human beings are not completely constituted by relation to one or two other persons, which necessitates the distinction between the act of loving and the loving subject, but in the case of the persons of the Trinity, "their existence as persons or hypostases is wholly filled by these specific mutual relations, so that they are nothing apart from them. Thus their existence as persons is coincident with the divine love, which is simply the concrete life of the divine Spirit, just as conversely the one reality of God as Spirit exists only in the mutual relations of the trinitarian persons and precisely for that reason is defined as love."[80] These relations come to their consummation in the perichoresis or mutuality of their ec-static indwelling, which is also the fulfillment of the life of the divine Spirit as love.[81]

For Pannenberg, the force field of the divine Spirit that constitutes the divine essence is differently manifested in different persons. In the person of the Father the sphere steps forth as the creative power of existence, which, however, always takes form only in relation to and in fellowship with the Son. Wherever there was reference to this divine power and mystery in Israel and other religions, the divine Logos was already at work although only in a "broken" way, the "fulness" of the Logos taking human form only in Jesus. Still, as mediator of all creaturely existence and essence, the Son was already the condition for the possibility of all human knowledge and talk about God.[82]

The "coming forth" of the Son from the Father is the basic fulfilment of divine love. It is so for the Father through the creative dynamic of the Spirit, the essence of Godhead, as it is also for the Son, as he knows that he has come forth and been sent, and as he distinguishes himself from the Father as "the divine origin of his existence" and honors him as the one God. "The essence of the Godhead is indeed Spirit. It is Spirit as a dynamic field, and as its manifestation in the coming forth of the Son shows itself to be the work of the Father, the dynamic of the Spirit radiates from the Father, but in such a way that the Son receives it as gift, and it fills him and radiates back from him to the Father."[83]

The Spirit comes forth as a distinct hypostasis as he comes over against the Father and the Son as the divine essence common to both which "actually unites them and also attests and maintains their unity in face of their distinction." A peculiarity of the Spirit is that he is never the specific object of love in the same way that the Son is the specific object of the Father's love and the Father the specific object of the Son's love, precisely because the Spirit is "the love *by which* the Father and the Son are mutually related even if as a hypostasis he stands over against both as the Spirit of love who unites them in their distinction. As a hypostasis, however, the Spirit is distinct from both Father and Son. Hence he can be at work in creation and he can also be shed abroad in the hearts of believers as a gift."[84]

The relation between the common divine essence and the three divine persons varies with each person, who represents the divine essence each in his own way. Just as the Spirit both represents the divine essence as the unifying dynamic of divine life and is a distinct person only in relation to the Father and the Son, so the Father represents the divine essence or the one God in his function as the "fount" of deity and is a distinct person only in relation to the Son. Of all the divine persons, however, the Son is most clearly distinct from the divine essence because he does not represent the Godhead as a whole as the Father and the Spirit do, only partaking of eternal deity through his relation to the Father and as filled by his Spirit. Still, in the person of the Son the one God also does come forth from his Godhead. The Son stands over against the Godhead in the form of the Father without losing his relation to the Father in the unity of the divine essence through obedience and self-distinction. In the self-relation of the Son to the Father the inner dynamic of the divine life finds concrete expression as Spirit and love.[85]

Pannenberg summarizes the dynamic, internal relations both between persons and the divine essence and among the persons themselves as well as between these two relations that constitute the heart of his trinitarian theology, as follows:

> The divine persons, then, are concretions of the divine reality as Spirit. They are individual aspects of the dynamic field of the eternal Godhead. This means that they do not exist for themselves but in ecstatic relation to the overarching field of deity which manifests itself in each of them and in their interrelations. But in this respect their reference to the divine essence that overarches each personality is mediated by the relations to the two other persons. The Son has a share in the eternal deity, and is the Son, only with reference to the Father; the Father has his identity as the Father, and is (Father) God, only with reference to the Son; the Father and Son have their unity, and therefore their divine essence, only through their relation to the Spirit; and the Spirit is a distinct hypostasis only by his relation to the distinction and fellowship of the Father and the Son in their differentiation. For the Spirit has full personal independence, not as proceeding from the Father, as radiating from his divine essence, but only in his distinction from the Father and the Son in their differentiation.[86]

Thus the unity of the divine life in its personal manifestations and relations is concrete and constituted by divine love. For Pannenberg the personal distinctions among Father, Son, and Spirit are not conclusions derived from an abstract concept of love but known only from the historical revelation of God in Jesus Christ, which presents the persons and their unity in the divine essence as "the concrete reality of the divine love that pulses through all things and which consummates the monarchy of the Father through the Son in the Holy Spirit."[87] All the attributes of God manifested in her action in the world are only attributes describing different aspects of the reality of divine love, which is not an abstract concept but "the concrete reality itself which unites all the aspects."[88]

The dynamic of divine love, then, provides a solution not only to the problem of the unity of the triune persons in the immanent Trinity but also to the problem of the unity of the immanent and the economic Trinity, of transcendence and immanence. It gives concrete form to the logic of the "true infinite" (Hegel) in that the ultimate motivation and power of God in creating and reaching out for the integrity and salvation of creatures is those of divine love. Only a trinitarianism of divine love "permits us so to unite God's transcendence as Father and his immanence in and with his creatures through Son and Spirit that the permanent distinction between God and creature is upheld."[89]

For Pannenberg, the trinitarian dynamic of divine love is literally and seriously the solution to every problem of dualism, including that between essence and attribute, essence and manifestation, and essence and existence. "Love is the essence that is what it is only in its manifestation [Erscheinung], in the forms of its existence, namely, in the Father, Son, and Spirit, presenting and manifesting [manifestiert] itself wholly and utterly in the attributes of its manifestation. Because God is love, having once created a world in his freedom, he finally does not have his own existence without the world, but over against it and in it in the process of its ongoing consummation."[90] The problem of the unity of the three persons raised by Nicea has received a solution in Pannenberg through the Johannine equation of God and love precisely because divine love has a trinitarian structure and enables us to think of the trinitarian life of God as an unfolding of his love as well as to think of God's relation to the world as grounded in God's own being.[91]

Cornelius Plantinga, Jr.: Generic Unity and Personal Differences

In addition to Moltmann and Pannenberg we also have a group of philosophical theologians who have been critical of the classical tradition on the issue of the unity of the three divine persons and who advocate instead a most explicit version of "social" trinitarianism, largely on the ground of philosophical clarity from the analytic perspective. These include Cornelius Plantinga, Jr., Richard Swinburne, and David Brown. Common to these social trinitarians is the acceptance of the three divine persons in their distinctness and the rejection of the classical tradition that each person is wholly divine in himself while the three persons together still constitute only one God. For these theologians, the identification of each person with the divine essence only abolishes the real distinction of persons. The main challenge to these social trinitarians, therefore, is how to provide a theory of unity that does not abolish the personal distinctions yet also avoids incurring the charge of tritheism.

Plantinga summarizes social trinitarianism in three propositions. (1) The Father, Son, and Holy Spirit are three "persons" in the full sense of the term, i.e., three "distinct centers of knowledge, will, love, and action" as well as "distinct centers of consciousness." (2) No theory of divine unity or simplicity should contradict this plurality of distinct persons. (3) The three persons must be regarded as closely enough related to one another to constitute "a particular social unit." "God" refers to the whole Trinity understood to be "one thing, even if it is a complex thing consisting of persons, essences, and relations."[92] We may go on to ask how "distinct" each person is from the others and what kind of unity can be attributed to them, and on what ground, so as to avoid tritheism.

For Plantinga, the Trinity is a "society or community" of three divine persons. What accounts for their unity? They are unified, first, by a common divinity, each possessing "the whole generic divine essence" including such properties as everlastingness, sublimely great knowledge, love, and glory; second, by "their joint redemptive purpose, revelation, and work"; and third, by their knowledge and love "directed not only to their creatures, but also primordially and archetypally to each other."[93] Each person is indeed a "distinct" person but not "an *individual* or *separate* or *independent* person. For in the divine life there is no isolation, no insulation, no secretiveness, no fear of being transparent to another. Hence there may be penetrating inside knowledge of the other as other, but as co-other, loved other, fellow. Father, Son, and Spirit are 'members one of another' to a superlative and exemplary degree."[94]

This means, warns Plantinga, that it is wrong to picture the Trinity as "a set of three miscellaneous divine persons each of whom discovers he has the generic divine essence and all of whom therefore form an alliance to get on together and combine their loyalties and work. We ought to resist every Congregational theory of Trinity membership." But why would it be wrong to picture the Trinity as an accidental collection of three independent individuals who first exist separately and later discover their common essence and decide on a common enterprise for a common goal? Plantinga responds that it is because in addition to a common or "generic" divinity each possesses, each also "bears a much closer relation to each other as well," i.e., a relation closer than the possession of a common generic essence indicated by "a derivation or origin relation that amounts, let us say, to a personal essence." The biblical language of Father and Son indicates "both kinship and derivation," which means both are "essentially related to each other not only generically but also in some quasi-genetic way." They are "not just members of the class of divine persons, but also members of the same family." Plantinga surmises that the Nicene "homoousios" meant something similar, namely, that they are not only generically wholly divine and equal but also related by quasi-genetic derivation.[95]

Unlike Pannenberg, then, who posits only one divine essence that at the same time manifests itself in the distinction and unification of three divine persons, but perhaps like Moltmann, who distinguishes between the *subsistence* of a person in the divine nature and his *existence* in relation to the others, Plantinga, holds that each person possesses two essences, "the whole generic divine essence and also a personal essence that distinguishes that person from the other two." Both essences unify. "The generic essence assures that each person is fully and equally divine. The personal essences, meanwhile, relate each person to the other two in unbreakable love and loyalty."[96]

We can, then, speak of "only one God" in three senses. First, we can speak of one God in the sense of God the Father as "only one font of divinity," in the same sense that the New Testament often means the Father when it speaks of God. Second, we can speak of one God in the sense of the divine essence taken as "only one generic divinity" or Godhead. This divine essence, however, is abstract, not concrete; it is a predicate adjective ("divine") indicating the "sort" of being it is, not a predicate nominative ("God"). This generic divine essence is "a set of excellent properties severally necessary and jointly sufficient for their possessor to be divine: Father, Son, and Spirit each *has* this essence, though none *is* it." We can say, therefore, that the Father is divine, that the Son is divine, and that the Spirit is divine, but not, as the Athanasian Creed claims, that the Father is God, that the Son is God, and that the Holy Spirit is God. Plantinga regards his view as a "typically Cappadocian view."[97] Third, we can speak of one God in the sense of one Trinity or one divine family. Each of these three ways is a perfectly acceptable view in the Christian tradition. Social trinitarianism is safely monotheistic.[98]

Against the objection that social trinitarianism posits the three persons as three "instances" of the divine essence and therefore three equally infinite divine beings—an absurd notion because it seems to imply mutual independence and struggle for domination—Plantinga argues that "just as it is a part of the generic divine nature to be everlasting, omnipotent, faithful, loving, and the like, so it is also part of the personal nature of each trinitarian person to be bound to the other two in permanent love and loyalty. Loving respect for the others is a personal essential characteristic of each member of the Trinity. Each divine person has general, generic *aseitas* vis-à-vis creation, but within the Trinity each essentially has interdependence, agapic regard for the other, bonded fellowship."[99] In the social Trinity, each person is not independent but essentially interdependent with the other two.

The crux of the difference between the classical Western tradition and social trinitarianism is that the latter refuses to identify each of the three persons with "the one divine essence or thing" lest it will reduce the Trinity to one person. Social trinitarianism cannot agree with the Athanasian Creed that "the Father is God, the Son is God, and the Holy Spirit is God; and yet they are not three Gods, but one God." How can three persons be "one" God both collectively and singly? Isn't this "the doctrine of the Trinity at its most incoherent," as David Brown laments?[100] If each person is distinct yet identical with the "one divine thing or reality," logic tells us that each is also identical with the others, meaning that there is only one God in the sense of one person. "How can three things identical with some fourth thing remain distinct?"[101] In Plantinga's view, however, the doctrine of divine simplicity which identifies each of the persons with the divine essence itself is not as established in the orthodox trinitarian tradition as is the doctrine of three distinct persons because the doctrine of simplicity as a philosophical, Neoplatonic theory is negotiable in a way that biblical statements are not. Instead of the doctrine of simplicity, social trinitarianism opts for a twofold essence in God, personal and generic, to do justice to both the unity and trinity in God: each person is an instance of the generic divine essence yet also distinguished from other instances by its own personal essence. Plantinga is aware that this idea of dual essences in God will be a point of contention between Aquinas and social trinitarianism.[102]

A Critique of Social Trinitarianism in Light of Aquinas

Rejecting the Classical Tradition

I begin with a comment on the terminology of "social" trinitarianism. Richard Swinburne distinguishes between "social" trinitarianism that stresses the "separateness" of the persons and "relative" trinitarianism that stresses the "unity" of the Godhead. He calls his own position "a moderate form" of social trinitarianism in that he also stresses "both the logical inseparability of the divine persons in the Trinity, and the absence of anything by which the persons of the Trinity are individuated except their relational properties,"[103] for which term Moltmann uses "particular individual natures" and Plantinga uses "personal essences." If there is anything common to the three positions presented above, it is that they all begin with the three divine persons as distinct agents and subjects each in his own right and seek their unity later in the unifying relations among them, in the perichoretic unity of the three (Moltmann), the divine essence constituted by the mutual love of the three persons (Pannenberg), and the unifying functions of both generic and personal essences (Plantinga). There are differences with regard to the kind of unity each seeks in order to guard itself against tritheism. Pannenberg was critical of Moltmann for the latter's distinction between the "constitution" and the "life" of the Trinity, by means of which Moltmann tried to eschew the question of the unity of the divine essence and appeal to the de facto perichoretic life and union of the three persons. I suspect Pannenberg would also be critical of Plantinga for resurrecting what is presumably the Cappadocian position with its emphasis on the "generic" unity of the persons and its liability to the charge of tritheism.[104]

However, if we allow a certain variation in the explanation of the kind of unity Moltmann, Pannenberg, and Plantinga posit among the three persons—and all of them seem to agree that neither the traditional doctrine of the divine essence or substance in its classical interpretation nor the modern doctrine of the divine subject can be the source of that unity—then we can define social trinitarianism simply as the view that begins with the three persons as three distinct agents and subjects (rather than with the self-knowledge and self-love of the one divine substance or the self-differentiation and self-identification of the one divine subject) and later seeks to find the unity of the Trinity in some relations of fellowship among such distinct subjects.

Before I go on to make specific comments on each of the three positions, let me provide three general comments bearing on all of them. The first comment has to do with their common rejection of the classical Trinity of substance in favor of social trinitarianism, the second with their common emphasis on the biblical starting point, and the third with their common failure to appreciate and explore the profound meaning of the monarchy of the Father, which in theory all three do acknowledge.

First, social trinitarianism rejects, for its starting point, both the monarchy of the Father, the presumed starting point of the Eastern approach, and the divine nature, the presumed starting point of the Western approach. It is afraid that the first would lead to subordinationism, the second to modalism. This, however, is a hasty conclusion. There is no a priori reason why this classical approach necessarily leads to such consequences, any more than there is an a priori reason why social trinitarianism necessarily leads to tritheism, as it is often accused of doing.

It would all depend. In the case of the classical Trinity of substance, it would depend on how trinitarian differentiation occurs on the basis of the one divine substance (of the Father); in the case of social trinitarianism, it would depend on how trinitarian unification occurs on the basis of the three distinct divine subjects. In the case of the classical position, it depends on whether it understands the process of trinitarian differentiation as intrinsically containing both the sharing of the numerically identical divine nature, which would avert subordinationism, and sufficiently irreducible differentiation, which would avert modalism. The classical position achieves the first task by conceiving the immanent processions as processes of the communication of the numerically identical divine nature of the Father, the second by conceiving the processes as self-differentiating in terms of the irreducible relations of opposition. In the case of social trinitarianism, the outcome depends on whether it understands the process of trinitarian unification as intrinsically containing a guarantee of unity sufficient to avert tritheism without canceling trinitarian differentiation. Social trinitarianism does this by positing an eternal fellowship of the three persons based on their perichoretic unity (Moltmann), the dialectic of self-pluralization of the divine essence as the unifying Spirit of love (Pannenberg), or the joint function of the generic and personal essences (Plantinga). Whether one begins with the unity or the plurality, Christian trinitarianism must grapple with both. The classical position cannot avoid the question of differentiation compatible with the unity of the divine nature; social trinitarianism cannot avoid the question of unification appropriate to the divine nature of the persons whose unity is at stake.

The central issue, in other words, is not so much whether one begins with the unity or with the differentiation, as how one proceeds and with what conceptualities. One may begin with the model of three human individuals in their distinctiveness, but if she does not take care to apply that model to God analogically, i.e., with negation and eminence, then she is likely to end up in tritheism: the three divine persons would be no more than three divine subjects united together in a loose collection with no essential connection. Again, one may begin with the model of substance or nature in its unity, but if she does not take care to apply that model likewise analogically, then she is likely to fall into modalism: the three divine persons would be no more than three aspects or modes of being of the one God. The model of three individuals who almost act like three human individuals in their all-too-obvious distinctiveness has the initial advantage of immediate empirical intelligibility, but such an advantage is also deceptive. Sooner or later it has to face the question of attributing a kind of unity to them that is also appropriate to beings with divine nature, which requires transcending the model in its human mode of signification. The model of one substance or nature, on the other hand, may have the initial disadvantage of accounting for intrinsic differentiation, but such a disadvantage can be turned into an advantage, depending on the nature of the substance at issue and whether one can appreciate the possibility of communicating the numerically identical divine nature in self-differentiating relations of irreducible opposition precisely as the privilege of the divine substance, which does require analogical imagination. Again, what counts is not so much where one begins as how and with what conceptualities one proceeds.

This also means that the whole debate concerning the relation between the treatise *de Deo uno* and the treatise *de Deo trino*—i.e., which treatise should come first and integrate the other—is not as crucial as it is often made out to be by its advocates. The order between the two is certainly not as decisive as the inherent adequacy, originality, and fruitfulness of the basic concepts used in both treatises in order to account for the unity of the divine essence and the trinity of the divine persons in ways that are faithful to the biblical and theological tradition as well as philosophically coherent. It is not so much a question, as Pannenberg claims, of simply "inferring" or "deriving" one from the other or "supplementing" one with the other,[105] as it is a question of devising concepts that will do justice to both unity and trinity and employing them as resourcefully and fruitfully as possible in the actual elaboration of the treatises. Not every approach that begins with the Trinity of persons and later seeks to integrate the unity of the divine essence into that Trinity, as does Pannenberg, is necessarily more successful—consider all the charges of tritheism and my criticisms below—than the classical approach in producing a genuine Christian doctrine of God who is both one and three.

My second general comment on the theologies of Moltmann, Pannenberg, and Plantinga concerns the point that all argue for social trinitarianism on biblical grounds. They are interested in revising the trinitarian doctrine in such a way that it will be more faithful to the witness of the Bible. This, however, is not really a new undertaking. The classical trinitarian doctrine was itself forged in the crucible of controversies bearing on biblical interpretation. The orthodox trinitarians from Athanasius and the Cappadocians to Augustine and Aquinas all appealed to Scripture as the norm for theology. Just look at the profuse quotations from Scripture dotting their pages. The difference between the classical tradition and contemporary social trinitarianism is not that the first was more philosophical and the latter more biblical; both positions are both biblical and philosophical. The difference lies rather in the kind of philosophies and related historical interests each brings into the very act of interpreting Scripture. The classical tradition wanted to reconcile the biblical teaching with prevailing Greek thought, and contemporary social trinitarians want to reconcile the biblical teaching with varying contemporary philosophies—Hegel, personalism, and analytic philosophy, for example—and their themes of equality, liberation, reconciliation of transcendence and immanence, and ecological interdependence.

All three argue that the Bible speaks of three divine agents or subjects and therefore three distinct persons, with which I don't think any trinitarian theologian will disagree. Moltmann argues that the Bible presents the three divine subjects or persons in relation and fellowship and therefore in the "form of the Trinity," and that it presents these in not only the familiar Father → Son → Spirit pattern but also the Father → Spirit → Son and the

Spirit → Son → Father patterns, thus indicating mutual mediation among the persons. Pannenberg, however, takes this idea of mutual mediation further in order to counteract the exclusive classical emphasis on the relation of origin, and turns mutual mediation into an affirmation of equal interdependence and reciprocity, regarding the relation of origin itself simply as a moment of this mutually mediating process. On this view, then, the monarchy of the Father is no longer the "presupposition" but the "result" of the common operation of the three persons.[106]

Pannenberg fails to notice, however, that mutual mediation does not always entail simple equality. It is true that the Father depends on the Son and the Holy Spirit for the execution of his plan for the creation, redemption, and consummation of the world, but he does so precisely as the source of the divinity and mission of the Son and the Spirit, which is different from the dependence of the Son and the Holy Spirit on the Father for their very divinity and economic mission. The Son and the Spirit are more dependent on the Father than the Father is dependent on the Son and the Spirit. Certainly this at least "functional" monarchy of the Father should be regarded as incontestably evident in the witness of the New Testament. Perhaps we should learn again to read Scripture on its own terms, with less immediate projection of our preoccupations with equality and our fears of subordinationism and patriarchy.

Third, it is no wonder, therefore, that all three of these theologians adopt the classical tradition in acknowledging the Father as the origin and fount of the divinity of the Son and the Spirit, but do nothing systematic with that crucial acknowledgment, still less explore the nature of that derivation—the meaning of "begetting"—for fear of falling into subordinationism. Moltmann sharply distinguishes between the "constitution" and the perichoretic "life" of the Trinity, restricting the monarchy of the Father to the level of constitution without exploring its implications precisely for the possibility of the perichoretic life of the triune persons, and declaring instead that the monarchy "has no validity within the eternal circulation of the divine life, and none in the perichoretic unity of the Trinity. Here the three Persons are equal; they live and are manifested in one another and through one another."[107] Pannenberg too is more interested in neutralizing the monarchy of the Father through a reciprocal mediation by the Son and the Spirit than in developing it for its positive implications for the mutual immanence and equality among the three persons.[108] Plantinga likewise refers to the "quasi-genetic derivation" of the Son and the Spirit from the Father, which he takes to mean that the three persons are "not just members of the class of divine persons, but also members of the same family," without, however, developing in full the meaning of such genetic derivation.

It is amazing how none of the three shows the slightest interest in exploring the profound content of the procession of the two persons from the Father which so impressed the classical tradition as the mystery of the communication of the numerically identical divine substance and total sharing among the persons, which also makes their perichoretic unity and mutual mediation possible. For Aquinas and the classical tradition, the monarchy of the Father as the source of the Trinity also makes both equality and differentiation possible: by communicating his numerically identical divine nature with the Son and the Spirit the Father produces two equal beings out of his own substance, and in doing so also produces differentiation as between the begetter and the begotten and between the spirator and the spirated.

The profundity of the classical doctrine of the monarchy of the Father is precisely that it is a *monarchy which cancels or sublates itself in its superiority in the very act of its exercise* because it is the privilege of a divine being alone to be able to share the totality of its own being or its divine substance with another in pure love whose first gift is that of self, thereby producing a being equal to itself. It is a giving that simultaneously posits and cancels the very distinction between giver and receiver by the kind of content that is given, the numerically identical divine nature of the Father himself. This idea, however, is completely lost in all three theologies. If we are going to preserve the monarchy of the Father—as I think any Christian trinitarianism must that is faithful to the biblical witness—and yet also avoid subordinationism, then we must find a way or principle within the monarchy of the Father and inherent in that monarchy whereby we can also transcend that monarchy: we must articulate a form of monarchy that is also capable of canceling itself into an affirmation of equality. This is precisely what the classical tradition from Athanasius to Aquinas has tried to do with its language of "generation" and "spiration" and the central notion of the divine procession as involving the communication of the numerically identical divine nature.[109]

Jürgen Moltmann

Let me now move on to specific observations on each of the three social trinitarians. With regard to Moltmann, I have two observations, one about the relation between person and relation, the other about the onto-logical basis of the trinitarian perichoresis. As we saw, for Moltmann relations neither "constitute" nor "manifest" personal existence. Relations do not constitute but presuppose personal existence, which is indeed relational but not reducible to relationality. Any reduction of personhood to relation, for Moltmann, is essentially modalistic. By the same token, relations do not merely manifest persons already complete in themselves apart from such relations to one another. Persons are irreducible to relations, but they cannot exist without relations either. For Moltmann, persons "subsist" in the divine nature, which keeps them from reduction to relations, but they "ex-ist" in essential relations to one another. "Subsistence" and "ex-istence" or substantiality and relationality are two essential, mutually irreducible components of the divine personhood, similar to Plantinga's "generic" and "personal" essences.

We may, however, push the question further and ask how these two principles of the divine persons are related to each other. Moltmann's answer is that they are so "genetically" connected as to arise "simultaneously and together." What, then, makes such genetic connection necessary between subsistence in the divine nature and totally relational existence? What exactly makes it possible and necessary for the divine persons to ex-ist, as distinct persons, "totally" in and through the others? Since there cannot be a third principle outside of God and therefore in addition to the two principles that can provide for the necessary connection between the two, the unifying principle must lie either in the one or the other principle. Moltmann, however, does not want to derive one from the other; in his view, deriving relationality from subsistence falls into modalism, while it is simply impossible to derive subsistence in the divine nature from relationality as such. In Moltmann, the two principles remain simply *given*, without further explanation.

One possible reason for this aporia is that Moltmann wishes to avoid modalism while also remaining purely univocal in his conception. Subsistence and relation are taken from the realm of finite, human experience, where indeed there remains an irreducible distinction between the two. The existence of a human being, for example, is indeed irreducible to relations; to reduce her existence to relations to others would be to deny her interiority, autonomy, and subjectivity as a person. A person can exist in and through the other only up to a point while also maintaining his integrity; he can exist totally in another only by being reduced to a "thing" either metaphorically as in the case of a complete slave, which is not possible, or literally as in the case of being incorporated into someone's body as food as in the case of cannibalism. The distinction between subsistence as a human being and relations to others remains irreducible in human beings. This is so, however, because of the "nature" of human beings as finite beings. For human "nature" in its finitude, the distinction between subsistence and relationality is something *given* in the created distinction between essence and existence, form and matter, subjectivity and objectivity, which no finite creature can cancel or sublate on its own. Materiality of essence makes others too opaque and external to us, and contingency of existence makes them too unpredictable, for us to find ourselves totally in them. To subsist in the created, finite, human nature does entail irreducible duality and alienation between substantiality and relationality. Being a human being is necessarily different from being a father or a son.

In God, however, these alienating dualities and distinctions do not exist. It is precisely subsistence in the divine nature that makes "total" existence of persons in one another in mutual perichoresis necessary and possible, necessary because there is only one intrinsically indivisible and therefore numerically identical divine nature or substance to be shared among the three, possible because only the divine persons can be so totally transparent and internal to one another and thus capable of total mutual sharing without alienation. If this is so, then subsistence in the divine nature and relations of total sharing among the persons need not be irreducibly different or opposed; rather, the total relationality of the persons follows precisely from their subsistence in the common divine nature. Which is to say, as Augustine and Aquinas have said, that divine persons are precisely "subsisting relations." Relations "constitute" the persons, who exist as relations subsisting in the divine nature. As divine, the three persons subsist in the divine nature, while as distinct persons, they are thoroughly and totally relational to one another. They are one in the numerically identical divine nature, distinct only with regard to their mutual relations, which makes their mutual, total perichoresis both possible and necessary.

For this analogical imagination, then, there is no irreducible dichotomy or alienation between person and relation in the divine mode of being. That imagination also provides the ontological foundation for the possibility and necessity of eternal mutual perichoresis among the persons while also obviating the dualism of "common divine nature" and "particular individual nature," substantiality and relationality, "constitution" and "life." It is true to say, with Moltmann, that the unity of the three persons is "already given with the fellowship of the Father, the Son, and the Spirit," but such a unity, wholly located by Moltmann in relationality, can be so given only because of the kind or nature of the being they are. Such a total mutual sharing is the privilege of the divine being and presupposes the numerical unity of the divine nature or substance.

Because Moltmann understands the monarchy of the Father only as the "constitutive" source of the Son and the Spirit without also appreciating the nature of that constitution as precisely the communication of the numerically identical divine nature and therefore also the incomprehensible depth of divine love which sublates or cancels the superiority of the source in one and the same act, he seeks to acknowledge the monarchy of the Father, which he cannot ignore because it is so pervasive in the New Testament, but to do so only in the order of "constitution" and to separate it from the perichoretic "life" of the three persons in which they are all immanent in and equal with one another. Just as he retains the unexplained dualism of subsistence and relationality in God, so also does he retain the inexplicable dualism of "constitution" and "life," which begs the question of how the three persons can be constituted in one way yet live in another. Does not the *life* of a thing reflect and express precisely its *constitution?* What makes the total mutual indwelling of the three persons possible and necessary except the divine nature of their constitution? Is it possible to abstract from the question of the divine nature and the constitution of the divine persons as divine in a discussion of the kind of total, infinite, mutual sharing and indwelling demanded by the concept of trinitarian perichoresis? After all, a being can only relate to another as it is constituted. Moltmann's problem, it seems, is that he tries to avoid modalism and subordinationism not by exploring the self-sublating nature of the monarchical constitution of the three persons but by isolating their constitution and their life.

Wolfhart Pannenberg

Pannenberg's Hegelian dialectical approach makes a straightforward critique difficult if not impossible. The assumptions of the philosophy of being and substance upon which the classical trinitarian tradition is based are quite different from those of the Hegelian dialectic upon which Pannenberg's trinitarian theology is based. The chief difference lies in the interpretation of being: Is being essentially self-sufficient and immutable, with relation and multiplicity as expressions of *finite* being—not being as such—or is it essentially self-unfolding and self-manifestation, with relation and multiplicity as intrinsic moments of being itself regardless of its finitude or infinity? In the first case, the divine essence would only be *shared* in its numerical identity among the three divine persons, while in the second, it would also be *actualized* in them in non-identical ways. The identity between the divine essence and the three persons is direct in the first case, dialectical in the second. In the first case the differences among persons are only "relational" and do not affect their very divine nature since they share the numerically identical divine nature, while in the second the differences do bear on their very divinity and mode of existence.

Pannenberg's innovations, therefore, verge on the revolutionary in relation to the classical tradition, and to the extent that they are revolutionary, also necessarily invite a number of methodological and substantive questions with regard to the way he tries to resolve the standard issues in trinitarian theology that every trinitarian theology must face. In particular I would like to raise issues about the ways he tries to argue from the economy to the eternal relations in the immanent Trinity, to account for the distinctive identity of each divine person, to interpret the role of the Son as the mediating Logos of creation, and to understand the relation between the divine essence and its manifestations both dialectically and by reconceptualizing the person of the Holy Spirit as both the divine essence itself and a distinctive person, reversing the classical "monarchy of the Father" into a "monarchy of the Holy Spirit." I will also point out problems with the model of the dialectic of self-manifestation.

Reduction of the immanent to the economic.   First, there is a tendency in Pannenberg to ignore the distinction between the human and the divine in Jesus and to project the relation of the human Jesus to the Father and the Holy Spirit, directly and without modification, onto the relation of the Son to the first and third persons in the immanent Trinity, thereby reducing the immanent to the economic Trinity. Pannenberg begins with the sound epistemological principle that God is in his eternal essence what he has shown himself to be in Jesus of Nazareth, a principle restated by Karl Rahner as the thesis of the identity of the economic and the immanent Trinity. Pannenberg goes on to say that the human Jesus showed himself to be the Son by refusing to identify himself with God, as Adam tried to do, and by distinguishing himself instead as a human creature and serving the lordship of the Father as the one God in complete obedience to his will. His sonship, therefore, consisted in creaturely obedience to the Father. Likewise, he was filled with the Holy Spirit from the conception to the resurrection. Pannenberg recognizes that it was in his human nature that Jesus showed his creaturely obedience to the Father and received the Holy Spirit, but also insists that he did so as the person of the eternal Son, making it, therefore, legitimate and necessary to read that relationship into the immanent Trinity. Thus, the eternal Son distinguishes himself from the eternal Father by "subjecting himself to the Father as the King of eternity," and "partakes of eternal deity only through his relation to the Father and as filled by the Spirit of the Father."[110] "In all eternity the Son gives the Father the honor of his kingly rule."[111] Even in the immanent Trinity the Son "receives it [the dynamic of the Spirit] as gift, and it fills him."[112]

The Christian tradition has always inferred from the saving presence of God in the life of the human Jesus to his eternal sonship in the immanent Trinity, regarding indeed the humanity of Jesus precisely as the finite manifestation of his divine sonship. It has, however, also always made a distinction between his humanity and divinity, interpreting what he did and suffered in his human nature as a finite sign of God's own salvific love for humanity, but never directly transposing it into the life of the eternal Son. It went so far as to affirm the "sharing or communication of attributes [communicatio idiomatum]" between the human and the divine on the basis of their hypostatic or personal union in the eternal Son but did not confuse the human and the divine as such. It is the divine Son indeed, but in his human nature, who was conceived by the power of the Holy Spirit, anointed with the Spirit at baptism, and guided in his life all the way to the cross and resurrection. God the Father was indeed lord and king to the human Jesus in his creaturely reality, as the human Jesus, in common with all creation, needed the empowering presence of the Holy Spirit. Insofar as it is the Son as a person who is involved in all the human experiences of Jesus, it is legitimate and necessary to transpose his basic filial relation to the Father into the immanent Trinity. But is it legitimate and necessary to transpose those aspects of his relation specifically derived from his humanity and creaturehood into the eternal life of God? Is it legitimate to argue that because God was king and lord to the human Jesus, the Father is also king and lord to the eternal Son; or that because the Father depended on the Son in some sense for the fulfillment of his lordship on earth, the Father does so in the immanent Trinity; or that because the human Jesus received the Holy Spirit, the eternal Son also does? Isn't this taking the Protestant emphasis on the economic lordship of the Father into the eternal divine relations themselves? Certainly, we cannot say that the Son is related to the Father in the immanent Trinity as a creature is related to the creator. Pannenberg tends to make a direct transfer from the relations in the economy to those in the immanent Trinity and to ignore the distinction between the two, thus reducing the identity between the economic and the immanent to an undifferentiated one.[113]

Distinctive identity of the divine persons. This leads, second, to the further question of what constitutes the distinctiveness of each person in the immanent Trinity and how such distinctiveness originates. We may recall that in the classical tradition, at least in Aquinas, it is relative oppositions—e.g., paternity and filiation—that constitute the distinctiveness of each person, and that such oppositions originate in the immanent processions of the intellect and will or the actions of generation and spiration. What would be Pannenberg's equivalents?

Pannenberg does agree with the classical tradition that persons are constituted by mutual "ec-static" relations,[114] but also insists that such relations are not reducible to the unilateral relations of origin from the Father. Rather, relations are constituted by mutual "self-distinctions" of the persons themselves. The Father distinguishes himself from the Son by "the generation and sending of the Son," while the Son distinguishes himself from the Father by "obedience to the sending of the Father, which includes recognition of his fatherhood," and the Holy Spirit distinguishes himself from the other two by "glorifying the Father in the Son and the Son as sent by the Father."[115] Pannenberg stresses that "the Father does not merely beget the Son. He also hands over his kingdom to him and receives it back from him. The Son is not merely [nicht nur] begotten of the Father. He is also obedient to him and he thereby glorifies him as the one God. The Spirit is not just breathed. He also fills the Son and glorifies him in his obedience to the Father, thereby glorifying the Father himself."[116] There is no one relation of origin to which a person can be reduced. Each is "a catalyst of many relations."[117] Thus, the three persons distinguish themselves from one another as persons and, for Pannenberg, in their deity as well. It is, for example, his self-distinction from the Father through obedience that is "constitutive for the eternal Son in his relation to the Father," while "in the act of self-distinction he receives his deity from the Father."[118]

Pannenberg is puzzling, however, on a number of issues. He consistently treats "generation" and "mission," "begetting" and "handing over his kingdom" as separable relations, and locates the relational identity of the Father in his lordship over the Son, not in his eternal generation of the Son, and that of the Son in his obedience to that lordship, not in his being begotten of the Father, determining their respective identities in terms of lordship and obedience that originate from their relations in the economy. Begetting appears to be just one relation among other relations, separable from the sending of the Son on his economic mission—as though the Father could distinguish himself from the Son by sending him without first generating him as Son, or as though the Son could distinguish himself from the Father by his obedience without first being begotten as Son. It would seem evident, however, that the self-distinction of the Son through obedience to the Father must presuppose his generation as Son from the Father: that the Son obeys because he is Son, and that he is first constituted as Son precisely through generation, not through obedience, which would only manifest his sonship; likewise, that the Son would receive his deity through generation, not through his obedient self-distinction from the Father, and that his mission would not be separable from but only follow from his eternal generation as Son.

If a person is indeed a "catalyst of many relations," it should be possible to specify the ontological bases of such relations as well as the ontological source of differences among them, neither of which Pannenberg provides. In any event, all the possible plural relations would presuppose the basic relation of origination from the Father as the source of the divinity of the Son and the Spirit; this relation would first constitute them as Son and Holy Spirit, after which they can then distinguish themselves. Yet, afraid of a reversion to the classical tradition, Pannenberg pays only lip service to the monarchy of the Father as the "divine origin" of the existence of the Son and the "fount" of the divine essence;[119] nowhere elaborating an ontology of this generation or making a systematic use of it. Pannenberg is only anxious to reduce the immanent Trinity with its eternal generation of the Son and eternal spiration of the Holy Spirit to the economic Trinity with its obedience and service of the Father's lordship, which in fact would undercut the ontological basis of the economic Trinity itself.

Furthermore, "obedience" and "service" to the "lordship" or "kingship" of the Father need not be distinctive of the Son; they can equally apply to any "creature," "servant," and "subject" (of a kingdom). If that obedience is to be distinctive of the "Son," it must reflect and presuppose—not constitute—his sonship as distinct from his creaturehood, servanthood, and subjecthood. But an elaboration of his sonship precisely as someone "begotten" of the Father and sharing his divinity—the focus of so much classical trinitarianism—is what Pannenberg fails to provide. Nor can such characterization of the identity of the Son avoid the danger of reducing the union of the Father and Son to a purely moral union without an ontological basis in the eternal generation of the Son.

The Son as mediator of creation.   Related to the issue of the origin of the personal distinctions is the issue of the specific roles of the Son and the Spirit in the economy. As Aquinas understands the economic roles of the three persons in terms of their place in the immanent logic of the eternal processions, so Pannenberg tries to relate the mediating role of the Son and the Spirit to their relations in the immanent Trinity. Pannenberg takes the Son as exemplar of all creation and locates that exemplarity in his eternal self-distinction from the Father through his kenotic self-subordination to the latter's lordship and majesty. Through "the humble and obedient acceptance of this distinction,"[120] the Son, without abandoning his deity, renounces equality with the Father, "moves out of the unity of the deity by letting the Father alone be God,"[121] takes the place of the creature, and becomes a human being "so as to overcome the assertion of the creature's independence in the position of the creature itself, i.e., without violating its independence."[122]

This subjection of the Son to the monarchy of the Father is "the basic law of the relation of creatures to the Creator. By it they can achieve an independent existence which is distinct from God and yet stay related to the origin of their life,"[123] without which they would fall into nothingness. The Son or Logos is "the generative principle of otherness" for all creation in that it exemplifies the model of the creature who refuses to identify itself with God in idolatry and accepts its creaturely otherness, but without absolutizing that otherness or independence in a false claim to self-sufficiency and infinity. This model is best exemplified in the human Jesus, who "actualizes in the course of his life the cosmic structure and destiny of all creaturely reality as in distinction from creation Jesus *assumes* his distinction from God the Father and totally affirms and accepts himself as God's creature, and God as his Father."[124] He refused to be like God or equal with God, instead accepting his creaturely finitude and honoring God as his own Father and creator, committing his entire existence to the service of his lordship. "In this obedience of the Son the structure and destiny of creaturely existence found their fulfillment in Jesus of Nazareth. In this way the eternal Son is the ontic basis of the creaturely existence of Jesus and all creaturely existence."[125]

Pannenberg's account of the mediating role of the Son as the Logos of creation immediately elicits three critical comments. First, it is clear that the Son's mediating role is limited to his moral exemplarity as the humble and obedient servant of the Father's lordship over all creation. Unlike the classical tradition that emphasized not only the moral but also the aesthetic, epistemological, and ontological functions of the Son as the Logos and Image of the Father in relation to creation, Pannenberg consistently and exclusively stresses the moral relation of self-distinguishing obedience between the Son and the Father as a model of all creation, assuming idolatry as the greatest evil, introducing the negation of idolatry as the highlight of the immanent relations themselves, and ignoring all other non-moral dimensions of divine and created existence.

This leads into the second comment, namely, that Pannenberg's is a thoroughly anthropocentric conception of mediation that limits salvation and reconciliation to the human, leaving the vast non-human creation simply theologically irrelevant. How would one apply the Son's moral exemplarity of obedience and humility to the non-human creatures of nature in all its vastness and mystery? How do the stars and plants and dogs distinguish themselves from the Father as creator of all things, unless one seeks, with the classical tradition, to introduce not only moral but also imaging and reflecting relations between the Son and the Father? Whereas Aquinas, along with the classical tradition, reflects on three personal names of the second person—Son, Word, and Image—with all their richness of implications for creation, Pannenberg tends to narrow his consideration to the purely moral relation of obedience, at the sacrifice of the Son's ontological relation as "begotten" of the Father. It may be recalled that this moral relation is originally a projection from the economic relations into the immanent. It is now being retrojected into the economic as its basic law, with the consequence that the whole of non-human creation is left out of the range of the effective mediation of the Son, thus failing to do justice both to God's comprehensive relation to the world and to the cry of all creation for liberation from sin and death, a cry getting louder in our ecological age.

Third, Pannenberg's account of the mediating function of the Logos also suffers from the fact that it overstresses the distinction between the

Father and the Son as well as the distinction of creator and creature and therefore also stresses only the negative relation between the two at the expense of positive relations of similarity and union. Out of the fundamental fear of idolatry Pannenberg accentuates the fact that Jesus did *not* equate himself with the Father but distinguished himself from the Father in obedience and humility. Pannenberg reads this fact of the economy into the immanent relations and makes this distinction between finite and infinite, human and divine, the basic law of all creation. The result is that he highlights only the fact that creatures are *not* God, that the finite is *not* infinite, that human beings are *not* divine. In contradiction to his own Hegelian principle of the "true infinite" that empowers the finite itself to share in its infinity, he fails to consider the positive aspects of both human and non-human creatures, their similitude to the divine, their movements toward the divine, and their varying capacity to image the divine, as Aquinas tried to do. He highlights what creatures are *not* at the expense of what they *are* in their relation to God.

Dialectic of the one divine essence and three divine persons and the monarchy of the Spirit.   In addition to the direct introduction of economic relations into the immanent, the neglect of the relations of origin in the constitution of persons, and a faulty hermeneutic of the mediating role of the Son with regard to creation, Pannenberg's reconstruction of trinitarian theology faces a fourth problem in his dialectical solution to the problem of the one divine essence and the three divine persons. The classical tradition saw either only simple identity as between the divine essence and the divine persons, or an "external" relation as between a created substance and its relations. Pannenberg, in a Hegelian departure from that tradition, posits "internal" or "constitutive" relations between the divine essence and the divine persons as between the essence and relations in general, sees the divine essence as dialectically manifesting itself and existing only in such relations,[126] interprets the divine essence itself as a "force field" and this force field as "love," and understands the unity of the divine essence dynamically as the *activity* of relating, uniting, and reconciling. The divine persons, the relations of the divine persons to the created world, and the various attributes of God revealed in that world are manifestations of the one divine essence in the unifying force field of divine love. Taken in itself, apart from the trinitarian tradition, there is a certain profundity, consistency, and dynamic vitality about Pannenberg's sophisticated approach that should be especially appealing to modern

sensibilities alienated from the classical tradition. I have several reservations, however, about Pannenberg's dialectical solution to the problem of
the unity and trinity in God.

First, Pannenberg's thoroughly Hegelian approach inverts the traditional "monarchy of the Father" into the "monarchy of the Spirit" without, however, explaining how the monarchy of the Spirit is compatible
with the monarchy of the Father he still seems committed to. In contrast
to the classical position where the Father represents both the divine
essence itself and a distinct person, Pannenberg sees the Spirit as both the
divine essence and a distinct person. The origination of the Son and the
Holy Spirit from the Father is replaced by the manifestations of the Spirit
as the divine essence. The Spirit is the divine essence in the dynamic sense
of the force field, movement, activity, and power of divine love that
relates and unites. He proceeds from the Father, is received by the Son, is
common to both, and provides the field on which and the gravitational
pull or love by which the Father and the Son are mutually related. As
such, the Spirit is "the one movement which embraces and permeates all
of them [the trinitarian persons],"[127] "the power and fire of love glowing
through the divine persons, uniting them, and radiating from them as the
light of the glory of God," and "the eternal power and deity which lives
in the Father, Son, and Spirit through their relations and which constitutes the unity of the one God in the communion of these persons." It is
also "the concrete reality of the divine love which pulses through all
things and which consummates the monarchy of the Father through the
Son in the Holy Spirit."[128] The Spirit is not only the divine essence but
also a particular person insofar as it is distinct from the two persons
whom it unites, provides the space and dynamic in which they are united,
and knows itself as united to both by glorifying the Son in the Father and
the Father through the Son.[129]

The relation between the divine essence and the divine persons is thoroughly dialectical. On the one hand, the unifying, essentializing Spirit of
love is not an independent power or a fourth entity apart from the three
persons; it is found "only" in the persons, yet not in each person taken
singly but rather in the persons taken in their concrete, internal, self-
transcending relations to one another. The divine "essence" exists only in its
"manifestations" in the persons.[130] "Love is the essence that is what it is
only in its manifestations, namely, in the Father, Son, and Spirit, presenting and manifesting itself wholly and utterly in the attributes of its manifestation."[131] The divine persons, on the other hand, are "the three forms

of the existence [Dasein] of God,"[132] "simply [nur] manifestations and forms—eternal forms—of the one divine essence,"[133] "the centers of action of the one movement which embrances and permeates all of them—the movement of the divine Spirit who has his existence only in them,"[134] "modes of being of the one divine life,"[135] the "concretions of the divine reality as Spirit,"[136] and "individual aspects of the dynamic field of the eternal Godhead."[137] As self-manifestations of the relating and uniting Spirit the persons are to be taken only in their self-transcending relationships to one another.

The contrast with the classical position is quite clear. Whereas, in the classical position, it is the dynamic of the self-knowledge and self-love of the Father in his divine essence and the communication or sharing of his numerically identical substance that move and unify the three persons in their mutual relations, in Pannenberg it is the unifying dynamic of the Spirit that governs the entire life of the Trinity and manifests itself in the mutual relations of the persons. In Aquinas, the Holy Spirit was the "formal effect" of the mutual love of the Father and the Son; here, in Pannenberg, the Spirit is, one cannot avoid the expression, the "efficient cause" of the entire life of the immanent Trinity, "the power and fire of love glowing through the divine persons, uniting them, and radiating from them as the light of the glory of God." For Pannenberg, "persons do not have power over love. It rises above them and thereby gives them their selfhood."[138] It is true that this divine power of love does not exist by itself but always only in and through its manifestations in the persons; by the same token, however, it seems clear that it is not reducible to any one person or even all three persons. There is, therefore, a clear distinction between the divine essence and the divine persons, as there is between an essence and its manifestations, a distinction made clearer by Pannenberg's insistence that persons do not have power over love but that love has power over persons. The Spirit as the divine essence and power of love is a power *over* the persons, inspiring each person to transcend himself and unite himself with the other two.

Is Pannenberg's attempt to reconcile the unity and trinity in God through the monarchy of the Spirit as the divine essence compatible, however, with the monarchy of the Father that Pannenberg recognizes and even at times insists on? Central to the monarchy of the Father are the notions of "generation" and "procession": the Son is begotten by the Father, while the Holy Spirit proceeds from the Father. What would generation and procession, a terminology Pannenberg still maintains, now mean in a trinitarian theology that understands the Spirit as the power of love that stands above the Father and inspires him to generate the Son and originate the Spirit, the power of love itself? Does the power of generation and origination maintain its meaning when it is itself empowered by a power above itself to generate and originate? Is this not in fact "subordination" of the Father to the Spirit? How could the Spirit both manifest itself in the Father as its *Dasein* and still proceed from the Father? It is never clear in what sense "the dynamic of the Spirit radiates from the Father."[139] Furthermore, how can the divine power of love empower the Father to originate itself, the divine power of love? I am not sure whether these problems can be brushed aside simply by invoking the "dialectical" understanding that affirms the mutuality of cause and effect or essence and manifestation; after all, dialectical thinking never affirms simple identity but always identity mediated by difference.

My second reservation, a corollary of the preceding consideration, questions whether Pannenberg can avoid the charge of positing the divine essence as an independent power over the persons and therefore as a fourth entity over and behind the three persons. Pannenberg insists that it is not an independent, fourth entity, asserting that it has its existence only in its manifestations. But does he succeed in avoiding the distinction between the three persons and the divine essence as the power that relates, unifies, permeates, and embraces them all? The power that relates and unifies must be distinct from the persons it relates and unifies. It will not do to say that the power exists "only" in the ec-static, self-transcending relations of the persons; the relations are still the products of the power of love, not the power itself, which moreover transcends any one of the relations, although it does not transcend all the relations in the immanent Trinity. The dialectic of essence and manifestation presupposes difference between the two. Christoph Schwöbel is quite right, therefore, in asking "how the three persons of the Trinity can be understood as presenting one divine essence without reducing them to moments or aspects of the one essential Godhead and without positing the divine essence as a fourth subject lurking behind the persons of Father, Son, and Spirit."[140]

Third, the dialectic of love as the power that empowers persons to transcend and relate themselves to others cannot explain the specific origin of the persons. There is a certain parallelism in structure between the dynamic of love and the dynamic of essence, which Pannenberg takes full advantage of. Just as love never exists by itself but only by manifesting itself in the persons who love, and in transcending and uniting those persons in reciprocal relations, so the essence never exists by itself but only in its manifestations, the persons, and in transcending and uniting those manifestations. There is something profoundly insightful and biblical in equating the divine essence precisely with the power of love as relating, transcending, and uniting power. This structure of the dynamic of love, however, can only tell us why each person is internally and constitutively related to another but not how or why each person is related to the other precisely in the specific ways of generation, procession, mission, reception of the Spirit, glorification, etc. The logic of love and the self-manifestation of the essence is purely formal and does not, by itself, provide its own material content. It can explain the interpersonal constitution of persons but neither the number of persons involved—why only three persons, not more?—nor the specificity of the relations and the identity of each person—why these specific persons and not others? It can explain why the essence as love must manifest itself but not why it must manifest itself in precisely these three specific ways but not others. Without this material content which specifies the relations and identities of each divine person, the persons, whom Pannenberg does call "modes of being" of the one divine essence, are in clear danger of being reduced to undifferentiated moments of the essence, with the certain implication of modalism.

Pannenberg is fully aware of this. He does admit that the concrete personal distinctions "cannot be derived from an abstract concept of love."[141] Such knowledge is available only from the historical revelation of God in Jesus Christ. He is optimistic, however, that the trinitarian distinctions known through that revelation are quite compatible with and can be integrated with his theory of the divine essence as the power of love, which is precisely the issue I am raising. The discussion of the three distinct divine persons is based on the biblical and classical trinitarian perspective; the discussion of the unity of the divine essence as the universal force field of love is based on a modern philosophical, especially Hegelian and personalist, perspective. I have tried to show how the traditional and the modern approach are incompatible in Pannenberg, giving the examples of the monarchy of the Spirit and the monarchy of the Father. Ingolf Dalferth, therefore, is quite right when he claims that "it is here that Pannenberg's account fails most conspicuously. He does not succeed in offering a trinitarian solution to the problem of the unity of God which is more than an eschatological postponement. Rather he gets stuck in a dualist cul-de-sac: on the one hand he develops the difference of Father, Son, and Spirit from his account of revelation in terms of Jesus' self-distinction from the God he calls Father; on the other hand he grounds the unity of God in a metaphysical concept of God's essence prior to and independent of revelation: the concept of God as Infinite."[142]

Pannenberg's failure to integrate the biblical perspective and philosophical models raises once again the question of the relation between the treatise *de Deo uno* and that *de Deo trino*, this time, however, not in the context of the classical tradition, the special object of his criticism, but in relation to his own approach. He charges Aquinas with separating the two treatises and basing the first on natural theology and the second on biblical revelation, thereby also allowing the domination of biblical revelation by natural theology.[143] As I have pointed out, however, Aquinas took the biblical revelation of the Father, Son, and Spirit and tried to elucidate the origination, specificity, and relations of the three persons in terms of the immanent operations of intellect and will and their unity in terms of generation and spiration both of which consist in the communication of the numerically identical divine substance of the Father. He did not leave the biblical revelation of the three divine persons and the philosophical notion of the divine essence as the unifying unity of love merely juxtaposed. The problem of the relation between the two treatises, therefore, is not so much which one precedes which as what philosophical conceptualities one uses.[144] Pannenberg's explicit claim to integrate the discussion of the one God into the discussion of the triune God does not free him from the charge of subordinating biblical revelation to philosophical, especially Hegelian and personalist, models. Pannenberg's own interpretation of the biblical revelation of the triune God is not uncontaminated by the philosophical ideas of internal, constitutive relations and mutual mediation.

Fourth, do the divine persons, in Pannenberg's theology, enjoy equality of essence? We may recall that the classical tradition from Athanasius to Aquinas tried to preserve the divinity of the three persons by insisting on the equal divinity of the three since the divine essence is indivisible and can only be shared equally. It therefore locates any identifying difference among them in mutual relations or pure mutual referentiality as external to or outside the divine essence—which as such cannot be the source of differentiation—while it also affirms the identity of essence and relation in God in the name of divine simplicity by way of negation and eminence. Pannenberg works with a different, dialectical conceptuality: the essence is not external to its relations through which it manifests itself. Nonetheless, he must answer the perennial question of trinitarian theology, i.e., in what sense the persons are equally divine. Even a dialectical metaphysics cannot avoid this question, although it may answer it in a different way; and Pannenberg, who is seriously concerned to avoid subordinationism, positively needs an answer on this issue.

There is a sense in which it is true to say that Pannenberg too tries to locate the personal differences in relations and especially in the equal reciprocity of relations. For him, it is not only that the Son serves the lordship of the Father but also that the Father depends on the Son for the execution of that lordship in the economy. It is not only that the Spirit proceeds from the Father but also that the Father depends on the Spirit for his eschatological fulfillment and glorification. The relations are equally reciprocal and constitute the equal deity of the persons. This much Pannenberg says on the basis of biblical revelation (although this interpretation is not immune to criticism, as I argued earlier). In his dialectical understanding of the divine essence, however, Pannenberg locates the identity of each person in his self-transcending and his self-relating to the other, which Pannenberg interprets as a manifestation of the essentializing activity of the Spirit—the unifying love that constitutes the divine essence. Moreover, he identifies the divine essence itself only with the "sum total" of such manifestations in which alone it has its existence.[145]

One cannot say, therefore, as in the classical position, that the whole divinity is present in each person or that the divinity of three persons is not greater than the divinity of one person. In Pannenberg, the difference of persons lies not only in their constitutive relations but also in their very deity constituted by their relations; this in contrast to the classical position in which the persons, not their deity, are constituted by their relations while their deity is simply the numerically identical divine essence of the Father only shared in relationally different ways. Pannenberg's dialectical understanding necessarily postulates that the divine essence is not identical with any one self-manifestation in the deity of a divine person but only with the "sum total" of the distinct deities of all three persons. The deities of the three persons together, therefore, are greater than the deity of any one person.

If this is so, we are in turn led to another question: In what sense is each person divine when each is possible only as a manifestation of the divine essence but is not identical with the divine essence? How is this position different from the Cappadocian position which Pannenberg accuses, unfairly in my view, of postulating three independently constituted individuals who yet share the same nature and participate in common action after the model of three human individuals? We seem justified in saying similarly that

Pannenberg's divine persons are both mutually distinct manifestations of the divine essence and themselves distinct from the divine essence itself and do not, to this extent, share the numerically identical—but only the specifically or generically identical—divine essence. This would in turn make them comparable to the three human individuals of the alleged Cappadocian position who are distinct and separate yet share, without exhausting, the same generic but not numerically identical human nature.

Such a position, however, raises the specter of the traditional trinitarian heresies. First, it is not different from tritheism. After all, the three persons have each his own deity distinct from that of the other two and only share in the unity of the divine essence—an essence they merely manifest without being identical with it—by sharing in its movement and activity. The deity of each, therefore, is different from the divine essence that manifests itself in the three and permeates and unites them all. The unity of Godhead is not really based on the identity of the divine essence or deity but only on the unity of the divine movement or action. Second, Pannenberg's position may also be in danger of subordinationism. As I argued earlier, it does subordinate the Father and Son to the monarchy of the Holy Spirit who, as the unifying, essentializing power of the divine essence, relate and unite the two as a superior power of love. Third, as also indicated earlier, Pannenberg's position is in danger of modalism.

The Dialectic as trinitarian model.   The basic problem with Pannenberg's trinitarian theology as a whole, then, may be the underlying Hegelian philosophical model itself of the dialectic of self-manifestation. The model is taken from the world of finite experience and finite being where indeed the essence of a thing, necessarily composite and potential, has to manifest itself externally in an essentially interdependent world, not only in any one manifestation but in fact in a plurality of manifestations, where it is true, therefore, to say that the essence is identical only with the "sum total" of its manifestations, without which it does remain more or less potential. The human essence is in need of actualizing and manifesting itself in many relational manifestations and is not to be identified with nor exhausted by any one manifestation in any one individual. We certainly cannot identify God with this sort of finite dialectic of self-manifestation. As an infinite being God does not need to manifest herself in any relation external to her own being. All necessary self-manifestation will have to be internal to herself according to the concrete inner logic of her own infinite, divine nature as the one God, while any external self-manifestation will be an expression of her freedom. Certainly God is not reducible to the sum total of all her external manifestations in the economy.

When we apply the dialectic of self-manifestation to God without negation and eminence as demanded by the analogical imagination, we run into numerous problems, even apart from the question of its biblical foundation. It means reducing the immanent to the economic Trinity, as Pannenberg also tends to reduce the divine essence itself to the sum total of its manifestations in the world and to project economic into the immanent relations. Insofar as Pannenberg posits the difference of the divine essence and its manifestations and regards the persons as "mere" manifestations of the divine essence with all its activity of relating and unifying, he runs not only the danger of modalism, but that of postulating the divine essence as the "fourth" entity above and beyond the three persons. Insofar as he posits the Spirit as the divine essence that relates and unifies as the power of love, he incurs the danger of replacing the monarchy of the Father with the monarchy of the Spirit and subordinating the Father and the Son to the Holy Spirit.

Likewise, the dialectic of self-manifestation can guarantee only that there will be a plurality of manifestations, but it cannot insure either that there will be only three manifestations or that each of these three manifestations has the distinctiveness of the Father, Son, and Spirit—two points Aquinas tried to establish by an analysis of the immanent activities of knowing and willing in God. Additionally, the dialectic of self-manifestation guarantees only that there will be a plurality of manifestations of the same essence, not that such manifestations will be equal manifestations of the essence, contrary to the teaching of Aquinas, with its concept of the communication of the numerically identical divine substance. In the case of the dialectic of the self-manifestation of the divine essence as the power of love, although the manifestations are thoroughly mutually relational since the divine essence of love manifests itself only in and through the mutual relations of the persons, such manifestations will not necessarily be equal manifestations of the divine essence, unless the divine essence is understood not only as a relating power and activity but also as an intrinsically indivisible power that can only be shared *in toto* or not at all.

Cornelius Plantinga, Jr.

Cornelius Plantinga's position raises two issues: his rejection of the classical doctrine of divine simplicity on the ground that it leads to the identification of each of the three persons with the one divine essence, and his separation of the divine essence into the generic and the personal.

Regarding the first issue, the identification of the divine persons with the divine essence in Aquinas, both Plantinga's and other social trinitarian critiques of Aquinas's position are, I am afraid, rather superficial and based on a lack of appreciation of the complexity and subtlety of the theological and metaphysical considerations underlying the identification. The criticism comes down to the conclusion of formal logic: If A, B, and C are each identical with D, then A, B, and C are identical with one another. If the Father, Son, and Holy Spirit are each identical with the divine essence so that the Father is God, the Son is God, the Holy Spirit is God, and so that they are one God, not three Gods, then there is no distinction between the three persons. The doctrine of the identity of the persons and the divine essence knows neither how to add nor how to argue in a logically coherent way, and ends up by reducing the triune God to one divine person.

As we noted previously, social trinitarians are not the first ones to make this criticism, to which Aquinas responded in an analogical way. For him, our only way of speaking about God—including the relation between the divine essence and divine persons—is the human mode of speaking based on the created likeness of God. In this human mode we speak of substance and accidents. If we are going to find a human way of speaking of genuine differences while also affirming total essential identity, as we must in the case of the triune God, we can do so only by locating the differences in the real relations of relative opposition while locating the identity in essence or substance. This is so for two reasons: (1) the peculiarity of relation among accidents, which denotes pure referentiality and, as such, does not endanger the simplicity of the essence; and (2) the reality of relative—not absolute—opposition, which renders relation real, not merely logical. This is the *ratio* of substance, relation, and relative opposition discovered from our created experience. We cannot, however, apply this *ratio* to God without negating its human mode of signification proper to finite, composite beings and without predicating it of God in an eminent mode. We do the first by saying that substance and relation (accident) are *not* two distinct principles of divine being as they are of finite being; in God they are really identical although logically different. We do the second by saying that we do not have an intuition of the divine essence in its identity with the divine relations here below; we can, therefore, only adore and worship God in all her divine incomprehensibility.

Nor is Aquinas guilty of logical incoherence as charged. As discussed in the preceding chapter, A, B, and C (the persons of the Father, Son, and Holy Spirit) would be identical with one another when each of them is identical with D (the divine essence) only if the identity of each of A, B, and C with D (of the persons with the divine essence) is both real and logical, i.e., exhaustive. For Aquinas, the identity of divine persons and the divine essence is not exhaustive. Divine persons are "really" or "existentially" identical with the divine essence insofar as the *esse* of the persons and the *esse* of the essence is indeed identical; there can be only one *esse* of the divine persons, i.e., that of the numerically identical divine essence. Divine persons are also distinct from the divine essence "formally" or "rationally," that is, in terms of their meaning or *ratio*, insofar as relations do not denote their reference to the subject in which they inhere so much as pure referentiality to one another. Just as, according to Aristotle, action and passion are really or materially the same yet rationally or formally distinct, so the divine essence and the divine persons are really identical yet also rationally distinct, in which case, then, the identity of each of the three persons with the divine essence does not entail reduction of the three persons to one person. They are identical with the one divine essence and remain "one God," but are distinct from the divine essence in their real and pure mutual referentiality, which also makes each really distinct from the others. To identify each of the persons with the essence, therefore, is to identify each with the one God but not with one another. It is, in fact, the only way of saving both the oneness of God and the threeness of persons, as far as classical ontology can allow.

Properly understood, Aquinas's doctrine of the essential identity and relational differences among the three divine persons is not about formal logic or knowing how to count, but is about the composite structure of finite being, the necessity and limitation of the human mode of predication of divine names, and the silent recognition of the incomprehensible transcendence of God in her infinite difference from finite, composite beings. One expression of this is to say that God is simple, not composed of multiple principles of being or material parts, and that all differences in God—differences among the Father, Son, and Holy Spirit—therefore must be looked for in the order of relations, not essence.

Plantinga mistakenly insists on the necessity and adequacy of the human mode of predication without the necessity of negation and eminence required by divine transcendence. He therefore wants to find a human mode of predication that is as such adequate to the transcendence of God, i.e., a mode of univocal predication, which, however, the entire classical tradition concurs simply does not exist. This is not to say that Aquinas's way of conceptualizing the relation between essence and relation is simply adequate and needs no improvement. As we saw in our discussion of Pannenberg, there is a strong current in modern thought from Hegel to Whitehead that sees an internal relation between essence and relation, not an external relation as in the case of the classical tradition. The modern current cannot be dismissed, although a controversy still remains as to whether the idea of internal relation can be applied indiscriminately to any relation, e.g., relations between the divine essence and divine persons, between the divine persons themselves, and between the divine essence and its economic or worldly manifestations, as it has been in Pannenberg. Plantinga's objection, however, is not to the adequacy of the category and use of internal relation but to the doctrine of divine simplicity itself that distinguishes the divine from the finite in the classical paradigm and to the anti-trinitarian reduction of God to one person in terms of formal logic.

The second issue in Plantinga's position is his separation of the divine essence into the generic and the personal. Unlike Aquinas who locates the identity among the persons in the one divine essence while placing differences in their relations, and unlike Pannenberg who locates the identity among the persons in the divine essence but places differences in the modes of the manifestation of the one divine essence, but like Moltmann who distinguishes between the "common divine nature" the three persons share and their "particular individual nature,"[146] Plantinga distinguishes between the "generic essence" common to the three persons and their "personal essence." By virtue of their generic divine essence the three persons share certain properties in common such as everlastingness, sublimely great knowledge, and infinity, while by virtue of their "personal essence" they are each related to one another essentially "not only generically but also in some quasi-genetic way," which makes the persons "not just members of the class of divine persons, but also members of the same family." The generic essence makes each person possessed of aseity fully and equally divine, and the personal essences distinguish each from the other two and relate each to the others in an essential interdependence of love and loyalty.

As in the case of Moltmann, positing twofold essences in God inevitably raises the question of their relation. What is the character of the relation between what each is in itself as divine and what each is in relation to the other two? Does the generic divinity of each person have any role in making the interpersonal relatedness among the persons—i.e., their personal essences—possible, and in fact making it possible to the degree of intimacy and sharing traditionally associated with the trinitarian perichoresis? If so, the personal essence would seem to be somehow derivative from the generic essence. If not, the degree of interdependence among the three persons is not clear. What does it mean to say that the relationship is "quasi-genetic"? (How is the Son generated from the Father?) What does it mean to say that the three persons are "members of the same family"? (What is the difference between members of a "human" family and those of a "divine" family?) Here again we find a pervasive lack of awareness of the radical difference between the infinite God and finite creatures, and how that radical difference is reflected in predicating essences, generic and personal, and family relations of the three divine persons.

Social trinitarianism cannot avoid the impression of taking the idea of three human individuals—who share the same generic human essence as human beings but also possess distinct characteristics as individuals—purifying it of the mutual separateness of human individuals by adding the notion of a personal essence, and applying the idea to the Trinity, but without asking about the difference of metaphysical structure between the divine and the human. Human essences necessarily include materiality and therefore essential divisibility and multiplicability. Human individuals have not only the common human essence but also individual characteristics. They are both more than their generic essence insofar as their individuality is not simply deducible from that essence, and less than their generic essence insofar as their individuality does not exhaust all the possibilities of the generic essence. They are not exhaustively identical with their human essence. It makes sense, therefore, to speak of a twofold essence, generic and personal, in the case of human beings. What sense, however, does it make to speak of a twofold essence in God, whose generic essence is infinite and immaterial and neither divisible nor separable? Does the generic divine essence require multiplication at all, still less in terms of three personal essences, not two or four or ten? Does it make sense to speak of three "infinite" beings whose essence is intrinsically inseparable and thus one in the sense of numerical identity? Can social trinitarianism, in that case, really avoid the charge of tritheism?[147] Because it focuses on the moment of similarity between God and human beings without maintaining an equal concern for the moments of negation and eminence, social trinitarianism must always run the risk of falling into sheer anthropomorphism.

Chapter Seven

TOWARD A DIALECTIC OF PROPHETIC AND SAPIENTIAL THEOLOGY

A Postcritical Retrieval of Aquinas

Dialectic of Suspicion and Retrieval

Over the centuries Aquinas has been much praised and blamed. He has been praised, largely by his Thomist followers, for the sheer scope, balance, objectivity, and daring of his theology; for his assertion of the primacy of the act of existing over essence; for his sensible respect for the creature; for his enduring sense of the limits of human knowledge and God's incomprehensibility; and for his confidence in divine providence. He has been blamed, largely by Protestant thinkers, for subordinating revelation to the demand of natural reason, which ultimately turns out to be Greek reason, and thus giving final form to the much deplored "Hellenization of dogma" already in operation since the post-apostolic period. His theology, it is said, is more philosophical than biblical; whatever biblical references there are in his *Summa* are no more than proof texts taken out of the living context of Scripture. Christology is treated only in the Third and last Part of the *Summa,* without any controlling influence on the doctrine of God in the First Part, which is treated according to the assumptions of human reason. Even when the Trinity is discussed, the emphasis is on the immanent, metaphysical Trinity; the economic Trinity revealed in Scripture is merely presupposed, not allowed to exercise control over the content of the immanent. What the life, death, and resurrection of Jesus reveals about the nature of God and how such revelation may transform our natural knowledge of God, not merely add externally to it, are simply not considered. Against these objections, there are others who praise Aquinas for his obvious theocentrism and who reject the christological concentration that Barthians consider to be the very test of the Christian authenticity of any theology. In recent decades Aquinas has also been criticized for extrinsecism of nature and grace by Rahner, for lack of God's internal relation to creation by process theologians, for sexism by feminists, and for classism by liberation theologians. I cannot go into all these controversies.[1]

Authentic retrieval of a past thinker requires, I believe, at least two things. The first is to recognize the historicity and historical limitations of that thinker and not to be too anxious to turn the thinker into our own contemporary, as though it were always a good thing for everyone to think like us. Being relevant to one's own time means being able to address certain essential issues of the time and entails accepting some of the dominant assumptions of that time in the light of which some issues are considered essential and others peripheral, even though such assumptions would inevitably be outdated at a later time. Furthermore, as we know in our critical and postmodern age, no theory is innocent. Conditioned by our social practices, our own theories often reflect and justify the distortions and oppressions contained in such practices. Historicity of theory means not only that it is limited and inadequate in its vision but also that it is often guilty of ideological distortion and oppression. The first order of business for a critical attempt to retrieve a tradition, therefore, is to clear it through a thoroughgoing hermeneutic of suspicion. No retrieval today can be precritical.

The second requirement is to allow the possibility that a thinker may harbor a way of thinking and a fund of insights which are indeed immersed in the perspectives of a particular age yet also speak to us beyond the limitations and intentions of the age and the thinker, and to try to recover those primordial possibilities rooted in the—often unconscious—depth and trajectories of his or her thought that still speak to our own contemporary needs. Gadamer, Ricoeur, and Tracy call "classics" those works that are rooted in the particularities of a past thinker yet retain a "surplus of meaning" beyond such particularities—disclosing enduring, fundamental, essential truths of the human condition and challenging and transforming later generations beyond subjectivism and relativism—a "concrete universal," in the language of Hegel, that is particular yet embodies something universal in its depth.[2] It is clear that this second task—the task of retrieval proper—requires self-clarification regarding our contemporary needs and confrontation between such needs and the possibilities of such a thinker, a "fusion of horizons" across the centuries of cultural difference.

In the process of the six preceding chapters I have done something of both the hermeneutic of suspicion and the hermeneutic of retrieval regarding Aquinas's theology insofar as such hermeneutics fall within the scope of this book. In the first chapter I called attention both to the lack in Aquinas of a concrete, dialectical sense of history as a limiting condition of theological reason and to the cosmological horizon of universal grace as antidote against both homocentrism arrogant enough to claim domination over nature and homocentrism anxiously preoccupied with its own sinfulness. In the second chapter I called attention to Aquinas's naivete in his belief about the extent of the spread of the knowledge of Christ as well as to his astonishingly "reasonable" interpretation of saving providence as ever so respectful of the "diversity of times and persons," allowing the possibility of implicit faith as a sufficient condition of salvation for most human beings. In the third chapter I tried to retrieve a "sacramental" theology of religions out of Aquinas's various theological assumptions, while also trying to deconstruct his doctrine of the reprobation of the majority of human beings. In the fourth chapter I presented his sapiential conception of theology in its positive relevance and the ambiguous heritage of its intellectualist anthropology and its method of formal distinctions. In the fifth and sixth chapters I not only presented his trinitarian theology but also confronted it with contemporary criticisms while also confronting such criticisms with the challenge of Aquinas and classical trinitarianism.

In this final chapter concerned with the contemporary retrieval of Aquinas, I begin with a critical analysis of the contemporary theological situation largely dominated by "prophetic" theologies of action, its limitations and excesses, go on to a twofold typology of theology into "prophetic" and "sapiential," using Aquinas as a classic example of the latter, and argue for a methodical tension or dialectic between the two, where the virtues of sapiential theology confront the limitations of prophetic theology and vice versa, based on a dialectic of suspicion and retrieval.

The State of Contemporary Theology

It would be an exaggeration to say that contemporary theology is one big chaos. It would not be an exaggeration to say that it is greatly bewildering, to say the least. For some thirty years we have seen a vigorous, growing pluralism of method, concern, agency/addressee, and indeed religion itself in theology. Partly in response to the demands of drastic social changes, and mostly out of the desire for liberation from political and theological oppression in the history of Western colonialism, Christian theology has been adding new voices, new agendas, and new methods. The illusion of classical Western theology with its claim to be the one, normative, universal theology has been unmasked. No one theology can ever again claim to be *the* universal theology. So we have been celebrating pluralism in theology for over thirty years now, and much has been gained by it. Ideological self-criticism, hermeneutic of suspicion, theological necessity of ethnic and gender liberations, democratization of the church and its greater involvement in the liberation of the world, rethinking the place of humanity in the cosmos, respect for the cultural and religious Other: these and perhaps much more have now become part of the heritage of all theologies.

By the same token, at the turn of the new millennium and new century we seem to be at another turning point in theology. On the one hand, one cannot avoid the impression that contemporary theology has now exhausted both its élan and its vision. Not much new impetus and not many new insights have been forthcoming in recent years. On the other hand, the sheer pluralism of theology has been generating a need for its own corrective, a sense of solidarity across the many human divisions, old and new, and a theology that would speak to all of us in our common humanity. The world, too, has been changing, bringing different nations and cultures together into the common space of the internet, forcing on everyone a compelling sense of the difference of the other and an equally compelling necessity of finding, at the same time, a way of living together with others. What is the theological significance of globalization? We live today in the *kairos* for a different kind of theology.

A cursory look at contemporary theology reveals, first of all, a pro-liferation of method. Just as the revolution of modernity began with Descartes' *Discourse on Method,* followed by treatises on critical episte-mology of early modern European philosophy, so the drastic changes in contemporary theology were ushered in through new methodologies. Hermeneutics, transcendental method, narrative, rhetoric, praxis, experi-ence, cultural linguistics, doxology, indigenization, deconstruction, post-colonialism: these are some of the new ways of doing theology. These are, however, not just methods. They are methods chosen precisely to steer theology in different directions and contain whole theologies in them-selves. Theologies of praxis are theologies that define Christian identity precisely in terms of the praxis of liberation. Cultural linguistic theology seeks to defend Christian identity in terms of its internal tradition and character over against the forces of secularization, including liberation. Doxology seeks to reorient the whole of theology in light of worship and its *lex orandi.* Each method contains a whole theology in itself, a theo-logical content it seeks to defend against certain perceived threats or in-adequacies, internal or external.

A multiplicity of methods hides a multiplicity of concerns in con-temporary theology. Beginning with the demand for the liberation of the oppressed poor in Latin America and African Americans in the United States, the demand for liberation has spread to women, to women of dif-ferent ethnic groups, to all ethnic minorities, native Americans, Hispan-ics, and Asian Americans, and now to nature itself. Then, there is the concern for respect for other religions and cultures with whom we have to live together in an increasingly interconnected world. Christianity in Asia and Africa still faces the task of inculturation. Over against these concerns to emphasize the involvement of Christianity in the world, there have also been concerns about such involvement as destructive of Christian identity and a corresponding anxiety to restore that identity by returning to its own tradition.

Just as theological methods hide theological contents and concerns, so theological concerns hide theological agents and addressees and their situations. In fact, it is these agents who articulate their theological con-cerns arising out of their own situations in methods best suited to such needs and concerns. In addition to the traditional white, European, male theologians, we have now the theological voices of those who until recently had been rendered voiceless in the long tradition of Western Christianity. So we have theological agents who are women and men of all ethnicities speaking to their own gender and ethnic groups out of the sufferings of their situations. There are now as many different ethnic theologies as there are ethnic groups, each articulating its own history of victimization, its own vision of Christianity, and its own hopes for the future, employing a variety of methods, from hermeneutics of suspicion and retrieval to narrative, deconstruction, and postcolonial theory.

These developments have been positive in many ways. The different methods disclose dimensions and aspects of Christianity that have long been suppressed, forgotten, or only inadequately developed, as different groups articulate and contribute their own visions of Christianity that have long been absent. As reactions to various historical oppressions as well as to the Western Christian tradition that has justified such oppressions by imposing its own particular vision on all, these theologies have been historically justifiable, compelling, and liberating. We have all become richer for these developments.

We often hear the complaint that with the passing of great theologians such as Karl Barth, Reinhold Niebuhr, Paul Tillich, Karl Rahner, and perhaps some others, we no longer enjoy the company of great theological "giants" today, those whose works were "classical" (Tracy) enough to give expression to the hopes and aspirations of an entire generation. What we have today instead, it is said, are theologians whose works have limited, regional significance for particular groups and interests, not the universal significance for the whole church that the "giants" were said to have in their own times. I think there is some justification to this complaint. We no longer seem to have theologians with the stature and impact of these giants.

There is also some illusion to that complaint. Giants as they were in their own ways, they were never so universal as to give expression to the aspirations of all groups in the church. They were, instead, giving voice largely to the dilemmas, hopes, and perspectives of white, male, European or North American intellectuals. Excluded from their purview were the experiences and perspectives of women, minorities, working people, and the oppressed, colonized peoples of the world. Despite their undoubted greatness, they were not as universal as they were thought to be. For the appearance of a truly universal giant we may have to wait until there is far more integration in the church than we have now of different groups and their interests. Certainly we will have to wait until there is enough integration and solidarity for a single, formidable thinker to grasp and articulate into a vision that would be as concrete as the particular sufferings and hopes of particular groups and as universal as the global situation to which they are commonly subjected and the basic Christian convictions that animate them all. The appearance of such a giant is not solely the function of the individual genius but, more importantly, that of the culture that demands, nurtures, and recognizes that genius. Until then, we may have to be content with "local" giants, of which we do have plenty.

This does not mean that there are no worrisome problems about contemporary theology as it is. There are. The most basic problem of all is a sheer fragmentation that is unworthy of theology. The difficulty is not that there is a multiplicity of theologies per se, each with its own perspective, agenda, and method; it is rather that each absolutizes its own perspective, agenda, and method and closes itself off from all the others, reducing theology to the politics, history, and sociology of a tribe. Different ethnic and gender groups do not listen to one another, even to other oppressed groups. The fear is that if each group does not speak for itself, its own perspective and interest, no one else will. Each group must, therefore, compete with the others for attention, resources, and power in the arena of the world. Any attempt to introduce some sense of unity, universality, or solidarity across the ethnic and gender boundaries is suspect, regarded as an attempt to reintroduce totalizing domination, and as such is to be unmasked and resisted. Each group must be for itself, for its own liberation, with suspicion and caution with respect to all the others. As a *sociology* of ethnic and gender relations at a time when equality for many groups still remains a distant goal and has to be fought for every inch of the way, there is nothing to be wondered at in this description.

As a description of the *theological* situation, however, it must be regarded as nothing short of disastrous. It is one thing to do theology from the perspective of a particular group with all its needs, which have been suppressed and absent in the long annals of theology. It is both appropriate and fair to contribute these perspectives to the ongoing theological reflection of the church universal. It is also appropriate and fair to subject the Christian theological tradition to a hermeneutic of suspicion from one's own perspective and to purge the tradition of oppressive ideologies and whatever inhumanities there still remain. It is altogether another thing to stop here, with the negative critique of the tradition and the absolutization of one's own perspective, producing theology, Christology, and soteriology that express the needs of only a particular group. The typical question runs: What do God, Christ, salvation, grace, and so on, mean to one specific group?

Such a procedure fails to take one more step, that of rebuilding and retrieving the genuine universality of God, Christ, and salvation that would indeed include one's own perspective and needs but also those of other groups through genuine dialogue. The point of a hermeneutic of suspicion is precisely to unmask the universal claims of a particular perspective, not to absolutize another particular perspective in its place or to justify complacency about one's own particularity. The perspective may be, in fact is and always will be, particular, but particularity of perspective is not something fixed; it is dynamic and open to expansion through dialogue and dialectic, just as universality is not something fixed but capable of varying degrees. One particular perspective may be less particular and try to be more universal than another perspective.

Furthermore, one must distinguish between *perspective,* that *from* which claims are made, and *content,* that which is *claimed* from that perspective. One can, does, and often should, make claims with a universal content, i.e., content that is relevant to many creatures including human beings, often to all creatures, although always from a particular perspective. All significant claims are universal. All claims bearing on God are universal by nature since "God" in the Christian tradition will not be "God" except as the universal provider for all things in their creation, redemption, and recreation. All theological statements, i.e., statements that include God as their ultimate reference and context, are likewise essentially universal, including statements about Christ, sin, salvation, grace, and the mission of the church. It is normal that a perspective is particular, but abnormal that a particular perspective should include and address only particular contents and needs. A statement that is relevant only to the particular needs and perspectives of one group may be sociological and historical, but it is certainly not theological. To fail to make this distinction between perspective and content is to reduce the God of all creation and all humanity to a tribal God and ultimately to destroy theology by reducing it to sociology.

The consequences of this fragmentation into a multiplicity of self-absolutizing particularities is nothing short of disastrous for theology. The reduction of theology to the needs and perspectives of particular groups means, first of all, the loss of genuine universality for the basic content of theology and thus the loss of the properly theological character of theology as such. We discuss what God, Christ, and salvation (should) mean for particular groups based on their respective perspectives and needs, but rarely what they should mean for all of us precisely in, through, and beyond such particularities. Every particular group now has its own—tribal—God adapted to its own needs and, in the process, also inescapably remade to its own image. The same is true of Christology and soteriology.

It is important here to remind ourselves of what Karl Rahner has to say about the meaning of the word "God." Regardless of whether one is a believer, an atheist, or a sceptic, the word has to mean something like "the ground of totality in its unity" if "God" is truly God. God cannot be conceived of as simply one being among others, or a collection of finite beings, or the ground of only some beings, but only as the ground of all beings in their unity. Without the transcendental horizon of God as the ground of totality, there is no transcendence of the given. Without the word "God," therefore, we lose the sense of totality, both of the world as a totality and of our existence as a totality. Without this sense of totality, however, we immerse and lose ourselves in the sheer particularities of the world without even knowing that they are particular. As the world is reduced to a collection of things present to the immediacy of sensation, no longer an intelligible totality of events and relations, so is our human life also reduced to a succession of isolated moments, no longer an intelligible unity about which questions of meaning and responsibility can be raised. The death of the word "God," therefore, is the death of human life in its genuine humanity. "God" cannot be God except as the ultimate ground of universality and totality, even if our conception of God may be particular and is in constant need of self-transcendence in order to really mean "God." Any deliberately and self-complacently particularist conception of God is a falsification of God.[3] For David Tracy this universality of God requires that theology be "public." Any theology that is private or particularist is unworthy of God, as any theology not anchored in the doctrine of a truly universal God may be good cultural discourse but is not theology.[4]

Second, the loss of universality for theology both reflects and encourages the profound antagonisms and alienations among different groups along the lines of class, gender, ethnicity, religion, nation, and culture. There is no sense of unity, solidarity, or common humanity across the boundaries of group identities. I as a Korean American male do not find myself included in the many ethnic and gender theologies—such as feminist, *mujerista*, womanist, African American, Hispanic, and Native American theologies—except at times as an object of criticism because I am male. Although these are all Christian theologies, and I am a

Christian theologian, they simply ignore and exclude me. I must, there-fore, do my own kind of theology, i.e., Korean American theology. Every significant group thus feels compelled to do its own theology, with no attempt to retrieve the sense of universality for God and the sense of solidarity for humanity in God which we already enjoy theologically through Christ in the Holy Spirit. While traditional theology suffered from the (implicit) ethnocentrism and gender-centrism of one theology, that is, white male Western theology, contemporary theology suffers from competition among many explicitly and self-consciously ethnocen-tric and gender-centric theologies.

Third, the fragmentation of contemporary theology into competing particularist ideologies also entails separation of theology from the churches with their comprehensive needs. As predominantly oriented toward liberation, contemporary theology considers liberation from oppression its main concern and all other things *sub ratione liberationis.* This also means that its attention is concentrated on and necessarily lim-ited to social issues of one sort or another and the human praxis bearing on them. As enduring institutions, on the other hand, the churches have comprehensive needs to attend to that go beyond the social and political.

Besides instruction on and praxis of human liberation and social jus-tice, which are indeed essential to their Christian identity, churches also have many other needs to consider. Religious education or catechesis, so essential to the identity and continuity of the church, must comprise the whole of Christian doctrine, not merely the doctrine of social justice. The liturgy should not only remind us of our obligations of social justice, but also thank God for the economy of salvation that includes but also tran-scends liberation, as well as praise and glorify God for her own excellence and majesty. The churches must care not only for the present and the future but also for the past and its tradition; this link with the tradition is especially important for the identity of Christianity, a religion that regards itself essentially as a historical religion. The churches must also nurture for all their members as a way of following Christ in the world a spirituality that deepens the heart so as to experience the triune God, that broadens the heart so as to include all creation and humanity in its love, and that empowers the heart so as to be ready for effective love in the world. The churches must also provide pastoral care and counseling for different groups in the congregation—the aged, the young, the sick and dying, the imprisoned, each group with its own needs which go beyond issues of social justice.

These and other necessary concerns of the churches transcend the purview of the needs of ethnic and gender liberation. A particular need, such as social justice, may be quite compelling and possess broad implications for other needs as well, but no particular need, including social justice, is so universal in its implications as to comprise all needs. When theology so confines its concern to one need as to neglect practically all others, two unhappy consequences follow. First, theology alienates itself from the churches whose needs it fails to meet. Second, the churches are deprived of the benefits of systematic and comprehensive reflection that theology alone can provide, and thus become victims of ad hoc, fashionable, and superficial substitutes. The result is the prevailing sense of chaos and helplessness we observe today in the mainline churches and the massive flight of the faithful to other sources of comfort and meaning.

Speaking of the worldly task of religion in the Hegelian context and its role in the crumbling of the Berlin Wall of 1989, one observer asks a challenging question about the future of a religion that has no content but the political:

A quiet revolution started under the guise of weekly prayer services for peace. It spilled out of the churches into the streets. One politician quietly ordered the troops not to fire on those chanting, "We are the people." A wall tumbled. A state crashed. Was all this the phenomenon of religion becoming "worldly"? Surely, but the churches in Leipzig are quiet and empty again. Is that what "religion" becoming "worldly" also means? If in 1989 the churches were the "moral space" of the disaffected and dissatisfied, what is their function now that disaffection finds a public voice? Should religion survive as a space of sacred protest? Can it do so without content?[5]

The wall of ethnic and gender oppression has by no means crumbled, yet the observation continues to challenge: What is the function and content of theology and the churches as problems of oppression become more and more a matter of secular politics increasingly independent of the churches? Is there a content to theology besides liberation? Is there life to theology after liberation?

The prevailing sense of fragmentation in contemporary theology is essentially the result of the loss of the sense of the whole that traditional theology used to provide, even if its content has been discovered not to be as universal as it claimed to be. We no longer seem to have a sense of God as the God of *all* creation and *all* humanity, the transcendent source of the totality of all things in their being, not a tribal, nationalist, or ethnocentric God. We no longer seem to have a sense of Christ as the image of the invisible God through whom *all* things have been created, the new Adam who lived, was murdered, and was raised for *all,* and in whom *all* die and rise; a sense of Christ as the head of the new humanity to which all are called as members of his body and thus as members of one another; a sense of Christ that is not just Christ for white women, Asians, or African Americans. We no longer seem to have a sense of humanity as a *whole,* a community of solidarity and mutual dependence with a common theological destiny and subject to certain common existential conditions of life; a sense of humanity as a communion of saints as well as sinners; a sense of humanity that is not one of just an antagonistic collection of men, women, African Americans, and other ethnic groups, often with radically different ultimate ends. We no longer seem to have a sense of the church *catholic,* the church in its universality of time, place, and needs: not just a church for a particular region, group, or gender, not just a church of action, but a church for all in all their needs precisely because the church is a sacrament of the unity of all creation and all humanity in the triune God. We no longer seem to have a sense of life as a *whole,* a whole of many dimensions, conditions, and needs, personal and social, active and contemplative, human and cosmic, mortal and immortal: a whole, not a mere collection of disparate needs.

Finally, we do need but lack today a compelling sense of the *common* global context for all significant human issues including the liberation of particular groups. The dynamics of the global capitalist economy brings different groups ever closer together into an infinitely complicating network of mutual dependence, making each sensitive to the otherness of the other and forcing each to find a way of living together with others. This same dynamics of the global market has been tearing down all the traditional walls of identity, commercializing the whole of life, enervating ethical commitments, relativizing national sovereignties, destroying nature, and creating new kinds of economic inequalities and instabilities. This is the common context to which all particular groups are subject regardless of their gender, ethnicity, class, nationality, religion, and culture, and which we can transform and humanize if at all only if we are united; we can certainly not do it if we are fragmented into our own particular ethnicities and genders.

The contemporary theological scene, however, evinces little evidence of a compelling sense of solidarity across the ethnic and gender boundaries in the face of common crises arising from the same global context in which we all live. We are very much locked into our own particularity. Destruction of nature remains the province only of the ecological theologians. None seems to care about the sweeping vulgarization of the whole of life going on today. No group seems terribly concerned over the suffering of the many third world nations imposed by the policies of the World Bank, the International Monetary Fund, and the World Trade Organization largely dominated by North Atlantic nations and corporations. No group seems terrified by the global consequences of the unilateralist imperialism of the United States now increasingly asserting itself in its nakedness. Each group remains preoccupied with its own ethnic or gender identity, retrieving its own suppressed past, anxious for its own liberation, while ignoring the very context that has been relativizing all identities, trivializing all cultural values, and creating new forms of oppression.

It is past time that we should have recovered some sense of the ultimacy of God and theological universality for Christology, theological anthropology, and ecclesiology; a sense of wholeness, totality, connectedness, and solidarity regarding our human destiny; and a sense of interdependence for all significant issues in a rapidly globalizing world which constitutes the common context for all struggles today. We should recover this sense of the whole, however, in a postcritical and not a precritical way, that is, without in any way turning deaf to the cry of the oppressed in all their particularity. I am not arguing for a simple, uncritical return to the deceptive universality of traditional, European theology. As I shall argue presently, without a sense of the whole, theology ceases to be *theology;* without the preferential concern for the oppressed it ceases to be *Christian.* We need both wholeness and particularity. What I have been criticizing is not particularity as such, but self-enclosed, self-complacent, and self-absolutizing particularity. How, then, do we go about retrieving this sense of wholeness without forgetting, for one moment, the imperative of liberation? By introducing the dimension of contemplative wisdom into contemporary theology, which has largely been a prophetic theology of liberating praxis, and maintaining a *tension*—not mere balance or complementarity—between the sapiential and the prophetic, the contemplative and the active, as two inseparably related moments of one and the same theology, not as two parallel types of theology.

Two Types of Theology: Prophetic and Sapiential

There are many ways and criteria for typologizing theology. We can divide theology into theologies of manifestation, proclamation, and historical action according to the anthropological-structural criteria of thinking, speaking, and acting (Tracy); into kerygmatic, transcendental, hermeneutic, liberationist, narrative, doxological, and other theologies according to methodological criteria; into Catholic, Orthodox, and Protestant theologies according to denominational criteria; into African American, Hispanic, native American, white feminist, womanist, and *mujerista* theologies according to ethnic/gender criteria; and in many other ways using different criteria. I prefer, however, to use the twofold typology of active/prophetic and contemplative/sapiential theology as most relevant to the dilemmas of the contemporary (theological) situation. The problems mentioned in the preceding section cut across all the methodological, denominational, ethnic, and gender boundaries and pose dilemmas for all of them.

My typology is based on the classical distinction between the contemplative, speculative, or theoretical intellect whose aim is wisdom, the contemplation and enjoyment of a vision of the whole in its ultimacy, totality, and necessity, and the active or practical intellect whose aim is prudence, appropriate action and transformation that fulfills human nature in the contingencies and particularities of history. The dynamism of the speculative intellect is to comprehend reality as it is, in its ultimacy and universality, as an object of receptive contemplation. The dynamism of the practical intellect is to comprehend reality as it should be, in its historical particularity, as an object of transformative action. Both the speculative and the practical contain intellectual reflection or thought. The contrast between the two is not between what is thoughtful and what is thoughtless, but between two distinct purposes of thought.[6] The purpose of the speculative intellect is to comprehend reality for its own sake, that of the practical intellect to comprehend reality as a means to action. Action is always historically determinate, i.e., particular in its circumstances, resources, aims, and consequences. Theology as a practical science at the service of action, therefore, is necessarily particular, regional, and limited in its aim, concern, and scope. By contrast, freed from the necessity of historical action, theology as a speculative science at the service of contemplation is necessarily universal in its aim and scope. Action requires particularization of theology in its concern and content, contemplation its universalization. Given the compelling contradictions of our day between the particularism of liberation and the universalism of theology, even Tracy's typology of manifestation (thinking), proclamation (speaking), and action, I believe, can be reduced to the tension between contemplative and active theologies, depending on with whom the theologies of proclamation align themselves, at least by default if not explicitly. Let me describe each type in some detail, beginning with prophetic theology.

As a theology of action or praxis, prophetic theology shares in the characteristics of action as such. First, as the end of action is always specific and determinate, so prophetic theology is centered on the solution to a specific problem of the time, the *kairos*. As Gustavo Gutierrez describes liberation theology, it arises "from concern with a particular set of issues" and is "vitally engaged in historical realities with specific times and places."[7] The specific problem may be forgetfulness of the cross, loss of genuine faith, political and economic oppression, sexism, or the fatal destruction of nature. Prophetic theology tries to discern the signs of the times and seeks to address an issue which is indeed specific but also central enough to be relevant to many other issues. Some sort of social analysis is regarded as necessary for the choice of the central issue it seeks to address. Prophetic theology arises out of a sense of crisis, out of the sense of something central to faith being at stake in the pressures of the time. Prophetic theology is essentially a theology of response to a determinate yet central crisis of the time. It is centered on the present crisis, and exhausts itself, by the same token, when our critical social consciousness of that crisis is over, then giving way to another theology to deal with a new perceived crisis.[8] The average life span of prophetic theology is the average life span of the critical perception of a central, historical crisis, perhaps some thirty years in the experience of the twentieth century.[9]

Second, because it is a theology responding to what it considers to be the central crisis of faith and the time, prophetic theology is deliberately one-sided in its attention. It considers a particular issue, for example, the liberation of a particular group, central to the whole of life and faith, sees the very identity of Christianity at stake in it, and seeks to devote all its theoretical and practical resources to respond to it. It evaluates all other things of faith and life only in relation to that overriding issue and simply neglects or ignores all issues that do not have a direct bearing on it. Partiality is thus built into the methodology of prophetic theologies. As Juan Luis Segundo succinctly puts it, "the Bible is not the discourse of a universal God to a universal man. Partiality is justified because we must find, and designate as the word of God, that *part* of divine revelation which *today*, in the light of our concrete historical situation, is most useful for the liberation to which God summons us. Other passages of that same divine revelation will help us tomorrow to complete and correct our present course towards freedom. God will keep coming back to speak to us from the very same Bible."[10] Any attempt to be systematic and comprehensive of all relevant issues and topics bearing on the whole of faith and life is suspect and considered a reactionary diversion from the most critical issue of the time.

Third, as a theology deliberately centered on a particular issue demanding action, prophetic theology is embodied and based in a particular group as its basic agents and addressees. The crisis becomes manifest and concrete in the sufferings of particular groups of people. We have thus particular theologies each with its own "preferential option" for a particular group. Prophetic theology arises out of the sufferings of a particular people, reflects on their experiences, seeks to respond to their needs, and appeals to them as both agents and addressees of their own theology. These experiences and needs in their particularity constitute the norm, even the "primary source," of prophetic theology.[11] What James Cone says about the hermeneutic principle of black theology applies to all prophetic theologies: "The norm of all God-talk which seeks to be black-talk is the manifestation of Jesus as the black Christ who provides the necessary soul for black liberation."[12] It is "only" to the black community that black theology is "accountable," as it "seeks to articulate the theological self-determination of blacks, providing some ethical and religious categories for the black revolution in America."[13] A certain organic link with or a certain existential participation in the experiences of the people, therefore, is considered essential for the integrity of prophetic theology. By its very nature and intention prophetic theology is particular and regional in its concern, agency, and addressee. To speak of suffering humanity as a whole or human suffering in general is excluded: it would be to trivialize the uniqueness and concreteness of the suffering of a particular group.

Fourth, as a theology intent on the practical solution to a crisis, prophetic theology is essentially activist: what is important is effective action that would produce results. It therefore stresses action and active engagement rather than passion and passive receptivity as a general response to life. It is based on an anthropology of action, of the human being as an agent in history, as distinct from the classical anthropology of thought, of the human being as a thinker or knower of being.[14] A favorite theme of prophetic theology is that human beings are the *subjects* of history, that history is not something given but is made by human beings, that what individuals cannot do as individuals, they can do together, and that structures of oppression can be undone. It therefore seeks to integrate systematic theology and/into ethics and promote the autonomous moral agency of oppressed peoples.[15] Prophetic theology is essentially political, aimed at the transformation and humanization of oppressive relations and structures of power. Its overriding virtue is hope—not eschatological hope but historical hope—its overriding temptation despair of history.

Fifth, as a theology committed to change and transformation, prophetic theology regards the past, the tradition, and history as a whole negatively and with suspicion, as something to be changed and transformed, not something to be positively affirmed and appreciated. Fully aware of the ideological complicity of the tradition in the scandal of oppression, it is more interested in the hermeneutic of suspicion than in the hermeneutic of retrieval. Committed to the urgency and centrality of liberation as the all-consuming goal, it tends to dismiss the *whole* of tradition partly because it contains oppressive ideologies and partly because the non-oppressive elements the tradition may still contain are considered irrelevant to the overriding urgencies of the present. In the interest of the present, prophetic theology tends to cut itself off from the tradition unless it finds something "usable" for the present in a highly selective way.[16] As James Cone puts it unambiguously, "black theology is concerned *only* with the tradition of Christianity that is *usable* in the black liberation struggle. As it looks over the past, it asks: 'How is the Christian tradition related to the oppression of blacks in America?'"[17] It does not find anything positive in the tradition for its own sake, in the tradition as tradition in its totality, in the tradition as the cumulative experiences and wisdom of our ancestors in faith and life. Its tendency is to focus on the contamination of a tradition by forms of oppression, to condemn the tradition as a whole—"the *entire* conceptual systems of theology and ethics, . . . tend to serve the interests of sexist society"[18]—and to condemn the whole tradition wholly, not partially, either explicitly or by silence about any of its redeeming aspects. Elizabeth Johnson dismisses the entire trinitarian tradition on these grounds: "The triune symbol has *not* functioned in this way [promoting loving relations in a community of equals] for the last thousand years in the West. It has been neglected, literalized, treated like a curiosity, or analyzed with conceptual acrobatics entirely inappropriate to its meaning. Consequently, the doctrine has become unintelligible and religiously irrelevant on a wide scale."[19]

Sixth, and last, centrally preoccupied with the practical solution of a historical problem through action on behalf of a particular group, prophetic theology tends to be anthropocentric, not theocentric. It deals primarily with the historical, human issues and only secondarily, if at all, with issues concerning God, her trinitarian life, her providing role in the whole of creation, God as the ultimate end and fulfillment of all things. When prophetic theology does deal with God and the Trinity, it does so precisely so as to adapt the doctrine of God to the needs of historical liberation and systematically reinterprets its traditional content so as to make it a theological justification of liberation, just as traditional theology was considered a justification of oppression. It may also need the functions of theology as wisdom and rational knowledge, but does so only insofar as they are redefined and resituated in relation to praxis as their starting point, content, and goal.[20] The reconstructions of prophetic theology thus tend to be reductionist, even projectionist. The meaning of Christian doctrine tends to be reduced to its ideological role in the promotion of human liberation. Moltmann, Leonardo Boff, and Elizabeth Johnson reconstruct the doctrine of the Trinity as a community of three equal persons and then immediately apply it as a critique of totalitarian oppression and a defense of democratic equality, doing unambiguous justice to Feuerbach's claim that our theology is after all the projection of our anthropology. James P. Mackey accuses Moltmann's trinitarian theology of "exporting these human characteristics [personhood as interpersonal dependence] and their practical implications into a God only to reimport them back to humanity again" and of "a very dangerous absolutizing" of our present understanding of things, a practice common to most prophetic theologies.[21]

Prophetic theology, then, is a deliberately partial and regional theology, not a comprehensive theology. It is centered on one historical crisis, not all religiously relevant issues, in a deliberately one-sided way, and speaks on behalf of a particular group, not all humanity. It is committed to action at the expense of contemplation, is cut off from the whole of tradition as tradition, and is anthropocentric, not theocentric. These are essential tendencies inherent in all prophetic theology. Sapiential theology, on the other hand, tends to be the exact opposite of prophetic theology in every respect. Using Aquinas's theology as a classic example, let me describe sapiential theology.

Sapiential theology consists in contemplative wisdom, the contemplation of God as the ultimate origin and end of all things, and the consideration and evaluation of all things *sub ratione Dei*, in their relation and movement to God. First of all, therefore, it is not centered on any one historical problem, but deals with all problems in their hierarchical relation to God, their ultimate end and fulfillment. Sapiential theology is primarily concerned with God and secondarily with all other things in relation to God. It deals with God, God's existence, God's attributes, God's trinitarian life, and God's creative and redeeming relation to all creation. It has room for all essential problems, not only human problems but also cosmological and even angelic problems, the problems of contingency, finitude, teleology, providence. When it deals with human problems, it deals with them in all their essential dimensions; thus it treats problems of eternal destiny as well as of historical liberation, problems of both existential and historical dichotomies, problems of both personal and social existence, problems of body and soul, problems of intellect, will, and feeling, problems of action and contemplation. As God is the ultimate origin and end of *all* things, a vision of totality is essential to sapiential theology.

Second, as a theocentric vision of totality, sapiential theology is deliberately all-sided, not one-sided, in its consideration of issues. It seeks to be systematic and comprehensive, to understand all things in their appropriate teleological relation to one another and to God. As a systematic and comprehensive vision, sapiential theology too needs some organizing principle; it cannot just enumerate and analyze all things simply ad hoc. Its organizing principle, however, is not some overriding historical issue that is particular by nature, but the universal, hierarchical, teleological relation of all things to God. If it highlights anything, it highlights precisely God, creation and redemption through divine grace, and Christ as the way from and to God. It does not even highlight the problem of human salvation but subsumes it under creation common to the relation of all creatures to God. It has room for everything in its proper teleological place in relation to God. We need only think of all the topics treated in the three Parts and some 611 Questions of the *Summa Theologiae*.

Third, as a vision of totality, sapiential theology is universalist in its consideration of contexts, agents, and addressees of theology. It does not lift up the concern and context of a particular group or limit itself to the agency and addressees of a particular group. These particular problems and concerns may well be the subject of special Christian ethics, but not of (systematic) theology. Instead, the proper concern of theology is to reflect on the common, universal context of all human beings in their teleological relation to God as their ultimate origin and end, i.e., on the creaturely, sinful conditions of human nature and existence. Theology does not concern itself with the contingent particularities of a given group but only with the universal necessities of all humanity, their ontological structure, their natural desire for the supernatural, their original sin or sin of nature, their healing and elevation through grace, their incorporation into Christ in the Holy Spirit, their virtues and vices, their final destination to the vision of God. A tribal conception of theology would be fundamentally untheological because it contradicts the very idea of God.

As part of this vision of the whole in God, sapiential theology is deliberately universalist in its conception of the possibilities of salvation without denying incorporation into Christ the Son as the revealed condition of salvation. We have seen in the first three chapters the rational, moral, and religious ways to God, respectively, and how Aquinas recognizes salvific potential in the three universal dimensions of human existence, reason, morality, and ritual. As a Christian theologian he recognizes the centrality of Christ in the creative and redemptive process of all creation and humanity and insists on the faith acceptance of Christ's redemptive work as condition of salvation. As a universalist sapiential theologian, however, he does not absolutize a particularist, contingent category, e.g., explicit faith in Christ as incarnate in the historical Jesus of some two thousand years ago, which it would be unreasonable to assume as a real possibility for all human beings of all ages. Instead, he wants to mediate the particularity of Christ's salvific work to the universality of his creative work and the universal possibilities of human existence in relation to God,—to reason in its search for the infinite truth, to moral experience as implicit affirmation of the ultimate end, and to visible signs and symbols as necessary mediations of all religious relations to God. For Aquinas, then, reason has been graced from the very beginning, moral experience embodies an implicit faith, and religious rituals are necessary windows to the world of God.

Fourth, as a vision of totality, sapiential theology is necessarily contemplative. Totality, universality, and ultimacy can only be recognized and appreciated for their own sake by contemplation, the infinite dynamism of the speculative intellect in its search for and knowledge of truth and in its enjoyment of that truth for its own sake. The practical intellect of prophetic theology, by nature aimed at action in the contingencies of particular history, is necessarily limited to the regional, particular, and partial in its issues and concerns. This does not mean that prophetic theology does not reflect on God and God's creative and redemptive relation to the world. It does do this, because it is precisely a theology centered on God's "prophetic" will to justice, peace, and reconciliation. But prophetic theology necessarily relates the theological vision of God's will to the particular and regional without reflecting on God's ultimacy and universality as valuable in itself. By the same token, sapiential theology does concern itself with the contingent particularities of history because one of the functions of wisdom is to judge the relativities of history. But it does so as its "secondary," not "principal" function, which is to contemplate the totality of reality in its ultimacy and breadth and to do so for its own sake.

Contemplation takes reality as *given,* tries to know it in all its aspects and implications, and enjoys both reality and our knowledge of that reality as an end in itself. Action, on the other hand, takes reality precisely as an object to be transformed through its own effort, never regarding reality or our knowledge of reality as an end in itself but only as a means to further transformation through action. For action, the world is something made, not given. For contemplation, the world in its totality, breadth, and ultimacy, is something given, to which it is our role as creatures to remain open and receptive. With regard to the basic structures, conditions, and dynamics of the world, human beings are far more passive than active. Whatever we can do through action is limited by the basic conditions of life. A constructive action is possible only under the given ontological conditions of life and only in actualizing the potentialities already given in those conditions. Whenever we act by violating such conditions, we are the first ones to suffer, as we now begin to realize in our ecological relation to nature. In a fundamental sense we do not, as modern homocentrism has claimed, either "make" or "constitute" the world. If we do either of these in any way, we do so only under conditions already given, not created by us. Contemplation thus relativizes the hubris of historicism.

Furthermore, for sapiential theology the world is not only given, but given precisely as a gift of God and therefore something fundamentally good. The world is a sacrament, a sign of God's creative and redeeming presence, a pointer to the transcendent. To be sure, there are evils in the world, but good and evil are not ontologically equal. The good is more fundamental and essential than evil, which exists only as negation and violation of the good immanent in the very structure of being and thus only as parasitic on the good. Contemplation of reality is supported by ontological confidence in the basic goodness of reality and ontological hope in the eschatological fulfilment of God's ends. We have not made the world, nor do we have to wholly remake it as though it were thoroughly evil and as though everything depended on us. We can leave the ultimate destiny of the world to the one who has created it, while doing what we can in the small corner of the universe that God's providence leaves us to tend according to our created nature and ability.

With a restored sense of perspective, sapiential theology spares us of the hubris of remaking the whole world, of the exaggerated hope in history, and of the anxiety and despair that comes from expecting everything from human effort alone. With confidence in God's graceful providence and a chastened, sober consciousness of our rather small place in a vast universe and an infinitely vaster divine mystery, we can rest and relax, enjoying God's creation and praising the creator. The point of contemplation is to know reality as it is given, to appreciate its fundamental goodness, to wonder at the mystery of being, to thank God for the gift of creation, and to glorify God in her incomprehensible majesty that "infinitely" transcends all things finite. Sapiential theology leads to doxology, mysticism, negative theology, spirituality, and dialogue with Asian religions, many of which are oriented towards contemplation rather than action. Contemplation of God and all things *sub ratione Dei* most befits human beings, who are far more creatures than creators.

Fifth, as a vision of the whole with a positive appreciation of reality as such, sapiential theology brings an affirmative attitude to the tradition. It does not isolate and absolutize the present but sees the present as possible only within the "effective history" of the tradition (Gadamer), as dependent on, continuous with, and building on the past. The past is not simply darkness and evil, ideology, intolerance, and obscurantism, but also the accumulation of experience and wisdom still illuminating the present. The tradition also has its evils and imperfections but no more so than does the present, whose own imperfections and evils will also be unmasked in due time. Sapiential theology tries to look at history as an enduring whole, not as a collection of unconnected events and episodes, with respect for the wisdom it embodies and tolerance for the faults it cannot escape from. It is not impressed by historical claims of novelty and originality, as it is not shocked by historical facts of scandal and foible. With a basic confidence in the goodness of the tradition, therefore, sapiential theology takes the tradition seriously as both the necessary vehicle and the enriching development of Christian faith. It does not consider the fullness of truth to reside only at the beginning of Christian faith with the subsequent history of faith as merely a history of distortion and degeneration. Without turning insensitive to the imperfections of the past, sapiential theology is more interested in the hermeneutic of retrieval than in the hermeneutic of suspicion, and periodically seeks to return to the tradition as source of insight, example, and renewal.

Sixth, and last, as a universalist, teleological vision, sapiential theology is essentially theocentric, not anthropocentric. Its basic concern is to contemplate God as the ultimate origin and end of all things, and all things not in themselves but only in relation to God. As such, it does not absolutize either nature as in much premodern culture or human history as in the modern, but God alone, relating both nature and history to God and thereby relativizing both. As critique of nature and history, sapiential theology constantly urges a sense of perspective and proportion in light of God and eternal life and warns us against complete immersion either in the immediacies of nature or in the priorities of history. The present is not the whole of history, nor is the whole of history the whole of created reality. Even the whole of created reality is not the whole of reality. There is the uncreated reality of God, the creative source and ultimate end of all things, present in all things yet "infinitely" transcending them all. It is this God who remains the primary object of theological contemplation. Only then is theology truly the *logos* of God and the *logos* about God.

I have described six contrasting characteristics of prophetic and sapiential theology. I have described them as two types of theology and, as in all typologies, only as two *ideal* types. As such, perhaps no existing theology perfectly embodies the ideality of the type to which it may belong, just as the typology does not perfectly fit any one existing theology. Rather, as ideal types they represent certain tendencies discernible in many theologies, and it is precisely these tendencies in existing theologies that demand serious theological attention because the very nature and goal of theology are at stake.

Toward a Dialectic of Prophetic and Sapiential Theology

The preceding discussion should make abundantly clear that each type of theology needs the other as a corrective that restrains and challenges. This is true of all six points of contrast. First, there is the tension between the prophetic tendency to focus on a particular historical issue as its central concern and the sapiential tendency to take seriously all essential religious issues in their teleological relation to God. Without the prophetic tendency sapiential theology would tend to ignore historical issues of critical importance for Christian faith always incarnated in the particularities of history, as classical European theologies have been accused of doing, with some justification. Without the sapiential tendency prophetic theology would tend to ignore perennial existential issues and lose its properly theological vision of the ultimate. Second, there is the tension between the prophetic tendency to absolutize its own historical concern and subordinate all else to that particular imperative and the sapiential tendency to be comprehensive and balanced with regard to all issues. Without the sapiential tendency prophetic theology would tend to be so one-sided as to lose its properly theological vision of totality. Without the prophetic tendency sapiential theology would tend to be so comprehensive and balanced as to fail to recognize historical priorities and historical conflicts as worthy themes of theological reflection.

Third, there is the tension between the prophetic tendency to identify exclusively with one particular group and its historical imperatives and the sapiential tendency to be universalist and all-embracing in its perspective and need. Without the sapiential tendency prophetic theology would tend to forget something essential in the Christian vision—the solidarity of all creation and all humanity before God in the body of Christ in the power of the Holy Spirit—and become another source of human division. Without the prophetic tendency sapiential theology would tend to ignore the seriousness of the suffering of particular peoples in all their historical conflicts and particularity and preach a precritical, purely moralistic peace and harmony that is irrelevant to the actual historical dynamics of any particular situation. Without the concrete particularity of prophetic theology, the immense potential of the doctrine of the universal solidarity of all in the body of Christ would remain undeveloped, without socio-historical content.

Fourth, there is the tension between the prophetic tendency to focus on human action in history and the sapiential tendency to focus on contemplation of all reality. Without the sapiential tendency prophetic theology tends to absolutize human action, to reduce everything else to an object of human exploitation or transformation, and to fluctuate between extremes of hope and despair. Without the prophetic tendency sapiential theology tends to use the joys of contemplation as an escape from the imperatives of historical action, often falling into the dualism of faith and politics in the name of the primacy of divine grace, and confusing hope in divine providence with a fatalistic acceptance of oppressive and inhuman historical reality that must always be most offensive to Christian love.

Fifth, there is the tension between the prophetic tendency to regard all tradition with suspicion and the sapiential tendency to sanctify all tradition as source of wisdom. Without the prophetic tendency sapiential theology tends to fall into a precritical affirmation of all tradition simply as given and inherited, and to justify the continuing oppressive consequences of the past on the present. Without the sapiential tendency prophetic theology tends to confine goodness and legitimacy to the present moment of liberating praxis, often absolutizing its own present perspectives and ideals, which are just as historically conditioned as any other. It thus cuts itself off from solidarity with the countless others in faith and life who constitute the great communion of both saints and sinners in God.

Sixth, and last, there is the tension between the anthropocentrism of prophetic theology and the theocentrism of sapiential theology. Without the sapiential tendency prophetic theology tends to exhaust itself with things human and historical and either lose its properly theological vision of God and all things in God or reduce theology to anthropology. Without the sapiential tendency prophetic theology also reduces all its work of liberation to a transient labor without enduring, ultimate, theological significance. Without the prophetic tendency sapiential theology tends to forget that even one's own conception of God is historically mediated and often contaminated and to ignore the possibility that the apparently compelling subordination of all things finite to God can hide an ideology of subordinating all things not to God herself but only to one's own historically contaminated *notion* of God. It can fall into the dualism of eternal and temporal, and become indifferent and even hostile to the urgencies of historical liberation in the name of perspective and proportion. Without the critical work of social and historical analyses on the part of prophetic theology, sapiential theology tends either to simply condemn reality for failing to measure up to the eschatological perfection or to issue abstract moral imperatives based on the general obligation of the creature to the creator and by the same token also rather irrelevant to the dynamic particularities of the concrete situation.[22] Without the *ratio Dei* of sapiential theology prophetic theology ceases to be theology, and without the prophetic critique of reality the *ratio Dei* remains historically ineffective, abstract, and even ideological.

To sum up, we are here undoubtedly dealing with two dimensions both of which are essential and indispensable to Christian theology. Without a contemplative vision of totality in its divine ultimacy, ontological universality, and spiritual depth, theology simply ceases to be *theology*. At best we have anthropocentrism and anthropology. Without a prophetic critique of all the sources of suffering in nature and history, theology ceases to be *Christian* theology. At best we have an ideology covering up the suffering of creation, an aesthetics functioning as the "opium of the people." The integrity of Christian theology requires that every theology must contain elements of both prophetic and sapiential theology, both the "not yet" and the "already," each serving as a corrective of the other. We need wisdom that is practical, and prudence that is contemplative. How can we conceive of the relation between the two? I suggest there are four ways of conceiving that relation: exaggeration, parallelism, balancing, and dialectical tension. Let me examine each in turn.

The first suggestion is to *exaggerate* the role and importance of the element regarded as minimized and underestimated in a theology, much as Kierkegaard tried to do in deliberately exaggerating the importance of individual subjectivity over against the objective, the social, and the historical. I do not think, however, that this is a viable suggestion. The function of a corrective is precisely to correct by removing distortions, not to create another distortion by an exaggeration that will require and waste the labor of another generation to correct it. Is it viable, then, to establish the two types of theology as *parallel* activities alongside of each other? This will not do, either, because merely parallel activities can easily ignore each other: existing simply side by side with each other, they do not have to engage and confront the challenge of each other; and indeed, many contemporary theologies do in fact exist side by side but without noticing or being noticed by one another.

The mutually corrective function can only be exercised from within the thing to be corrected. The corrective and the corrected, however, can remain external to each other, as, in our case, two types of independent theology. From two types of theology, therefore, they must become two dialectical moments of one and the same theology within which they can challenge, confront, and correct each other. If they are going to truly confront and correct each other, however, it will not do to try to restore a *balance* between the two, as we often speak of a balance between action and contemplation, particularity and universality. Balance means peace and harmony between the two, but mutual confrontation and challenge between two ways and paradigms of theology with opposing ultimate claims and tendencies are not conducive to peace and harmony. The relation between the corrective and the corrected, therefore, can only be conceived in terms of a dialectic or *tension* between the two, where each remains internal to the other, is not minimized by the other, seeks to preserve its integrity over against the other, and yet also challenges and corrects the other. In other words, the proper corrective function is possible only when prophetic and sapiential theology become two moments in mutual tension within one and the same theology. Only a tension will prevent each of the two moments from being complacent about itself or absolutizing itself against the other, without at the same time enervating the dynamism of each. Each type of theology may have its own method or hermeneutic circle. It is imperative that prophetic theologies build into their methods and circles the critical moment of sapiential mediation, as it is imperative that sapiential theologies build into theirs the critical moment of prophetic mediation.[23]

This mutually corrective relation between prophetic and sapiential moments is not an accidental necessity; it is based on the dialectical structure of human existence in the world. As pointed out in chapter 4, human existence is not an external collection of intellect and sense, theory and praxis, transcendence and historicity, but a concrete totality, a dynamic unity in which these elements mediate each other. There is neither pure sensation unmediated by intellectuality nor pure intellection unmediated by sensation, except as a limit. The self which transcends in search of eschatological salvation in the vision of God, and the self which struggles for liberation in and of history are not two separate selves but *one* self. It is because the self is transcendent that human existence is possible as history, not merely as nature, just as human existence as transcendence is possible only because and to the extent that history poses both a challenge and a limitation for us to transcend.

Human existence is the concrete unity or totality of the intrinsic, mutual mediation of historicity and transcendence with all their harmonies and contradictions. Redemption in the theological sense, therefore, must be the liberation of human existence in its concrete totality, i.e., both historical liberation and eschatological salvation in intrinsic, mutual mediation. We are indeed destined to seek the vision of God by our "intellectual" nature, but by our "embodied" nature we are destined to seek it only in and through history. Upon this structural dialectic of transcendence and historicity are based all the other dialectics: particularity and universality, action and contemplation, finitude and infinitude, partiality and wholeness, anthropocentrism and theocentrism. The dialectic or tension between prophetic action and sapiential contemplation is not just a tension between two theologies that happen to be different but a tension that reflects the very structure and dynamics of human existence itself as created by God.[24]

Kierkegaard put the dialectic of human existence in a way quite relevant to our discussion. For him human existence is a synthesis of finite and infinite. If we were only finite, we would be creatures of pure immediacy with no awareness of problems. If we were only infinite, we would be certain, positive, and complete in our existence. Problems of life—uncertainty, negativity, and incompleteness—arise because of the synthesis and the resulting tension of finitude and infinity, finitude that seeks to limit, infinity that seeks to expand, our existence. If we try to dissolve this tension by removing one of the poles, we also cease to be human. Such has been the temptation of inauthentic modes of existence: the aesthetic, which tries to remove the infinite pole and live in the pure immediacy of the finite, fully subject to the immanent laws of psychology; and speculation, which tries to remove the finite pole and live in the eternity of pure thought. In either case, the synthesis is dissolved, and the human being becomes a mere thing or a pure spirit. This dialectic or tension, furthermore, must be reflected, with all its ambiguity, negativity, and paradox, in any existence, reflection, and communication that seeks to do justice to the truth of human existence. Holding the two poles in tension without dissolving the synthesis, however, is a matter of art and passion. Hence the need for "training in existence," subjective reflection, and indirect communication.[25]

Likewise, according to Rahner, all our statements about God are caught in an irreducible tension between their categorical or historical origin on the one hand and their self-transcendence to God, to which they point on the other. Such a tension is not a secondary product of our logic trying to avoid univocity and equivocity but a primordial tension which we *are* as spiritual subjects who can have a history only through transcendence and can transcend only through history. As the condition of the possibility of all categorical experience transcendence is more original than categorical, univocal concepts. Analogy in its most primordial sense is none other than this transcendental movement of the spirit itself; it is not a subsequent midpoint, a hybrid, between univocity and equivocity, which are deficient modes of the more original analogical relationship to transcendence. Analogy indicates the tension between our categorical existence and the incomprehensibility of God. We *exist* the analogical tension between historicity and transcendence. It can be said that Tracy's "analogical imagination," which seeks to discern similarities in difference, is itself derived from our "analogical existence."[26]

The tension between action and contemplation, history and transcendence, is an essential "existential" of human existence, which as such must be reflected in all theology that seeks to do justice to the truth of human life. Christian theological reflection must be analogical enough to appreciate this existential tension, artistic enough to articulate it in all its complexity and difference, and passionate enough to uphold it in all its seriousness. The temptation to surrender to the self-complacency of either prophetic theology or sapiential theology is an enduring temptation that only a truly analogical theology can discern and only a great theological passion can resist, just as giving expression to the full implications of the tension requires art. Christian theology is possible today only as an analogical theology, only as a methodically practiced tension or dialectic between prophetic and sapiential theology. This, I submit, is the demand of the *kairos* in which we live today.

Theology "of" liberation can be taken in two different ways. It can be taken in the sense of a theology of a specific domain, dimension, or aspect of human life, as we speak of the theology of marriage, the theology of laity, or the theology of baptism. In this sense, theology of liberation would be theological reflection on human liberation as one domain or topic among others. It can also be taken in the sense of a totalizing theological perspective or paradigm, i.e., theological reflection on the whole of theology from the perspective of a particular paradigm. In this sense, "liberation" is no longer one special domain among others but is rather the paradigm from whose perspective all theological topics or domains of life are considered. It makes all the difference whether we interpret liberation as a particular domain within theology or as a totalizing paradigm.

The problem of prophetic theology has been precisely to take liberation, essentially a specific domain of human life and by no means its totality, as a totalizing paradigm of a comprehensive theology, thereby reducing all of life to the imperatives of a particular historical action. The demand of the *kairos* is to "sublate" prophetic theology in the Hegelian sense of *aufheben*, i.e., to negate its claims to comprehensive totality but preserve its prophetic power as a specialized theology precisely by bringing it into the self-transcending tension with the universalism of sapiential theology. Likewise, the problem of sapiential theology has been to ignore the problems of human suffering in history in the name of a universalist comprehensive theology not based on a particular human paradigm but on the *ratio* of a self-revealing God. The demand of the *kairos* is to sublate sapiential theology by negating its claim to the divine perspective but preserving its human aspirations as a comprehensive theology by bringing and keeping it in tension with the scandal of prophetic particularity.

Concretely, this task entails institutionalizing critical mediation by the other into an essential moment of the methodology of each theology. Sapiential theology tends to reflect on the universal elements of all reality and human existence—God as creator and end of all things, the contingency of all beings including the human, sin, salvation, grace, and eschatology. In addition to the retrieval of this sapiential moment of the biblical, theological, and philosophical tradition, every sapiential theology should also consider as part of its own method subjection of the retrieved content to the critique and mediation of prophetic suspicion so as to ensure that its content should also contribute to our historical liberation and at least that it should not contribute to our historical oppression. Sapiential theology must recognize that for all its transcendence, its content always exists in historically concrete forms: for example, God in the specific concepts of ancient Hebrews, ancient Romans and Greeks, or modern Germans; or sin in the specific forms of the European genocide of indigenous peoples in America, the historic slavery of African Americans, the Jewish Holocaust, the sexual slavery of East Asian women during World War II, and the historically enduring oppression of the poor, women, and powerless minorities. In view of the prophetic mediation these concrete concepts of God need constantly to be reviewed and these concrete forms of sin constantly to be condemned.

By the same token, it is imperative that prophetic theology institutionalize as an essential moment of its own method the critical mediation by sapiential theology. It is not enough to analyze the empirical facts of oppression and injustice or to subject all tradition to a hermeneutic of suspicion. Prophetic theology must also subject its own assumptions, often atomistic, individualistic, and particularistic, to the communalizing, interconnecting, and universalistic critique of sapiential theology. Empirical conceptions of God may be particular, but they should be understood and evaluated as pointing beyond themselves to a reality *semper major*. Sins are indeed always concretized in particular forms of violated human relations, but sins receive their theological significance as "sins," not just "crimes" or "errors," precisely because of the violated relation to God and violated human solidarity embodied in such forms but also transcendent of them.

Ultimately, particularity as such cannot be the basis for critique and condemnation of oppression. I cannot say that it is wrong for you to oppress me because I am a Korean, a woman, or a Christian, to which others can oppose their own particularities. Only transcendence and universality can provide such a basis; I can say that it is wrong for you to oppress me because I am a human being created and redeemed by God, which makes me more than a thing, and because I am meant to fulfill my transcendent destiny only in historical solidarity with others who are like me and to share the same destiny, which makes me more than an isolated individual, although I may differ from others in gender, ethnicity, class, and other empirical marks of identity. Oppression violates this transcendence and this solidarity. Through this tensive mediation by the rich resources of sapiential theology, prophetic theology is constantly reminded of its own transcendent, theological basis and universal, human context, thus providing theological depth and universal solidarity for its cause.[27]

Notes

Introduction

For the most frequently cited works of Aquinas I use the following abbreviations. References made without the citation of a title are to *Summa Theologiae*.

SCG	*Summa contra Gentiles*
CT	*Compendium Theologiae*
Boethius on the Trinity	*Expositio super librum Boethii de Trinitate*

1. It was a symposium in honor of Richard C. Dales and devoted to the theme "Issues in Medieval Philosophy," organized by my colleague at Claremont Graduate University, Nancy Van Deusen, through the Claremont Consortium for Medieval and Early Modern Studies, and held at Claremont Graduate University, Claremont, California, February 22–23, 1996. My paper entitled "The Theological Legacy of Thomas Aquinas: A Post-Critical Appreciation" was subsequently published with other papers in Nancy Van Deusen, ed., *Issues in Medieval Philosophy: Essays in Honor of Richard C. Dales* (Ottawa: Institute of Mediaeval Music, 2001). This paper, revised and expanded, now constitutes the first chapter of this book. I thank Nancy for her invitation to participate and for her permission to reprint my essay here.

2. I, 62, 3 ad 3.

3. I, 23, 8.

4. SCG, 3, 47.

5. Aloysius Pieris, *An Asian Theology of Liberation* (Maryknoll, NY: Orbis, 1988), 64.

6. I have elaborated on the concept and theology of the "solidarity of Others" in *The Solidarity of Others in a Divided World: A Postmodern Theology after Postmodernism* (New York: T & T Clark International, 2004) and "From Autobiography to Fellowship of Others: Reflections on Doing Ethnic Theology

Today," in Peter Phan, ed., *Journeys at the Margin* (Collegeville, MN: Liturgical Press, 1999), 135–159.

7. I, 62, 3 ad 3.

8. Hans Küng, "What Is True Religion? Toward an Ecumenical Criteriology," in Leonard Swidler, ed., *Toward a Universal Theology of Religion* (Maryknoll, NY: Orbis, 1987), 236.

9. For readable, straightforward, and comprehensive accounts of Aquinas's theology, see Brian Davies, *The Thought of Thomas Aquinas* (Oxford: Clarendon Press, 1992), and Fergus Kerr, *After Aquinas: Versions of Thomism* (Malden, MA: Blackwell, 2002). For a comprehensive discussion of Aquinas's metaphysics, so essential to an understanding of Aquinas's theology but no longer widely available in the training of theologians, I recommend John F. Wippel, *The Metaphysical Thought of Thomas Aquinas: From Finite Being to Uncreated Being* (Washington, DC: The Catholic University of America Press, 2000).

Chapter 1.   Reason and Creation in Theology and Faith

1. Emil Brunner and Karl Barth, *Natural Theology* (London: Centenary Press, 1946), 51–60. The exchange between Brunner and Barth, translated here, originally took place in 1934.

2. See Brunner and Barth, *Natural Theology*, 76.

3. John Cobb, Jr., *A Christian Natural Theology: Based on the Thought of Alfred North Whitehead* (Philadelphia: Westminster Press, 1965), 252–284.

4. See James Barr, *Biblical Faith and Natural Theology*, 1991 Gifford Lectures (Oxford: Clarendon Press, 1993); "The Theological Case against Biblical Theology," in Gene M. Tucker, David L. Petersen, and Robert R. Wilson, eds., *Canon, Theology, and Old Testament Interpretation* (Philadelphia: Fortress Press, 1988), 3–17, which is a critique of Brevard Childs's biblical theology movement; and Dietrich Ritschl, *The Logic of Theology*, trans. John Bowden (Philadelphia: Fortress Press, 1987), 67–77. For a recent discussion of the possibility, methodology, and significance of natural theology, see Eugene Thomas Long, ed., *Prospects for Natural Theology* (Washington, DC: Catholic University of America Press, 1992). The editor's introduction provides a good history of natural theology from a philosophical perspective. For a fuller and insightful history and analysis of "natural theology" from a theological perspective including a critique of Barth, see Wolfhart Pannenberg, *Systematic Theology*, I, trans. Geoffrey W. Bromiley (Grand Rapids, MI: Eerdmans, 1991), 73–118.

5. See Edward Farley and Peter C. Hodgson, "Scripture and Tradition," in Peter C. Hodgson and Robert H. King, eds., *Christian Theology: An Introduction to Its Traditions and Tasks,* rev. ed. (Philadelphia: Fortress Press, 1985), 61–87; and Peter C. Hodgson, "Introduction: The End of Salvation History,"

chapter 1 of *God in History: Shapes of Freedom* (Nashville, TN: Abingdon Press, 1989), 11–50.

6. See Jürgen Moltmann, *God in Creation: A New Theology of Creation and the Spirit of God* (San Francisco: HarperSanFrancisco, 1991), 53–56, and Anselm Kyongsuk Min, "Asian Theologians," in Donald W. Musser and Joseph L. Price, eds., *A New Handbook of Christian Theologians* (Nashville, TN: Abingdon, 1996), 24–50.

7. See John Polkinghorne, "The New Natural Theology," *Studies in World Christianity* 1.1 (1995): 41–50.

8. For recent discussions of these controversies, see Hermann Dembowski, "Natürliche Theologie—Theologie der Natur: Erwägungen in einem weiten Feld," *Evangelische Theologie* 45.3 (1985): 224–248; Gerhard Ludwig Müller, "Hebt das Sola-Fide Prinzip die Möglichkeit einer natürlichen Theologie auf?" *Catholica* 40.1 (1986): 59–96; Michael Kappes, " 'Natürliche Theologie' als innerprotestantisches und ökumenisches Problem? Die Kontroverse zwischen Eberhard Jüngel und Wolfhart Pannenberg und ihr ökumenischer Ertrag," *Catholica* 49.4 (1995): 276–309; and Eberhard Jüngel, "Die Möglichkeit theologischer Anthropologie auf dem Grunde der Analogie," *Evangelische Theologie* 9.22 (1962): 535–557.

9. For a history of interpretations of "sacra doctrina" in Aquinas from Cardinal Cajetan to Gerald F. Van Ackeren, see James A. Weisheipl, "The Meaning of *Sacra Doctrina* in *Summa Theologiae* I, q. 1," *Thomist* 38 (1974): 49–80; also Thomas Gilby, "Sacra Doctrina," in St. Thomas Aquinas, *Summa Theologiae*, vol. 1, *Christian Theology*, ed. Thomas Gilby (New York: McGraw-Hill, 1964), 58–66.

10. For an illuminating discussion of Aquinas's theory of revelation as conferral of a new divine light and a new species of knowledge issuing in the judgment, see Thomas Hughson, "Dulles and Aquinas on Revelation," *Thomist* 52.3 (1988): 445–471.

11. I, 12, 13 ad 3.

12. *Boethius on the Trinity*, 3, 1 ad 4; also *On Truth*, 14, 1 and 3. On the role of this "light" of faith, see Ludger Oeing-Hanhoff, "Gotteserkenntnis im Licht der Vernunft und des Glaubens nach Thomas von Aquin," in Ludger Oeing-Hanhoff, ed., *Thomas von Aquin: 1274/1974* (München: Kösel Verlag, 1974), 115–120. As Oeing-Hanhoff puts it: "As the light of reason is the a priori preconcrete knowledge of being that makes possible our concrete knowledge of the world and principles, so the grace-given light of faith is a preconcrete a priori immediate knowledge of God that makes it possible to see the articles of faith accepted a posteriori through hearing as worth believing, i.e., in their attestation through the first truth, and so to accept them with the absolute certainty of faith" (117, my translation).

13. See I, 1, 1; I, 1, 3; II-II, 1, 8; II-II, 2, 7; II-II, 2, 5; II-II, 1, 4 ad 2 and ad 3; II-II, 1, 5, ad 1; I, 32, 1 ad 2; II-II, 1, 4 and 5; II-II, 6, 1; SCG, 1, 8; *Boethius on*

the Trinity, 2, 1 ad 5, and 2, 2. For a sophisticated discussion, from and for the analytic perspective, of the nature of faith, especially its irreducible transcendence over human reason and the problem of reference that such transcendence raises, see Victor Preller, *Divine Science and the Science of God: A Reformulation of Thomas Aquinas* (Princeton, NJ: Princeton University Press, 1967), 179–265. Preller somewhat underestimates the role of reason in faith.

14. I, 1, 6; *Boethius on the Trinity,* 2, 2.

15. See I, 1, 1; I, 1, 3.

16. For a contemporary discussion of this difference between philosophy and theology, see Helmut Hoping, "Understanding the Difference of Being: On the Relationship Between Metaphysics and Theology," *Thomist* 59.2 (1995): 189–221.

17. See SCG, 2, 4.

18. I, 1, 1 ad 2.

19. I, 1, 3; I, 1, 4.

20. I, 1, 4.

21. See I, 1, 5.

22. I, 1, 7.

23. I, 1, 7; II-II, 1, 1.

24. See further Eugene F. Rogers, Jr., *Thomas Aquinas and Karl Barth: Sacred Doctrine and the Natural Knowledge of God* (Notre Dame, IN: University of Notre Dame, 1995), 48–49.

25. On the distinction between theology and philosophy, between faith and reason, see further Etienne Gilson, *The Christian Philosophy of St. Thomas Aquinas,* trans. L. K. Shook (New York: Random House, 1956), 7–25.

26. II-II, 1, 5, ad 3.

27. See I, 1, 7; also II-II, 1, 1.

28. See I, 1, 7.

29. *Boethius on the Trinity,* 3, 1.

30. On the distinction between the revealed [*revelata*] and the revealable [*revelabilia*], see Gilson, *Christian Philosophy,* 9–25; Michel Corbin, *Le chemin de la theologie chez Thomas D'Aquin* (Paris: Beauchesne, 1974), 727–743; and Ulrich Kuhn, *Via Caritatis: Theologie des Gesetzes bei Thomas von Aquin* (Göttingen: Vandenhoeck & Ruprecht, 1965), 21–29. About "theology's transforming incorporation of philosophy" in Aquinas, see further Mark D. Jordan, "Theology and Philosophy," and Jan A. Aertsen, "Aquinas's Philosophy in its Historical Setting," in Norman Kretzmann and Eleonore Stump, eds., *The Cambridge Companion to Aquinas* (Cambridge: Cambridge University Press, 1993), 232–251 and 12–37 respectively.

31. For a recent, illuminating discussion of the concept of *scientia* as applied to theology in Aquinas and in comparison with the same concept in Aristotle's *Posterior Analytics,* see John I. Jenkins, *Knowledge and Faith in Thomas Aquinas*

(Cambridge: Cambridge University Press, 1997). Eugene F. Rogers, Jr., provides an elaborate analysis of part I, question 1 of the *Summa Theologiae,* trying to show how Aquinas's conception of theology both preserves and transcends Aristotle's conception of science and how the more Aristotelian his theology was, the more "christoform" it became; see his *Thomas Aquinas and Karl Barth,* 17–70. For a detailed textual study of the development of the concept of theology in relation to philosophy in Aquinas, see Michel Corbin, *Le chemin de la theologie chez Thomas D'Aquin.*

32. See I, 1, 2. On the status and terminological history of "articles of faith," see Joseph Goering, "Christ in Dominican Catechesis: The Articles of Faith," in Kent Emery, Jr., and Joseph Wawrykow, eds., *Christ Among the Medievel Dominicans: Representations of Christ in the Texts and Images of the Order of Preachers* (Notre Dame, IN: University of Notre Dame Press, 1998), 132–133.

33. I, 1, 8, ad 2.

34. In discussing the functions of theological reason in theology in Aquinas, I am heavily indebted to Yves Congar, *History of Theology,* trans. Hunter Guthrie (Garden City, NY: Doubleday, 1968), 91–114. See also Marie-Dominique Chenu, *Is Theology a Science?,* trans. A. H. N. Green-Armytage (New York: Hawthorne Books, 1959), 48–96; Reginald Garrigou-Lagrange, *Reality: A Synthesis of Thomistic Thought* (St. Louis, MO: B. Herder, 1950), 64–70.

35. II-II, 1, 5.

36. I, 32, 1; II-II, 1, 5; II-II, 2, 10; SCG, 1, 2 and 9.

37. *Boethius on the Trinity,* 2, 3; I, 1, 8; SCG, 1, 7.

38. I, 1, 8.

39. I, 1, 8; II-II, 1, 5; *Boethius on the Trinity,* 2, 2. For an illuminating recent essay that defends Aquinas against Luther's charge that Aquinas's heavy reliance on the syllogism or demonstrative argument makes him a theologian of glory, see Denis Janz, "Syllogism or Paradox: Aquinas and Luther on Theological Method," *Theological Studies* 59 (1998): 3–21. I have only small reservations about the essay, in particular about the claim that "from creation to the entire economy of salvation to eschatology—none of this can in the strict sense be proven. None of these matters possess any internal necessity. They are as they are only because God has willed them to be such, and in God's will there is no internal necessity. The whole body of *sacra doctrina* is made up of truths radically contingent on God's will" (11). Janz includes the mystery of the Trinity under this stricture. One reservation is that the reason for unavailability of proofs in matters of faith is not only that they are radically contingent, which would be true of many historical events, but also that we do not have an intuition into the essence of God whose will indeed determines all those matters of faith. The second reservation is that the Trinity does have its own internal necessity, except that *we* do not have an intuition into that necessity.

40. *Boethius on the Trinity*, 2, 1 ad 5; I, 1, 8; I, 32, 1. On the preliminary, explicative, and apologetic function of reason in theology, see also *Boethius on the Trinity*, 2, 3.

41. I, 1, 8.

42. *Boethius on the Trinity*, 2, 3.

43. *Boethius on the Trinity*, 2, 3 ad 2.

44. I-II, 109, 1, ad 1.

45. I, 1, 6; SCG, 1, 7.

46. *Boethius on the Trinity*, 2, 1 and 3.

47. Mark D. Jordan illustrates theology's "transforming incorporation of philosophy," using the examples of the two Aristotelian concepts of virtue and causality as incorporated into the theological contexts of infused virtues and sacramental causality respectively; theology is not merely a repetition of philosophy but its transformation. See his "Theology and Philosophy" and his *Ordering Wisdom: The Hierarchy of Philosophical Discourses in Aquinas* (Notre Dame, IN: University of Notre Dame Press, 1986), 197–201.

48. *Boethius on the Trinity*, 2, 3 ad 5.

49. I, 1, 5: SCG, 2, 4.

50. On the controversy of whether Aquinas was primarily a theologian or a philosopher, see Anton C. Pegis, " *Sub Ratione Dei:* A Reply to Professor Anderson," *New Scholasticism* 39.2 (April 1965): 141–157. The quotations are found on 153 and 156 respectively. The quotation from Maritain is originally from Jacques Maritain, *La philosophie morale* (Paris: Gallimard, 1960), 8–9.

51. For an illuminating critique of the many misinterpretations of the function of the "proofs" in the *Summa* from this perspective, see Richard A. Muller, "The Dogmatic Function of St. Thomas' 'Proofs': A Protestant Appreciation," *Fides et Historia* 24 (Summer 1992): 15–29. From what has been argued in this section—the intrinsic indemonstrability, by natural reason, of the content of faith, the necessity of the "light" of faith, and the controlling horizon of revelation in theology—it should be clear that the usual charges of subjecting revealed to natural theology and making "anthropology the essential framework within which *all* theological activity is conducted" are simply groundless or at best based on a very limited reading of the texts. See, e.g., Kenneth Surin, "Creation, Revelation, and the Analogy Theory," *Journal of Theological Studies* 32.2 (1981): 421.

52. For an excellent discussion that tries to mediate the positions of Aquinas and Barth on the theological significance of natural theology, see Thomas F. Torrance, "The Problem of Natural Theology in the Thought of Karl Barth," *Religious Studies* 6.2 (1970): 121–135. Torrance makes it clear that the heart of the dispute is not whether theology can avoid the use of metaphysics nor whether natural theology can be included and illuminated by revealed theology—on both issues Aquinas and Barth agree—but whether natural theology or knowledge of God achieved by human reason independently of and in abstraction from divine

revelation can be considered legitimate and whether such knowledge does not tend to become the hermeneutic horizon for the interpretation of revelation itself. Barth's fear is that any admission of the independent validity of natural theology leads to the denial of the monistic sovereignty of the self-revealing God in both creation and incarnation. The heart of the issue still remains the theological significance of the *nature* of human reason and its activities in theology. Can and should rational reflection on the created world be totally subordinated to the monism of divine revelation, as Barthians tend to claim? Or, is it possible to see a basic harmony between the God revealed in creation and the God revealed in the incarnation while also interpreting the former in light of the latter, as the Catholic tradition since Aquinas tends to claim?

53. For example, Aertsen, "Aquinas's Philosophy in its Historical Setting," 34–35.

54. I-II, 91, 2.

55. I, 44, 4.

56. SCG, 3, 19.

57. I, 6, 1.

58. I, 6, 4.

59. Kenneth Surin makes the interesting argument that the analogies of attribution and proportionality in Aquinas are meaningful only on the basis of a "generic likeness" between God and creatures established by God's creation of creatures in her image, a doctrine also found in Aquinas, and that the latter doctrine of the *imago Dei* can reconcile the Thomistic analogy of being with the Barthian analogy of faith. My account in this section of a trinitarian, christological, iconic theology of participation should go a long way towards clarification of the relation between being and imaging, and in some sense reinforce Surin's argument, although I have some reservations about his interpretation of the Thomistic theories of analogy and the role causality plays in understanding both being and the content of revelation; see his "Creation, Revelation, and the Analogy Theory."

60. SCG, 3, 20.

61. *On Truth*, 10, 7.

62. We may note here that Aquinas is not always terminologically consistent. He sometimes distinguishes sharply among vestige, image, grace, and glory (I, 33, 3 and 93, 6), but also deals with them as four degrees of similitude and image (I, 33, 3 and SCG, III, 19), taking even "vestiges" as imperfect "images" (I, 93,2), and image, grace, and glory as three different ways of imaging God (I, 93, 4). Still, there is a certain logical consistency in considering all four ways as degrees of likeness and image. Likeness or *similitudo* is the most general category under which vestige, image (in the strict sense), grace, and glory are subsumed. However, "image" in the broad sense is also as general a category as is likeness. Aquinas does define image in the proper sense as likeness according to species or form, not just any likeness or likeness according to genus and causality (I, 93, 2)

or *per modum effectus* (I, 93, 6), and he locates the *ratio* of image in the representation of the species or form of the exemplar. However, he does consider likeness and image as ultimately implying each other. The image is possible only as a mode of likeness, and likeness is possible only as a mode of image, i.e., some sort of representation of the form or nature of the exemplar. Just as likeness admits of a variety, so does the image. Both allow analogical applications. The likeness of non-intellectual creatures to God, which Aquinas classifies as "vestige," not "image" in the strict sense, is based on the generic similarity of the created effect to the creating cause. Even causality implies communication of some kind of form of the agent insofar as all agents bring about something similar to themselves [omnis agens agit simile sibi]. The effect reflects in some way the form of the generator as the end of generation (SCG, 3, 19). It is no wonder that Aquinas calls all created things "a kind of images" [quaedam imagines] of God as the first agent (SCG, 3, 19), and concedes the name of "image" to non-intellectual creatures insofar as they bear a certain likeness to God, although they remain "imperfect" images insofar as they do not represent God's intellectual nature, as do images in the proper sense. What is imperfect participates in what is perfect (I, 93, 2).

63. SCG, 3, 19.

64. I, 93, 1; 93, 5.

65. I, 35, 2.

66. I, 93, 5; my emphases.

67. I, 93, 4.

68. I, 93, 4.

69. I-II, 109, 9; III, 62, 2.

70. I, 33, 3.

71. III, 53, 3.

72. I, 62, 3. Jürgen Moltmann has been critical of the traditional two-term, dual dogmatics common to both Catholicism ("nature" and "grace") and Protestantism ("creation" and "covenant") for falling into both triumphalism (by construing "glory" that perfects nature as already inherent in grace) and homocentrism (by subordinating nature to grace rather than subordinating both to glory). See his *God in Creation*, 7–8. It is clear that this critique of medieval theology does not quite apply to Aquinas, who is here clearly proposing a three-term, not a two-term, dialectic. It is also clear that the characteristic difference between Catholicism and Protestantism remains between Aquinas and Moltmann. For Moltmann, "grace does not perfect but prepares nature for eternal glory; grace is not the perfection of nature but the messianic preparation of the world to the reign of God [gratia non perficit, sed praeparat naturam ad gloriam aeternam; gratia non est perfectio naturae, sed praeparatio messianica mundi ad regnum Dei] (ibid., 8), whereas, for Aquinas, grace *both* perfects nature by healing its wounds and restoring its natural integrity *and* elevates nature ultimately

for participation in glory. The Protestant distrust of nature is evident in Molt-mann, the Catholic embrace of nature in Aquinas.

73. Yves Congar, *The Mystery of the Church*, trans. A. V. Littledale (Baltimore: Helicon Press, 1960), 107.

74. For a recent study of the ontological perfecting of nature by grace, see Aertsen, *Nature and Creature*, 384–390.

75. I-II, 113, 10.

76. *On Evil*, q. 2, a. 11 and a. 12.

77. I, 12, 4 ad 3.

78. Earlier in SCG, 3, 57, Aquinas says that "every intellect naturally desires the vision of the divine substance, but natural desire cannot be incapable of fulfillment. Therefore, any created intellect whatever can attain to the vision of the divine substance." He could say this only because he had presupposed the work of prevenient grace.

79. *Summa Theologiae*, vol. 30, *The Gospel of Grace*, ed. Cornelius Ernst (New York: McGraw-Hill, 1972), 199. See also Ernst's review of Henri de Lubac's *The Mystery of the Supernatural* in *Journal of Theological Studies* 20.1 (1969): 365–367.

80. III, 34, 1; I, 34, 2; I, 35, 2, respectively.

81. I, 34, 3.

82. II, 3, 8.

83. SCG, 4, 42.

84. SCG, 4, 42.

85. *Super 1 Epistolam B. Pauli ad Corinthios lectura*, c. 11, l. 1, also cited in Jean-Pierre Torrell, "Le Christ dans la 'spiritualité' de saint Thomas," in Kent Emery and Joseph Wawrykow, eds., *Christ Among the Medieval Dominicans: Representations of Christ in the Texts and Images of the Order of Preachers* (Notre Dame, IN: University of Notre Dame Press, 1998), 214. Torrell's essay contains an excellent discussion of the ontological and moral exemplarity of Christ for all creation.

86. I, 33, 3; I, 34, 3; III, 3, 8, respectively.

87. I-II, 93, 4 ad 2.

88. I-II, 91, 1, and 93, 1.

89. I-II, 93, 1 ad 2.

90. I-II, 93, 3; 93, 3 ad 2; 93, 5.

91. III, 3, 8.

92. III, 3, 8.

93. SCG, 4, 42.

94. III, 3, 8.

95. SCG, 4, 42.

96. III, 8, 1; 7, 13.

97. III, 48, 1.

98. I-II, 114, 6.

99. III, 23, 3.

100. III, 3, 8.

101. See III, 24, 1 ad 2; III, 24, 3; III, 24, 4.

102. I, 2, prologue, and III, prologue, respectively. For the important connection between these prologues and John 14:6 ("I am the way, the truth, and the life"), see Jean-Pierre Torrell, "Le Christ dans la 'spiritualité' de saint Thomas," 197–198.

103. III, 9, 2.

104. SCG, 4, 55, [2].

105. Rogers, *Thomas Aquinas and Karl Barth*, 17–70.

106. Michel Corbin makes a convincing argument about the placing of Christology in the Third Part of the *Summa Theologiae*, a subject of much disagreement. Instead of the traditional exitus/reditus scheme, which finds it difficult to explain the placing of Christology in the last part of the *Summa*, Corbin argues for the scheme of the divine exemplar and the human image dealt with respectively in the First and the Second Parts and the appropriateness of discussing Christ, the revealing unity of God and humanity, exemplar and image, in the last, crowning part of theology. See his *Le chemin de la theologie chez Thomas D'Aquin*, 782–806.

107. I, 37, 2.

108. I, 45, 6.

109. I, 32, 1.

110. I-II, 68, 8.

111. SCG, 4, 20–22.

112. I, 38, 1.

113. I, 43, 7.

114. I-II, 106, 1.

115. I, 45, 7; SCG, 4, 26, [8].

116. III, 23, 2.

117. III, 23, 2.

118. III, 8, 1.

119. II-II, 2, 8.

120. T. C. O'Brien, in Thomas Aquinas, *Summa Theologiae*, vol. 27, *Effects of Sin, Stain and Guilt*, ed. T. C. O'Brien (New York: McGraw-Hill, 1974), 131 (the editor's commentary on I-II, 89, 6).

121. The prologue to I, 2; prologue to I-II. For an insightful discussion of Aquinas's doctrine of creation as a "trinitarian" theology, see David A. Walker, "Trinity and Creation in the Theology of St. Thomas Aquinas," *The Thomist* 57.3 (1993): 443–455. For a historical study of the development of the doctrine of the image of the Trinity in Aquinas, see D. Juvenal Merriell, *To the Image of the Trinity: A Study in the Development of Aquinas' Teaching* (Toronto:

Pontifical Institute of Medieval Studies, 1990). For a detailed, informative discussion of whether, to what extent, and how Aquinas regards woman as image of God, see Joseph Francis Hartel, *Femina ut Imago Dei: On the Integral Feminism of St. Thomas Aquinas* (Rome: Editrice Pontificia Universita Gregoriana, 1993).

122. I, 45, 3, and I, 45, 6.

123. I, 62, 4.

124. Joyce A. Little, *Toward a Thomist Methodology* (Lewiston, NY: Edwin Mellen Press, 1988). Her work is significantly indebted to the insights of Donald J. Keefe, S.J., *Thomism and the Ontological Theology of Paul Tillich: A Comparison of Systems* (Leiden: E. J. Brill, 1971), 43–134. On Rahner's distinction between being "intrinsic" and being "constitutive," see his *Foundations of Christian Faith: An Introduction to the Idea of Christianity* (New York: Seabury, 1978), 185. My own reservation about Little's work stems from its lack of a more adequate trinitarian account.

125. Marie-Dominique Chenu, *Toward Understanding Saint Thomas,* trans. A. M. Landry and D. Hughes (Chicago: Henry Regnery, 1964), 310–318; Thomas F. O'Meara, *Thomas Aquinas Theologian* (Notre Dame, IN: University of Notre Dame Press, 1997), 56–64.

126. Chenu, *Toward Understanding Saint Thomas,* 315; Otto Hermann Pesch, *Thomas von Aquin: Grenze und Grosse mittelalterlicher Theologie* (Mainz: Matthias-Grunewald-Verlag, 1988), 381–394.

127. Corbin, *Le chemin de la theologie chez Thomas d'Aquin,* 782–806.

128. Jean-Pierre Torrell, "Le Christ dans la 'spiritualité' de saint Thomas," 202.

129. SCG, 3, 19.

130. Pesch, *Thomas von Aquin,* 399.

131. III, 3, 8.

132. III, 1, 2, and SCG, 4, 54. For a detailed discussion of the motifs of incarnation, see chapter 3.

133. For a critique of Protestant misunderstandings of Aquinas by a Reformed theologian on the nature of faith, evidentialism, natural theology, and the relation between nature and grace, see Arvin Vos, *Aquinas, Calvin and Contemporary Protestant Thought: A Critique of Protestant Views on the Thought of Thomas Aquinas* (Grand Rapids, MI: Eerdmans, 1985).

134. I, 62, 3 ad 3.

135. Pannenberg, *Systematic Theology,* I, 74–75, 79.

136. Pannenberg, *Systematic Theology,* I, 75.

137. Pannenberg, *Systematic Theology,* I, 75.

138. The Second Vatican Council, *The Pastoral Constitution on the Church in the Modern World,* #22 and #11 respectively.

139. Küng, "What Is True Religion?", 107–109.

140. Thomas Gilby, introduction to Thomas Aquinas, *Summa Theologiae,* vol. 1, *Christian Theology,* ed. Thomas Gilby (New York: McGraw-Hill, 1964), 49.

141. I, 1, 9 and I, 43, 7 respectively.

142. I, 23, 8.

143. Cornelius Ernst, introduction to Thomas Aquinas, *Summa Theologiae,* vol. 30, *The Gospel of Grace,* ed. Cornelius Ernst (New York: McGraw-Hill, 1972), xx–xxi.

144. I-II, 109, 2 ad 2 and I-II, 109, 8 respectively.

145. SCG, 3, 126.

146. Brunner and Barth, *Natural Theology,* 46.

147. See II-II, 1, 7; 1, 8; 1, 10.

148. See I, 1, 2; II-II, 2, 5.

149. II-II, 1, 2.

150. I-II, 113, 7. Armand Maurer tries to show how Aquinas is open to accepting the historicity of reason and truth by saying that for Aquinas, truth "always has the mark of history upon it, for it lives and develops in a mind that is historically situated." See his *St. Thomas and Historicity* (Milwaukee: Marquette University Press, 1979), 33. To what extent or in what sense does Aquinas accept this historical situation? For him, truth is the relation of conformity of subject and object. If the object changes (e.g., Socrates sits), then our judgment too must change (to "Socrates sits"), or else it becomes false (if we say, "Socrates stands"). That human beings are rational is true only as long as the human race exists; if it ceases to exist, we must say instead that they *were* rational. In this sense, *secundum variationem temporis sunt diversi intellectus.* Furthermore, there is progress from one age to another in the discovery and understanding of truth, a slow progress from the sensible to the intelligible, from the more extrinsic to the more intrinsic, from the more particular to the more universal, and Aquinas admits his indebtedness to Aristotle and the Fathers. See Maurer, *St. Thomas and Historicity,* 30–33. See also Aertsen, *Nature and Creature,* 196–201.

This, however, is also the extent to which Aquinas accepts historicity, which still operates within the Aristotelian conception of time as mere change, an accident which does not "cut into" being (Whitehead). It remains extrinsic to nature. As Maurer himself notes, "not that time itself contributes anything, . . . but help comes with time"(32). Neither the temporality of existence (Kierkegaard, Heidegger) which constitutes the inner *horizon* of the subject nor the historicity of social existence (Hegel, Marx) which constitutes the *ideologies* of a society—both of which operate as the a priori, intrinsic condition of reason—come into view in Aristotle and Aquinas. Intellectual changes which come with time are merely *factual* and incidental to the operation of reason and its relation to the object, or *deducible* from the composite nature of humanity. Both subject and object are already constituted in their essential reality prior to such changes, while there is no possibility of paradigm changes in human knowledge, including the very notion of human nature.

151. See Karl Barth, *Church Dogmatics*, vol. I, *The Doctrine of the Word of God*, part 1, trans. G.W. Bromiley, 2nd ed. (Edinburgh: T & T Clark, 1975), 295–306; Karl Rahner, *The Trinity*, trans. Joseph Donceel (New York: Seabury, 1974), 15–21; Jürgen Moltmann, *The Trinity and the Kingdom*, trans. Margaret Kohl (San Francisco: HarperSanFrancisco, 1991), 16–20; Pannenberg, *Systematic Theology*, I, 288–308; Vladimir Lossky, *Orthodox Theology: An Introduction* (Crestwood, NY: St. Vladimir's Seminary Press, 1978), 19–22; Thomas F. Torrance, *The Christian Doctrine of God, One Being Three Persons* (Edinburgh: T & T Clark, 1996), 10; Catherine Mowry LaCugna, *God for Us: The Trinity and Christian Life* (San Francisco: HarperSanFrancisco, 1991), 143–169.

152. Barth, *Church Dogmatics*, vol. I, part 1, 303.

153. Brunner and Barth, *Natural Theology*, 20, 24–27.

154. Brunner and Barth, *Natural Theology*, 58.

155. For the distinction between "existentials" and "categories," see Martin Heidegger, *Being and Time*, trans. John Macquarrie and Edward Robinson (New York: Harper & Row, 1962), 70.

156. I, 96, 2.

157. I-II, 95, 2; I-II, 91, 2, and 3 ad 2; I-II, 93, 1 ad 3.

158. I, 61, 3; I, 96, 1 and 2; I, 103, 5; SCG, 3, 78; SCG, 3, 81; SCG, 3, 112. It is more than curious that it is only some thirty years ago that Catholic theology was celebrating the "turn to the subject" or "anthropocentric turn," with people like Rahner and Johannes Baptist Metz arguing that such a turn began not so much with Descartes as with Aquinas. See Karl Rahner, *Theological Investigations*, IX (New York: Seabury, 1973), 28–42 ("Theology and Anthropology").

159. I, 65, 1.

160. I, 20, 4, ad 2.

161. I, 20, 3.

162. I, 20, 4.

163. SCG, 3, 19.

164. I, 6, 1.

165. I, 62, 3 ad 3.

166. On the contemporary appropriateness of the category of " being," see Elizabeth A. Johnson, *She Who Is: The Mystery of God in Feminist Theological Discourse* (New York: Crossroad, 1992), 236–240; Martin Bieler, "The Future of the Philosophy of Being," *Communio* 26 (Fall 1999): 455–485. On the intuition of "being," see Jacques Maritain, *Existence and the Existent: An Essay on Christian Existentialism* (Garden City, NY: Doubleday Image Books, 1956), 20–55.

167. SCG, 3, 47; also CT, I, 105.

168. See I, 1, 7.

169. SCG, 1, 8.

170. I, 1, 9; also SCG, 1, 5.

171. II-II, 81, 4.

172. *On Power,* 7, 5 ad 14, in *Selected Writings,* 316.

173. I, 12, 13 ad 1.

174. Karl Rahner, "Thomas Aquinas on the Incomprehensibility of God," *Journal of Religion,* S109 (1978): 107–125; also his *Theological Investigations,* XVI (New York: Seabury, 1979), 244–254.

175. I provide a more elaborate discussion of the limits of human knowledge of God and God's incomprehensibility in chapter 4.

Chapter 2.   The Implicit Salvation of Non-Christians

1. The literature on exclusivism and inclusivism is vast. Let me simply refer to two excellent surveys: Alan Race, *Christians and Religious Pluralism: Patterns in the Christian Theology of Religions* (London: SCM Press, 1983), and Paul F. Knitter, *No Other Name? A Critical Survey of Christian Attitudes toward the World Religions* (Maryknoll, NY: Orbis, 1985). For excellent historical surveys of the official Catholic position on the issue, see Francis A. Sullivan, *Salvation outside the Church? Tracing the History of the Catholic Response* (Mahwah, NJ: Paulist, 1992); Jerome P. Theissen, *The Ultimate Church and the Promise of Salvation* (Collegeville, MN: St. John's University Press, 1976), 1–64; and Jacques Dupuis, *Toward a Christian Theology of Religious Pluralism* (Maryknoll, NY: Orbis, 1997), 25–202. The second part of Dupuis' book is also the most recent statement of what might be called pluralistic inclusivism.

2. To this typology I add a new type of my own, called "dialectical" pluralism. See Anselm K. Min, "Dialectical Pluralism and Solidarity of Others: Towards a New Paradigm," *Journal of the American Academy of Religion* 65.3 (Fall 1997): 587–604; idem, *The Solidarity of Others in a Divided World: A Postmodern Theology after Postmodernism* (New York: T & T Clark International, 2004), 156–197.

3. For a portrayal of changing times and frontiers in Aquinas's day, see Otto Hermann Pesch, *Thomas von Aquin,* 52–65. On the extent and nature of Aquinas's contact with non-Christian religions, see Thomas F. O'Meara, *Thomas Aquinas Theologian,* 235–237, and idem, "The Presence of Grace Outside Evangelization, Baptism and Church in Thomas Aquinas' Theology," in Michael F. Cusato and F. Edward Coughlin, eds., *That Others May Know and Love: Essays in Honor of Zachary Hayes* (St. Bonaventure, NY: Franciscan Institute, 1997), 91–95. I would like to acknowledge my great indebtedness to this essay for introducing me to the issue of the salvation of the non-Christian in Aquinas, and to hereby express my gratitude to Fr. O'Meara for sharing it with me prior to its publication.

4. II-II, 2, 3.

5. SCG, 3, 118.

6. II-II, 1, 8; II-II, 1, 6.

7. II-II, 2, 5.

8. II-II, 1, 7; also II-II, 1, 8.

9. II-II, 2, 5.

10. II-II, 2, 7.

11. II-II, 2, 7.

12. II-II, 2, 7.

13. II-II, 2, 7, ad 3. For Aquinas, the belief in the Incarnation contains the belief in the Trinity. Thus, the preceding remarks about the necessity and explicitness of faith in Christ also apply to faith in the Trinity. See II-II, 2, 8. Aquinas's belief that the mystery of redemption in Christ was probably revealed to many pagans as well even before the coming of Christ is as old as *On Truth*, 14, 11, ad 5.

14. See 3 *Sent.*, d.25, q.2, a.1, ad 1; *On Truth*, 14, 11, ad 1; *Super Epistolam B. Pauli ad Romanos Lectura*, c. 10, l. 3.

15. II-II, 10, 4.

16. In this regard, Max Seckler seems a little too definitive in his interpretation that *after* the Incarnation, Aquinas demands an explicit faith of *all* in the mysteries of Christ regardless of whether such mysteries have become *known* to them. See his "Das Heil der Nichtevangelisierten in thomistischer Sicht," *Theologische Quartalschrift* 140.1 (1960): 43; this excellent article forms the last chapter of his book, *Instinkt und Glaubenswille nach Thomas von Aquin* (Mainz: Matthias-Grünewald-Verlag, 1961); also George Sabra, *Thomas Aquinas' Vision of the Church: Fundamentals of an Ecumenical Ecclesiology* (Mainz: Matthias-Grünewald-Verlag, 1987), 162. Sabra also raises an important issue of whether Aquinas requires for culpable unbelief merely hearing the *fama* or report about the Gospel or *effective* encounter with the Gospel through the proclamation of an established church (166–168). I do not think these exhaust the alternatives for Aquinas, who was sensitive to the disparity between subjective dispositions and objective conditions and the possibility of erroneous conscience even in the matter of belief in Christ (I-II, 19, 5). It is quite possible not to have an "effective" subjective encounter with the Gospel even when the Gospel has been preached in churches and on radio and television for decades as in contemporary America. My suspicion is that for Aquinas, effective encounter with the Gospel and culpable unbelief require not only objective but also subjective conditions appropriate to faith.

17. O'Meara, "Presence of Grace," 106.

18. II-II, 10, 1.

19. II-II, 10, 1.

20. Sullivan, *Salvation Outside the Church?*, 57.

21. II-II, 10, 4; III, 69, 4.

22. II-II, 10, 5.

23. II-II, 10, 6.

24. *De Veritate,* 14, 11.

25. II-II, 2, 7.

26. Seckler, "Das Heil der Nichtevangelisierten in thomistischer Sicht," 48 and 45.

27. I, 43, 7.

28. SCG, 3, 113.

29. I-II, 113, 3.

30. III, 61, 1.

31. I, 62, 5.

32. I-II, 114, 2.

33. SCG, 4, 55, [4].

34. II-II, 2, 7.

35. II-II, 174, 6.

36. II-II, 1, 7.

37. II-II, 2, 3.

38. I-II, 19, 15.

39. I, 43, 7.

40. SCG, 4, 55, [4].

41. III, 61, 1. Aquinas makes the same argument from human nature for the necessity of sacraments in SCG, 4, 56: "Just as he does for all other things, so also for the human being, God provides according to his condition. . . . Now, the human being's condition is such that he is brought to grasp the spiritual and intelligible naturally through the senses. Therefore, spiritual remedies had to be given to men under sensible signs."

42. III, 67, 3.

43. III, 60, 5.

44. Seckler, "Das Heil der Nichtevangelisierten in thomistischer Sicht," 50–51.

45. 3 *Sent.,* d. 25, q. 2, a.1, as translated in O'Meara, "Presence of Grace," 97.

46. Ibid. Aquinas's discussion of the necessity of explicit faith in Christ for salvation in his commentary on the *Sentences* sets the general principle for all his later works: On the one hand, an explicit faith in Christ is necessary in principle so as to direct our life to our ultimate end, but on the other the degree of explicitness required depends on different times such as before the fall, before the coming of Christ, and after the coming of Christ, and on the intellectual capacities and official responsibilities of the persons involved, such as official teachers and simple folks. See further 3 *Sent.,* d. 25, q. 2, a. 2.

47. *On Truth,* 14, 11.

48. *On Truth,* 14, 11.

49. *On Truth,* 24, 14.

50. *On Truth,* 24,12; 24,15.

51. *Super Epistolam B. Pauli ad Romanos Lectura,* c. 10, l. 3, as translated in O'Meara, "Presence of Grace," 98.

52. *Super Epistolam B. Pauli ad Romanes Lectura,* c. 2, l. 3.

53. Seckler, "Das Heil der Nichtevangelisierten in thomistischer Sicht," 45.

54. I-II, 89, 6.

55. I-II, 88, 1.

56. For an excellent commentary on the supernatural significance of the first moral act as discussed in I-II, 89, 6, see T. C. O'Brien's editorial commentary in Saint Thomas Aquinas, *Summa Theologiae,* vol. 27, *Effects of Sin, Stain and Guilt,* ed. T. C. O'Brien (New York: McGraw-Hill, 1974), 125–133. Fr. Francis Sullivan finds it "puzzling that with regard to this person who arrives at justification through his first moral decision (aided, of course, by grace) there is no mention of the necessity of an act of faith," but only because he assumes that Aquinas held "explicit" faith in Christ "absolutely necessary for all in his day" (61), which I do not think is true. Aquinas's remarks in II-II, 2, 7, ad 3, discussed earlier, should clearly demonstrate that for him, implicit faith in saving providence was sufficient for the salvation of those who have never heard the gospel, including, therefore, the pagans of his own day.

57. I-II, 109, 5.

58. I-II, 109, 6.

59. I-II, 109, 1; 109, 9.

60. I-II, 109, 2; 109, 8; 109, 9; 111, 2.

61. I-II, 109, 3.

62. I-II, 109, 6; 109, 7.

63. I-II, 109, 9; 109, 10; also *Boethius on the Trinity,* 1, 1.

64. I-II, 110, 2.

65. I-II, 109, 1.

66. I-II, 109, 1.

67. For exposition and clarification of the traditional division of grace into habitual and actual, sufficient and efficacious, see Reginald Garrigou-Lagrange, *Reality: A Synthesis of Thomistic Thought,* trans. Patrick Cummins (St. Louis: B. Herder, 1950), 293–317; also idem, *De Gratia: Commentarius in Summam Theologicam S. Thomae Iae IIae qq. 109–114* (Torino: R. Berruti, 1947); Karl Rahner, "Grace," in *Encyclopedia of Theology: The Concise Sacramentum Mundi,* ed. Karl Rahner (New York: Crossroad, 1982), 587–595; Roger Haight, *The Experience and Language of Grace* (New York: Paulist, 1979), 54–78.

68. I-II, 110, 2.

69. I-II, 110, 4; *On Truth,* 27, 6.

70. I-II, 110, 3. For an insightful discussion of the idea of the "light of grace" [lumen gratiae] in Aquinas, see Ludwig Hödl, " 'Lumen gratiae,' Ein Leitgedanke der Gnadentheologie des Thomas von Aquin," in Heribert Rossmann and Joseph

Ratzinger, eds., *Mysterium der Gnade: Festschrift für Johann Auer* (Regensburg: Friedrich Pustet, 1975), 238–250.

71. For a further discussion of Aquinas's concept of divine motion or pre-motion as distinct from habitual grace, see Joseph P. Wawrykow, *God's Grace and Human Action: "Merit" in the Theology of Thomas Aquinas* (Notre Dame, IN: University of Notre Dame Press, 1995), 146, 172, 231–232, 249–254; he refers to divine motion simply as the grace of *auxilium.*

72. I-II, 109, 6.

73. I-II, 112, 2.

74. I-II, 111, 2.

75. I-II, 113, 3.

76. I-II, 109, 7.

77. I-II, 109, 2 ad 2.

78. I-II, 109, 8.

79. I-II, 72, 4.

80. II-II, 2, 3; I-II, 109, 2, 8, and 9.

81. I-II, 113, 2.

82. *On Truth*, 24, 12.

83. See also Seckler, "Das Heil der Nichtevangelisierten in thomistischer Sicht," 53.

84. Seckler, "Das Heil der Nichtevangelisierten in thomistischer Sicht," 53.

85. Seckler, "Das Heil der Nichtevangelisierten in thomistischer Sicht," 68.

86. II-II, 2, 7, ad 3.

87. I-II, 113, 4.

88. II-II, 10, 4.

89. Seckler, "Das Heil der Nichtevangelisierten in thomistischer Sicht," 59–66; Jacques Maritain, *The Range of Reason* (New York: Charles Scribner's Sons, 1942), 66–85 ("The Immanent Dialectic of the First Act of Freedom").

90. Rahner, *Foundations of Christian Faith*, 97–102, and "Grace," 594–595.

91. E.g., Seckler, "Das Heil der Nichtevangelisierten in thomistischer Sicht," 55, 63.

Chapter 3. A Sacramental Theology of Religions

1. I, 31, 2.

2. I, 45, 6.

3. I, 44, 4; III, 23, 1.

4. I, 33, 2; I, 38, 2.

5. I, 34, 3.

6. I, 33, 3.

7. III, 24, 3.

8. I, 37, 2.

9. I, 39, 8; I, 45, 6; III, 23, 2; III, 23, 3.

10. I, 37, 2.

11. LaCugna, *God for Us,* 164–65.

12. III, 1, 1.

13. I, 44, 4.

14. In questioning the plausibility of the idea of one universal savior of all humanity, John Hick, Paul Knitter, and Stanley Samartha ask whether a *finite* being could express the *infinite* exhaustively, to which the obvious answer is "no." By the same token they fail to ask the only relevant question in the whole debate, namely whether the *infinite* can *empower* a finite being to embody in a *definitive* although not an exhaustive way both God's saving love and human acceptance of that love in solidarity with all creation and humanity, which is the soteriological meaning of the hypostatic union. A finite being by itself is not capable of such a hypostatic union, but an infinite being *can* enter into an hypostatic union with a finite being. See Paul Knitter, *Jesus and the Other Names* (Maryknoll, NY: Orbis, 1996), 37, 73–75; Stanley Samartha, *One Christ—Many Religions: Toward a Revised Christology* (Maryknoll, NY: Orbis, 1991), 4; John Hick, *The Metaphor of God Incarnate: Christology in a Pluralistic Age* (Louisville, KY: Westminster/John Knox Press, 1993), 76.

15. III, 2, 6; III, 2, 10; III, 2, 11.

16. III, 1, 2; III, 1, 3.

17. SCG, 4, 54, [5].

18. Thomas Aquinas, *Commentary on Saint Paul's First Letter to the Thessalonians and the Letter to the Philippians,* 80–81.

19. SCG, 4, 55, [2]. On a slightly different formulation of the lessons of the incarnation, see Thomas Aquinas, *The Three Greatest Prayers,* 56–57.

20. Thomas Aquinas, *Commentary on the Gospel of St. John,* 92.

21. III, 1, 2; III, 2, 11.

22. III, 1, 2; SCG, 4, 54.

23. SCG, 4, 55, [4].

24. On the intimate connection between the incarnation and our attainment of the ultimate end in the vision of God, see further Torrell, "Le Christ dans la 'spiritualité' de saint Thomas," 200–202. It is important to note here, as Philip Quinn reminds us, that although "satisfaction for sin" is mentioned only as one among other reasons for the incarnation, all other reasons also "pertain to the remedy for sin. For if man had not sinned, he would have been endowed with the light of divine wisdom, and would have been perfected by God with the righteousness of justice in order to know and carry out everything necessary" (III, 1, 3 ad 1). It is equally important to note, however, as Quinn does not seem to, that "remedy for sin" in Aquinas is a much broader concept than "satisfaction for sin." See Philip L. Quinn, "Aquinas on Atonement," in Ronald J. Feenstra and Cornelius

Plantinga, Jr., eds., *Trinity, Incarnation, and Atonement: Philosophical and Theological Essays* (Notre Dame, IN: University of Notre Dame Press, 1989), 155.

25. III, 1, 3.

26. See the discussion of the concept of "mission" in chapter 5.

27. III, 3, 5 on how any of the three divine persons "could" have assumed flesh.

28. SCG, 4, 42, [3].

29. SCG, 4, 42, [1]-[2].

30. III, 3, 8; Aquinas, *Commentary on the Sentences,* I, prologue, in *Selected Writings,* 51–54. For a detailed analysis of III, 3, 8 (on the fittingness of the incarnation of the Son as the "power and wisdom of God") and a development of its implications for the whole of Christology and even the very concept of theology in I, 1, 1, see Joseph Wawrykow, "Wisdom in the Christology of Thomas Aquinas," in Kent Emery, Jr., and Joseph P. Wawrykow, eds., *Christ Among the Medieval Dominicans: Representations of Christ in the Texts and Images of the Order of Preachers* (Notre Dame, IN: University of Notre Dame Press, 1998), 175–196.

31. Karl Rahner, *The Trinity,* trans. Joseph Donceel (New York: Seabury, 1974), 11; *Foundations of Christian Faith,* 214–215.

32. Rahner, *Foundations of Christian Faith,* 217–218.

33. Rahner, *Foundations of Christian Faith,* 222–23.

34. Rahner, *Foundations of Christian Faith,* 223–225.

35. III, 1, 1.

36. III, 1, 2.

37. For a detailed discussion of the nature and uses of the argument from "fittingness" or "convenience [convenientia]" in Aquinas's theology, see Gilbert Narcisse, O.P., "Les enjeux epistemologiques de l'argument de convenance selon saint Thomas d'Aquin," in Carlos-Josaphat Pinto de Oliveira, O.P., ed., *Ordo Sapientiae et Amoris* (Fribourg: Editions Universitaires, 1993), 143–167; Alain Contat, "Destin de l'homme et incarnation du Verbe selon St. Thomas d'Aquin," *Atti del IX Congresso Tomistico Internazionale,* 5 (1991), 255–272; John Milbank and Catherine Pickstock, *Truth in Aquinas* (London: Routledge, 2001), 60–65.

38. III, 4, 5.

39. III, 48, 1.

40. III, 46, 1; for a clear summary of Aquinas's theology of atonement, see Quinn, "Aquinas on Atonement."

41. Aquinas, *The Three Greatest Prayers,* 58–60.

42. III, 46, 2; III, 46, 3.

43. III, 56, 1.

44. III, 56, 1.

45. III, 56, 1.

46. III, 56, 1.

47. III, 53, 1 ad 3.

48. III, 56, 2; III, 62, 5.

49. III, 56, 1.

50. III, 56, 1 ad 1.

51. III, 56, 2.

52. III, 56, 1.

53. Thomas Aquinas, *Commentary on Saint Paul's First Letter to the Thessalonians and the Letter to the Philippians,* 85.

54. III, 19, 4.

55. III, 8, 3.

56. III, 8, 4; III, 19, 4. I cannot go into Aquinas's ecclesiology here, but I just mention some contemporary studies of his ecclesiology as follows. For an interpretation of the church as the "people of God"—so prominent in Vatican II—in the texts of Aquinas, see Yves Congar, "'Ecclesia' et 'Populus (Fidelis)' dans l'Ecclesiologie de S. Thomas," in *St. Thomas Aquinas, 1274–1974, Commemorative Studies,* vol. 1 (Toronto: Pontifical Institute of Medieval Studies, 1974), 159–173. For a christological, non-institutionalist interpretation of Aquinas's ecclesiology by a Protestant theologian, see Sabra, *Thomas Aquinas' Vision of the Church.* For a pneumatological interpretation of the church, see John Mahoney, "The Church of the Holy Spirit in Aquinas," *The Heythrop Journal* 15.1 (1974): 18–36.

57. On the moral and ontological exemplarity of Christ for all humanity, see Torrell, "Le Christ dans la 'spiritualité' de saint Thomas," 202–213.

58. III, 8, 1; III, 8, 6.

59. III, 19, 4 ad 3.

60. III, 48, 2.

61. I-II, 81, 1 and 3 ad 3; *On Evil,* 4, 1. For a careful defense of Aquinas's theology of the mystical body against the juridical, authoritarian, or totalitarian interpretation it has often suffered, see H. Rikhof, "Corpus Christi Mysticum: An Inquiry into Thomas Aquinas' Use of a Term," *Bijdragen* 37 (1976): 149–71. For a Christology of the mystical body, see Emile Mersch, *The Theology of the Mystical Body* (St. Louis, MO: B. Herder, 1951), 197–246.

62. Aquinas, *The Three Greatest Prayers,* 80–83.

63. Sabra, *Thomas Aquinas' Vision of the Church,* 182; Mersch, *The Theology of the Mystical Body* 250–270.

64. III, 48, 1.

65. III, 49, 1.

66. III, 46, 5.

67. III, 48, 4.

68. III, 69, 2; III, 1, 4 ad 3. Although this is no place for a full-scale discussion of the validity of the idea of "vicarious" satisfaction for sins of others, it seems necessary to respond, however briefly, to Quinn's two criticisms regarding Aquinas's theology of atonement: (1) that the very idea of vicarious satisfaction

does not make sense because "debts of punishment for serious sins simply cannot be transferred from one person to another," and (2) that the use of the organic metaphor of the body and its members—e.g., a person redeeming himself, through the good industry of his hands, from a sin committed with his feet (III, 49, 1)—fails because the metaphor only involves one person redeeming himself through one part of his body from a sin committed with another part and does not involve one person making satisfaction for the sin of another person; see Quinn, "Aquinas on Atonement," 173–174. With regard to the first criticism Aquinas might respond by saying that it assumes an individualistic conception of the agent of sin, and with regard to the second by saying that the point of the organic metaphor is not to compare the two parts of the body as though they were two individual persons, in which case it would cease to be a metaphor, but precisely to disclose the theological depth of mutual dependence and solidarity not apparent at the empirical level of individual interaction. The perception of the validity of the idea of "vicarious" satisfaction depends on whether one can appreciate the depth of the *theological* solidarity of all humanity, and indeed of all creation, in Christ the head and exemplar, a solidarity that transcends the possibilities and responsibilities of the free acts of individuals. This, I think, is the whole point of the traditional doctrine of the communion of saints.

69. III, 48, 6.

70. III, 26, 2.

71. III, 49, 3; III, 49, 5.

72. III, 48, 6 ad 2; III, 56, 1 ad 3.

73. II-II, 2, 2; II-II, 2, 3.

74. III, 62, 5.

75. Aquinas, *The Three Greatest Prayers*, 74.

76. III, 49, 1 ad 5; III, 52, 6.

77. II-II, 23, 1; II-II, 23, 2; II-II, 23, 3; II-II, 24, 2.

78. II-II, 4, 3; II-II, 23, 6 ad 2; II-II, 23, 8.

79. III, 60, 2.

80. III, 60, 3; III, 62, 1; III, 62, 4; III, 62, 5; *On Truth*, 27, 4.

81. III, 61, 1; III, 60, 4.

82. III, 61, 1.

83. III, 49, 1; III, 61, 1. For a defense of Aquinas's theology of the sacrament against the charge of ontotheology raised by Louis-Marie Chauvet in his *Symbol and Sacrament* (Collegeville, MN: Liturgical Press, 1995), see Liam G. Walsh, "The Divine and the Human in St. Thomas's Theology of Sacraments," in Carlos-Josaphat Pinto de Oliveira, O.P., ed., *Ordo Sapientiae et Amoris* (Fribourg: Editions Universitaires, 1993), 321–354.

84. III, 61, 3.

85. III, 68, 1.

86. III, 52, 7.

87. III, 49, 3.

88. III, 73, 3.

89. III, 61, 2.

90. III, 61, 3.

91. III, 61, 4.

92. III, 61, 4.

93. III, 62, 6; III, 70, 4.

94. III, 64, 3.

95. III, 64, 7; also III, 67, 5.

96. III, 60, 5.

97. III, 8, 3 ad 3; III, 62, 6.

98. I-II, 106, 1 ad 3.

99. III, 66, 11.

100. III, 66, 12.

101. III, 68, 2.

102. III, 73, 3.

103. III, 68, 1.

104. III, 68, 2. For a further discussion of the different modes of incorporation into Christ as a condition of salvation, see Colman E. O'Neill, "St. Thomas on the Membership of the Church," *Thomist* 27 (1963): 88–140; Jerome Toner, "The Salvation of Non-Christians in the Writings of St. Thomas Aquinas," *The Living Word* 77.5 (September–October 1971): 221–227.

105. III, 68, 1.

106. II-II, 2, 7 ad 3.

107. Heinz Robert Schlette, *Towards a Theology of Religions* (New York: Herder & Herder, 1966), 81.

108. On the idea of the Church as a basic sacrament, see Karl Rahner, *The Church and the Sacraments* (New York: Herder & Herder, 1963). On non-Christian religions as ways of salvation, see Karl Rahner, *Theological Investigations,* XVIII (New York: Crossroad, 1983), 288–295 ("On the Importance of the Non-Christian Religions for Salvation").

109. III, 60, 5.

110. For discussions of pluralistic inclusivism based on the presence of the Holy Spirit in other religions, see Gavin D'Costa, "Christ, the Trinity and Religious Plurality," in Gavin D'Costa, ed., *Christian Uniqueness Reconsidered: The Myth of a Pluralistic Theology of Religions* (Maryknoll, NY: Orbis, 1990), 16–29. See also Dupuis, *Toward a Christian Theology of Religious Pluralism.*

111. For a typology of religious pluralisms prevailing today, see my essay, "Dialectical Pluralism and Solidarity of Others: Towards a New Paradigm," *Journal of the American Academy of Religion* 65.3 (Fall 1997): 587–604.

112. Charles Taylor, *Multiculturalism and "The Politics of Recognition,"* ed. Amy Guttmann (Princeton, NJ: Princeton University Press, 1992), 73.

113. On the incarnational dynamic of grace, see Karl Rahner, *Theological Investigations,* XII (New York: Crossroad, 1974), 161–178 ("Anonymous Christianity and the Missionary Task of the Church").

114. II-II, 5, 3.

115. II-II, 1, 1.

116. II-II, 1, 4; II-II, 1, 5; II-II, 2, 3; II-II, 5, 2; II-II, 5, 3.

117. Aquinas, *Commentary on Sentences* I, 1, 3, solution 2 ad 1, in *Selected Writings,* 62.

118. II-II, 2, 2.

119. II-II, 5, 3.

120. I, 1, 1.

121. I, 1, 8; I, 32, 1.

122. II-II, 2, 10.

123. II-II, 5, 3.

124. II-II, 10, 1.

125. See Bruce D. Marshall, "Aquinas as Postliberal Theologian," *Thomist* 53.3 (July 1989): 353–402. For criticisms of Marshall and Marshall's response, see Louis Roy, "Bruce Marshall's Reading of Aquinas," *Thomist* 56.3 (1992): 473–480; Frederick J. Crosson, "Reconsidering Aquinas as Postliberal Theologian," *Thomist* 56.3 (1992): 481–498; and Bruce D. Marshall, "Thomas, Thomisms, and Truth," *Thomist* 56.3 (1992): 499–524.

126. *On Truth,* 14, 11.

127. I tried to provide in my own way this kind of theology of solidarity in *The Solidarity of Others in a Divided World: A Postmodern Theology after Postmodernism* (New York: T & T Clark International, 2004).

128. See Sullivan, *A Salvation Outside the Church?,* 54–55; Seckler, "Das Heil der Nichtevangelisierten in tomistischer Sicht," 39; O'Meara, "The Presence of Grace," 31; Pesch, *Thomas von Aquin,* 53. In a similar context, it may be noted that Wawrykow argues for a shift in Aquinas's position on merit from his *Commentary on the Sentences* to *Summa Theologiae,* where he fully introduces the overriding concept of predestination, and that this shift reflects Aquinas's reading of the late Augustine on predestination and the gift of perseverance. Wawrykow does not consider this a "pessimistic" turn. As I argue in the later part of this section, however, the theme of predestination and reprobation already occurs in *Summa contra Gentiles,* about which Wawrykow remains completely silent. See his *God's Grace and Human Action,* 260–276.

129. II-II, 2, 5.

130. II-II, 10, 1.

131. III, 52, 7.

132. III, 8, 3.

133. All preceding quotations are from I, 23, 3.

134. I, 22, 1.

135. I, 22, 3; I, 23, 8 ad 2.
136. I, 22, 4; 23, 5 ad 3; 23, 7 ad 2; 23, 8 ad 2; 47, 1; 47, 2; 47, 3.
137. I, 19, 6; 22, 2.
138. I, 19, 8.
139. I, 19, 6; 22, 4.
140. I, 22, 2 ad 5.
141. I, 19, 9.
142. I, 19, 9 ad 3.
143. I, 22, 2 ad 2; 48, 2 ad 3; 49, 2.
144. I, 23, 1.
145. I, 23, 4.
146. I, 23, 4 ad 1.
147. I, 23, 5.
148. I, 23, 5.
149. I-II, 114, 5.
150. I-II, 114, 5.
151. I, 23, 8.
152. I, 23, 7.
153. I, 23, 7.
154. I, 23, 3.
155. I, 19, 2.
156. I, 19, 3.
157. I, 19, 6 ad 1; 23, 4 ad 3.
158. I, 20, 2.
159. I, 19, 6 ad 1; 23, 4 ad 3.
160. I., 20, 2 ad 4; 20, 3; 20, 3 ad 1; 20, 4.
161. I, 21, 1; 21, 1 ad 2.
162. I, 21, 1 ad 3; 21, 2.
163. I, 23, 5 ad 3.
164. I-II, 109, 8; SCG, 3, 160; *On Truth*, 24, 12.
165. I, 23, 3.
166. I, 23, 3 ad 2 and ad 3.
167. *On Evil*, 2, 12 ad 6; 3, 1; 3, 2; I, 20, 2 ad 4; 49, 2 ad 2.
168. SCG, 3, 161.
169. I, 23, 5 ad 3; 49, 2.
170. II-II, 4, 4.
171. I-II, 79, 3; emphasis added.
172. I-II, 79, 4.
173. SCG, 3, 163.
174. SCG, 3, 161.
175. SCG, 3, 161.
176. In light of this doctrine of predestination and reprobation Joseph P. Wawrykow argues that when Aquinas makes universal statements about the

"ordination" of human beings to the end of eternal life (I-II, 112, 2), he should be interpreted as saying that all human beings are "capable" of attaining their end. Whether they will "actually" attain the end will depend on God's own predestining and reprobating will. Although I believe that the word "ordination" has a much stronger theological and soteriological meaning than mere "capacity," I do think that Wawrykow is calling attention to a crucial but often neglected aspect of Aquinas's theology. See his *God's Grace and Human Action,* 157–159

177. I-II, 109, 1.

178. I-II, 112, 2.

179. I-II, 112, 3; my emphasis.

180. SCG, 4, 163.

181. See Sullivan, *Salvation Outside the Church?,* 28–43.

182. Pesch, 153.

183. Pesch, 155.

184. SCG, 3, 19.

185. III, 46, 2.

186. I, 23, 5.

187. I, 23, 3; 23, 4.

188. I, 23, 7.

189. I, 23, 5.

190. For a discussion of different positions on predestination (Peter Aureol, William of Ockham, and Gregory of Rimini) in the century after Aquinas, see James Halverson, "Franciscan Theology and Predestinarian Pluralism in Late Medieval Thought," *Speculum* 70.1 (January 1995): 1–26.

191. *On Evil,* 5, 1 ad 1.

192. Karl Rahner, *The Content of Faith: The Best of Karl Rahner's Theological Writings,* ed. Karl Lehmann and Albert Raffelt, and trans. Harvey D. Egan (New York: Crossroad, 1992), 635–636.

193. III, 67, 3.

194. For a classical exposition and defense of Aquinas's doctrine of predestination and reprobation, see Reginald Garrigou-Lagrange, *The One God: A Commentary on the First Part of St. Thomas' Theological Summa,* trans. Bede Rose (St. Louis, MO: B. Herder Book Co., 1943), 653–717.

Chapter 4.   Theology as Contemplative Wisdom

1. For a history of the concepts of theory and praxis, see Nicholas Lobkowicz, *Theory and Practice: History of a Concept from Aristotle to Marx* (Notre Dame, IN: University of Notre Dame Press, 1967); Richard J. Bernstein, *Praxis and Action: Contemporary Philosophies of Human Activity* (Philadelphia: University of Pennsylvania Press, 1971); and Jürgen Habermas, *Theory and Practice* (Boston: Beacon Press, 1973).

2. For a typology of the relation between theory and praxis in contemporary Christian theology, see Matthew Lamb, "The Theory-Praxis Relationship in Contemporary Christian Theologies," *Proceedings of the Catholic Theological Society of America* 31 (1976): 149–178. For the relation between theory and praxis in liberation theologies in particular, see my *Dialectic of Salvation: Issues in Theology of Liberation* (Albany: State University of New York Press, 1989), 37–78.

3. See II-II, 47, 10.

4. Jürgen Moltmann, *Theology of Hope: On the Ground and the Implications of a Christian Eschatology* (New York: Harper & Row, 1975), 15.

5. Hans Urs von Balthasar, *Explorations in Theology,* vol. 1, *The Word Made Flesh* (San Francisco: Ignatius Press, 1989), 160.

6. Balthasar, *Explorations in Theology,* vol. 1, 109.

7. Frans Jozef van Beeck, *God Encountered: A Contemporary Catholic Systematic Theology,* vol. 1, *Understanding the Christian Faith* (San Francisco: Harper & Row, 1989), 145–177, and "Trinitarian Theology as Participation," in Stephen Davis, Daniel Kendall, and Gerald O'Collins, eds., *The Trinity* (New York: Oxford University Press, 1999), 295–325.

8. See Geoffrey Wainwright, *Doxology: The Praise of God in Worship, Doctrine and Life* (New York: Oxford University Press, 1980).

9. Ritschl, *The Logic of Theology,* 288.

10. See David Tracy, *The Analogical Imagination: Christian Theology and the Culture of Pluralism* (New York: Crossroad, 1981), 202–207, 376–386.

11. See Matthew Fox, *Sheer Joy: Conversations with Thomas Aquinas on Creation Spirituality* (San Francisco: HarperSanFrancisco, 1992), 30–37, and A. N. Williams, "Mystical Theology Redux: The Pattern of Aquinas' *Summa theologiae,*" *Modern Theology* 13.1 (January 1997): 53–74.

12. Josef Pieper, *Leisure: The Basis of Culture* (New York: Pantheon Books, 1952).

13. Jürgen Moltmann, *The Coming of God: Christian Eschatology* (Minneapolis: Fortress, 1996).

14. See Jürgen Moltmann, *The Church in the Power of the Spirit* (San Francisco: HarperSanFrancisco, 1991), 261–288; *The Trinity and the Kingdom* (San Francisco: HarperSanFrancisco, 1991), 152–153; *God in Creation: A New Theology of Creation and the Spirit of God* (San Francisco: HarperSanFrancisco, 1991), 276–280, 285–296; *The Spirit of Life: A Universal Affirmation* (Minneapolis: Fortress, 1992), 200–202, 301–305; *The Coming of God,* 323–339.

15. Otto H. Pesch, "Existential and Sapiential Theology: The Theological Confrontation between Luther and Thomas Aquinas," in Jared Wicks, ed., *Catholic Scholars Dialogue with Luther* (Chicago: Loyola University Press, 1970), 61–81.

16. Pesch, "Existential and Sapiential Theology," 81; also Otto H. Pesch, *Thomas von Aquin,* 49–50. For an ecumenical rapprochement in the interpreta-

tion of Aquinas and Luther in the 1960s through figures such as Stephanus Pfurtner, Otto Hermann Pesch, and Hans Vorster, and a possible contribution of Aquinas to Lutheran theology, see Ulrich Kuhn, "Thomas von Aquin und die evangelische Theologie," in Ludger Oeing-Hanhoff, ed., *Thomas von Aquin 1274–1974* (München: Kosel Verlag, 1974), 13–32.

17. Thomas Aquinas, *Commentary on the Sentences* I, q.1, art. 3, solution 1, in *Selected Writings*, 60.

18. I-II, 57, 2 ad 1; I-II, 66, 5 ad 4.

19. Aquinas, *Commentary on the Metaphysics*, preface, in *Selected Writings*, 719–721; *Commentary on the Sentences* I, art. 1, in *Selected Writings*, 55–57; SCG, I, 1, (1); SCG, 2, 24, (4); I, 1, 6; I, 1, 6, ad 2; I, 1, 6 ad 3; I-II, 66, 5 ad 1; II-II, 45, 1.

20. I, 39, 7 and 8.

21. SCG, 4, 11, (15).

22. CT, I, 216.

23. I, 34, 3.

24. III, 3, 8; SCG, 4, 13, (7) and (9).

25. III, 3, 8.

26. Aquinas, *Commentary on the Sentences* I, prologue, in *Selected Writings*, 51–54.

27. I, 39, 8; I, 22, 1.

28. SCG, 4, 20.

29. SCG, 4, 22, (5).

30. SCG, 4, 22, (6); also SCG, 4, 21 and 22.

31. I, 1, 3 ad 1.

32. I, 1, 3.

33. I, 14, 16, ad 2.

34. I, 1, 4.

35. II-II, 1, 8.

36. II-II, 2, 7; also II-II, 2, 5.

37. See I, 1, 1; also II-II, 2, 3; SCG 1, 5.

38. On the distinction between the content of revelation in the strict sense and *revelabilia*, see Etienne Gilson, *The Christian Philosophy of St. Thomas Aquinas*, 9–14. See the distinction between *revelata* and *revelabilia* in chapter 1.

39. I, 1, 1; II-II, 2, 4; SCG I, 4.

40. II-II, 180, 4.

41. See I, 1, 5.

42. I-II, 72, 4 ad 1.

43. II-II, 45, 3; II-II, 45, 3 ad 2 and 3; II-II, 45, 6.

44. I, 2, Prologue to the Three Parts of the *Summa Theologiae*. For a discussion of the plan of the *Summa Theologiae* around the exitus-reditus scheme and the place of the Incarnation in that scheme, see Marie-Dominique Chenu, *Toward Understanding Saint Thomas*, 310–318, and Jean-Pierre Torrell, *Saint*

Thomas Aquinas, vol. 1, *The Person and His Work,* trans. Robert Royal (Washington, DC: Catholic University of America Press, 1996, 145–159; Pesch, *Thomas von Aquin,* 381–400. For a different scheme, the exemplar and image scheme, as the plan of the *Summa,* see Michel Corbin, *Le chemin de la theologie chez Thomas D'Aquin,* 782–806. For grace as an organizing principle of the *Summa,* see Thomas F. O'Meara, "Grace as a Theological Structure in the *Summa Theologiae* of Thomas Aquinas," *Recherches de theologie ancienne et medievale* 55 (1988): 130–153. See the discussion of the structure of the *Summa* in chapter 1.

45. I, 62, 3, ad 3.
46. SCG, 3, 20, (2).
47. SCG, 3, 24, (8); SCG, 3, 21 and 22.
48. I-II, 2, 7.
49. SCG, 3, 28; I-II, 2, 2.
50. SCG, 3, 29; I-II, 2, 3.
51. SCG, III, 30; I-II, 2, 1.
52. SCG, 3, 31; I-II, 2, 4.
53. SCG, 3, 27, (10).
54. SCG, 3, 32; I-II, 2, 5.
55. SCG, 3, 33; I-II, 2, 6.
56. I-II, 2, 7.
57. SCG, 3, 34.
58. SCG, 3, 35.
59. SCG, 3, 36.
60. SCG, 3, 48; I-II, 2, 8; I-II, 3, 2 ad 4; I-II, 5, 3.
61. I-II, 3, 2.
62. I-II, 3, 2.
63. I-II, 3, 3.
64. SCG, 3, 26; I-II, 3, 4.
65. I, 82, 3 and 4.
66. SCG, 3, 26 (emphasis added)
67. SCG, 3, 25 (emphasis added).
68. II-II, 182, 1.
69. SCG, 3, 25, (9).
70. I-II, 3, 5 and 6.
71. SCG, 3, 26, (8) (emphasis added).
72. SCG, 3, 25, (3) (emphasis added).
73. SCG, 3, 25, (3).
74. SCG, 3, 37, (8).
75. SCG, 3, 37.
76. See II-II, 179, 2.
77. SCG, 3, 26 (emphasis added).
78. II-II, 182, 1.

79. See SCG, 3, 26.

80. SCG, 3, 37.

81. CT, I, 104.

82. I-II, 3, 8; CT, I, 103. For an elaborate recent analysis of the "natural desire to know" and its ontological/epistemological dynamics, see Jan Aertsen, *Nature and Creature: Thomas Aquinas's Way of Thought*, trans. Herbert Donald Morton (Leiden: E. J. Brill, 1988).

83. SCG, 3, 38.

84. SCG, 3, 3.

85. SCG, 3, 40.

86. I, 12, 5.

87. SCG, 3, 47; also CT, I, 105.

88. See I, 1, 7.

89. SCG, 1, 8.

90. I, 1, 9; also SCG, 1, 5.

91. I-II, 5, 5.

92. II-II, 81, 4.

93. I, 12, 4 ad 3.

94. *Boethius on the Trinity*, 1, 2.

95. I, 12, 5.

96. I, 12, 6; *On Truth*, 10, 11.

97. I, 12, 7; *Commentary on the Gospel of St. John*, 102–103; *Commentary on Saint Paul's First Letter to the Thessalonians and the Letter to the Philippians*, 103.

98. I, 12, 8 ad 4.

99. I, 12, 1–13; SCG, 3, 51–63.

100. Pierre Rousselot, *The Intellectualism of St. Thomas*, trans. James E. O'Mahony (New York: Sheed and Ward, 1935), 38–42.

101. Aquinas, *The Three Greatest Prayers*, 87–88.

102. For a very succinct summary of the epistemology of our knowledge of God through reason and faith, divine incomprehensibility, and the vision of the divine essence, see Emilio Brito, "Connaissance et inconnaisance de Dieu selon Thomas D'Aquin et Hegel," *Ephemerides theologicae lovanienses* 63.4 (1987): 327–338. For an Orthodox understanding of the vision of God, see Vladimir Lossky, *The Vision of God* (Crestwood, NY: St. Vladimir's Seminary Press, 1983). For a thorough recent textual discussion of why we cannot have a knowledge of what God is or a quidditative knowledge of God, see John F. Wippel, *The Metaphysical Thought of Thomas Aquinas*, 502–542.

103. I, 62, 4.

104. I, 62, 3 ad 3. On Rahner's distinction between being "intrinsic" and being "constitutive," see *Foundations of Christian Faith*, 185. It is precisely the whole point of Henri de Lubac, *The Mystery of the Supernatural*, trans.

Rosemary Sheed (New York: Herder and Herder, 1967), that, for Aquinas, by virtue of divine grace our "natural" desire is for the "supernatural," the beatific vision of God, not for the "natural," as Cajetan and Suarez taught. For further discussion of the natural desire for the supernatural, see Aertsen, *Nature and Creature*, 361–390; Stephen J. Duffy, *The Graced Horizon: Nature and Grace in Modern Catholic Thought* (Collegeville, MN: Liturgical Press, 1992), 66–84; Georges Cottier, "Desir naturel de voir Dieu," *Gregorianum* 78.4 (1997): 679–698; A. Vanneste, "Saint Thomas et le problème du surnaturel," *Ephemerides theologicae lovanienses* 64.4 (1988), 348–370.

105. See SCG, 3, 63, (10).

106. I-II, 66, 5 ad 2. I have throughout used "speculative," "theoretical," and "contemplative" as synonyms in Aquinas. See Torrell, *St. Thomas Aquinas*, vol. 1, 157.

107. I-II, 3, 6.

108. Aquinas, *Commentary on the Gospel of St. John*, 23–26.

109. II-II, 180, 1 ad 2; II-II, 180, 7. On mysticism as the fruit and crowning part of Aquinas's intellectualism, see Rousselot, *The Intellectualism of St. Thomas*, 190, 217.

110. II-II, 182, 1 ad 2; *Commentary on Metaphysics*, Lesson 1, 32, Lesson 2 and Lesson 3, in *Selected Writings*, 731–738.

111. Aristotle, *Metaphysics*, 1.2.

112. II-II, 182, 1; also 181, 1; SCG, 3, 25 and 37.

113. II-II, 182, 1. On the superiority of contemplation over action, see II-II, 182, 1 and SCG, 3, 37.

114. II-II, 182, 2.

115. See II-II, 182, 2.

116. II-II, 4, 2. Aristotle, *De Anima*, 3.10.

117. II-II, 180, 2; also 182, 4.

118. See I-II, 58, 5 ("Can there be intellectual virtue without moral virtue?"). For Aristotle's similar view, see Nicholas Lobkowicz, *Theory and Practice*, 12–14.

119. On the notion of immanence and self-presence as the essence and nobility of the intellect, see further Rousselot, *The Intellectualism of St. Thomas*, 17–33.

120. This, of course, is one of the classic criticisms of "sense certainty" in Hegel's *Phenomenology of Spirit*. On the human identity and mutual mediation of sense and intellect within the Thomist tradition, see Karl Rahner, *Spirit in the World*, trans. William Dych (New York: Herder & Herder, 1968), 32–33, 65–67, 117–118; *Hörer des Wortes*, ed. Johannes B. Metz (Münich: Kösel, 1963), 159 and 173–184; *Schriften zur Theologie*, VI (Einsiedeln: Benziger, 1965), 171–184 and 185–214.

121. See SCG, 3, 48.

122. *The Marx-Engels Reader,* 2nd ed., ed. Robert W. Tucker (New York: W. W. Norton, 1978), 54.

123. I am borrowing these arguments, in simplified form, from Camus' critique of the Kierkegaardian "leap of faith" in his *The Myth of Sisyphus* and Hegel's critique of dualistic otherworldliness in his *Phenomenology of Spirit.*

124. For further discussion of the dialectic of theory and praxis, see Clodovis Boff, *Theology and Praxis: Epistemological Foundations* (Marynoll, NY: Orbis, 1987), 159–194.

125. Etienne Gilson, *Reason and Revelation in the Middle Ages* (New York: Charles Scribner's Sons, 1938; repr., 1966), 70. Here Gilson is eulogizing Aquinas for solving the conflict between rationalism and fideism by "distinguishing" the order of nature and the order of grace. See also Leo XIII's eulogy of Aquinas in his encyclical, *Aeterni Patris.*

126. I tried to develop an outline of a philosophical anthropology of "concrete totality" in some of my previous works: "Praxis and Liberation: Toward a Theology of Concrete Totality" (Ph. D. diss., Vanderbilt University, 1989), 74–178; *Dialectic of Salvation: Issues in Theology of Liberation* (Albany, NY: SUNY Press, 1989), 163–169; *The Solidarity of Others in a Divided World: A Postmodern Theology after Postmodernism* (New York: T & T Clark International, 2004), 100–107.

Chapter 5.   Contemplating the Triune God

1. William J. Hill, *The Three-Personed God* (Washington, DC: Catholic University of America Press, 1982), 68–69; Gustave Martelet, "Theologie und Heilsökonomie in der Christologie der 'Tertia,' in Johannes B. Metz, Walter Kern, Adolf Darlapp, and Herbert Vorgrimler, eds., *Gott in Welt: Festgabe für Karl Rahner,* II (Freiburg: Herder, 1964), 5–10.

2. I, 32, 1 ad 3.

3. Aquinas, *Boethius on the Trinity,* 1, 4, in *Selected Writings,* 122–126; *On Truth,* 10, 13.

4. Richard of St. Victor actually claims, at the end of book 3 of his *De trinitate* (3, 25), that "behold now we have proved [probavimus] by clear and manifold reasons how true that is which we are commanded to believe, namely, that we venerate 'one God in trinity and trinity in unity,'" in Richard of St. Victor, *The Twelve Patriarchs, The Mystical Ark, Book Three of the Trinity,* trans. Grover A. Zinn (New York: Paulist, 1979), 397.

5. John Milbank and Catherine Pickstock, *Truth in Aquinas,* 52. One of the sources of the misunderstanding of Aquinas in this matter of the two uses of reason—adequately proving [probare] and merely showing [ostendere, manifestare] congruity—is the mistranslation in the five-volume work of the English Dominicans of "ratio quae inducitur ad manifestationem Trinitatis" as "reasons

avail to prove the Trinity" in the crucial passage of I, 32, 1 ad 2. There is a misleading confusion of *manifestare* with *probare*. For a thorough textual discussion of whether Aquinas is himself observing this distinction in his trinitarian theology, see Robert L. Richard, S.J., *The Problem of an Apologetical Perspective in the Trinitarian Theology of St. Thomas Aquinas* (Rome: Gregorian University Press, 1963).

6. On Richard of St. Victor's argument on the "necessity" of the Trinity on the basis of the nature of perfect charity as the highest goodness, see book 3 of his *De trinitate.* For Richard Swinburne's recent revival of the same argument, see his *The Christian God* (Oxford: Clarendon Press, 1994), 190. To Aquinas's critique of Richard of St. Victor, John O'Donnell adds that "his [Richard of St. Victor's] approach does not show why the community of persons in the Trinity has three and only three persons nor does this approach indicate the order of the processions. These limits reveal that the community model taken alone is insufficient to illumine the total reality of the Trinity"; see John O'Donnell, "The Trinity as Divine Community: A Critical Reflection Upon Recent Theological Developments," *Gregorianum* 69.1 (1988): 10.

7. Walter Kasper, *The God of Jesus Christ* (New York: Crossroad, 1984), 268.

8. For this discussion of our knowledge of the Trinity, see I, 32, 1, and I, 12, 13 ad 1; SCG, 4, 1, [10]; LaCugna, *God for Us,* 168.

9. I, 29, 3 ad 1, and 32, 2 ad 1; I, 36, 2 ad 1; I, 39, 2 ad 2.

10. I, 13, 2. For analogy, see I, 12, 12, and the whole of I, 13. The literature on analogy in Aquinas is vast. For some of the older works, see Gerald B. Phelan, *Saint Thomas and Analogy* (Milwaukee: Marquette University Press, 1948), and George P. Klubertanz, *St. Thomas Aquinas on Analogy: A Textual Analysis and Systematic Synthesis* (Chicago: Loyola University Press, 1960). For some recent discussions, see John F. Wippel, *The Metaphysical Thought of Thomas Aquinas,* 543–571; Philip A. Rolnick, *Analogical Possibilities: How Words Refer to God* (Atlanta: Scholars Press, 1993); Gregory P. Rocca, "Aquinas on God-Talk: Hovering over the Abyss," *Theological Studies* 54.4 (1993): 641–661; Kenneth Surin, "Creation, Revelation, and the Analogy Theory"; William P. Alston, "Aquinas on Theological Predication: A Look Backward and a Look Forward," in Eleonore Stump, ed., *Reasoned Faith: Essays in Philosophical Theology in Honor of Norman Kretzmann* (Ithaca, NY: Cornell University Press, 1993), 145–178; Nicholas Lash, "Ideology, Metaphor and Analogy," in Brian Hebblethwaite and Stewart Sutherland, eds., *The Philosophical Frontiers of Christian Theology: Essays Presented to D. M. Mackinnon* (Cambridge: Cambridge University Press, 1982), 68–94; Henry Chavannes, *The Analogy between God and the World in Saint Thomas Aquinas and Karl Barth,* trans. William Lumley (New York: Vantage Press, 1992); Joseph Palakeel, *The Use of Analogy in Theological Discourse: An Investigation in Ecumenical Perspective* (Rome: Editrice Pontificia Universita Gregoriana, 1995).

11. I, 13, 3. Gregory P. Rocca, O.P., reminds us that for Aquinas all names that denote finitude as such, not only materiality, should be predicated of God metaphorically, not analogically. See his *Speaking the Incomprehensible God: Thomas Aquinas on the Interplay of Positive and Negative Theology* (Washington, DC: Catholic University of America Press, 2004), 318–322.

12. I, 13, 4.

13. I, 39, 2; 39, 4; 39, 5.

14. I, 27, 1.

15. St. Thomas Aquinas, *The Three Greatest Prayers,* 51.

16. SCG, 4, 24, [5].

17. Aquinas, *The Three Greatest Prayers,* 52.

18. I, 12; I, 27, 1. For a discussion of the diversity of emanation or procession consequent on the diversity of natures and the correspondence between the perfection of the nature of the principle and the degree of immanence of what proceeds in the principle, see SCG, 4, 11, [1]–[5]. On the relation between the internal and the external word, see further *On Truth,* 4, 1.

19. I, 27, 5 ad 3; SCG, 4, 26, [2].

20. Aquinas, *Commentary on the Gospel of St. John,* 34.

21. I, 27, 3.

22. I, 27, 2; SCG, 4, 11, [9]–[13], and 26, [6] for an earlier discussion of the generation of the Son on the model of intellectual conception in God.

23. I, 27, 4.

24. SCG, 4, 23, [13].

25. I, 27, 4 ad 1, ad 2 and ad 3; I, 30, 2 ad 2; SCG, 4, 19, [9].

26. I, 28, 3; SCG, 4, 14, [12].

27. I, 28, 4.

28. I, 40, 2; David S. Cunningham, "Developing Alternative Trinitarian Formulas," *Anglican Theological Review* 80.1 (Winter 1998), 18.

29. SCG, 4, 24, [7]; *On Power,* 7, 8, in *Selected Writings,* 327–330.

30. Cunningham, "Developing Alternative Trinitarian Formulas," 16.

31. LaCugna, *God for Us,* 153.

32. I, 28, 1; SCG, 4, 14, [11]; I, 13, 7; I, 45, 3. For an illuminating recent discussion of the Thomistic notion of relation and its implications for the issue of whether God's relation to the world can be real, not merely logical, see Earl Muller, "Real Relations and the Divine: Issues in Thomas's Understanding of God's Relation to the World," *Theological Studies* 56.4 (1995): 673–695.

33. I, 28, 2.

34. Cunningham, "Developing Alternative Trinitarian Formulas," 15.

35. Aquinas, *On Power,* 7, 8.

36. Cornelius Plantinga, Jr., "Social Trinity and Tritheism," in Ronald J. Feenstra and Cornelius Plantinga, Jr., eds., *Trinity, Incarnation, and Atonement* (Notre Dame, IN: University of Notre Dame Press, 1989), 40.

37. I, 28, 3 ad 1.

38. I, 29, 1; I, 29, 2; I, 29, 2 ad 1 and ad 2; I, 30, 1 ad 1. For a discussion of the terminology of "substance" in classical trinitarian theology and some contemporary criticism of that terminology, see William P. Alston, "Substance and the Trinity," in Stephen Davis, Daniel Kendall, and Gerald O'Collins, eds., *The Trinity* (Oxford: Oxford University Press, 1999), 179–201.

39. I, 29, 3.

40. I, 29, 4.

41. I, 30, 1.

42. I, 30, 2.

43. I, 30, 3.

44. I, 30, 4.

45. I, 31, 1 ad 1.

46. I, 31, 2.

47. I, 31, 3.

48. I, 32, 2.

49. I, 32, 3.

50. I, 32, 2.

51. LaCugna, *God for Us,* 164.

52. I, 39, 5 ad 6.

53. I, 33, 1. For a discussion of different kinds of ordering of one thing to another—such as in quantified things, time, learning, and production of things—and the meaning of "principle" in each case, see Aquinas, *Commentary on the Gospel of St. John,* 36–37.

54. Leonardo Boff, *Trinity and Society* (Maryknoll, NY: Orbis, 1987), 141–144. For a study of Aquinas's early reflections on the Father as principle, see Gilles Emery, "Le Père et l'oeuvre de creation selon le Commentaire des Sentences de S. Thomas d'Aquin," in Carlos-Josaphat Pinto de Oliveira, O.P., ed., *Ordo Sapientiae et Amoris* (Fribourg: Editions Universitaires, 1993), 85–118.

55. I, 33, 1.

56. I, 33, 2; SCG, 4, 11, [16] and [17].

57. Aquinas, *Commentary on Saint Paul's Epistle to the Ephesians,* 139; *Super Epistolam B. Pauli ad Ephesios lectura,* c. 3, l. 4; *De Veritate,* 4, 4.

58. John D. Zizioulas, "The Doctrine of the Holy Trinity: The Significance of the Cappadocian Contribution," in Christoph Schwöbel, ed., *Trinitarian Theology Today: Essays on Divine Being and Act* (Edinburgh: T & T Clark, 1995), 60; Thomas F. Torrance, *The Christian Doctrine of God,* 137–141, 157–161, 193.

59. For example, Janet Martin Soskice claims that for Aquinas "father" was a metaphor as applied to God; see her essay, "Can a Feminist Call God 'Father'?" in Alvin F. Kimel, Jr., ed., *Speaking the Christian God: The Holy Trinity and the Challenge of Feminism* (Grand Rapids, MI: Eerdmans, 1992), 83. See also Thomas Marsh, *The Triune God: A Biblical, Historical, and Theological Study* (Mystic,

CT: Twenty-Third Publications, 1994), 189. I am concerned here only with "father" in the sense of "begetter" who shares the same nature with the begotten, not in the sense of a male parent. On the issue of the sexism of the trinitarian language in Aquinas, see chapter 6, "The Problem of Sexist Language."

60. *Super Epistolam B. Pauli ad Ephesios lectura,* c. 1, l. 2.

61. *Super Epistolam B. Pauli ad Ephesios lectura,* c. 3, l. 4.

62. I, 33, 3; Wolfhart Pannenberg, *Systematic Theology,* I, 325–26.

63. I, 33, 4.

64. For the development of the concept of "word" in Aquinas, see A. F. von Gunten, O.P., "In Principio Erat Verbum: Une evolution de saint Thomas en theologie trinitaire," in Carlos-Josaphat Pinto de Oliveira, O.P., ed., *Ordo Sapientiae et Amoris* (Fribourg: Editions Universitaires, 1993), 119–141.

65. I, 34, 1; *On Truth,* 4, 2.

66. I, 34, 1 ad 3.

67. Aquinas, *Commentary on the Gospel of St. John,* 34.

68. I, 34, 2 ad 4.

69. SCG, 4, 13, [7]; *On Truth,* 4, 4.

70. Aquinas, *Commentary on the Gospel of St. John,* 36, 52, 66–69; SCG, 4, 13, [11].

71. I, 34, 3; I, 13, 7; *On Truth,* 4, 5.

72. I, 35, 1.

73. I, 35, 2.

74. SCG, 4, 11, [16].

75. I, 35, 2 ad 3.

76. Charles Andre Bernard, S.J., "Mystère trinitaire et transformation en Dieu," *Gregorianum* 80.3 (1999): 454; see SCG, 4, 11, [14].

77. Aquinas, *Commentary on the Gospel of St. John,* 79; *Super Evangelium S. Ioannis lectura,* c. 6, l. 5.

78. Aquinas, *Commentary on the Gospel of St. John,* 35; I, 34, 2 ad 1 and ad 3.

79. On the etymology of "spirit" in Aquinas, see SCG, 4, 23, [2].

80. I, 36, 1; SCG, 4, 19, [10]–[11].

81. SCG, 4, 24, [2] and [7].

82. SCG, 4, 24, [12].

83. SCG, 4, 24, [13].

84. SCG, 4, 24, [4] and [14], and 25, [5].

85. For these arguments why the Holy Spirit also proceeds from the Son, see I, 36, 2; I, 36, 4; SCG, 4, 24, [9] and [10].

86. SCG, 4, 24, [11].

87. I, 36, 4 ad 1; I, 37, 1 ad 3. For a thorough historical, biblical, and theological study of the Holy Spirit as the mutual love of the Father and the Son, see Patrick Coffee, "The Holy Spirit as the Mutual Love of the Father and the Son," *Theological Studies* 51.2 (June 1990): 193–229. For a historical study of Aquinas's

indebtedness to the patristic tradition on the Filioque, see Jaroslav Pelikan, "The Doctrine of Filioque in Thomas Aquinas and Its Patristic Antecedents," *St. Thomas Aquinas 1274–1974: Commemorative Studies* (Toronto: Pontifical Institute of Medieval Studies, 1974), 315–336.

88. Jürgen Moltmann, *The Trinity and the Kingdom*, 167.

89. I, 36, 3. See also William J. Hill, *The Three-Personed God*, 73–77, for Aquinas's rejection of the Dionysian idea that the Father was *fons divinitatis* prior to the generation of the Son and the spiration of the Holy Spirit.

90. I, 37, 1.

91. I, 37, 2.

92. SCG, 4, 21, 2; Bernard, "Mystère trinitaire et transformation en Dieu," 458–461.

93. I, 38, 1.

94. I, 38, 1.

95. I, 38, 2.

96. I, 39, 1.

97. I, 39, 2.

98. I, 39, 3.

99. *On Truth*, 7, 3 (my translation); see Karl Barth, *Church Dogmatics*, vol. I, part 1, 373.

100. I, 39, 7; SCG, 4, 12, [3]–[4].

101. I, 39, 5 ad 6.

102. I, 39, 8; *On Truth*, 7, 3. For a discussion of the appropriation of transcendentals to the Trinity, especially "truth" to the Son, see Norman Kretzmann, "Trinity and Transcendentals," in Ronald J. Feenstra and Cornelius Plantinga, Jr., eds., *Trinity, Incarnation, and Atonement* (Notre Dame, IN: University of Notre Dame Press, 1989), 79–100.

103. I, 39, 8; Leonardo Boff, *Trinity and Society*, 141.

104. I, 45, 6. On the early development of the idea in Aquinas that the eternal divine processions are the cause and reason for the procession of creatures, and a comparative study of Albert the Great, Bonaventure, and Aquinas on the subject, see Gilles Emery, "Trinité et creation: le principe trinitaire de la creation dans les commentaires d'Albert Le Grand, de Bonaventure et de Thomas d'Aquin sur les *Sentences*," *Revue des sciences philosophiques et theologiques* 79 (1995): 405–430.

105. I, 45, 6; *Commentary on the Gospel of St. John*, 51.

106. I, 45, 7.

107. LaCugna, *God for Us*, 165–166.

108. Robert W. Jenson, *The Triune Identity: God According to the Gospel* (Philadelphia: Fortress, 1982), 126. Wolfhart Pannenberg repeats the same charge against Aquinas; see his *Systematic Theology*, II, 26.

109. I, 32, 1 ad 3.

110. I, 40, 1.

111. I, 41, 1.

112. I, 41, 2.

113. *Super Evangelium S. Ioannis lectura,* c. 3, l. 5.

114. I, 41, 3.

115. I, 41, 5.

116. I, 41, 5 ad 1, 2, and 3.

117. SCG, 4, 26, [4].

118. SCG, 4, 13, [1] and 26, [2].

119. SCG, 4, 26, [5]; I, 30, 2 ad 4.

120. I, 41, 6.

121. SCG, 4, 13, [3]–[4], and 26, [2].

122. See the comparative discussion of Rahner and Lonergan on the question of the self-consciousness among the divine persons by Walter Kasper, *The God of Jesus Christ,* 289; John O'Donnell, "The Trinity as Divine Community," 33.

123. I, 42, 1.

124. I, 42, 4. For a discussion of the sharing of the numerically identical divine nature as the ontological foundation of the perichoresis of the divine persons in Athanasius and the Cappadocians, see Thomas F. Torrance, *The Christian Doctrine of God,* 125–127.

125. I, 42, 4 ad 3.

126. I, 30, 1 ad 4.

127. I, 42, 2; SCG, 4, 11, [18], and 14, [3]; *Commentary on the Gospel of St. John,* 38–39.

128. I, 42, 3.

129. I, 42, 5.

130. I, 42, 5; SCG, 4, 14, [4].

131. Torrance, *The Christian Doctrine of God,* 176.

132. Torrance, *The Christian Doctrine of God,* 178.

133. Torrance, *The Christian Doctrine of God,* 176–190; Torrance identifies his position emphasizing being or ousia rather than person, and the monarchy of the Trinity rather than the monarchy of the Father, with that of Athanasius and Gregory of Nazianzen over against Basil and Gregory of Nyssa, who presumably emphasized person and the monarchy of the Father rather than ousia and the monarchy of the Trinity. Let me simply register my serious reservation about this interpretation of Athanasius and the three Cappadocians.

134. Torrance, *The Christian Doctrine of God,* 193.

135. I, 41, 5.

136. I, 41, 3.

137. I, 42, 3.

138. I, 39, 5 ad 6.

139. I cannot go into the details of the trinitarian discussion among the Fathers, but I find it imperative to call attention to the fact that Athanasius, the Cappadocians, Hilary of Poitier, and Augustine have all found the terminology of father and son—already given in Scripture—and the analogy of generation the most fruitful paradigm in suggesting the identity of nature and relational difference constitutive of the immanent Trinity. See, for example, Athanasius, *Contra Arianos,* I, 9, 16, 26, 28; III, 1, 3, 6, 9, 20; IV, 1–5; Gregory of Nazianzen, *Oratio* XXIX, 10, 15; XXX, 11, 20; Gregory of Nyssa, *Contra Eunomium,* I, 14–16, 22, 32, 33, 34, 38, 39; II, 1, 9; III, 3, 4, 7; Hilary of Poitier, *De Trinitate,* I, 17; II, 3; III, 3, 4, 23; IV, 4, 6; XII, 17, 21, 23, 25, 32; Augustine, *De Trinitate,* II, 2.

140. See the next chapter for a detailed discussion of Moltmann and Pannenberg on this and other points.

141. I, 41, 5 ad 1, 2, and 3. For a defense of Thomas Torrance against Colin Gunton on a related issue, see Paul D. Molnar, *Divine Freedom and the Doctrine of the Immanent Trinity: In Dialogue with Karl Barth and Contemporary Theology* (London: T & T Clark, 2002), 317–330.

142. I, 43, 1.

143. I, 43, 2.

144. I, 8, 3.

145. I, 43, 3.

146. I, 43, 4.

147. I, 43, 5.

148. For an excellent discussion of how this renewal takes place in us in relation to each of the three persons, see Charles Andre Bernard, S.J., "Mystère trinitaire et transformation en Dieu," 441–467.

149. I, 43, 6; on the effects of the Holy Spirit in us, SCG, 4, 20–22.

150. SCG, 4, 23, [4].

151. I, 43, 7.

Chapter 6.   Contemporary Trinitarian Discussions in Light of Aquinas

1. On Aquinas's trinitarian theology as a synthesis of East and West, see Walter Kasper, *The God of Jesus Christ,* 298.

2. Kasper, *The God of Jesus Christ,* 311; Nicholas Lash, "Considering the Trinity," *Modern Theology* 2.3 (1986): 183.

3. For a survey of contemporary issues in trinitarian theology, see Gerald O'Collins, "The Holy Trinity: The State of the Questions," in Stephen Davis, Daniel Kendall, and Gerald O'Collins, eds., *The Trinity* (Oxford: Oxford University Press, 1999), 1–25; Ted Peters, *God as Trinity: Relationality and Temporality in Divine Life* (Louisville, KY: Westminster/John Knox Press, 1993), 27–80; Christoph Schwöbel, *Trinitarian Theology Today,* 1–30; articles by Elizabeth A.

Johnson, Donald H. Juel, Colon Gunton, Ian A. McFarland, James P. Mackey, and Ellen T. Charry in *Theology Today* 54.3 (October 1997): 299–380.

4. Rudolf Steiner, *The Redemption of Thinking: A Study in the Philosophy of Thomas Aquinas,* trans. A. P. Shepherd and Mildred Robertson Nicoll (London: Hodder and Stoughton, 1956), 23.

5. Moltmann, *The Trinity and the Kingdom,* 170.

6. Ruth C. Duck, for example, claims that all names of God are not "literal" but "metaphorical," whether "rock" or "father," without making a further distinction between univocal and analogical, and in fact reduces analogy to similarity without the "tension of identity and difference" characteristic of the metaphor, practically identifying the metaphor with Aquinas's analogical predication but without making Aquinas's further distinction between analogy and metaphor. See her *Gender and the Name of God: The Trinitarian Baptismal Formula* (New York: Pilgrim Press, 1991), 13, 22.

7. A critique of the sexism of language, especially theological language, as both source and reflection of sexism in culture, has been central to feminist theology since Mary Daly's *Beyond God the Father,* and the literature on the subject has grown vast. For a comprehensive survey of the feminist critique of theological language, especially trinitarian language, see Duck, *Gender and the Name of God.*

8. Robert W. Jenson, "The Father, He . . ." in Alvin F. Kimel, Jr., ed., *Speaking the Christian God: The Holy Trinity and the Challenge of Feminism* (Grand Rapids, MI: Eerdmans, 1992), 96.

9. Kimel, editor's introduction, *Speaking the Christian God,* ix.

10. Thomas F. Torrance, "The Christian Apprehension of God the Father," in Kimel, *Speaking the Christian God,* 140; also Augustine J. DiNoia, "Knowing and Naming the Triune God: The Grammar of Trinitarian Confession," in Kimel, *Speaking the Christian God,* 183–186.

11. Elizabeth Achtemeier, "Exchanging God for 'No Gods': A Discussion of Female Language for God," in Kimel, *Speaking the Christian God,* 6. See also Jenson, "The Father, He . . . ," 103.

12. Achtemeier, "Exchanging God for 'No Gods,' " 8–15; Robert W. Jenson, *The Triune Identity* (Philadelphia: Fortress, 1982), 15.

13. Pannenberg, *Systematic Theology,* I, 262.

14. DiNoia, "Knowing and Naming the Triune God," 186–187; Jenson, "The Father, He . . . ," 108; Jenson, *The Triune Identity,* 15.

15. SCG, 4, 11, [19]

16. I–II, 81, 5.

17. Jenson, *The Triune Identity,* 16.

18. DiNoia, "Knowing and Naming the Triune God," 183–186.

19. Jenson, *The Triune Identity,* 16.

20. Jenson, *The Triune Identity,* 18.

21. Peter van Inwagen, "And Yet They Are Not Three Gods But One God," in Thomas V. Morris, ed., *Philosophy and the Christian Faith* (Notre Dame, IN: University of Notre Dame Press, 1988), 247.

22. Jenson, *The Triune Identity*, 17; Torrance, "The Christian Apprehension of God the Father," 141.

23. Donald Bloesch, *The Battle for the Trinity* (Ann Arbor, MI: Servant Publications, 1985), 50; Duck, *Gender and the Name of God*, 174; Torrance, "The Christian Apprehension of God the Father," 141; Wainwright, *Doxology*, 353.

24. DiNoia, "Knowing and Naming the Triune God," 172.

25. DiNoia, "Knowing and Naming the Triune God," 172.

26. Duck, *Gender and the Name of God*, 185–189.

27. Duck, *Gender and the Name of God*, 166.

28. Duck, *Gender and the Name of God*, 163–166.

29. Duck, *Gender and the Name of God*, 55–57.

30. Duck, *Gender and the Name of God*, 56–57.

31. Jürgen Moltmann, *The Trinity and the Kingdom*, 19.

32. Moltmann, *The Trinity and the Kingdom*, 10–19. For a critique of Barth and Rahner as representatives of the "reflection trinity of the absolute subject," see 139–148.

33. Moltmann, *The Trinity and the Kingdom*, 19.

34. Moltmann, *The Trinity and the Kingdom*, 64.

35. Moltmann, *The Trinity and the Kingdom*, 75.

36. Moltmann, *The Trinity and the Kingdom*, 83.

37. Moltmann, *The Trinity and the Kingdom*, 88.

38. Moltmann, *The Trinity and the Kingdom*, 94–95.

39. Moltmann, *The Trinity and the Kingdom*, 95–96.

40. Moltmann, *The Trinity and the Kingdom*, 150; *Trinität und Reich Gottes: Zur Gotteslehre* (München: Christian Kaiser, 1980), 167.

41. Moltmann, *The Trinity and the Kingdom*, 150.

42. Moltmann, *The Trinity and the Kingdom*, 157–158.

43. Moltmann, *The Trinity and the Kingdom*, 165.

44. Moltmann, *The Trinity and the Kingdom*, 165.

45. Moltmann, *The Trinity and the Kingdom*, 165–166.

46. Moltmann, *The Trinity and the Kingdom*, 168.

47. Moltmann, *The Trinity and the Kingdom*, 170.

48. Moltmann, *The Trinity and the Kingdom*, 170.

49. Moltmann, *The Trinity and the Kingdom*, 172.

50. Moltmann, *The Trinity and the Kingdom*, 173.

51. Moltmann, *The Trinity and the Kingdom*, 172.

52. Moltmann, *The Trinity and the Kingdom*, 173; *Trinität und Reich Gottes*, 189.

53. Moltmann, *The Trinity and the Kingdom*, 173; *Trinität und Reich Gottes*, 190.

54. Moltmann, *The Trinity and the Kingdom*, 175.

55. Moltmann, *The Trinity and the Kingdom*, 175; emphases are mine.

56. Moltmann, *The Trinity and the Kingdom*, 176.

57. Moltmann, *The Trinity and the Kingdom*, 178.

58. For a good summary presentation of his position, see Jürgen Moltmann, "Some Reflections on the Social Doctrine of the Trinity," in James M. Byrne, ed., *The Christian Understanding of God Today* (Dublin: Columba, 1993), 104–111.

59. Pannenberg, *Systematic Theology*, I, 294–299.

60. Pannenberg, *Systematic Theology*, I, 335.

61. Pannenberg, *Systematic Theology*, I, 336.

62. Pannenberg, *Systematic Theology*, I, 334.

63. Pannenberg, *Systematic Theology*, I, 321.

64. Pannenberg, *Systematic Theology*, I, 300–320.

65. Pannenberg, *Systematic Theology*, I, 325; emphasis added.

66. Pannenberg, *Systematic Theology*, I, 325; emphasis added.

67. Pannenberg, *Systematic Theology*, I, 327; emphasis added.

68. Pannenberg, *Systematic Theology*, I, 335.

69. Pannenberg, *Systematic Theology*, I, 272, 278, 283.

70. Pannenberg, *Systematic Theology*, I, 333–336.

71. Pannenberg, *Systematic Theology*, I, 359; *Systematische Theologie*, I (Göttingen: Vandenhoeck & Ruprecht, 1988), 388.

72. Pannenberg, *Systematic Theology*, I, 358; *Systematische Theologie*, I, 388.

73. Pannenberg, *Systematic Theology*, I, 383; *Systematische Theologie*, I, 415.

74. Pannenberg, *Systematic Theology*, I, 383–384.

75. Pannenberg, *Systematic Theology*, I, 385.

76. Pannenberg, *Systematic Theology*, I, 385; *Systematische Theologie*, I, 417.

77. Pannenberg, *Systematic Theology*, I, 426–427.

78. Pannenberg, *Systematic Theology*, I, 428.

79. Pannenberg, *Systematic Theology*, I, 428.

80. Pannenberg, *Systematic Theology*, I, 431.

81. Pannenberg, *Systematic Theology*, I, 428.

82. Pannenberg, *Systematic Theology*, I, 428.

83. Pannenberg, *Systematic Theology*, I, 429.

84. Both quotations are from Pannenberg, *Systematic Theology*, I, 429; emphasis has been added.

85. Pannenberg, *Systematic Theology*, I, 430.

86. Pannenberg, *Systematic Theology*, I, 430.

87. Pannenberg, *Systematic Theology*, I, 432.

88. Pannenberg, *Systematic Theology*, I, 432, 392.

89. Pannenberg, *Systematic Theology*, I, 445.

90. Pannenberg, *Systematic Theology*, I, 447; *Systematische Theologie*, 482.

91. Pannenberg, *Systematic Theology*, I, 447. For a summary of Pannenberg's doctrine of God, see Stanley J. Grenz, *Reason for Hope: The Systematic Theology of Wolfhart Pannenberg* (New York: Oxford University Press, 1990), 44–78. I would like to mention three other creative steps Pannenberg takes in his trinitarian theology which I have not had room to discuss in this section. They are (1) the application of the metaphysics of divine self-manifestation to God's economic relations to the world through the mediation of the concept and structure of "action," (2) the systematic introduction of the Hegelian concept and logic of the "true infinite" into the interpretation of the divine attributes and the economic trinity, and (3) the interpretation of the trinitarian movement as the concrete source and fulfilment of the logic of the true infinite.

92. Cornelius Plantinga, Jr., "Social Trinity and Tritheism," in Ronald J. Feenstra and Cornelius Plantinga, Jr., eds., *Trinity, Incarnation, and Atonement* (Notre Dame IN: University of Notre Dame Press, 1989), 22.

93. Plantinga, "Social Trinity and Tritheism," 27–28.

94. Plantinga, "Social Trinity and Tritheism," 28.

95. Plantinga, "Social Trinity and Tritheism," 28–29.

96. All the quotes in this paragraph are from Plantinga, "Social Trinity and Tritheism," 28–29.

97. For a critique of this "social" interpretation of the Trinity in at least Gregory of Nyssa, see Sarah Coakley, " 'Persons' in the 'Social' Doctrine of the Trinity: A Critique of Current Analytic Discussion," in Stephen T. Davis, Daniel Kendall, and Gerald O'Collins, eds., *The Trinity* (Oxford: Oxford University Press, 1999), 124–144.

98. All the quotes in this paragraph are from Plantinga, "Social Trinity and Tritheism," 31.

99. Plantinga, "Social Trinity and Tritheism," 36.

100. David Brown, *The Divine Trinity* (London: Duckworth, 1985), 291.

101. Plantinga, "Social Trinity and Tritheism," 40.

102. Plantinga, "Social Trinity and Tritheism," 37–42. For similar versions of social trinitarianism, see Richard Swinburne, "Trinity," in *The Christian God* (Oxford: Clarendon Press, 1994), 170–191; David Brown, "The Coherence of the Trinity," in *The Divine Trinity*, 272–304; Peter van Inwagen, "And Yet They Are Not Three Gods But One God," in Thomas V. Morris, ed., *Philosophy and the Christian Faith* (Notre Dame, IN: University of Notre Dame Press, 1988), 271–272.

103. Swinburne, "Trinity," 189.

104. Pannenberg, *Systematic Theology*, I, 272, 278, and 283.

105. Pannenberg, *Systematic Theology*, I, 283, 288.

106. Pannenberg, *Systematic Theology*, I, 325.

107. Moltmann, *The Trinity and the Kingdom*, 176.

108. For this reason I don't quite understand how one can speak of Pannenberg's "emphasis on the monarchy of the Father," as does Roger Olson, "Wolfhart Pannenberg's Doctrine of the Trinity," *Scottish Journal of Theology* 43.2 (1990): 203.

109. See also Juan A. Martinez Camino, "Wechselseitige Selbstunterscheidung? Zur Trinitätslehre Wolfhart Pannenbergs," in Hans-Ludwig Ollig and Oliver J. Wietz, eds., *Reflektierter Glaube* (München: Verlag Dr. Hansel-Hohenhausen, 1999), 142–145. Camino speaks of the monarchy of the Father as the power of giving one's entire essence so as to invalidate the opposition between the relation of origin and the reciprocity of relations that Pannenberg insists on.

110. Pannenberg, *Systematic Theology*, I, 421 and 429 respectively.

111. Pannenberg, *Systematic Theology*, II, 390.

112. Pannenberg, *Systematic Theology*, I, 429; also 317. On the idea of the self-distinction of the Son from the Father and the mutual self-distinction of the divine persons, see his *Systematic Theology*, I, 300–326, and II, 20–34 and 372–396.

113. Hill, *The Three-Personed God*, 159.

114. Pannenberg, *Systematic Theology*, I, 428.

115. Pannenberg, *Systematic Theology*, I, 428.

116. Pannenberg, *Systematic Theology*, I, 320.

117. Pannenberg, *Systematic Theology*, I, 320.

118. Pannenberg, *Systematic Theology*, I, 310 and 311 respectively.

119. Pannenberg, *Systematic Theology*, I, 429.

120. Pannenberg, *Systematic Theology*, II, 386.

121. Pannenberg, *Systematic Theology*, II, 22.

122. Pannenberg, *Systematic Theology*, I, 421.

123. Pannenberg, *Systematic Theology*, I, 421.

124. Pannenberg, *Systematic Theology*, II, 24.

125. Pannenberg, *Systematic Theology*, II, 24.

126. On the internal relation between essence and relation in Pannenberg, see his *Systematic Theology*, I, 335 and 367.

127. Pannenberg, *Systematic Theology*, I, 385.

128. Pannenberg, Systematic Theology, I, 432.

129. Pannenberg, *Systematic Theology*, I, 383–384, 429.

130. Pannenberg, *Systematic Theology*, I, 335, 358–359, 428.

131. Pannenberg, *Systematic Theology*, I, 447.

132. Pannenberg, *Systematic Theology*, I, 358–359.

133. Pannenberg, *Systematic Theology*, I, 383; *Systematische Theologie*, I, 415.

134. Pannenberg, *Systematic Theology*, I, 385.

135. Pannenberg, *Systematic Theology*, I, 385.

136. Pannenberg, *Systematic Theology*, I, 430.

137. Pannenberg, *Systematic Theology*, I, 430.

138. Pannenberg, *Systematic Theology,* I, 428.

139. Pannenberg, *Systematic Theology,* I, 429.

140. Christoph Schwöbel, "Wolfhart Pannenberg," in David F. Ford, ed., *The Modern Theologians: An Introduction to Christian Theology in the Twentieth Century,* 2nd ed. (Cambridge, MA: Blackwell, 1997), 192.

141. Pannenberg, *Systematic Theology,* I, 432.

142. Ingolf F. Dalferth, "The Eschatological Roots of the Doctrine of the Trinity," in Christoph Schwöbel, ed., *Trinitarian Theology Today: Essays on Divine Being and Act* (Edinburgh: T & T Clark, 1995), 154.

143. Pannenberg, *Systematic Theology,* I, 288ff.

144. Pannenberg seems to concede as much when he allows for the possibility of beginning with a treatise on the one God and proceeding to the treatise on the triune God, even with "a trace" of the derivation of the trinitarian distinctions from the divine unity, without this "trace" necessarily determining the systematic treatment of the doctrine of God, as long as the unity of God initially at stake is clearly understood, from the beginning, to be the unity of the trinitarian God, a possibility that Pannenberg believes was demonstrated in the case of Gregory of Nyssa and John of Damascus. See Pannenberg, *Systematic Theology,* I, 289.

145. Pannenberg, *Systematic Theology,* I, 358; Pannenberg makes this identification of the essence with the "sum total" of its manifestations in the context of God's self-manifestation in the world, but I take this also to apply to his conception of the relation of the divine essence to its manifestations in the divine persons as well, since the same dialectical understanding is operative in his understanding of the divine essence and the persons and since he does not anywhere, as far as I know, indicate the rejection of that application.

146. Moltmann, *The Trinity and the Kingdom,* 172.

147. For a more detailed critique of contemporary "social trinitarians" such as Richard Swinburne, David Brown, and Cornelius Plantinga, see Brian Leftow, "Anti Social Trinitarianism," in Stephen Davis, Daniel Kendall, and Gerald O'Collins, eds., *The Trinity* (Oxford: Oxford University Press, 1999), 203–249.

Chapter 7.   Toward a Dialectic of Prophetic and Sapiential Theology

1. On these issues, see Chenu, *Toward Understanding St. Thomas,* 301–322; Per Erik Persson, *Sacra Doctrina: Reason and Revelation in Aquinas,* trans. Ross Mackenzie (Philadelphia: Fortress, 1970), 285–290; Kuhn, *Via Caritatis,* 225–272, which provides a detailed response to standard Protestant objections over the issue of law and gospel; and Rogers, *Thomas Aquinas and Karl Barth,* which interprets Aquinas "in the direction of Karl Barth" (3).

2. On the notion of a "classic," see David Tracy, *The Analogical Imagination,* 99–153.

3. See Rahner, *Foundations of Christian Faith,* 46–51.

4. Tracy, *Analogical Imagination,* 51–52.

5. Michael Vater, "Religion, Worldliness, and *Sittlichkeit,*" in David Kolb, ed., *New Perspectives on Hegel's Philosophy of Religion* (Albany: State University of New York Press, 1992), 212.

6. II–II, 179, 1 ad 2; II–II, 179, 2; II–II, 181, 1; I, 79, 7.

7. Gustavo Gutierrez, *A Theology of Liberation: History, Politics, and Salvation,* 15th anniversary ed. (Maryknoll, NY: Orbis, 1988), 11 and 10 respectively.

8. For an excellent analysis of the concept of the historical "relevance" of theology, see Clodovis Boff, *Theology and Praxis: Epistemological Foundations* (Maryknoll, NY: Orbis, 1987), 175–185.

9. I make a distinction here between the critical "perception" or "consciousness" of a crisis as a crisis and the "crisis" itself. We may no longer perceive a crisis as a central crisis (e.g., the plight of African Americans) either (1) because the crisis has been resolved, (2) because we are too tired to pay sustained attention to the crisis that still persists, (3) because the crisis has become part of a larger global crisis in the course of historical change and demands a new critical perspective, or (4) because of a combination of (2) and (3). I believe the theological perception of the crisis of African Americans belongs to (4).

10. Juan Luis Segundo, *The Liberation of Theology* (Maryknoll, NY: Orbis, 1976), 33.

11. Ada María Isasi-Díaz, *En la Lucha, In the Struggle: Elaborating a Mujerista Theology* (Minneapolis: Fortress, 1993), 175.

12. James H. Cone, *A Black Theology of Liberation,* 2nd ed. (Maryknoll, NY: Orbis, 1986), 38.

13. Cone, *A Black Theology of Liberation,* 10.

14. See my *Dialectic of Salvation* (Albany: State University of New York Press, 1989), 27–28, 163–169.

15. Isasi-Díaz, *En la Lucha, In the Struggle,* 4–5.

16. See Letty M. Russell, *Human Liberation in a Feminist Perspective: A Theology* (Philadelphia: Westminster, 1974), 72–103 ("Search for a Usable Past"). Thus, for example, Elizabeth A. Johnson, who, as a Thomist feminist, is more sympathetic to the tradition than most feminist theologians are, singles out the classical doctrines of divine incomprehensibility, analogy, and the many names of God as useful resources for emancipatory speech about God. See her *She Who Is: The Mystery of God in Feminist Theological Discourse* (New York: Crossroad, 1992), 104–123.

17. Cone, *A Black Theology of Liberation,* 35; emphases added.

18. Mary Daly, *Beyond God the Father: Toward a Philosophy of Women's Liberation* (Boston: Beacon Press, 1973), 4.

19. Elizabeth A. Johnson, "Trinity: To Let the Symbol Sing Again," *Theology Today* 54:3 (October 1997): 300–301.

20. Gutierrez, *A Theology of Liberation,* 11.

21. James P. Mackey, "The Preacher, the Theologian, and the Trinity," *Theology Today* 54.3 (October 1997): 364; for a similar critique, see also Colin Gunton, "The God of Jesus Christ," *Theology Today* 54.3 (October 1997): 329. See the respective reconstructions of the concepts of God and the Trinity in Elizabeth A. Johnson, *She Who Is;* Leonardo Boff, *Trinity and Society;* Jürgen Moltmann, *The Trinity and the Kingdom;* and James H. Cone, *A Black Theology of Liberation.* In another essay Mackey elaborates on his critique of Moltmann: "What is wrong . . . is the projection of current ideas of human relationships into the divine being, resulting in an 'immanent' Trinity which then, of course, becomes normative (and not merely inspiring) for the reconstruction of human relationships in civic and ecclesiastical societies. This process turns our present perception of 'good relationships' into absolutes, and that is not a good thing even for our present perception of the good 'Christian' relationships, that is, those we believe that Jesus as Risen Lord still tries to foster in our midst, for of such processes ideologies are made." See James P. Mackey, "Are There Christian Alternatives to Trinitarian Thinking?" in James M. Byrne, ed., *The Christian Understanding of God Today* (Dublin: Columba, 1993), 67.

22. For a critique of the abstract conception of faith and the eschatological proviso, see Juan Luis Segundo, *The Liberation of Theology,* 125–153.

23. Among the many contemporary prophetic theologians, Jon Sobrino seems especially sensitive to this tension between transcendence and historicity. See his *Jesus in Latin America* (Maryknoll, NY: Orbis, 1987), 10–11.

24. On this dialectic of transcendence and historicity as constitutive of human existence, see Rahner, *Spirit in the World, Hörer des Wortes,* and *Foundations of Christian Faith,* 24–43.

25. Søren Kierkegaard, *Concluding Unscientific Postscript,* trans. David F. Swenson and Walter Lowrie (Princeton, NJ: Princeton University Press, 1941), 74–84, 176–178, 223, 232, 314.

26. Rahner, *Foundations of Christian Faith,* 71–73.

27. For a critique of the fragmentation of contemporary theologies and the use of the traditional paradigm of "the body of Christ" as a resource for overcoming that fragmentation, see further my essay, "Solidarity of Others in the Body of Christ: A New Theological Paradigm," *Toronto Journal of Theology* 12.2 (Fall 1998): 239–254. The whole of my *The Solidarity of Others in a Divided World* is an attempt to overcome fragmentation.

Works Cited

For a recent, up-to-date, and relatively comprehensive bibliography on Aquinas, see Brian Davies, *Aquinas* (New York: Continuum, 2002), xi–xxii.

Works by Thomas Aquinas

S. Thomae de Aquino Opera Omnia. Available in electronic version prepared by Roberto Busa, S.J., under the general supervision of Enrique Alarcon of the University of Navarro, Pamplona, Spain, in 2001 on the internet at www.unav.es/filosofia/alarcon/amicis/ctopera.html. This contains, among other works, the following editions of the works consulted in this book:
> *Scriptum super Sententiis.* Parma edition of 1856.
> *Summa contra Gentiles.* Taurini edition of 1961.
> *Summa Theologiae.* Leonine edition of 1888.
> *De Veritate.* Leonine edition of 1970.
> *De Potentia.* Taurini edition of 1953.
> *De Malo.* Taurini edition of 1953.
> *Compendium Theologiae.* Taurini edition of 1954.
> *Expositio super librum Boethii de Trinitate.* Bruno Decker edition of 1959.
> *Super Epistolam B. Pauli ad Romanos lectura.* Taurini edition of 1953.
> *Super Epistolam B. Pauli ad Hebraeos lectura.* Taurini edition of 1953.
> *Super 1 Epistolam B. Pauli ad Corinthios lectura.* Taurini edition of 1953.
> *Super Evangelium S. Ioannis lectura.* Taurini edition of 1952.
Commentary on the Gospel of St. John. Translated by Fabian R. Larcher. Albany, NY: Magi Books, 1980.
Commentary on Saint Paul's Epistle to the Ephesians. Translated by Matthew L. Lamb. Albany, NY: Magi Books, 1966.

Commentary on Saint Paul's First Letter to the Thessalonians and the Letter to the Philippians. Translated by F. R. Larcher and Michael Duffy. Albany, NY: Magi Books, 1969.

Compendium of Theology. Translated by Cyril Vollert. St. Louis, MO: B. Herder, 1947.

Faith, Reason and Theology. Translated by Armand Maurer. Toronto: Pontifical Institute of Medieval Studies, 1987.

On Evil. Translated by John A. Oesterle and Jean T. Oesterle. Notre Dame, IN: University of Notre Dame Press, 1995.

On Truth. Translated by Robert W. Mulligan, James V. McGlynn, and Robert W. Schmidt. 3 vols. Chicago: Henry Regnery, 1954. Reprint, Indianapolis: Hackett, 1994.

Selected Writings. Translated and edited by Ralph McInerny. London: Penguin Books, 1998.

Summa contra Gentiles. Translated by Anton C. Pegis, James F. Anderson, Vernon J. Bourke, and Charles J. O'Neil. 5 vols. New York: Doubleday, 1955–1957. Reprint, Notre Dame, IN: University of Notre Dame Press, 1975.

Summa Theologiae. 4 vols. Matriti, Italy: Biblioteca de Autores Cristianos, 1955–1958.

Summa Theologica. Translated by the Fathers of the English Dominican Province. 5 vols. New York: Benziger Brothers, 1948. Reprint, Westminster, MD: Christian Classics, 1981.

The Three Greatest Prayers: Commentaries on the Our Father, the Hail Mary, and the Apostles' Creed. Translated by Laurence Shapcote. Westminster, MD: Newman, 1956.

Works on Aquinas and Related Subjects

Achtemeier, Elizabeth. "Exchanging God for 'No Gods': A Discussion of Female Language for God." In *Speaking the Christian God: The Holy Trinity and the Challenge of Feminism,* edited by Alvin F. Kimel, Jr. Grand Rapids, MI: Eerdmans, 1992. 1–16.

Aertsen, Jan A. "Aquinas's Philosophy in Its Historical Setting." In *The Cambridge Companion to Aquinas,* edited by Norman Kretzmann and Eleonore Stump. Cambridge: Cambridge University Press, 1993. 12–37.

———. *Nature and Creature: Thomas Aquinas's Way of Thought.* Translated by Herbert Donald Morton. Leiden: E. J. Brill, 1988.

Alston, William P. "Aquinas on Theological Predication: A Look Backward and a Look Forward." In *Reasoned Faith: Essays in Philosophical Theology in Honor of Norman Kretzmann,* edited by Eleonore Stump. Ithaca, NY: Cornell University Press, 1993. 145–178.

———. "Substance and the Trinity." In *The Trinity*, edited by Stephen Davis, Daniel Kendall, and Gerald O'Collins. Oxford: Oxford University Press, 1999. 179–201.

Athanasius, Saint. *Select Writings and Letters of Athanasius, Bishop of Alexandria.* Edited by Archibald Robertson. NPNF, 2nd ser., 4. Grand Rapids, MI: Eerdmans, 1980.

Augustine, Saint. *The Trinity.* Translated by Edmund Hill, O.P. Brooklyn, NY: New City Press, 1991.

Balthasar, Hans Urs von. *Explorations in Theology.* Vol. 1, *The Word Made Flesh.* San Francisco: Ignatius Press, 1989.

Barr, James. *Biblical Faith and Natural Theology.* 1991 Gifford Lectures. Oxford: Clarendon Press, 1993.

———. "The Theological Case against Biblical Theology." In *Canon, Theology, and Old Testament Interpretation*, edited by Gene M. Tucker, David L. Petersen, and Robert R. Wilson. Philadelphia: Fortress, 1988. 3–19.

Barth, Karl. *Church Dogmatics.* Vol. I, *The Doctrine of the Word of God*, part 1. Translated by G. W. Bromiley. 2nd ed. Edinburgh: T & T Clark, 1975.

Beeck, Frans Jozef van. *God Encountered: A Contemporary Catholic Systematic Theology.* Vol. 1, *Understanding the Christian Faith.* San Francisco: Harper & Row, 1989.

———. "Trinitarian Theology as Participation." In *The Trinity*, edited by Stephen Davis, Daniel Kendall, and Gerald O'Collins. New York: Oxford University Press, 1999. 295–325.

Bernard, Charles Andre, S.J. "Mystère trinitaire et transformation en Dieu." *Gregorianum* 80.3 (1999): 441–467.

Bernstein, Richard J. *Praxis and Action: Contemporary Philosophies of Human Activity.* Philadelphia: University of Pennsylvania Press, 1971.

Bieler, Martin. "The Future of the Philosophy of Being." *Communio* 26 (Fall 1999): 455–485.

Bloesch, Donald. *The Battle for the Trinity.* Ann Arbor, MI: Servant Publications, 1985.

Boff, Clodovis. *Theology and Praxis: Epistemological Foundations.* Maryknoll, NY: Orbis, 1987.

Boff, Leonardo. *Trinity and Society.* Maryknoll, NY: Orbis, 1988.

Brito, Emilio. "Connaissance et inconnaissance de Dieu selon Thomas d'Aquin et Hegel." *Ephemerides theologicae lovanienses* 63.4 (1987): 327–338.

Brown, David. *The Divine Trinity.* London: Duckworth, 1985.

Brunner, Emil, and Karl Barth. *Natural Theology.* London: Centenary Press, 1946.

Byrne, James M., ed. *The Christian Understanding of God Today.* Dublin: Columba, 1993.

Camino, Juan A. Martinez. "Wechselseitige Selbstunterscheidung? Zur Trinitätslehre Wolfhart Pannenberg." In *Reflektierter Glaube*, edited by

Hans-Ludwig Ollig and Oliver J. Wietz. München: Verlag Dr. Hansel-Hohenhausen, 1999. 131–149.

Charry, Ellen T. "Spiritual Formation by the Doctrine of the Trinity." *Theology Today* 54.3 (October 1997): 367–380.

Chauvet, Louis-Marie. *Symbol and Sacrament.* Collegeville, MN: Liturgical Press, 1995.

Chavannes, Henry. *The Analogy between God and the World in Saint Thomas Aquinas and Karl Barth.* Translated by William Lumley. New York: Vantage Press, 1992.

Chenu, Marie-Dominique. *Is Theology a Science?* Translated by A. H. N. Green-Armytage. New York: Hawthorne Books, 1959.

———. *Toward Understanding Saint Thomas.* Translated by A. M. Landry and D. Hughes. Chicago: Henry Regnery, 1964.

Coakley, Sarah. "'Persons' in the 'Social' Doctrine of the Trinity: A Critique of Current Analytic Discussion." In *The Trinity,* edited by Stephen T. Davis, Daniel Kendall, and Gerald O'Collins. Oxford: Oxford University Press, 1999. 123–144.

Cobb, John B., Jr. *A Christian Natural Theology: Based on the Thought of Alfred North Whitehead.* Philadelphia: Westminster Press, 1965.

Coffee, Patrick. "The Holy Spirit as the Mutual Love of the Father and the Son." *Theological Studies* 51.2 (June 1990): 193–229.

Cone, James H. *A Black Theology of Liberation.* 2nd ed. Maryknoll, NY: Orbis, 1986.

Congar, Yves. "'Ecclesia' et 'Populus (Fidelis)' dans l'Ecclesiologie de S. Thomas." In *St. Thomas Aquinas, 1274–1974, Commemorative Studies,* vol. 1. Toronto: Pontifical Institute of Medieval Studies, 1974. 159–173.

———. *History of Theology.* Translated by Hunter Guthrie. Garden City, NY: Doubleday, 1968.

———. *The Mystery of the Church.* Translated by A. V. Littledale. Baltimore: Helicon Press, 1960.

Contat, Alain. "Destin de l'homme et incarnation du Verbe selon St. Thomas d'Aquin." In *Atti del IX Congresso Tomistico Internazionale,* 5 (1991): 255–272.

Corbin, Michel. *Le chemin de la theologie chez Thomas D'Aquin.* Paris: Beauchesne, 1974.

Cottier, Georges. "Desir naturel de voir Dieu." *Gregorianum* 78.4 (1997): 679–698.

Crosson, Frederick J. "Reconsidering Aquinas as Postliberal Theologian." *Thomist* 56.3 (1992): 481–498.

Cunningham, David S. "Developing Alternative Trinitarian Formulas." *Anglican Theological Review* 80.1 (Winter 1998): 8–29.

Dalferth, Ingolf F. "The Eschatological Roots of the Doctrine of the Trinity." In *Trinitarian Theology Today: Essays on Divine Being and Act,* edited by Christoph Schwöbel. Edinburgh: T & T Clark, 1995. 147–170.

Daly, Mary. *Beyond God the Father: Toward a Philosophy of Women's Liberation.* Boston: Beacon Press, 1973.

Davies, Brian. *The Thought of Thomas Aquinas.* Oxford: Clarendon Press, 1992.

Davis, Stephen, Daniel Kendall, and Gerald O'Collins, eds. *The Trinity.* New York: Oxford University Press, 1999.

D'Costa, Gavin, ed. *Christian Uniqueness Reconsidered: The Myth of a Pluralistic Theology of Religions.* Maryknoll, NY: Orbis, 1990.

Dembowski, Hermann. "Natürliche Theologie—Theologie der Natur: Erwägungen in einem weiten Feld." *Evangelische Theologie* 45.3 (1985): 224–248.

DiNoia, Augustine J. "Knowing and Naming the Triune God: The Grammar of Trinitarian Confession." In *Speaking the Christian God: The Holy Trinity and the Challenge of Feminism,* edited by Alvin F. Kimel, Jr. Grand Rapids, MI: Eerdmans, 1992. 162–187.

Duck, Ruth C. *Gender and the Name of God: The Trinitarian Baptismal Formula.* New York: Pilgrim Press, 1991.

Duffy, Stephen J. *The Graced Horizon: Nature and Grace in Modern Catholic Thought.* Collegeville, MN: Liturgical Press, 1992.

Dupuis, Jacques. *Toward a Christian Theology of Religious Pluralism.* Maryknoll, NY: Orbis, 1997.

Emery, Gilles. "Le Père et l'oeuvre de creation selon le Commentaire des Sentences de S. Thomas d'Aquin." In *Ordo Sapientiae et Amoris,* edited by Carlos-Josaphat Pinto de Oliveira, O.P. Fribourg: Editions Universitaires, 1993. 85–118.

———. "Trinité et creation: le principe trinitaire de la creation dans les commentaries d'Albert Le Grand, de Bonaventure et de Thomas d'Aquin sur les *Sentences.*" *Revue des sciences philosophique et theologiques* 79 (1995): 405–430.

Emery, Kent, Jr., and Joseph Wawryknow, eds. *Christ Among the Medieval Dominicans: Representations of Christ in the Texts and Images of the Order of Preachers.* Notre Dame, IN: University of Notre Dame Press, 1998.

Ernst, Cornelius, ed. *The Gospel of Grace.* New York: McGraw-Hill, 1972.

———. "Review of *The Mystery of the Supernatural,* by Henri de Lubac." *Journal of Theological Studies* 20.1 (1969): 365–367.

Farley, Edward, and Peter C. Hodgson. "Scripture and Tradition." In *Christian Theology: An Introduction to Its Traditions and Tasks,* edited by Peter C. Hodgson and Robert H. King. Rev. ed. Philadelphia: Fortress Press, 1985. 61–87.

Feenstra, Ronald J., and Cornelius Plantinga, Jr., eds. *Trinity, Incarnation, and Atonement: Philosophical and Theological Essays.* Notre Dame, IN: University of Notre Dame Press, 1989.

Ford, David F., ed. *The Modern Theologians: An Introduction to Christian Theology in the Twentieth Century.* Cambridge, MA: Blackwell, 1997.

Fox, Matthew. *Sheer Joy: Conversations with Thomas Aquinas on Creation Spirituality.* San Francisco: HarperSanFrancisco, 1992.

Garrigou-Lagrange, Reginald. *De Gratia: Commentarius in Summam Theologicam S. Thomae Iae IIae qq. 109–114.* Torino: R. Berruti, 1947.

———. *The One God: A Commentary on the First Part of St. Thomas' Theological Summa.* Translated by Bede Rose. St. Louis, MO: B. Herder, 1943.

———. *Reality: A Synthesis of Thomistic Thought.* Translated by Patrick Cummins. St. Louis, MO: B. Herder, 1950.

Gilby, Thomas. "Sacra Doctrina." In St. Thomas Aquinas, *Summa Theologiae.* Vol. 1, *Christian Theology,* edited by Thomas Gilby. New York: McGraw-Hill, 1964. 58–66.

Gilson, Etienne. *The Christian Philosophy of St. Thomas Aquinas.* Translated by L. K. Shook. New York: Random House, 1956.

———. *Reason and Revelation in the Middle Ages.* New York: Charles Scribner's Sons, 1938.

Goering, Joseph. "Christ in Dominican Catechesis: The Articles of Faith." In *Christ Among the Medieval Dominicans: Representations of Christ in the Texts and Images of the Order of Preachers,* edited by Kent Emery, Jr., and Joseph Wawrykow. Notre Dame, IN: University of Notre Dame Press, 1998. 132–133.

Gregory of Nazianzus. *Select Orations of Saint Gregory Nazianzen.* Translated by Charles Gordon Browne and James Edward Swallow. NPNF, 2nd ser., 7. Grand Rapids, MI: Eerdmans, 1996.

Gregory of Nyssa. *Select Writings and Letters of Gregory, Bishop of Nyssa.* Translated by William Moore and Henry Austin Wilson. NPNF, 2nd ser., 5. Grand Rapids, MI: Eerdmans, 1954.

Grenz, Stanley J. *Reason for Hope: The Systematic Theology of Wolfhart Pannenberg.* New York: Oxford University Press, 1990.

Gunten, A. F. von, O.P. "*In Principio Erat Verbum*: Une evolution de saint Thomas en theologie trinitaire." In *Ordo Sapientiae et Amoris,* edited by Carlos-Josaphat Pinto de Oliveira, O.P. Fribourg: Editions Universitaires, 1993. 119–141.

Gunton, Colin. "The God of Jesus Christ." *Theology Today* 54.3 (October 1997): 325–334.

Gutierrez, Gustavo. *A Theology of Liberation: History, Politics, and Salvation.* 15th anniversary ed. Maryknoll, NY: Orbis, 1988.

Habermas, Jürgen. *Theory and Practice.* Boston: Beacon Press, 1973.

Haight, Roger. *The Experience and Language of Grace.* New York: Paulist, 1979.

Halverson, James. "Franciscan Theology and Predestinarian Pluralism in Late Medieval Thought." *Speculum* 70.1 (January 1995): 1–26.

Hartel, Joseph Francis. *Femina ut Imago Dei: On the Integral Feminism of St. Thomas Aquinas.* Rome: Editrice Pontificia Universita Gregoriana, 1993.

Hebblethwaite, Brian, and Stewart Sutherland, eds. *The Philosophical Frontiers of Christian Theology: Essays Presented to D. M. Mackinnon.* Cambridge: Cambridge University Press, 1982.

Heidegger, Martin. *Being and Time.* Translated by John Macquarrie and Edward Robinson. New York: Harper & Row, 1962.

Hick, John. *The Metaphor of God Incarnate: Christology in a Pluralistic Age.* Louisville, KY: Westminster/John Knox Press, 1993.

Hilary of Poitiers. *St. Hilary of Poitiers.* Translated by Philip Schaff and Henry Wace. NPNF, 2nd ser., 9. Peabody, MA: Hendrickson Publishers, 1994.

Hill, William J. *The Three-Personed God.* Washington, DC: Catholic University of America Press, 1982.

Hodgson, Peter C. *God in History: Shapes of Freedom.* Nashville, TN: Abingdon Press, 1989.

Hödl, Ludwig. "'Lumen gratiae,' Ein Leitgedanke der Gnadentheologie des Thomas von Aquin." In *Mysterium der Gnade: Festschrift für Johann Auer,* edited by Heribert Rossmann and Joseph Ratzinger. Regensburg: Friedrich Pustet, 1975.

Hoping, Helmut. "Understanding the Difference of Being: On the Relationship between Metaphysics and Theology." *Thomist* 59.2 (1995): 189–221.

Hughson, Thomas. "Dulles and Aquinas on Revelation." *Thomist* 52.3 (1988): 445–471.

Inwagen, Peter van. "And Yet They Are Not Three Gods But One God." In *Philosophy and the Christian Faith,* edited by Thomas V. Morris. Notre Dame, IN: University of Notre Dame Press, 1988. 241–278.

Isasi-Díaz, Ada María. *En la Lucha, In the Struggle: Elaborating a Mujerista Theology.* Minneapolis: Fortress, 1993.

Janz, Denis. "Syllogism or Paradox: Aquinas and Luther on Theological Method." *Theological Studies* 59 (1998): 3–21

Jenkins, John I. *Knowledge and Faith in Thomas Aquinas.* Cambridge: Cambridge University Press, 1997.

Jenson, Robert W. 'The Father, He . . ." In *Speaking the Christian God: The Holy Trinity and the Challenge of Feminism,* edited by Alvin Kimel, Jr. Grand Rapids, MI: Eerdmans, 1992. 95–109.

———. *The Triune Identity: God According to the Gospel.* Philadelphia: Fortress, 1982.

Johnson, Elizabeth A. *She Who Is: The Mystery of God in Feminist Theological Discourse.* New York: Crossroad, 1992.

———. "Trinity: To Let the Symbol Sing Again." *Theology Today* 54.3 (October 1997): 299–311.

Jordan, Mark D. *Ordering Wisdom: The Hierarchy of Philosophical Discourses in Aquinas.* Notre Dame, IN: University of Notre Dame Press, 1986.

———. "Theology and Philosophy." In *The Cambridge Companion to Aquinas,* edited by Norman Kretzmann and Eleonore Stump. Cambridge: Cambridge University Press, 1993. 232–251.

Juel, Donald. "The Trinity and the New Testament." *Theology Today* 54.3 (October 1997): 312–324.

Jüngel, Eberhard. "Die Möglichkeit theologischer Anthropologie auf dem Grunde der Analogie." *Evangelische Theologie* 9.22 (1962): 535–557.

Kappes, Michael. "'Natürliche Theologie' als innerprotestantische und ökumenische Problem? Die Kontroverse zwischen Eberhard Jüngel und Wolfhart Pannenberg und ihr ökumenischer Ertrag." *Catholica* 49.4 (1995): 276–309.

Kasper, Walter. *The God of Jesus Christ.* New York: Crossroad, 1984.

Keefe, Donald J., S.J. *Thomism and the Ontological Theology of Paul Tillich: A Comparison of Systems.* Leiden: E. J. Brill, 1971.

Kerr, Fergus. *After Aquinas: Versions of Thomism.* Malden, MA: Blackwell, 2002.

Kierkegaard, Søren. *Concluding Unscientific Postscript.* Translated by David F. Swenson and Walter Lowrie. Princeton, NJ: Princeton University Press, 1941.

Kimel, Alvin F., Jr., ed. *Speaking the Christian God: The Holy Trinity and the Challenge of Feminism.* Grand Rapids, MI: Eerdmans, 1992.

Klubertanz, George P. *St. Thomas Aquinas on Analogy: A Textual Analysis and Systematic Synthesis.* Chicago: Loyola University Press, 1960.

Knitter, Paul F. *Jesus and the Other Names.* Maryknoll, NY: Orbis, 1996.

———. *No Other Name? A Critical Survey of Christian Attitudes toward the World Religions.* Maryknoll, NY: Orbis, 1985.

Kolb, David, ed. *New Perspectives on Hegel's Philosophy of Religion.* Albany: State University of New York Press, 1992.

Kretzmann, Norman. "Trinity and Transcendentals." In *Trinity, Incarnation, and Atonement: Philosophical and Theological Essays,* edited by Ronald J. Feenstra and Cornelius Plantinga, Jr. Notre Dame, IN: University of Notre Dame Press, 1989. 79–100.

Kuhn, Ulrich. "Thomas von Aquin und die evangelische Theologie." In *Thomas von Aquin 1274–1974,* edited by Ludger Oeing-Hanhoff. München: Kosel Verlag, 1974. 13–32.

———. *Via Caritatis: Theologie des Gesetzes bei Thomas von Aquin.* Göttingen: Vandenhoeck & Ruprecht, 1965.

Küng, Hans. "What Is True Religion? Toward an Ecumenical Criteriology." In *Toward a Universal Theology of Religion,* edited by Leonard Swidler. Maryknoll, NY: Orbis, 1987. 231–250.

LaCugna, Catherine Mowry. *God for Us: The Trinity and Christian Life.* San Francisco: HarperSanFrancisco, 1991.

Lamb, Matthew. "The Theory-Praxis Relationship in Contemporary Christian Theologies." *Proceedings of the Catholic Theological Society of America* 31 (1976): 149–178.

Lash, Nicholas. "Considering the Trinity." *Modern Theology* 2.3 (1986): 183–196.

———. "Ideology, Metaphor and Analogy." In *The Philosophical Frontiers of Christian Theology: Essays Presented to D.M. Mackinnon,* edited by Brian Hebblethwaite and Stewart Sutherland. Cambridge: Cambridge University Press, 1982. 68–94.

Leftow, Brian. "Anti Social Trinitarianism." In *The Trinity*, edited by Stephen Davis, Daniel Kendall, and Gerald O'Collins. Oxford: Oxford University Press, 1999. 203–249.

Leo XIII, Pope. "On the Restoration of Christian Philosophy according to the Mind of St. Thomas Aquinas, the Angelic Doctor." In St. Thomas Aquinas, *Summa Theologica,* translated by the Fathers of the English Dominican Province, vol. 1. Westminster, MD: Christian Classics, 1981. Reprint of the revised Benziger edition of 1948. ix–xviii.

Little, Joyce A. *Toward a Thomist Methodology.* Lewiston, NY: Edwin Mellen Press, 1988.

Lobkowicz, Nicholas. *Theory and Practice: History of a Concept from Aristotle to Marx.* Notre Dame, IN: University of Notre Dame Press, 1967.

Long, Eugene Thomas, ed. *Prospects for Natural Theology.* Washington, DC: Catholic University of America Press, 1992.

Lossky, Vladimir. *Orthodox Theology: An Introduction.* Crestwood, NY: St. Vladimir's Seminary Press, 1978.

———. *The Vision of God.* Crestwood, NY: St. Vladimir's Seminary Press, 1983.

Lubac, Henri de. *The Mystery of the Supernatural.* Translated by Rosemary Sheed. New York: Herder and Herder, 1967.

Mackey, James P. "Are There Christian Alternatives to Trinitarian Thinking?" In *The Christian Understanding of God Today,* edited by James M. Byrne. Dublin: Columbia, 1993. 66–75.

———. "The Preacher, the Theologian, and the Trinity." *Theology Today* 54.3 (October 1997): 347–366.

Mahoney, John. "The Church of the Holy Spirit in Aquinas." *The Heythrop Journal* 15.1 (1974): 18–36.

Maritain, Jacques. *Existence and the Existent: An Essay on Christian Existentialism.* Garden City, NY: Doubleday Image Books, 1956.

———. *La philosophie morale.* Paris: Gallimard, 1960.

———. *The Range of Reason.* New York: Charles Scribner's Sons, 1942.

Marsh, Thomas. *The Triune God: A Biblical, Historical, and Theological Study.* Mystic, CT: Twenty-Third Publications, 1994.

Marshall, Bruce D. "Aquinas as Postliberal Theologian." *Thomist* 53.3 (July 1989): 353–402.

———. "Thomas, Thomism, and Truth." *Thomist* 56.3 (1992): 499–524.

Martelet, Gustave. "Theologie und Heilsökonomie in der Christologie der 'Tertia'." In *Gott in Welt: Festgabe für Karl Rahner,* vol. 2, edited by Johannes B. Metz, Walter Kern, Adolf Darlapp, and Herbert Vorgrimler. Freiburg: Herder, 1964. 3–42.

Maurer, Armand. *St. Thomas and Historicity.* Milwaukee: Marquette University Press, 1979.

McFarland, Ian A. "The Ecstatic God: The Holy Spirit and the Constitution of the Trinity." *Theology Today* 54.3 (October 1997): 335–346.

Merriell, D. Juvenal. *To the Image of the Trinity: A Study in the Development of Aquinas's Teaching.* Toronto: Pontifical Institute of Medieval Studies, 1990.

Mersch, Emile. *The Theology of the Mystical Body.* St. Louis, MO: B. Herder, 1951.

Metz, Johannes B., Walter Kern, Adolf Darlapp, and Herbert Vorgrimler, eds. *Gott in Welt: Festgabe für Karl Rahner,* II. Freiburg: Herder, 1964.

Milbank, John, and Catherine Pickstock. *Truth in Aquinas.* London: Routledge, 2001.

Min, Anselm Kyongsuk. "Asian Theologians." In *A New Handbook of Christian Theologians,* edited by Donald W. Musser and Joseph L. Price. Nashville, TN: Abingdon, 1996. 22–48.

————. *Dialectic of Salvation: Issues in Theology of Liberation.* Albany: State University of New York Press, 1989.

————. "Dialectical Pluralism and Solidarity of Others: Towards a New Paradigm." *Journal of the American Academy of Religion* 65.3 (Fall 1997): 587–604.

————. "From Autobiography to Fellowship of Others: Reflections on Doing Ethnic Theology Today." In *Journeys at the Margin,* edited by Peter Phan. Collegeville, MN: Liturgical Press, 1999. 135–159.

————. "Praxis and Liberation: Toward a Theology of Concrete Totality." Ph.D. diss., Vanderbilt University, 1989.

————. "Solidarity of Others in the Body of Christ: A New Theological Paradigm." *Toronto Journal of Theology* 12.2 (1998): 239–254.

————. *The Solidarity of Others in a Divided World: A Postmodern Theology after Postmodernism.* New York: T & T Clark International, 2004.

Molnar, Paul D. *Divine Freedom and the Doctrine of the Immanent Trinity: In Dialogue with Karl Barth and Contemporary Theology.* London: T & T Clark, 2002.

Moltmann, Jürgen. *The Church in the Power of the Spirit.* San Francisco: HarperSanFrancisco, 1991.

————. *The Coming of God: Christian Eschatology.* Minneapolis: Fortress, 1996.

————. *God in Creation: A New Theology of Creation and the Spirit of God.* San Francisco: HarperSanFrancisco, 1991.

————. "Some Reflections on the Social Doctrine of the Trinity." In *The Christian Understanding of God Today,* edited by James M. Byrne. Dublin: Columba, 1993. 104–111.

————. *The Spirit of Life: A Universal Affirmation.* Minneapolis: Fortress, 1992.

————. *Theology of Hope: On the Ground and the Implications of a Christian Eschatology.* New York: Harper & Row, 1975.

————. *Trinität und Reich Gottes: Zur Gotteslehre.* München: Christian Kaiser, 1980.

————. *The Trinity and the Kingdom.* Translated by Margaret Kohl. London: SCM Press, 1981.

Morris, Thomas V., ed. *Philosophy and the Christian Faith.* Notre Dame, IN: University of Notre Dame Press, 1988.

Muller, Earl. "Real Relations and the Divine: Issues in Thomas's Understanding of God's Relation to the World." *Theological Studies* 56.4 (1995): 673–695.

Müller, Gerhard Ludwig. "Hebt das Sola-Fide Prinzip die Möglichkeit einer natürlichen Theologie auf?" *Catholica* 40.1 (1986): 59–96.

Muller, Richard A. "The Dogmatic Function of St. Thomas' 'Proofs': A Protestant Appreciation." *Fides et Historia* 24 (Summer 1992): 15–29.

Narcisse, Gilbert, O.P. "Les enjeux epistemologiques de l'argument de convenance selon saint Thomas d'Aquin." In *Ordo Sapientiae et Amoris,* edited by Carlos-Josaphat Pinto de Oliveira, O.P. Fribourg: Editions Universitaires, 1993. 143–167.

O'Brien, T. C., ed. *Summa Theologiae,* Vol. 27, *Effects of Sin, Stain and Guilt.* New York: McGraw-Hill, 1974.

O'Collins, Gerald. "The Holy Trinity: The State of the Questions." In *The Trinity,* edited by Stephen Davis, Daniel Kendall, and Gerald O'Collins. Oxford: Oxford University Press, 1999. 1–25.

O'Donnell, John. "The Trinity as Divine Community: A Critical Reflection Upon Recent Theological Developments." *Gregorianum* 69.1 (1988): 5–34.

Oeing-Hanhoff, Ludger. "Gotteserkenntnis im Licht der Vernunft und des Glaubens nach Thomas von Aquin." In *Thomas von Aquin: 1274–1974,* edited by Ludger Oeing-Hanhoff. München: Kösel Verlag, 1974. 97–124.

———, ed. *Thomas von Aquin 1274–1974.* München: Kösel Verlag, 1974.

Oliveira, Carlos-Josaphat Pinto de, O.P., ed. *Ordo Sapientiae et Amoris.* Fribourg: Editions Universitaires: 1993.

Ollig, Hans-Ludwig, and Oliver J. Wietz, eds. *Reflektierter Glaube.* München: Verlag Dr. Hansel-Hohenhausen, 1999.

Olson, Roger. "Wolfhart Pannenberg's Doctrine of the Trinity." *Scottish Journal of Theology* 43.2 (1990): 175–206.

O'Meara, Thomas F. "Grace as a Theological Structure in the *Summa theologiae* of Thomas Aquinas." *Recherches de theologie ancienne et medievale* 55 (1988): 130–153.

———. "The Presence of Grace Outside Evangelization, Baptism and Church in Thomas Aquinas' Theology." In *That Others May Know and Love: Essays in Honor of Zachary Hayes,* edited by Michael F. Cusato and F. Edward Coughlin. St. Bonaventure, NY: Franciscan Institute, 1997. 91–131.

———. *Thomas Aquinas Theologian.* Notre Dame, IN: University of Notre Dame Press, 1997.

O'Neill, Colman E. "St. Thomas on the Membership of the Church." *Thomist* 27 (1963): 88–140.

Palakeel, Joseph. *The Use of Analogy in Theological Discourse: An Investigation in Ecumenical Perspective.* Rome: Editrice Pontificia Universita Gregoriana, 1995.

Pannenberg, Wolfhart. *Systematic Theology,* I. Translated by Geoffrey W. Bromiley. Grand Rapids, MI: Eerdmans, 1991.

———. *Systematic Theology,* II. Translated by Geoffrey W. Bromiley. Grand Rapids, MI: Eerdmans, 1994.

———. *Systematische Theologie,* I. Göttingen: Vandenhoeck & Ruprecht, 1988.

Pegis, Anton C. "*Sub Ratione Dei*: A Reply to Professor Anderson." *New Scholasticism* 39.2 (April 1965): 141–157.

Pelikan, Jaroslav. "The Doctrine of Filioque in Thomas Aquinas and Its Patristic Antecedents." In *St. Thomas Aquinas 1274–1974: Commemorative Studies.* Toronto: Pontifical Institute of Medieval Studies, 1974. 315–336.

Persson, Per Erik. *Sacra Doctrina: Reason and Revelation in Aquinas.* Translated by Ross Mackenzie. Philadelphia: Fortress, 1970.

Pesch, Otto Hermann. "Existential and Sapiential Theology: The Theological Confrontation between Luther and Thomas Aquinas." In *Catholic Scholars Dialogue with Luther,* edited by Jared Wicks. Chicago: Loyola University Press, 1970. 61–81.

———. *Thomas von Aquin: Grenze und Grösse mittelalterlicher Theologie.* Mainz: Matthias-Grünewald-Verlag, 1988.

Peters, Ted. *God as Trinity: Relationality and Temporality in Divine Life.* Louisville, KY: Westminster/John Knox Press, 1993.

Phelan, Gerald B. *Saint Thomas and Analogy.* Milwaukee: Marquette University Press, 1948.

Pieper, Josef. *Leisure: The Basis of Culture.* New York: Pantheon Books, 1952.

Pieris, Aloysius. *An Asian Theology of Liberation.* Maryknoll: Orbis, 1988.

Plantinga, Cornelius, Jr. "Social Trinity and Tritheism." In *Trinity, Incarnation, and Atonement: Philosophical and Theological Essays,* edited by Ronald J. Feenstra and Cornelius Plantinga, Jr. Notre Dame, IN: University of Notre Dame Press, 1989. 21–47.

Polkinghorne, John. "The New Natural Theology." *Studies in World Christianity* 1.1 (1995): 41–50.

Preller, Victor. *Divine Science and the Science of God: A Reformulation of Thomas Aquinas.* Princeton, NJ: Princeton University Press, 1967.

Quinn, Philip L. "Aquinas on Atonement." In *Trinity, Incarnation, and Atonement: Philosophical and Theological Essays,* edited by Ronald J. Feenstra and Cornelius Plantinga, Jr. Notre Dame, IN: University of Notre Dame Press, 1989. 153–177.

Race, Alan. *Christians and Religious Pluralism: Patterns in the Christian Theology of Religions.* London: SCM Press, 1983.

Rahner, Karl. *The Church and the Sacraments.* New York: Herder & Herder, 1963.

———. *The Content of Faith: The Best of Karl Rahner's Theological Writings.* Edited by Karl Lehmann and Albert Raffelt. Translated by Harvey D. Egan. New York: Crossroad, 1992.

———. *Foundations of Christian Faith: An Introduction to the Idea of Christianity.* Translated by William Dych. New York: Seabury, 1978.

———. "Grace." In *Encyclopedia of Theology: The Concise Sacramentum Mundi*, edited by Karl Rahner. New York: Crossroad, 1982. 587–595.

———. *Hörer des Wortes*, ed. Johannes B. Metz. München: Kösel, 1963.

———. *Schriften zur Theologie*, VI. Einsiedeln: Benziger, 1965.

———. *Spirit in the World.* Translated by William Dych. New York: Herder & Herder, 1968.

———. *Theological Investigations*, IX. New York: Seabury, 1973.

———. *Theological Investigations*, XII. New York: Crossroad, 1974.

———. Theological Investigations, XVI. New York: Seabury, 1979.

———. *Theological Investigations*, XVIII. New York: Crossroad, 1983.

———. "Thomas Aquinas on the Incomprehensibility of God." *Journal of Religion* S109 (1978): 107–125.

———. *The Trinity.* Translated by Joseph Donceel. New York: Seabury, 1974.

Richard of St. Victor. *The Twelve Patriarchs, The Mystical Ark, Book Three of the Trinity.* Translated by Grover A. Zinn. New York: Paulist, 1979.

Richard, Robert L., S.J. *The Problem of an Apologetical Perspective in the Trinitarian Theology of St. Thomas Aquinas.* Rome: Gregorian University Press, 1963.

Rikhof, H. "Corpus Christi Mysticum: An Inquiry into Thomas Aquinas' Use of a Term." *Bijdragen* 37 (1976): 149–171.

Ritschl, Dietrich. *The Logic of Theology.* Translated by John Bowden. Philadelphia: Fortress Press, 1987.

Rocca, Gregory P. "Aquinas on God-Talk: Hovering over the Abyss." *Theological Studies* 54.4 (1993): 641–661.

———. *Speaking the Incomprehensible God: Thomas Aquinas on the Interplay of Positive and Negative Theology.* Washington, DC: Catholic University of America Press, 2004.

Rogers, Eugene F., Jr. *Thomas Aquinas and Karl Barth: Sacred Doctrine and the Natural Knowledge of God.* Notre Dame, IN: University of Notre Dame Press, 1995.

Rolnick, Philip A. *Analogical Possibilities: How Words Refer to God.* Atlanta: Scholars Press, 1993.

Rousselot, Pierre. *The Intellectualism of Saint Thomas.* Translated by James E. O'Mahony. New York: Sheed and Ward, 1935.

Roy, Louis. "Bruce Marshall's Reading of Aquinas." *Thomist* 56.3 (1992): 473–480.

Russell, Letty M. *Human Liberation in a Feminist Perspective.* Philadelphia: Westminster, 1974.

Sabra, George. *Thomas Aquinas' Vision of the Church: Fundamentals of an Ecumenical Ecclesiology.* Mainz: Matthias-Grünewald Verlag, 1987.

Samartha, Stanley. *One Christ—Many Religions: Toward a Revised Christology.* Maryknoll, NY: Orbis, 1991.

Schlette, Heinz Robert. *Towards a Theology of Religions.* New York: Herder & Herder, 1966.

Schwöbel, Christoph, ed. *Trinitarian Theology Today: Essays on Divine Being and Act.* Edinburgh: T & T Clark, 1995.

———. "Wolfhart Pannenberg." In *The Modern Theologians: An Introduction to Christian Theology in the Twentieth Century,* edited by David F. Ford. Cambridge, MA: Blackwell, 1997. 180–208.

Seckler, Max. "Das Heil der Nichtevangelisierten in thomistischer Sicht." *Theologische Quartalschrift* 140.1 (1960): 38–69.

———. *Instinkt und Glaubenswille nach Thomas von Aquin.* Mainz: Matthias-Grünewald-Verlag, 1961.

Second Vatican Council. *The Documents of Vatican II.* Edited by Walter M. Abbott, S.J. New York: America Press, 1966.

Segundo, Juan Luis. *The Liberation of Theology.* Maryknoll, NY: Orbis, 1976.

Sobrino, Jon. *Jesus in Latin America.* Maryknoll, NY: Orbis, 1987.

Soskice, Janet Martin. "Can a Feminist Call God 'Father'?" In *Speaking the Christian God: The Holy Trinity and the Challenge of Feminism,* edited by Alvin F. Kimel, Jr. Grand Rapids, MI: Eerdmans, 1992. 81–94.

Steiner, Rudolf. *The Redemption of Thinking: A Study in the Philosophy of Thomas Aquinas.* Translated by A. P. Shepherd and Mildred Robertson Nicoll. London: Hodder and Stoughton, 1956.

Stump, Eleonore, ed. *Reasoned Faith: Essays in Philosophical Theology in Honor of Norman Kretzmann.* Ithaca, NY: Cornell University Press, 1993.

Sullivan, Francis A. *Salvation Outside the Church? Tracing the History of the Catholic Response.* Mahwah, NJ: Paulist, 1992.

Surin, Kenneth. "Creation, Revelation, and the Analogy Theory." *Journal of Theological Studies* 32.2 (1981): 401–422.

Swinburne, Richard. *The Christian God.* Oxford: Clarendon Press, 1994.

Taylor, Charles. *Multiculturalism and "The Politics of Recognition."* Edited by Amy Guttmann. Princeton, NJ: Princeton University Press, 1992.

Theissen, Jerome P. *The Ultimate Church and the Promise of Salvation.* Collegeville, MN: St. John's University Press, 1976.

Toner, Jerome. "The Salvation of Non-Christians in the Writings of St. Thomas Aquinas." *The Living Word* 77.5 (September–October 1971): 221–227.

Torrance, Thomas F. "The Christian Apprehension of God the Father." In *Speaking the Christian God: The Holy Trinity and the Challenge of Feminism,* edited by Alvin F. Kimel, Jr. Grand Rapids, MI: Eerdmans, 1992. 120–143.

———. *The Christian Doctrine of God, One Being Three Persons.* Edinburgh: T & T Clark, 1996.

———. "The Problem of Natural Theology in the Thought of Karl Barth." *Religious Studies* 6.2 (1970): 121–135.

Torrell, Jean-Pierre. "Le Christ dans la 'spiritualité' de saint Thomas." In *Christ among the Medieval Dominicans: Representations of Christ in the Texts and Images of the Order of Preachers,* edited by Kent Emery and Joseph Wawrykow. Notre Dame, IN: University of Notre Dame Press, 1998. 197–219.

———. *Saint Thomas Aquinas.* Vol. I, *The Person and His Work.* Translated by Robert Royal. Washington, DC: Catholic University of America Press, 1996.

Tracy, David. *The Analogical Imagination: Christian Theology and the Culture of Pluralism.* New York: Crossroad, 1981.

Tucker, Robert W., ed. *The Marx-Engels Reader.* 2nd ed. New York: W. W. Norton, 1978.

Vanneste, A. "Saint Thomas et le probleme du surnaturel." *Ephemerides theologicae lovanienses.* 64.4 (1988): 348–370.

Vater, Michael. "Religion, Worldliness, and *Sittlichkeit.*" In *New Perspectives on Hegel's Philosophy of Religion,* edited by David Kolb. Albany: State University of New York Press, 1992. 201–216.

Vos, Arvin. *Aquinas, Calvin and Contemporary Protestant Thought: A Critique of Protestant Views on the Thought of Thomas Aquinas.* Grand Rapids, MI: Eerdmans, 1985.

Wainwright, Geoffrey. *Doxology: The Praise of God in Worship, Doctrine and Life.* New York: Oxford University Press, 1980.

Walker, David A. "Trinity and Creation in the Theology of St. Thomas Aquinas." *Thomist* 57.3 (1993): 443–455.

Walsh, Liam G. "The Divine and the Human in St. Thomas's Theology of Sacraments." In *Ordo Sapientiae et Amoris,* edited by Carlos-Josaphat Pinto de Oliveira, O.P. Fribourg: Editions Universitaires, 1993. 321–354.

Wawrykow, Joseph P. *God's Grace and Human Action: "Merit" in the Theology of Thomas Aquinas.* Notre Dame, IN: University of Notre Dame Press, 1995.

———. "Wisdom in the Christology of Thomas Aquinas." In *Christ among the Medieval Dominicans: Representations of Christ in the Texts and Images of the Order of Preachers,* edited by Kent Emery, Jr., and Joseph P. Wawrykow. Notre Dame, IN: University of Notre Dame Press, 1998. 175–196.

Weisheipl, James A. "The Meaning of *Sacra Doctrina* in *Summa Theologiae* I, q. 1." *Thomist* 38 (1974): 49–80.

Williams, A. N. "Mystical Theology Redux: The Pattern of Aquinas' *Summa theologiae.*" *Modern Theology* 13.1 (January 1997): 53–74.

Wippel, John F. *The Metaphysical Thought of Thomas Aquinas: From Finite Being to Uncreated Being.* Washington, DC: Catholic University of America Press, 2000.

Zizioulas, John D. "The Doctrine of the Holy Trinity: The Significance of the Cappadocian Contribution." In *Trinitarian Theology Today: Essays on Divine Being and Act,* edited by Chrisoph Schwöbel. Edinburgh: T & T Clark, 1995. 44–60.

Index of Names

Index of Subjects

Professor of philosophy of religion and theology at Claremont Graduate University, **ANSELM K. MIN** is the author of, among other works, *Dialectic of Salvation: Issues in Theology of Liberation* and *The Solidarity of Others in a Divided World: A Postmodern Theology after Postmodernism.*